The Globalisation of Chinese Business

CHANDOS
ASIAN STUDIES SERIES

Series Editor: Professor Chris Rowley,
Centre for Research on Asian Management, Cass Business School,
City University, UK; HEAD Foundation, Singapore
(email: *c.rowley@city.ac.uk)*

Chandos Publishing is pleased to publish this major Series of books entitled *Asian Studies Series*. The Series Editor is Professor Chris Rowley, Director, Centre for Research on Asian Management, City University, UK and Director, Research and Publications, HEAD Foundation, Singapore.

Asia has clearly undergone some major transformations in recent years and books in the Series examine this transformation from a number of perspectives: economic, management, social, political and cultural. We seek authors from a broad range of areas and disciplinary interests: covering, for example, business/management, political science, social science, history, sociology, gender studies, ethnography, economics and international relations, etc.

Importantly, the Series examines both current developments and possible future trends. The Series is aimed at an international market of academics and professionals working in the area. The books have been specially commissioned from leading authors. The objective is to provide the reader with an authoritative view of current thinking.

New authors: we would be delighted to hear from you if you have an idea for a book. We are interested in both shorter, practically orientated publications (45,000+ words) and longer, theoretical monographs (75,000–100,000 words). Our books can be single, joint or multi-author volumes. If you have an idea for a book, please contact the publishers or Professor Chris Rowley, the Series Editor.

Dr Glyn Jones
Chandos Publishing
Email: *g.jones.2@elsevier.com*

Professor Chris Rowley
Cass Business School, City University
Email: *c.rowley@city.ac.uk*
www.cass.city.ac.uk/faculty/c.rowley

Chandos Publishing: Chandos Publishing is an imprint of Elsevier. The aim of Chandos Publishing is to publish books of the highest possible standard: books that are both intellectually stimulating and innovative.

We are delighted and proud to count our authors from such well-known international organisations as the Asian Institute of Technology, Tsinghua University, Kookmin University, Kobe University, Kyoto Sangyo University, London School of Economics, University of Oxford, Michigan State University, Getty Research Library, University of Texas at Austin, University of South Australia, University of Newcastle, Australia, University of Melbourne, ILO, Max-Planck Institute, Duke University and the leading law firm Clifford Chance.

A key feature of Chandos Publishing's activities is the service it offers its authors and customers. Chandos Publishing recognises that its authors are at the core of its publishing ethos, and authors are treated in a friendly, efficient and timely manner. Chandos Publishing's books are marketed on an international basis, via its range of overseas agents and representatives.

Professor Chris Rowley: Dr Rowley, BA, MA (Warwick), DPhil (Nuffield College, Oxford) is Subject Group leader and the inaugural Professor of Human Resource Management at Cass Business School, City University, London, UK, and Director of Research and Publications for the HEAD Foundation, Singapore. He is the founding Director of the multi-disciplinary and internationally networked Centre for Research on Asian Management (*http://www.cass.city.ac.uk/cram/index.html*) and Editor of the leading journal *Asia Pacific Business Review* (*www.tandf.co.uk/journals/titles/13602381.asp*). He is well known and highly regarded in the area, with visiting appointments at leading Asian universities and top journal Editorial Boards in the UK, Asia and the US. He has given a range of talks and lectures to universities, companies and organisations internationally with research and consultancy experience with unions, business and government, and his previous employment includes varied work in both the public and private sectors. Professor Rowley researches in a range of areas, including international and comparative human resource management and Asia Pacific management and business. He has been awarded grants from the British Academy, an ESRC AIM International Study Fellowship and gained a 5-year RCUK Fellowship in Asian Business and Management. He acts as a reviewer for many funding bodies, as well as for numerous journals and publishers. Professor Rowley publishes extensively, including in leading US and UK journals, with over 370 articles, books, chapters and other contributions.

The Globalisation of Chinese Business

Implications for multinational investors

EDITED BY
ROBERT TAYLOR

AMSTERDAM • BOSTON • CAMBRIDGE • HEIDELBERG • LONDON
NEW YORK • OXFORD • PARIS • SAN DIEGO
SAN FRANCISCO • SINGAPORE • SYDNEY • TOKYO
Chandos Publishing is an imprint of Elsevier

Chandos Publishing
Elsevier Limited
The Boulevard
Langford Lane
Kidlington
Oxford OX5 1GB
UK
store.elsevier.com/Chandos-Publishing-/IMP_207/

Chandos Publishing is an imprint of Elsevier Limited

Tel: +44 (0) 1865 843000
Fax: +44 (0) 1865 843010
store.elsevier.com

First published in 2014

ISBN: 978-1-84334-768-2 (print)
ISBN: 978-1-78063-449-4 (online)

Library of Congress Control Number: 2014946704

British Library Cataloguing-in-Publication Data.
A catalogue record for this book is available from the British Library.

Project management by Neil Shuttlewood Associates, Gt Yarmouth, Norfolk, UK

Contents

List of figures and tables

Figures

Tables

List of abbreviations

ABC	Agricultural Bank of China
ADF	Augmented Dickey-Fuller
AMC	Asset Management Corporation
APEC	Asia-Pacific Economic Cooperation
ASEAN	Association of South East Asian Nations
AVIC I	Aviation Industry Corporation I
AVIC II	Aviation Industry Corporation II
B2B	Business-to-Business
B2C	Business-to-Consumer
BIS	Basic Insurance Scheme
BoC	Bank of China
BRIC	Brazil, Russia, India, China
CASS	Chinese Academy of Social Science
CBRC	China Banking Regulatory Commission
CCB	China Construction Bank
CCP	Chinese Communist Party
CCTV	China Central TeleVision
CDM	Clean Development Mechanism
CHIPs	Chinese Household Income Project survey
COB	Country Of Brand
COD	Country Of Design
COM	Country Of Manufacture
COMAC	COMmercial Aircraft Corporation of China
COO	Country Of Origin
CPC	Communist Party of China
CPI	Consumer Price Index
CSR	China's South Locomotive and Rolling Stock Industry Corporation
CSRC	China Securities Regulatory Commission
DS	Developmental State
EBIT	Earnings Before Interest and Taxes
EHESS	École des Hautes Études en Sciences Sociales

EMEA	Europe, Middle East and Africa
ENAC	Ecole Nationale de l'Aviation Civile
ENSMA	Ecole Nationale Supérieure d'Aéronautique et d'Aérotechnique
ETDZ	Economic and Technological Development Zone
EU	European Union
FB	Family Business
FDI	Foreign Direct Investment
FESCO	Foreign Enterprise Service COmpany
FMSH	Fondation Maison des Sciences de l'Homme
FSB	Financial Stability Board
GDP	Gross Domestic Product
GIS	Government Insurance Scheme
GM	Genetically Modified
HR	Human Resources
HRM	Human Resource Management
HS	Hang Seng
HS	Harmonized Commodity Description and Coding System
HS	High Speed
ICBC	Industrial and Commercial Bank of China
ICT	Information and Communication Technology
IFPRI	International Food Policy Research Institute
INRIA	Institut National de Recherche en Informatique et en Automatique
ISAE	Institut Supérieur de l'Aéronautique et de l'Espace
KHI	Kawasaki Heavy Industry
LED	Light Emitting Diode
LGFV	Local Government Financial Vehicle
LIS	Labor Insurance Scheme
LTCM	Long Term Capital Management
M&A	Merger and Acquisition
MBO	Management By Objectives
MID	Marshallian Industrial District
MMNE	Medium-size MultiNational Enterprise
MNC	MultiNational Company
MRE	MultiRegional Enterprise
MSA	Medical Saving Account
NFB	Non Family Business
NPL	Non Performing Loan
ODI	Overseas Direct Investment

OECD	Organization for Economic Cooperation and Development
OLS	Ordinary Least Squares
PBOC	People's Bank Of China
PI	Public Insurance
POE	Private Owned Enterprise
PPP	Purchasing Power Parity
PRC	People's Republic of China
PURH	Presses Universitaires de Rouen et du Havre
PV	PhotoVoltaic
QFII	Qualified Foreign Institutional Investor
R&D	Research and Development
RAI	Radiotelevisione Italiana
RMB	RenMinBi
ROA	Return On Assets
ROE	Return On Equity
ROIC	Return On Invested Capital
RSDAIDS	Restricted Source Differentiated Almost Ideal Demand System
S&T	Science and Technology
SAIC	State Administration for Industry and Commerce
SASAC	State Assets Supervision and Administration Commission
SD	Standard Deviation
SEZ	Special Economic Zone
SH	SHanghai Composite
SIB	Social Insurance Bureau
SME	Small and Medium Enterprise
SOE	State Owned Enterprise
SP	Standard and Poor's 500
ST	Straits Times
STIPs	S&T Industrial Parks
TBI	Technology Business Incubator
TFP	Total Factor Productivity
TNC	TransNational Corporation
UNIDO	United Nations Industrial Development Organization
UNSW	University of New South Wales
VAR	Vector AutoRegressive
VoC	Varieties of Capitalism
WTO	World Trade Organisation
XPP	Xiao Piao Piao Food Company Limited

Acknowledgements

The chapters in this book are based on papers first presented at the 18th Euro-Asia Research Conference, held in Venice in late January and early February 2013 and their original presentation would not have been possible without the excellent organisation and kind hospitality provided by academic and administrative colleagues at the School of Asian Studies and Business Management at Ca' Foscari University. I am also indebted to editors at Chandos for their assistance in the preparation of this book.

Preface

Recent global events attest to China's growing voice in international affairs, as witnessed by the country's enhanced economic role and increasing national self-confidence. No region of the world is unaffected by the nature and volume of China's trade and investment. Ever since the initiation of China's economic reform in the 1980s, China has been seen as a huge market by foreign traders and investors, with increased focus following the recent recession in the Eurozone and the United States. In addition, commodity and mineral-rich Asian and African countries have become increasingly economically dependent on China. Thus, China is not only a locus for inward investment, its domestic companies are also outward investors.

Nevertheless China's economic reform process is not complete and there are serious obstacles to sustaining the high growth rates of the past. At meetings of Chinese Communist Party (CCP) and government leaders in late 2013 and early 2014 measures were announced to accelerate the ongoing policy of rebalancing the economy from investment towards consumption, a key component being the injection of further competition, both in manufacturing and services. For example, deregulation of the banking sector through permitting non-governmental entrants is designed to facilitate funding of private enterprise, hitherto at a disadvantage when raising capital from state banks. Monopolistic state-owned manufacturing enterprises are to be subjected to greater competition from the private sector, with intended positive impact on goods and services (Chance, 2014). Moreover, as China's economy matures, services loom larger and, importantly, will provide increased employment for both rural migrants to the cities and better educated urban university graduates.

Such policies are thus responding to the ongoing maturation of the Chinese economy and present both challenges and opportunities for foreign multinational investors whose operations are discussed in the following chapters.

Reference

Chance, G. (2014) China moving up to the next level. *China Daily European Weekly*, 21–27 March 2014.

About the editor

Robert Taylor was formerly Director of the Centre for Chinese Studies and Reader in Modern Chinese Studies at the University of Sheffield. His research interests focus on China's domestic and foreign policy, especially Chinese business management and foreign economic relations as well as Sino-Japanese relations. He has published widely in such academic journals as the *Asia Pacific Business Review* and *Asian Business and Management.*

He has contributed to media programmes relating to contemporary Asia. His publications include *China's Intellectual Dilemma* (University of British Columbia Press, 1981), *Greater China and Japan* (Routledge, 1996) and he edited *International Business in China* (Routledge, 2012).

He also engages in management consultancy.

About the contributors

Lara Agnoli has a PhD in Wine Economics and Rural Development. She is research fellow at the Department of Business Administration, University of Verona (Italy). Her research activity is focused on discrete choice modelling in demand analysis and food and wine marketing. She holds seminars in courses at the University of Verona on consumption behaviour and food choice. Her recent publications include a book chapter on the management of food and wine events, and scientific articles on alcoholic beverage consumption models relating to the young, novice wine consumer decision-making process, the role played by the value system in food choice, and packaging strategies in wine industry.

Bruno Amann is Professor in Management Sciences at the University Paul Sabatier of Toulouse (France). He is the Director of the Management and Cognition Research team of that University. He has published several contributions in leading academic journals on family business, corporate governance, and international management. His most recent publications have been released in the *International Journal of Human Resource Management* (2013), *Asia Pacific Business Review* (2011), *Journal of Transition Economies* (2010), *Ebisu* (2010, 2013), *Journal of Family Business Strategy* (2010) and *Family Business Review* (2008).

Bernadette Andreosso-O'Callaghan is Visiting Professor (Chair of East-Asian Economics) at the Fakultät für Wirtschaftswissenschaft, Ruhr Universität Bochum and Jean Monnet Chair of Economics, Euro-Asia Centre and Kemmy Business School, University of Limerisk. She has published extensively in the areas of comparative economic integration – Asia and Europe – and of structural change in East-Asian countries. Her most recent publications include the following: *Economic/Social Exclusion and Collective Action in Europe and Asia*, Springer Publishing Group: Heidelberg (2013) coedited with F. Royall; 'How red is China's red capitalism? Continuity and change in China's financial services sector during the global crisis,' (2013) *Asia Pacific Business Review*, with Joern

Carsten Gottwald; and 'Regional moderator: a new role for South Korea,' (2013) *ASIEN (The German Journal on Contemporary Asia)*, special issue on the G20 and Asia.

Vincenzo Atella is Associate Professor of Economics at the University of Rome 'Tor Vergata' where he teaches Macroeconomics and courses in Applied Health Economics at graduate and postgraduate levels and Adjunct Associate of the Center for Health Policy at Stanford. Currently, he is also Scientific Director of the Farmafactoring Foundation, member of SIVEAS (Health Care Services National Evaluation System) of the Ministry of Health and chief economist of the Italian Association of General Practitioners (SIMG). His most recent research activity has focussed on poverty, income distribution and health economics. The results of this research activity have been published in several international refereed journals and books.

Diego Begalli, PhD, is Full Professor in Agricultural Economics at the University of Verona's Department of Business Administration (Italy). He has more than 25 years of academic experience in the field of agribusiness and food and wine marketing. He teaches courses in Wine Business Management and Wine Marketing. He is director of a post-graduate course in Wine Marketing. His research activity is focused on agro-food business management, consumer behaviour, and wine and food product branding. His recent publications include articles on collective brand strategies in food and wine territorial systems, wine consumer behaviour, and analysis of impacts of climate change on wine business performance.

Agar Brugiavini is Professor of Economics at Ca' Foscari University of Venice. She is Director of the Ca' Foscari International College and Dean of the Venice International University (VIU). She is a Research Affiliate of the Institute for Fiscal Studies (IFS), London. She received a PhD in Economics at the London School of Economics (UK) under the supervision of Prof. Mervyn King, and was Visiting Professor at Northwestern University (USA). She has been co-editor of *Research in Economics*. She has contributed to many volumes of the NBER project *Social Security around the World*. Her research interests include the behaviour of individuals and households in the areas of consumption, saving and labour supply, pension reforms and insurance markets. She plays a key role in the SHARE project (Survey of Health, Ageing and Retirement in Europe). More recently she has been carrying out research on the economics of ageing, looking at the relationship between health conditions and economic behaviour, and on gender economics as well.

Roberta Capitello, PhD, is Associate Professor in Agricultural Economics at the University of Verona's Department of Business Administration (Italy), where she teaches courses on food economics and business management. Her special research interests are in consumer behaviour, marketing and communication in the wine industry. Her recent publications include a book chapter on the management of food and wine events and scientific articles on the analysis of wine consumer decision-making process, with a focus on emerging wine markets, winery online communication, and wine experience and tourism.

Francesca Checchinato is Assistant Professor in the Department of Management at the Ca' Foscari University of Venice. She received her PhD at the same university in 2006, where she studied the benefits and pitfalls of co-branding strategies. Her main research field is marketing, with particular focus on communication and brand. In 2008 her focus of study turned to business models used to enter the Chinese market; currently, she is involved in research projects related to marketing in China. She is the author of a number of papers in international publications and conference proceedings about the marketing strategies of foreign firms in China.

Hao Chen was born in 1982 in Shandong Province, China. He spent his first 23 years in China. In 2005, he obtained aBachelor's Degree in Mathematics at Shandong University, one of the best universities in China. After his undergraduate study, he went to Italy to further his academic career. He spent 7 years in Italy and finally got a Doctor's Degree in Economics at Ca' Foscari University of Venice (Italy). His PhD thesis focussed on Chinese reform effects on household saving performance. He is currently studying Asset Management. His research interests include the latest series of Chinese reforms and their effects on the real world economy.

Cinzia Colapinto is Assistant Professor of Management at Ca' Foscari University of Venice (Italy). She obtained a PhD in Business History and Management from the University of Milan (Italy), where she has been post-doc fellow. She was a Visiting Researcher at the Department of Media and Communications, London School of Economics and Political Science (UK), and at the Centre for Research in Transnational Education, Leadership and Performance, University of Canberra (Australia). She continues to be research active, with current interests in media management, decision making and innovation management. Her main publications appear in the *European Journal of Operational Research*, *Annals of Operations Research*, *Physica A* and *Media, Culture and Society*.

Joseph Coughlan is currently Head of School of Accounting & Finance at the College of Business, Dublin Institute of Technology (Ireland) where he leads a multi-disciplinary research team on business-to-business relationships. He is interested in corporate governance, particularly in the public sector. Recent papers have appeared in *Industrial Marketing Management*, *Journal of Services Marketing* and *Journal of International Management*.

Guilhem Fabre is a China scholar with a PhD in Chinese Studies (University Paris 7, 1980) and a PhD in Socio-economy (EHESS, 1992). He is currently Professor of Chinese Civilisation and East Asian Economics at the University of Le Havre, and co-responsible for the BRIC seminar at FMSH/EHESS. His research and publications concern the cultural revolution, the Yan'an period, the political economy of reforms, contemporary and classical chinese poetry, drug trafficking and money laundering, intellectual property, R&D and innovation. He is the author of *Criminal Prosperity: Drug Trafficking, Money Laundering and Financial Crisis after the Cold War* (RoutledgeCurzon, 2003), *Chine, crises et mutations* (L'Harmattan, 2002), *Propriété intellectuelle, contrefaçon et innovation: les multinationales face à l'économie de la connaissance* (PURH, 2009), and *Instants éternels: Cent et quelques poèmes connus par cœur en Chine*, (Paris, La Différence, 2014).

Lingfang Fayol-Song got her bachelor and master degree from Fudan University in Shanghai, then did her PhD degree in Poitiers University in France. She now works at France Business School. She teaches marketing and cross-cultural management courses in different programs such as MBA, graduate and undergraduate programs. Her research interests are consumer behaviours, luxury marketing, cross-cultural management, expatriation, and management localisation. She also runs an MBA program. Her recent publications are "The reasons behind management localisation: a case study of China" (*Journal of Asia Pacific Business Review*, Special Issue, International Business in China, November, 2011, 455–72); "Internationalization of Chinese executives" (*Global Journal of Business Research*, 6(1), 2012, 47–54); and "Targeting vulnerable new consumers in China" (a chapter in *Ethics in Marketing and Communications: Towards a Global Perspective*, Palgrave, pp. 81–96).

Qi Feng is a Teaching Assistant of Tianjin Foreign Studies University, China. He is currently preparing his PhD in the University of Pau (France). His research interests are in Strategic Human Resource Management in Chinese enterprises. He has already published a paper in a Chinese academic journal in HRM in the finance and bank industry. He is currently preparing other academic publications, both in English and in Chinese.

Alice Giusto is an Italian-educated young researcher with 7 years experience of living and working in China, now living in Beijing. She completed her MA(Hons) at Ca' Foscari University of Venice in Italy in 2010 and during her time at that university had the opportunity to study at Beijing Capital Normal University (China) and Taipei Fu-ren Catholic University (Taiwan). After working as a research assistant for Venice University in Asia, she is now taking a PhD at Peking University's School of Journalism and Communication, focussing her research on food safety and risk communication in China, with special attention to usage of social media in this field. This is her first international publication.

Jörn Gottwald is Professor of East Asian Politics at Ruhr University Bochum, Germany. He holds a PhD in Political Science from FU Berlin and a Habilitation from University of Trier where he was appointed Assistant Professor in Political Science from 2000 to 2006 before working at the Irish Institute of Chinese Studies, National University of Ireland, Cork. He has published internationally on various topics in the fields of political and economic development in East Asia, particularly in China, on EU–China relations and the politics of financial market regulation.

Qianxuan Huang is currently a research assistant at Kedge Business School, France. In 2013, she received her PhD in Management Science from the University of Pau (France), where she also obtained a lot of teaching experience. While a PhD student, she published a joint paper with Prof. Jacques Jaussaud on the subject of Chinese Family Businesses in the Chinese academic journal, *Technoeconomics & Management Research*. The article has been cited several times in Chinese publications. Her ongoing research includes the resilience of family businesses in China. Other research interests include International Management, Family Business study and HRM.

Jacques Jaussaud is Professor of Management, University of Pau, France, and Director of the CREG Research team in Management of this university.

His research interests are in the areas of business strategy, organization, control, and human resource management, with a particular focus on Japan, China, and other Asian countries. He has published widely in these areas, including in such academic journals as the *International Journal of Human Resource Management*, *Asian Business and Management*, *Asia Pacific Business Review*, *Journal of International Management*, *Transition Studies Review*. He has also co-edited several books, including *The Changing Economic Environment in Asia: Firms' Strategies in the Region* (Palgrave, 2001), *Economic Dynamism and Business Strategy of Firms in Asia: Some Recent Developments* (China Publishing Economic House, Beijing, 2006) and *Evolving Corporate Structures and Cultures in Asia* (ISTE Publishing, London, 2008).

Cuiling Jiang is a post-doc research fellow at KEDGE Business School in France. She holds a PhD in Management at the University of Pau. Her research focusses on international human resource management, evolution of organizational forms, multinational companies in Asian emerging markets and knowledge management in the context of cross-border mergers and acquisitions. She teaches courses on International Human Resource Management, Asian Emerging Markets, International Strategic Management, Cultural Management and International Business, Introduction to Management, etc..

Su Qian Kong has a PhD in Financial Economics (with a major in Econometrics) at the College of Business at Dublin Institute of Technology (Ireland). Her main research interests are the field of market contagion and economic and financial instability in world economies. At present she is workng in the Chinese stock market to understand market connections and levels of integration and their impact on the country's level of growth and development. She is also interested in understanding global financial linkages with macroeconomic fundamentals and how they can be used for policy making. She holds a Master's Degree in Finance, attends international conferences and is currently preparing work for publication.

Xueming Liu is Associate Professor at the Groupe ESC Larochelle (La Rochelle Business School, France). He is a Doctor in Management of the University of Poitiers, France. His research interest is Human Resource Management, with a special focus on China. He has published several papers in English in the *Asia Pacific Business Review* as well as book chapters. He has also published in French in the *Revue de Gestion des Ressources Humaines*.

Lucía Morales is a Lecturer in Finance at Dublin Institute of Technology (Ireland). She holds a PhD in Economics and several postgraduate degrees at the master level in Economics, Finance, Financial Markets and Education. She is an active researcher in financial economics and applied econometrics with an interest in market integration, economic and financial crises, volatility and market instability and implications for economic development and growth. She has been published in the *Journal of Asian Economics*, *Journal of Economics and Finance* and other specialist journals. She has participated in conferences at the international level in Economics and Finance and more recently in Education.

Noemi Pace is currently Assistant Professor at the Department of Economics, Ca' Foscari University of Venice (Italy) and Stanford Health Policy Adjunct Associate at the Centre for Health Policy, Stanford University (California). She is also fellow at the Centre for Economic and International Studies at University of Rome Tor Vergata. She was previously Research Fellow at the Centre for International Health and Development at University College London and Research Fellow at LUISS Guido Carli University (Rome). Her fields of interest are Applied Microeconomics, Health Economics and Experimental Economics. The results of her research activities have been published in several refereed journals, such as *The Lancet*, *Economics and Human Biology*, *Journal of Risk and Uncertainty* and *Theory and Decision*. She holds a BA in Economics, a Master's Degree in Development Economics and a PhD in Economic Theory and Institutions from the University of Rome Tor Vergata.

Andrea Pontiggia is Full Professor of Organization Theory and Design at Ca' Foscari University of Venice, Italy; SDA Professor of Organization and Human Resource Management at School of Business Administration, Bocconi University, Milan; Co-Director of the International Management to Asia Laboratory – IMA Lab. His main research interests concern Organizational Design of International and Global Companies, Human Resource Management and the Global Labor Market. He is a member of several scientific committees of European research centers. He has been a visiting professor at US, European and Asian universities. He extensively publishes on strategic and organizational models and is conducting several research projects with European and Chinese universities.

Tiziano Vescovi is Full Professor of Management at Ca' Foscari University of Venice, Italy; Co-Director of the International Management to Asia

Laboratory – IMA Lab; Co-Director of the ELIM (Entrepreneurial Leadership and International Management) Institute, Ca' Foscari University of Venice and Zhejiang University, China. He teaches Cross-Cultural Marketing, Market Opportunities and Marketing Communication. He is a member of the Steering Committee of the Italian Management Society. He is Director of Masters in Sport Management and Marketing and Scientific Director of the Italian Booksellers Management School, Rome. His research interests are International Management and International Marketing. He has been a visiting professor at US, European and Chinese universities.

Valeria Zanier. After working as a consultant for foreign companies and institutions in China for several years, she embarked on an academic career and contributed to the growth of contemporary Chinese studies at Ca' Foscari University of Venice, where she has been teaching Political Economy (China) and History of Economic Relations in East Asia since 2008. Her main fields of research include the PRC's economic and industrial policy; formal and informal institutions; migration and economic change; China–Europe economic and trade relations. Dr Zanier is currently affiliated to the London School of Economics and Political Science as a Marie Curie Fellow Researcher.

Introduction and overview

Robert Taylor

Abstract: The evolution of management in China is taking place in the context of the globalisation of Chinese business, itself spurred by both domestic and external forces. The economic recession in Western countries has impacted upon business in China, and Chinese manufacturers are being impelled to move from labour-intensive production to high-tech innovation to maintain competitiveness. In addition, high Chinese domestic economic growth has been at the expense of growing regional and personal income inequalities. Now emphasised is a shift from investment to consumption, with innovation and labour productivity gains seen as the key to the avoidance of the 'middle income trap'. A pacesetter in innovation is private enterprise, stimulating consumer demand by raising personal income. Increases in state social welfare and the institution of the statutory minimum wage will also release income for consumption. Growth of the services sector will present challenges and opportunities for both Chinese management and foreign ventures.

Key words: consumption, innovation, minimum wage, multinational investors, private sector, services.

The following chapters are derived from papers presented at the Eighteenth Euro-Asia Research Seminar held in Venice in early 2013, focused on the globalisation of Asian markets and the implications for multinational investors. This book, however, examines the evolution of business management in China, an increasingly major Asian and global player, driven by both domestic and external forces.

Since 2008 the economic recession in Western countries has impacted on Chinese business, even though some of the following trends were already in evidence. Until recently multinational investors came to China to take advantage of low wages in order to export cheap labour-intensive goods. Potential tariff barriers, for example, against China's textiles in Europe and the context of recession necessitate Chinese moves towards high-tech value-added production. Consequently, Chinese management must address the challenge of innovation. Even though in such areas of production Western countries will retain an advantage in the immediate term, increased investment in those sectors as well as services by both domestic and multinational companies could create a major Chinese competitor in the long term, especially on China's own domestic market.

In addition to external impetus to change, the very success of China's reform programme since 1978 has engendered problems which its leadership must face. In recent years China's economic growth rates have been the envy of Western countries, with at the time of writing 7.5 per cent being targeted in 2013 (Sheridan, 2013). There have, however, been costs, both economically and socially.

The focus to date on growth in gross domestic product (GDP) has, for instance, led to high spending by competing local and provincial governments which have borrowed heavily from a number of financial sources such as state and commercial banks and even individuals. Significantly, local governments' difficulty in repaying debt is derived in part from slow growth in land income which has in the past accounted for more than 70 per cent of their revenue. They have also been earning money by selling land to real estate developers. Such evidence has been cited by S.P. Kothari of the Massachusetts Institute of Technology (MIT) Sloan School of Management (Wang, 2013). The localities and provinces, like the state-owned enterprises (SOEs), know that, in the event of indebtedness, they may ultimately appeal for rescue by the central government. Consequently, development has been unbalanced, particularly to the disadvantage of the private sector, the motor of growth in innovation and potentially personal consumer wealth, which has found it difficult to secure state bank funding, having to resort to informal sources like family funds and even the infamous shadow banking loan lenders. In short, capital flow to the private sector should be facilitated (Luo, 2013; Sheridan, 2013).

In turn this brings into focus the issue of competitiveness and concomitant effective markets where a healthy private sector which, as previously noted may prove a pacesetter in innovation, can play a major role. Its role is also crucial, as discussed later, in the Chinese government's shift in emphasis from investment to consumption. There are nevertheless barriers to achieving that objective; economic development has brought growing regional and personal income inequalities, with consequent impact on the distribution of consumption (Zhu, 2013). In 2010 a Chinese economist, Wang Xiaolu, noted that the top 2 per cent of Chinese households earned 35 per cent of national urban income, an issue that must be addressed if social dissent born of rising expectations is to be prevented (Sheridan, 2013). The key to sustainable consumption is increased labour productivity through technological innovation and industrial upgrading which, from a macroeconomic perspective, is the way to overcome the so-called 'middle income trap'. Thus increased consumption is made possible by growth derived from productivity gains (Moody and Chang, 2013b).

The importance of increasing labour productivity is also underlined by demographic change, occasioned at least in part by the one-child policy. One source has stated that the number of people aged between 15 and 59 fell by 3.45 million in 2012 (Lau and Green, 2013). Thus there is an impending labour shortage, especially in high-tech skill areas. To date labour-intensive industries have been absorbing rural migrants but the imparting of advanced technological innovative skills demands not only scientists and engineers trained in higher education but the induction, training and mentoring of the unskilled arriving from the countryside. Attention is now turned to the policies with which the Chinese leadership is addressing these challenges.

In the 12th Five Year Plan (2011–15) the Chinese leadership seeks to rebalance China's economy in a move from investment towards greater emphasis on consumption in an attempt to avoid the kind of overheating which occurred in Japan in the 1990s. This objective is necessarily reflected in current strategic priorities as outlined in a policy document following a meeting of the State Council, China's cabinet, in May 2013. Included are fiscal system reforms and marketisation of interest rates as well as other measures designed to encourage investment by private enterprises. The government has sought, for example, to assist entrepreneurship by abolishing taxes on small businesses with incomes lower than US $3300 per month. There are, however, no immediate plans to fundamentally reduce the role of state enterprises (Fu, 2013; Moody and Chang, 2013a; Summers, 2013). These policies are designed to stimulate consumption; private enterprise, for instance, can serve as a motor of growth in personal incomes.

It could nevertheless be argued that this consumption-driven policy has social as well as economic ramifications because, given the need to reduce income inequality and secure greater equity, livelihood issues have come to the fore (Summers, 2013). Accordingly, the following narrative broadly encompasses those problem areas which were highlighted earlier in this introduction and may be subsumed under the province of services.

A concomitant of the expansion of consumer demand is the high-tech service sector which can be much less polluting than the energy-intensive smokestack industries created by earlier overinvestment. To this end the State Council outlined punitive sanctions in August 2013 against polluters, implicitly emphasising the link between environmental protection and the people's well-being. Although there is a pending shortage of skilled workers, parts of the service sector are more labour intensive and can employ city-bound rural migrants who can easily be trained in menial occupations. The burgeoning IT sector, which is being promoted through the expansion of broadband and licensing, requires highly skilled scientific and technological personnel (Li, 2013). Such well-paid operatives are potentially high spenders but in a rapidly expanding field need extensive training. It is here that a major role is being played by central government initiative, witness the launching of the National High Technology (863)[1] Programme in March 1986 which prioritises such areas as information and manufacturing technology and automation. Since the mid-1990s the trajectory has been shifted towards cutting edge technological products and processes like the Tianhe-IA supercomputer. An extension of the 863 Programme is the indigenous innovation strategy, a part of the 2006 National Medium to Long Term Plan (MLP) for the Development of Science and Technology (2005–20), the sectors in focus being, for example, electronics, semiconductors, telecommunications, pharmaceuticals and clean technology, with personnel being trained at home and abroad (Raska, 2013).

Moves towards high-tech industry and its highly qualified workforce are in tandem with another spur to consumption, the government's urbanisation policy, the objective being to move 300 million people into cities in the next two decades, taking account of growing skilled service employment in urban centres. Moreover, if migrant workers bring their families to live in the cities, they are likely to spend more rather than remitting their wages back to the countryside (Moody and Chang, 2013a). As high-tech industry and urban inhabitants' wealth increases, so will demand for such services as IT telecom and healthcare. In the case of the latter more effective provision through state welfare subsidies will facilitate consumption of affordable consumer goods, as the development of state social insurance will reduce the need for personal saving to fund healthcare (Fu, 2013).

The development of healthcare is a focus of the 12th Five Year Plan but medical reform began in 2009, the objective being to establish universal provision by 2020. Until recently medical services were an urban phenomenon; there were few modern rural hospitals. Now the aims are affordable public hospitals and a system of national medical insurance which is as yet in its infancy. The central government is targeting 400 million yuan to be spent by 2020 to improve rural healthcare, create a digital public health information network and train more doctors (Liu and Zhang, 2013b).

Finally, a number of financial and social legislative measures enacted by government may well prove a more important stimulus to personal consumption. For instance, ongoing reform to the banking system could well make consumer credit more widely available. Moreover, in recent years labour legislation has not only furthered secure tenure of employment but instituted and increased the statutory minimum wage which may nevertheless vary across provinces according to local pay. Significantly, the government aims to raise the minimum wage by an average of at least 13% per year. Moves towards a universal pension system are also likely to maintain consumption (Lau and Green, 2013; Song, 2013).

Moreover, as an economy matures, the role of services grows; in China labour legislation and consumer protection law, for instance in relation to advertising, are leading to demand for legal and insurance specialists. It is in these areas that Western experts may contribute expertise and investment.

Ongoing trends, already in evidence even before the 12th Five Year Plan, demonstrate how the above policies are being realised in practice. Encouraging consumption depends on both foreign and domestic investment in manufacturing but also in its increasingly important adjunct, services. China is seen as a major location of investment by far-seeing multinational investors because of its long-term potential as a marketplace. A number of examples may be cited. By 2015 Ford Motor aims to double its capacity in China; its capital investment will create employment which will in turn increase the ability to consume of both blue-collar and white-collar employees. Given China's consumption potential, service providers like advertising agencies are following manufacturers (Steinbock, 2013). As living standards rise, a greater concern among consumers for quality health provision, for instance, emerges, a trend which has not escaped the notice of foreign pharmaceutical manufacturers. A case in point is GlaxoSmithKline, a British company which has invested over a billion yuan in research and development (R&D) over the last 20 years, engaging in cooperative drug-manufacturing projects with Chinese clinical research centres. Similarly, the Danish healthcare provider, Novo Nordisk, is carrying out extensive R&D in China. The Chinese government's recent decision to increase public health insurance, with the objective of covering 95% of the rural population, can only enhance consumer demand for patent medicines (Liu and Zhang, 2013a, b).

The following statistics bear out the shift in foreign direct investment (FDI) towards services. FDI flows into China totalled US $124 billion in 2011, when, for the first time, the service share of FDI exceeded that for manufacturing (Steinbock, 2013).

The private sector, even though that term must be used advisedly in China, given links to local government for funding, has been making a contribution to the growing service sector. A main focus of Wahaha, the retail giant, is the shopping mall, a venue for the sale of mid-market affordable European luxury quality products and foods, designed to attract the growing number of young middle-class consumers with purchasing power. While demand is likely to grow, marketeers must increase public recognition of European brands, hitherto unknown in China. There is also scope for greater diversification beyond first-tier cities where retail sector competition is already fiercely competitive (Liu and Zhang, 2013c). In general, distribution and delivery, especially of foods, through e-commerce will in turn stimulate consumption. Thus, via, for instance, its involvement in retail markets, the private sector is becoming a key player in economic rebalancing, accounting for over half of China's GDP through both services and manufacturing. Thus it is helping to improve the population's living standards through higher wages, spurred by entrepreneurial initiative. The caveat must be entered, however, that if the private sector is to continue to further the process of economic rebalancing it must have enhanced access to new sources of capital (Fuhrman, 2013).

If private enterprise has been a pacesetter in the growth of services, the regional distribution of the latter sector has been uneven across China. In Shanghai, for instance, services accounted for 61.7 per cent of the area's economy in the first half of 2013. During the same period in Shanghai, GDP grew by 7.7 per cent year on year but the equivalent figure for services was 9.6 per cent. Significantly, turnover in the online retail sector grew by 57.4 per cent over the same time span. In Beijing, not surprisingly given the presence of government offices and research institutes, services accounted for 76.4 per cent of the local economy in the first half of 2013. Similarly, in Zhejiang, a coastal province, the tertiary sector was growing more quickly year on year than manufacturing in early 2013.

In contrast, in Hebei, an inland province, heavily involved in steel production, services currently accounted for 34.6 per cent of GDP as opposed to industry's 55 per cent in 2013. In addition, service-driven provinces are likely to benefit from government funding incentives in the years to come, intensifying the regional division of labour (Zhang, 2013).

While in the past the tertiary sector has not always paid high-tech wages, there is now demand for highly qualified scientific personnel who will contribute to high-tech manufacturing in exchange for remuneration commensurate with their skills. Additionally, local authorities may set the minimum wage above the national level, resulting in substantial differentiation between provinces. This has put upward pressure on salaries, for example, in Shenzhen, a magnet for the ambitious, in order to retain a skilled workforce. A survey conducted in Shenzhen showed that company directors often expressed a wish to move inland to provinces like Jiangxi where wages were lower.

A mobile labour force and salary increases in coastal cities are already pushing up wage costs in inland provinces, even though regional differentials and social inequalities are being exacerbated (Lau and Green, 2013).

In summary, this introduction has examined Chinese government policy in rebalancing the economy by shifting focus from investment to consumption, even though the two are not necessarily mutually exclusive. Within the above overall context brief reference is now made to the content of the following chapters which reflect the above concerns in their discussion of how Chinese management is evolving, whether in manufacturing or services, both in domestic and foreign-invested ventures.

Against this background the early chapters in this book (Part 1) relate to management in the manufacturing sector, covering such areas as corporate strategy and human resources. In his contribution Guilhem Fabre shows how crucial innovation is for Chinese enterprises, since growth has become more limited in the wake of the global economic recession. His study shows how government has taken the lead in promoting indigenous innovation through state-owned enterprises in key sectors. China's innovation strategy is analysed through the three case studies of high-speed trains, aeronautics and clean energy. An issue raised is the awareness of foreign investors regarding China's growing pioneering role in R&D and its implications for global markets.

While the need for innovation will present challenges for management in foreign-invested and domestic enterprises alike, Valeria Zanier, in her chapter, breaks new ground by focusing on the economies of Chinese districts and the role they have played in China's economic growth. As a case study the nature and structure of the Wenzhou district is examined, with focus on the roles played by endogenous and exogenous factors in the process of globalisation.

Qi et al. move to a broader focus to offer an original contribution to the study of human resource practices in Chinese enterprises. Unlike most previous research their concern is to compare human resource management in Chinese private and state-owned enterprises, and their research suggests that there may be convergence between practices in the two categories.

Following the theme of management in Chinese domestic enterprises, Amann et al. compare performance in family and non-family businesses. They conclude that where family control is strong, profitability, liquidity and financial viability are enhanced.

In contrast, Pontiggia and Vescovi examine a sample of Italian medium-sized multinational enterprises (MMNEs), with two major concerns: first, the strategic and governance models adopted in Chinese businesses and markets and, second, the relationship between headquarters and overseas branches in China. In conclusion, the results show that the MMNEs under review tend to replicate their existing business models.

Continuing this theme of adaptation to the Chinese context, Jiang conducts a detailed analysis of human resource practices in eight French multinational companies in China. Her empirical research findings indicate that French subsidiaries tend to adopt the parent company's human resource practices to a considerable degree.

In this introduction the growing role of services has been emphasised. Accordingly, later chapters (Part 2) look at diverse areas in that category. Andreosso-O'Callaghan and Gottwald discuss one of the latest stages in China's ongoing reform, that relating to financial services. This is examined through reference to sector restructuring, supported by statistical analysis. The chapter concludes that this reform brings risks and challenges, notably, political control and vested interests, with implications for further internationalisation of the sector.

Kong et al. pursue a similar theme, the effects of the global financial crisis on the Shanghai stock market. Their analysis examines the contagion and/or spillover effects originating in the United States' financial sector. They conclude that the Chinese stock market was able to react more quickly to instability, since the authorities introduced stimulus measures to enhance national investment together with policies to encourage domestic demand, itself facilitated by high levels of savings in the economy.

The following chapters also raise financial issues but specifically in relation to consumer spending. It has often been argued that the high rate of personal saving in China has been furthered by the absence of nationwide state social security. Atella et al. modify this view in their analysis of Chinese healthcare reforms and household savings patterns.

Their research was based on data collected through the Chinese Household Income Project (CHIP), conducted by the Chinese Academy of Social Sciences. They concluded that public insurance coverage, as currently constituted, might actually induce households to save more.

The next contribution, by Taylor, deals with the emergence of a consumer culture in China and its impact on marketing strategy. The study stresses that growth in, especially, discretionary urban incomes has led to greater diversification of taste, while the emergence of civil society and the passing of, for instance, food safety laws have heightened consumer awareness, with implications for the marketing strategy of foreign and domestic producers.

In similar vein Fayol-Song's research concerns the extent to which country of origin affects consumer preferences and selection of foreign branded products. Qualitative research was conducted through interviewing of respondents of differing sex, age, educational background, income and occupation. She suggests that the results of her research may assist companies in more effective market targeting.

Crucial to targeting the consumer market is advertising. In their contribution Checchinato et al. focus on the advertising strategies adopted by companies in the three luxury sectors of clothing, cosmetics and jewellery. The study's objective was to determine the importance of local culture for advertising content by comparing advertisements appearing in the Italian and Chinese editions of the magazine *Vogue*. Through an examination of standardisation and adaptation it was concluded that advertising should take account of such features as language, product category and clientele.

Similarly, Capitello et al.'s chapter relates to another luxury product, wine, increasingly in demand, given the growth of China's affluent urban middle class. Thus the factors driving demand for wine imports are examined. While the reputation of French wines remains paramount, the chapter provides insights as to how consumer discernment and product differentiation may offer opportunities for competitive new foreign suppliers.

The studies summarised above, ranging across areas as diverse as innovation strategy, district economies, state and private enterprises, family and non-family business, multinational investors, human resource management practices, financial services, healthcare, consumer markets and advertising, bear witness to how foreign direct investment has contributed to technological transfer, enhancing the global competitiveness of Chinese business. China, however, is now increasingly the focus of indigenous innovation, a process in tandem with China's outward direct investment (ODI), the theme of this book's epilogue.

Note

1. The 863 Program is so called because it began in the 3rd month (March) of 1986.

References

Fu, J. (2013) Growth factor. *China Daily European Weekly*, 6–12 September.

Fuhrman, P. (2013) New capital drought threatens growth. *China Daily European Weekly*, 21–27 June.

Lau, K. and Green, S. (2013) Wages reach a point of no return. *China Daily European Weekly*, 10–16 May.

Li, K.Q. (2013) On course for sustainable growth. *China Daily European Weekly*, 13–19 September.

Liu, C. and Zhang, C.Y. (2013a) Healthcare's Chinese elixir. *China Daily European Weekly*, 10–16 May.

Liu, C. and Zhang, C.Y. (2013b) Feeling the pulse in China. *China Daily European Weekly*, 10–16 May.

Liu, C. and Zhang, C.Y. (2013c) Wahaha woos Europe with WAOW. *China Daily European Weekly*, 17–23 May.

Luo, J.X. (2013) Investment strategy must change. *China Daily European Weekly*, 9–15 August.

Moody, A. and Chang, L.V. (2013a) A fine balance. *China Daily European Weekly*, 31 May–6 June.

Moody, A. and Chang, L.V. (2013b) More investment boosts consumption. *China Daily European Weekly*, 31 May–6 June.

Raska, M. (2013) China's [secret] civil-military megaprojects. Available from: RSIS Commentary 163/2013, RSIS Publications *<rsis_pubn_update@ntu.sg.* 2 September [accessed 2 September 2013].

Sheridan, M. (2013) Riddle of the faltering dragon. *Sunday Times*, 18 August.

Song, Y. (2013) Likonomics is about reform and growth. *China Daily European Weekly*, 2–8 August.

Steinbock, D. (2013) New growth model, new investment. *China Daily European Weekly*, 24–30 May.

Summers, T. (2013) China's current reform agenda. Available from: *asia@email.chathamhouse.org* 25 June [accessed 26 June 2013].

Wang, C. (2013) Debts, derivatives and discipline. *China Daily European Weekly*, 9–15 August.

Zhang, E. (2013) Driven by the new or shackled by the old. *China Daily European Weekly*, 9–15 August.

Zhu, N. (2013) The next best thing. *China Daily European Weekly*, 31 May–6 June.

Part 1
The evolution of Chinese management

1

The Real Leap Forward: China's R&D and innovation strategy

Guilhem Fabre[1]

Abstract: R&D and innovation have become much more strategic for China, as investment and export-led growth have shown their limits in the context of the global crisis. A Real Leap Forward has been accomplished since the turn of the millennium, not only in terms of scientific demography at the college and university level, but also with the definition of a National Plan for Science and Technology Development (2006–20) which puts the emphasis on indigenous innovation, mainly led by state-owned enterprises (SOEs) in key sectors. At the same time, access to the Chinese market is more and more linked to technology transfers, especially for transnational corporations, which tend to develop a part of their R&D in China. The country's catching-up strategy is analysed through three sectors (high-speed trains, aeronautics, clean energy) with a discussion of its potential impact on world industry.

Key words: R&D, innovation, technology, high-speed trains, aeronautics, clean energy, IT.

Introduction

In 2010, China became the world's largest manufacturing nation (19.8 per cent of world manufacturing output) bypassing the US (19.4 per cent), thus ending its 110-year run as the largest producer of goods.[2] After joining the WTO in 2001, China's growth during its golden period (2002–7) was driven mainly by fixed asset investment and exports, whose average annual growth rates were respectively 29 and 24 per cent. Following the spread of the US financial crisis around the world, the fall of global demand revealed China's high-export dependency. Meanwhile, the government's stimulus package, based on an expansionary fiscal and monetary policy to maintain economic growth, raised the investment rate to 48 per cent of GDP in 2010 and 2011, leading to overcapacity in certain sectors, a decline in efficiency (Yu, 2009), inflation and wage pressure, which reflect the general imbalance between investment and consumption.

China's investment and export-led growth is largely dependent on the supply of cheap labor from the hinterland, in a context of stunted urbanization resulting from Maoist policies (1949–79). This compelling illustration of Arthur Lewis' development model, whereby the transfer of an unlimited supply of labor in the traditional sectors feeds accumulation in the modern sectors through urbanization dynamics (Lewis, 1954) has been challenged for several reasons. First of all, in 2004 and 2007 there was a shortage of labor, partly due to the absence of any social insurance for the massive migrant population, in the Pearl River Delta Region of Guangdong province, which concentrates some 30 per cent of foreign investments and exports, and 10 per cent of GDP between Canton, Shenzhen and Zhuhai, the two special economic zones at the borders of Hong Kong and Macao (Fabre and Rodwin, 2011). Although this shortage of labor often takes the form of high turnover rates, and an imbalance of female employment, generally more docile and required for precision processing than male employment (the ratio between young women and men is of the order of 117 to 100), this trend will increase in the future. United Nations projections show that in the 15 years from 2010 to 2025, the pool of 15 to 24-year-olds, which provides the bulk of labor-intensive activities, will fall, as a result of the one-child policy, by 56 million people to a total of 173 million (United Nations, WDI Database).

Second, China has seen double-digit annual growth of real salaries, partly due to the multiplication of work conflicts before and after the slowdown of 2008–9. According to a Chinese survey in Shandong province, 80 per cent of migrants in 2007 were paid less than 800 yuan (US $105) per month, and nearly two thirds of them were working 56 hours per week without any day off per month (Xu, 2007). In 2012, the average salary for the 163 million trans-provincial migrants reached 2290 yuan (US $375).[3] Some local economists underline China's loss of competitivity for labor-intensive products: according to the Ministry of Commerce, China's urban workers' salaries rose at an average of 33 per cent in the last three years, and minimum salaries rose for the last two years at an average of 20 per cent in most of the provinces (Xinhua News Agency, 27 April 2012). These higher salaries profit mainly half of the 260 million migrant workers, born after 1980, who are better educated, with an average education of about ten years, more demanding than their parents and familiar with the Internet and new technologies.[4]

Third, since 2000, the cost of land has increased drastically, and even more so after the 2008 crisis, when land was used to finance the local part of the stimulus package, which led to a predictable property bubble, in the absence of any land tax. Last, but not least, the cost of energy, which accounts for a third of the cost of grain production, has also risen dramatically, to the point that China's crude oil imports, in 2011, represent 2.7 per cent of its GDP. If we add the competitiveness loss due to revaluation of the yuan to the US dollar, and the relative fall of the euro, it is clear that China's high investment and export-led growth model is no longer sustainable.

This quadruple shock, in terms of costs, exchange rate, labor, energy and land, has put to the forefront the role of China's R&D and innovation policy for sustaining growth while climbing up the value chain, as Japan and the four dragons had previously done in the mid-1980s. The US Department of Commerce estimates that 75 per cent of the growth in the American economy since World War II is due to technological innovation (Glassman, 2010).

Basic research is the field of the 'know why', from abstract mathematical demonstrations to the highly theoretical world of quantum physics and quantum mechanics, or the discovery of the gene structure for life sciences. Applied research is the field of the 'know-how', based on the corpus of basic science. The laser, the semiconductor industry and the IT revolution are thus applications of quantum physics and quantum mechanics. Development is about products, the conception and construction of prototypes and the standardization of industrial production. These fields are not separate; they are strong interactions between basic and applied research, as well as between applied research and development.

The broader concept of innovation takes into account these interactions. Although 'innovation can be based on investment of complementary assets beyond R&D such as software, human capital and organizational structures', most of product innovation is linked to R&D.[5] In advanced economies, the return of industrial policy has occurred mainly in the form of innovation policies (Dhont-Peltrault and Lallement, 2011). Innovations do not only concern new products, but mostly the improvement of existing products in terms of efficiency, energy use, etc. These are 'incremental innovations' as opposed to 'breakthrough innovations', which have large spillover effects in terms of productivity. Simply speaking, the former are about improving the candle while the latter concern the uses of electricity. In fact, the distinctions between basic and applied research, and between breakthrough innovations and incremental innovations can be misleading, as there are numerous interactions between the two fields: the Internet, a breakthrough innovation which has dramatic effects on productivity, exchanges, culture and everyday life, is an application of the digital revolution, and biology and informatics, which develop along an incremental path, may also produce other breakthrough innovations.

Let us put definitions to one side and illustrate the interactions between basic and applied sciences. It is useful to remember that scientific research and development has historically been a tool of war. From theoretical discussions on nuclear energy to the Manhattan Project and the making of the atomic bomb, there was just a span of a quarter of century (Rhodes, 1986).

The Real Leap Forward

The transition from low-cost labor to technology-intensive growth

Although science and technology were a key part of the 'four modernisations' program launched by Deng Xiaoping when he rose to power in 1978–9, the 'Real Leap Forward' in S&T (science and technology) began after 2000. It contrasts drastically with the catastrophic Great Leap Forward of 1958–60, which was based on the negation of science and technology, and more generally on simple practical evidence. Nowadays, China's leaders are extremely accurate on technology issues, as in 2012, eight of the nine members of the Communist Party Political Bureau had engineering degrees. They perceive innovation and competition as two sides of the same coin, and consider technological innovation as a strong means to fuel long-term growth.

Following intense debates at the central level, the release of the 'National Medium and Long-term Plan for Science and Technology Development (2006–2020)' in early 2006, (hereafter the 2020 Plan), aims to derive by the end of the decade 60 per cent or more of China's economic growth from technological progress, and to catch up with more advanced countries. 'Innovation with Chinese characteristics' or 'indigenous innovation' became the motto of the 'second stage of the opening and reform policy' led by the tandem Hu Jintao–Wen Jiabao (McGregor, 2011).

The turn of the millennium

The best proof of China's radical evolution in the last decade is the dramatic increase in higher education and human resources mostly in engineering. The percentage of young-age cohorts enrolled in university curricula, between 2000 and 2008, rose from 11 to 35 per cent, and the number of graduates increased from 1.7 million to more than 7 million. About 39 per cent of students concentrate on a scientific curriculum in comparison to 5 per cent in the US. There were 700,000 Chinese graduates in engineering degrees in comparison to 80,000 in the U.S. The share of the active population with a university-level education is now comparable to the Eurozone (26 per cent), but the absolute number is striking (now more than 100 million), as well as the number of currently enrolled Chinese students (25 million out of 140 million worldwide) (Artus, 2011, pp. 17, 292).

Between 2000 and 2010, China's R&D expenditure doubled as a share of GDP (0.8–1.75 per cent) and R&D personnel increased from about one million (full-time equivalent) to 2.8 million (Wu, 2010, 2011). At the end of the decade, China's share of total global R&D spending equaled Japan's in purchasing power parity (12.3 per cent) just behind the US (34.4 per cent) and Europe (23.3 per cent). China's world share of researchers was equal to the US (20 per cent, with 1.4 million) in 2007, just behind Europe (30 per cent, with 2.1 million) but the rapid increase of R&D personnel during the crisis allowed it to catch up with Europe. Nobel Prize–winning economist Robert Fogel of the University of Chicago estimates that in the US, a high school–educated worker is 1.8 times as productive and a college graduate, 3 times as productive as someone with a ninth-grade education. On this basis, he believes that the increase in highly skilled workers will substantially boost China's annual growth rate for a generation (Grueber, 2010; Wu, 2011).

The quality of China's education has also improved, with the creation of the C9 League, a club like the US Ivy League, which includes the top universities and has adopted a bold policy of internationalization of studies. In 2011, the total number of Chinese students and scholars attending foreign universities or research institutes rose to 340,000, 15 times more than in 1999. Chinese students comprise the highest share of foreign students in the US, the European Union as well as Japan. At the end of 2010, China had the largest oversea student population in the world, with 1.27 million Chinese studying or having studied abroad, among whom many do not return. According to the latest census data, more than 700,000 highly skilled residents in OECD countries were Chinese born, 57% of whom were living in the United States (Chinese Ministry of Education; Chen, 2011; Schaaper, 2009, p. 4).

Nothing is more symptomatic of the qualitative change of the last decade than the recent activism of China towards intellectual property. According to the World Intellectual Property Organization (WIPO), the applications for international patents by China have more than tripled between 2006 and 2011, representing 9 per cent of the world total, after Germany (10.2 per cent), Japan (21.4 per cent) and the USA (26.7 per cent) (WIPO Statistics Data Base, March 2012). They concern mainly electrical engineering, telecommunication and informatics (58 per cent), chemicals, biotechnology and drugs (21 per cent) (Carta IEDI, 2011). As for scientific publication, China has more than doubled its share of world papers in the last decade (more than 20 per cent, just behind the USA), despite the fact that their average impact remains much lower than the world average. China is stronger in physical sciences and mathematics, engineering and technology, weaker in molecular biology, but 'it is now diversifying its research base into the life sciences, and will become equally competitive in these key areas' (Adams, 2012).[6]

TNCs and R&D

Transnational corporations are key players since they account for about half of global R&D and at least two thirds of business R&D expenditures (estimated at US $450 billion in 2005). R&D spending of some large TNCs is higher than that of many countries, as six of them, concentrated in a few industries (IT hardware, automotive, pharmaceutical and biotechnology) spent more than US $5 billion on R&D in 2003 (Ford, Pfizer, Daimler Chrysler, Siemens, Toyota, GM). The share of R&D of their majority-owned foreign affiliates varied from 13 per cent for the US to 43 per cent in the case of Sweden, in the first years of the new century. During the period 2002–4, developing Asia and Oceania took over half of the FDI projects involving R&D worldwide, and China, which had already around 700 foreign R&D units in 2005, was mentioned by the largest number of TNCs as the main destination for R&D future expansion, before the US and India (WIR, 2005).

The internationalisation of R&D in China was driven by the need to adapt products and processes to key host markets (*adaptive R&D*). Internationalisation might create potential tensions between TNCs and host country governments 'in that the former may seek to retain proprietary knowledge while the latter seeks to secure as many spillovers as possible'. The key determinant is therefore the *absorptive capacity* of the host country, the type of R&D conducted, and its links to production. 'The more a TNC interacts with a host developing country's local firms and R&D institutions, and the more advanced the country's national innovation system, the greater the likelihood of positive effects on a host economy' (WIR, 2005, pp. xxvi–xxxii). In other words, there are no longer closed frontiers or strict labor divisions between the 'innovators' and the 'commodity providers'. The commodity providers at low prices may also become innovators at low prices – for example, for competitive products targeting emerging markets.

TNCs are expanding R&D in China to tap the vast pool of talents and ideas and to stay abreast of competitors in the increasingly sophisticated markets of China and Asia. The supply of talented manpower exceeds the demand of foreign firms; universities and research institutes are eager to get funding from private firms. High-technology parks, governmental incentives and the potential to reduce costs across all the stages of the R&D value chain tend to shift TNC R&D labs from support and adaptation to full-scale R&D work using China's emerging technologies and talent pools (WIR, 2005, p. 16). TNC involvement was confirmed in the second half of the decade, as the pace of R&D investment growth in China was 20 per cent a year, on average, between 2000 and 2010, versus 3.2 per cent on average in G7 markets.

The top 25 TNCs by reported R&D investment, collectively responsible for nearly US $84 billion R&D investment in 2010, have a tendency to globalise their activities in research-intensive industries such as pharmaceuticals and technology hardware. Pfizer, the world's second-leading corporate R&D investor (at US $7.4 billion), has its own R&D centre in Shanghai and research partnerships with leading Chinese universities. General Electric has had research facilities since 2000. Ten years later, 1500 of its global 2800 research staff are based in China. Philips has 1800 research and development staff in China, 110 of them working on high-level research. Microsoft employs 3750 full-time researchers and developers in China, over 300 coming from the US and Europe, and 7000 outside the company, working on a contract basis. Ninety per cent of its R&D activity is for global products, with only 5 to 10 per cent for local products. Intel, which established its China Research Center in 1998, has announced new equity investments in clean technology and healthcare software in China. IBM launched the China Analytics Solutions Centre in 2009, to support its expansion in the region. This tendency may accelerate in the next decade, as students of Chinese origin now receive 11 per cent of all US scientific and engineering doctoral degrees, with more than 4000 PhDs in 2007, twice as many as students of Indian origin, and as global R&D investment is shifting toward growth markets (Gilman, 2010).

Returning members of the Chinese diaspora play a key role in these R&D centres where locally recruited researchers provide the main manpower. In Shanghai, over 353 TNC R&D centers had been established by 2010 (WIR, 2005, pp. 142, 185). Between 2004 and 2010, R&D-related FDI stock at the national level increased from US $4 billion to US $12.8 billion, according to the Chinese Ministry of Commerce. R&D centers established by foreign affiliates, generally wholly owned by their parent company, are mainly focusing on adaptive innovations for the Chinese market, especially in the electronic and ICT (information and communication technology) industries, with Beijing and Shanghai as the main centers. But this stage can evolve into global innovative R&D in certain cases: since the 1990s China's mobile telecommunications has become the world's largest, in terms of network capacity as well as number of subscribers. Many telecom equipment makers have invested in production facilities as well as in R&D. Motorola set up its first R&D center in 1990 and had 15 centres with 1300 R&D employees in 2004. At the same time, Nokia had five centres with 800 R&D personnel while Ericsson had 9 centers with 700 R&D personnel. Certain models of mobile phones for the Asia Pacific market or the world market, including for 3G technologies, have been developed both for the Chinese market and the world market, in the R&D centres of Nokia or Ericsson.

Although labor rates in engineering were about a fifth of those in the US or Europe before the global crisis of 2008, they reached about 40 per cent in 2011, and might eventually become similar with the quick rise in the costs of living in Shanghai or Beijing, where most of the R&D centers are based. In this new environment, the balance between cost and performance of products and processes, what Eric Thun calls 'frugal engineering', and the choice of the best Chinese suppliers in terms of costs and quality will certainly increase local R&D competition, and adapt it to the constraints of emerging markets (Moody, 2011; Thun, 2011).

The 2020 Plan for S&T and the key role of state-owned enterprises

The current policy adopted in the Medium and Long-Term Plan for S&T (2006–20) aims to increase R&D intensity to 2.5 per cent of GDP in 2020, and to bring the contribution of S&T to 60 per cent of growth. This plan represents a radical change from the previous policy as it looks to decrease the country's reliance on foreign technology by 30 per cent or below, and to develop 'indigenous innovation'. Technology development is now based on an import/assimilate/re-innovate model. This is a far cry from the previous division of labor as noted by the Executive Vice-President of IBM for innovation and technology, Nicholas M. Donofrio, who declared in 2005: 'the global innovation–commoditization cycle has never been more pronounced than it is today, and it forces distinct choices. Winners can be the innovators – those with the capacity to invest, manage and leverage the creation of intellectual capital – or the commodity players, who differentiate through low prices, economies of scale and efficient distribution of other parties' intellectual capital' (Fabre, 2008, p. 203). The previous low-skilled and low-paid worker thus reincarnates into an engineer, who re-innovates through the re-appropriation of intellectual capital. A clear illustration of the process of climbing up the value chain.

To reach these objectives, the country must give priority to technological development in 11 key sectors (energy; water resources; environmental protection; ICT; nanosciences and nanotechnology; health; food, agriculture and fisheries; biotechnology; aeronautics and aerospace; new materials; security and defense), as well as improve the national Intellectual Property System and its enforcement, and encourage enterprises to play a key role in innovation through state projects, tax incentives and other financial support.[7] Sixteen megaprojects had already been carried out during the 11th Five Year Plan (2006–10) in key sectors. In the 12th Five Year Plan (2011–15), the emphasis is put on life sciences (in particular, drug discovery) and infectious diseases, which have strong societal and economical potential, an area where China needs to upgrade.

In addition to S&T programs which play a signaling role to enterprises in terms of priority directions, in S&T-intensive sectors such as IT, new materials, new energy, biotech and environmental technology, the government favours S&T Industrial Parks (STIPs) and Technology Business Incubators (TBIs) to promote academia–industry partnerships, through both commercialisation and internationalisation of R&D (Schaaper, 2009, p. 31). Zhongguancun Science Park, in the northwest of Beijing Haidian district, is the largest science park, home to 40 universities and 130 research institutes. By 2004, it had attracted 41 foreign-invested R&D centres, 60 per cent of them in the ICT industry, with funding coming from leading TNCs such as Hewlett-Packard, IBM,

Motorola, Nokia, Nortel, Oracle, Samsung, Siemens, Sony, Sun Microsystems and Toshiba, to name a few.

A striking feature of China's innovation system is the expanded role of enterprises, and their orientation toward development activities. Government research institutes, which are supposed to carry out basic as well as applied research, represent less than 20 per cent of R&D expenditure, and 18 per cent of R&D personnel (2006). In 2005, nearly 95 per cent of their expenditure was concentrated in natural sciences and high tech–related fields. The higher education sector, where applied research is predominant, concentrates less than 10 per cent of R&D expenditures, and 16 per cent of R&D personnel, mainly based in the top 50 universities (66 per cent of expenditures) on a few key disciplines in natural sciences and engineering. The business sector provides a large share of its funding, and plays an important role in research–industry linkage.

The bulk of R&D, 71 per cent, is almost self-financed by the business sector, mainly state-owned and state-holding enterprises which employ nearly 66 per cent of R&D personnel on experimental development in diverse industrial sectors (communication, computer, electronic equipment, instruments, chemicals, etc.). According to the first national survey of firm innovation conducted by the State Statistical Bureau in 2007, state-owned and state-holding enterprises are the main actors of innovation in China, since they account for 81 per cent of total business R&D in 2006, mainly in pharmaceuticals, instrument and office machines, tobacco, communication and electronic equipment, and special measuring equipment (Schaaper, 2009, p. 56; Wu, 2010, 2011, pp. 7–8). In order to bridge the technology gap with OECD countries, state-owned enterprises which include the country's 80 to 100 big corporations were chosen as the foundations of the country's micro-economy as well as key components of the indigenous innovation policy.

SOEs have been the core of China's 'going global strategy' since its launch in 2000, and they play a dominant role, after being restructured in the 1990s in capital-intensive and strategic sectors such as petroleum, coking, nuclear fuel, raw chemical material, transport equipment, mining, electric and heat power, gas and water. Their profits increased nearly fourfold between 2000 and 2009, and in 2007 they represented 83 per cent of stock market capitalization (Lee, 2009; *The Economist*, 3 September 2011).

As in the higher education sector, R&D activities are often carried out on a project basis. The share of basic and applied research expenditures over total R&D spending dropped to 17 per cent in 2010, compared with

OECD countries which have an average level of 50 per cent. Basic research represents less than 6 per cent of total R&D spending, with a slight decline in recent years, to be compared with an average of 20 per cent in OECD countries. The present step-by-step catching-up strategy is clearly focused on development (83 per cent of R&D) in order to reduce technological dependency on OECD countries and to compete with them on innovative products. New technology–intensive growth aims at higher economic efficiency, lower energy consumption, less pollution and better use of human resources.

Access to the market and technology transfer: a cat-and-mouse game

As the 2020 Plan aims at indigenous innovation and reducing the dependency on foreign technology, it is legitimate to ask if the internationalisation of R&D, as the next stage of outsourcing, will turn into a win–win situation. Large public investment toward important areas of research has put China on the map in genomics, nanotechnology, clean energy, space science, supercomputing and defense technology. Apart from dramatic successes in these strategic sectors of R&D, China's relies on the size of its potential consumption market, the scale of its public investment and procurement, the competitiveness of its labor force and the dynamics of its R&D and innovation policy to ask for technology transfer in exchange for market access (Gordon et al. 2011).

Some oppose strong arguments against such deals. The belief that high-tech sectors like alternative energy are supposed to revive economic growth in OECD countries leads Gary P. Pisano from the Harvard Business School to underline the fact that the US 'has lost or is in the process of losing the ability to manufacture many of the cutting-edge products it invented. These include the batteries that power electric and hybrid cars, light-emitting diodes (LEDs) for the next generation of energy-efficient lighting, critical components of solar panels, advanced displays for mobile phones and new consumer electronics products like Amazon's Kindle e-reader, and many of the carbon-fiber components for Boeing's new 787 Dreamliner'. He opposes the idea of separating R&D and manufacturing which has prevailed in the last 25 years. Innovation needs a two-way feedback, from R&D to production but also from production to R&D, because 'the act of production creates knowledge about the process and the product design'. There are of course exceptions where R&D and manufacturing are separable, but in the vast majority of high-tech products, 'when manufacturing capabilities migrate from a country, design and R&D capabilities eventually follow' (Pisano, 2009).

In fact, producing in China is the only way for foreign companies to get access to the market. In 2007, foreign capital firms were responsible for about 25 per cent of total industrial production for domestic use (Gaulier et al., 2011). But, at the same time, as author Nirmal Chandra underlines, citing the 11th Five Year Plan for Use of Foreign Investment, China will 'encourage foreign enterprises – especially large-scale multinationals – to transfer the processing and manufacturing processes with higher technology levels and higher added-value and research and development organizations to China [...] to develop a technology spillover effect, and strengthen the independent innovation ability of Chinese enterprises [...] The overall strategic objective of use of foreign investment in China is to [...] change the (previous) emphasis from making up the shortage of capital and foreign exchange to introducing advanced technology' (Chandra, 2012).

In the new landscape of indigenous innovation, quite different from the previous one, the question for most foreign capital corporations is less to attempt to control 'the stealing of IPR' by counterfeiters than to organize the extent of technology transfer while keeping their core technology. There is no way to capture the real dimensions of these transfers, since the Chinese government does not publish any balance of payments for technology. Some studies conclude that as the skill intensity of exports increases, the percentage of the value of the final product that derives from imported components rises sharply: for electronic devices (85.2 per cent), telecommunication equipment (91.6 per cent) and computers (96.1 per cent). China would have remained 'a low value-added assembler of more sophisticated inputs imported from abroad, a "workbench" economy' (Moran, 2011). The dominance of foreign firms and the large share of imported materials in processing trade 'raise the question whether China's high-tech industries are really high-tech and whether the high-tech industries in China are really Chinese'. These conclusions may be excessive, as noted by Chandra. Since the threshold of foreign equity is only 10 per cent, many foreign enterprises may be controlled by state-owned enterprises, and these figures do not reveal the potential of China's domestic firms, as China has become the regional hub for the production of high-tech goods. After all, Korea's Samsung and LG began assembling electronic components as subcontractors of US majors, before rising to the status of global leaders (Chandra, 2012).

According to the first national survey of firm innovation conducted by the State Statistical Bureau in 2007, state-owned and state-holding enterprises are the main actors of innovation in China, since they account for 81 per cent of total business R&D in 2006, mainly in pharmaceuticals, instrument and office machines, tobacco, communication and electronic equipment, and special measuring equipment (Schaaper, 2009, pp. 56, 62; Wu, 2010, 2011, pp. 7–8). SOEs have been the core of China's 'going global strategy' since its launch in 2000, and – as has already been pointed out – they have played a dominant role, after being restructured in the 1990s, in capital-intensive and strategic sectors such as petroleum, coking, nuclear fuel, raw chemical material, transport equipment, mining, electric and heat power, gas and water. Their profits increased nearly fourfold between 2000 and 2009, and in 2007 they represented 83 per cent of stock market capitalization (Lee, 2009; *The Economist*, 3 September 2011).

In light of these contradictory statements, it may be useful to look at such examples as high-speed trains, aeronautics and clean energy to grasp the dynamic of China catching up in key sectors.

Catching up in high-potential sectors

High-speed trains

The high-speed (HS) railway program is a very interesting example of China's indigenous innovation policy led by SOEs. The first HS railway, the Beijing–Tianjin intercity line, covering the 120 km distance in 30 minutes, was opened for service on 1 August 2008. With the global financial crisis of 2008, China's leaders turned the project into part of the economic stimulus package, speeding construction, including bringing forward completion of the US $33 billion Beijing–Shanghai line by a year. By the end of 2009, total HS operating length had reached 6552 km, and the Ministry of Railways had an additional 10,000 km of HS rails under construction (Xinhua, 3 July 2010).

The *People's Daily* presented the development of China's high-speed railways as an example of domestic innovation after incorporating advanced technology from developed nations (Li Hujun, Caixin Online, 23 June 2011). In 2004 the Railway Minister signed deals to buy trains from Kawasaki Heavy Industry (KHI), which transferred production facilities and know-how for its 200 km/h bullet train for US $760 million. Alstom and Bombardier signed similar deals for their first or second-generation bullet trains rolling at 200–50 km/h, and in 2005 Siemens transferred technologies for a 300 km/h HS train. Engineers trained by Kawasaki in Japan later helped to build the Qingdao factory of China's South Locomotive and Rolling Stock Industry Corporation

(CSR), which now produces about 200 trains a year, some of them rolling at 300 km/h. Paraphrasing Bernard de Chartres and Isaac Newton, a CSR senior engineer declared: 'Real innovation is rare. We attained our achievements in high-speed train technology by standing on the shoulders of past pioneers' (Shirouzu, 2010).

While its competitors from Bombardier, Siemens and Alstom preferred to keep silent in a market which is expected to account for more than half of global railway spending until 2020 (according to World Bank estimates), Kawasaki Heavy Industries (KHI) openly denied China's claim that it had created its own technology. The firm issued a public communiqué to the effect that the CRH2 bullet train in operation today is practically the same as the original Japanese one. Kawasaki Heavy Industry (KHI) hopes to settle the issue through commercial talks, but contests the IPR of its Chinese partner to export the technology (Shirouzu, 2010). The Chinese Ministry of Railways has organized a team of lawyers to examine how vulnerable state companies would be to IP lawsuits in outside markets. But some foreign companies have already accepted forming partnerships with the Chinese groups bidding on HS projects all over the world. In 2010, for instance, Siemens dropped its own bid to build and operate a line in Saudi Arabia so it could join a Chinese consortium.

Although competitors mostly believe that China has in a way 'metabolized' imported technology, the Chinese have taken charge of the competition between different foreign groups in order to obtain a larger share of technology than has been publicly admitted. Foreign industry executives estimate than around 90 per cent of the HS technology used in China derives from partnerships or equipment developed by foreign companies, while for such programs the Chinese government says this is 30 per cent, which means officially that 70 per cent of (digested) technology is Chinese (Anderlini, 2010).

Although tarnished by the dismissal and arrest for corruption of Liu Zhijun (the Railways Minister) in February 2011 and later the tragic collusion of two trains in Wenzhou which caused 40 deaths and hundreds of casualties (July 2011), the Chinese HS train program, with all the excesses that accompany a top–down strategy, illustrates the huge investment in 'indigenous innovation' that was allocated by the stimulus package following the global crisis of 2008. The rhythm of the indigenous innovation policy has clearly accelerated since 2008, reflecting the evolution of the leadership's choices in favor of strategic sectors such as aircraft and spacecraft (where R&D represents 15.39 per cent of added value), electronic and communications equipment (where its share is 6.78 per cent), medical equipment and metre manufacturing (6.28 per cent), pharmaceuticals (4.66 per cent), computers and office equipment (3.87 per cen) (Wu, 2011).

Aeronautics

If we turn to the aircraft and aerospace industry, which is the top priority of China's innovation policy, it is striking to observe the asymmetry between the Chinese government's strategic will and the relative passivity of US and European governments which tend to relegate policy developments in this area to private parties, or even to follow their own initiatives. In May 2008 China announced that it had 'established a homegrown company to make passenger jumbo jets . . . to become less dependent on Boeing and Airbus'. A new consortium was formed, the Commercial Aircraft Corporation of China (COMAC), with a capitalisation of US $2.72 billion and the participation of the two leading aircraft companies in China, China Aviation Industry Corporation I (AVIC I) and China Aviation Industry Corporation II (AVIC II), which including their subsidiaries have about 491,000 employees between them. China already has the muscle to support such an ambition with six companies devoted to 'air frame assembly', eight 'engine companies', 28 entities involved with components, and 20 research institutes (Herrnstadt, 2010).

In the same year (2008), China signed an agreement with Airbus to build a plant in Tianjin, which is now successfully assembling 10 per cent of A320 production. The European aircraft manufacturer delivered 110 A320s to China in 2011, accounting for one fifth of the company's deliveries worldwide, and sold the first of five superjumbo A380 aircraft to China Southern Airline. Airbus remains optimistic about prospects in the Chinese market, since it is the second largest aircraft manufacturer in the world and should be the first by 2020, according to its projections (Xinhua, 15 October 2011). In the interval, in April 2009 the first design of the planned Chinese jumbo jet, the new C919 was released, with the first test flight announced for 2014 and the first delivery for 2016. The country would be capable of producing 150 domestically made jumbo aircraft each year. 'Although Western companies are seeking to become suppliers to the program, even if they are successful, question remains regarding how much of those contracts will be supported by production outside China' asked an aircraft expert (Herrnstadt, 2010).

Two agreements recently signed provide an answer and suggest the same digestive proportion as for HS trains: 70 per cent of indigenous innovation and 30 per cent of foreign technology dependence will apply in the aircraft industry. In September 2011, AVIC, the supplier of the C919 project, signed a 50/50 joint venture with General Electric to develop a new generation of the latter's avionic operating system (the 'brains' guiding navigation, communication and other operations on an airplane), which is already on board the Boeing 787 (Bussey, 2011b). The same month (i.e., September 2011) the French government created, along the lines of the Ecole Centrale de Pékin (one of its best engineering universities), the Sino-French Institute of Nuclear Energy and the Sino-European Institute of Aviation Engineering in Tianjin, the latter a consortium of the Ecole Nationale de l'Aviation Civile (ENAC), the Institut Supérieur de l'Aéronautique et de l'Espace (ISAE) and the Ecole Nationale Supérieure d'Aéronautique et d'Aérotechnique (ENSMA), which will be staffed by 100 engineers in 2013. French officials tend to insist on the francophone curriculum (*Les Echos*, 27 September 2011), while the Chinese authorities are more motivated by other perspectives. The C919, if successful, would be the first new model of the Chinese aircraft industry and may compete with Boeing and Airbus in the market for 150-seat and larger commercial aircraft. But the two Western companies believe that their technological sophistication and manufacturing capacities will keep them ahead of innovation. The 100-seat regional jet sector is already crowded. There is fierce competition between Bombardier, with its CRJ700/900/1000 family and the new CSeries at 110 and 130 seats (rollout in 2013); Embraer, with the E-Jet family; Sukhoi, with its Superjets 100 and 171; Mitsubishi, with the 70 and 90-seat MRJ family (rollout in 2015). It will be quite hard for the Comac ARJ21, the last creation of the Chinese aircraft industry in the 100-seat market segment to bypass the local Chinese market. The future of the 150 to 190-seat C919 (rollout in 2016), which depends on active collaboration with General Electric and Safran, may be linked with the performance of the ARJ21 (Morris, 2012; Rabinovitch, 2012).

Clean energy

The HS train program and the C919 project are clear examples of the Chinese art of creating competition between TNCs while restricting the latter's share of big public procurement contracts through indigenous innovation, as well as by organizing bidding processes in favor of Chinese SOEs. Clean energy is another priority of the 2020 Plan, not only for obvious domestic reasons (China being the largest issuer of CO_2), but *also because by 2020 it will be one of the world's biggest industries, estimated at US $2.3 trillion* (Gordon et al., 2010, p. 1) China leads the world in terms of renewable electricity capacity, with 16 per cent of its electricity from hydropower and wind power at the end of 2009, despite the fact that between 20 and 30 per cent of its wind power capacity is still not connected to the very fragmented and maladapted electric network. The wind power sector has been growing rapidly through the Kyoto Protocol clean development mechanism (CDM), which allowed advanced countries to offset their emissions at home by investing in clean energy projects and transferring technology to developing countries such as China. The surge in investment that followed in the very attractive domestic market was such that major wind manufacturers rapidly grew in number from a mere 5 or 6 to 70 in 2008, leading the Chinese government to revise its 2007 national target of, respectively, 10 GW and 30 GW of installed wind capacity for 2010 and 2020, as 20 GW were already installed by the end of 2009! Despite the surge in investment by foreign corporations, the authorities persisted in imposing a 70 per cent local requirement for wind power equipment according to the standard of indigenous innovation. The result was that the share of foreign suppliers in this fast-growing market dropped from 75 per cent in 2004 to 13.8 per cent in 2009. This requirement has finally been dropped following complaints from foreign manufacturers at the beginning of 2010, but it served its purpose since there is now concern about wind-manufacturing overcapacity among Chinese wind firms and the race for exports. Today, only domestic or joint venture firms with at least 50 per cent Chinese ownership can operate or develop offshore wind farms. The American Chamber of Commerce and the European Chamber of Commerce in China have openly complained since 2010 about the plethora of constantly changing rules, which have had the effect of restricting access to the local market in a lot of sectors (Areddy, 2011; ECC, 2010; Gordon, 2011, pp. 29–30; McGregor, 2011, p. 33).[8]

As for solar energy, China is the leading manufacturer of photovoltaic (PV) panels, having captured 57 per cent of world production; the PVs are mainly for export. At the end of 2009, the country had just 0.3 MW of installed power capacity, but following major policies to stimulate the sector, China's PV market grew by 230 per cent in 2011 over 2010, with a surge of installed power capacity (1.6 GW) and exports, especially to Europe (€21 billion). Europe initiated an anti-dumping complaint at the WTO, as did the US, under pressure from manufacturers, especially Solar World, the German leader of photovoltaic production. As of 2012, 5 of the top 10 companies in photovoltaic production were Chinese (*http://www.solarbuzz.com*).[9] China's competitiveness in the production of PV panels is not limited to its exports, it is also highly effective at attracting foreign firms. Applied Materials, one of the world's leading suppliers of equipment to make semiconductors, solar panels and flat-panel displays, has set up an entire solar panel assembly line in Xi'an, northern China, as part of a research centre dedicated to advanced research into solar panel manufacture. The choice of Xi'an was motivated by an attractive discount on a 75-year land lease, 5-year subsidies covering a quarter of the lab's operating costs, and a supply of low-cost engineers with master's degrees who can be hired for US $730 per month. The development phase of global research will be done in Xi'an and will be a 360-employee operation, while at the same time the company has resolved to reduce employment from 10 to 12 per cent, or 1300 to 1500 jobs, in the US and Europe (Bradsher, 2010).

Conclusion

Until recently, China's R&D and innovation policy has been mainly analysed by comparing it with that of Japan and the four dragons in terms of climbing up the value chain. This type of analysis underestimates the scale of China's impact. It is more than just the new scientific and engineering demography created by the Real Leap Forward of the 2000s; there is also China's manufacturing capacity which has already bypassed that of the US, the growing internal market and the rising presence of Chinese TNCs in emerging markets.

If we add to these factors national sovereignty, which plays a key role in the sensitive sector of defence, it is clear that China's R&D and innovation strategy, presented in 2006 as the second stage of the opening up and reform policy, is slowly changing the global landscape of technology, and moving the frontiers. Although China's wish to reduce its technology dependency is perfectly legitimate, indigenous innovation as set out in the 2020 Plan is viewed by many international technology companies as a 'blueprint for technology theft on a scale the world has never seen before' … Some analysts remain pessimistic as regards the consequences of this new techno-nationalism coupled with a reduction of market access: 'As the belief by foreign companies that large financial investments, the sharing of expertise and significant technology transfers would lead to an ever opening China market is being replaced by boardroom banter that win–win in China means China wins twice', we are heading toward 'contentious trade disputes and inflamed political rhetoric on both sides' (McGregor, 2011, pp. 4 and 6).

The top–down model of R&D and innovation has been strongly criticised by prominent Chinese scientists, from inside and outside China, for giving bureaucrats too much power over them.[10] The postponement of the HS train program, following a fatal HS train crash in July 2011 illustrates the limits of this new techno-nationalism.

However, it would be a mistake to focus on indigenous innovation without considering the entire R&D landscape, which is much more open than it seems at first sight. Although there are conflicting views in some strategic sectors, such as aeronautics, clean energy vehicles, HS trains, where 'the Chinese government exerts leverage where it can and foreign firms do what they can to limit the loss of their core technologies', R&D is not reducible to this cat-and-mouse game (Thun, 2011). In other sectors such as chemistry, life sciences, IT, and nanotechnology, things appear much more open. The constant flow of foreign researchers, now facilitated with Chinese green cards, or researchers of Chinese origin from the US and Europe wanting to return to China brings about a new climate of hybrid R&D and innovation, such as the one that already exists in other East Asian countries.

Some TNC executives are convinced that China is the new frontier of innovation. Andrew Lewis, the CEO of Dow Chemicals is confident that 'innovation has followed manufacturing to China [...] Over time, when companies decide where to build R&D facilities, it will make more and more sense to do things like product support, upgrades and next generation design in the same place where the product is made [...] That is one reason why Dow has 500 Chinese scientists working in China, earning incredibly good money, and who are already generating more patents per scientist than our other locations' (Bussey, 2011a). The Chinese president's speech at the APEC summit in Hawaii illustrates the strong political will of the leadership in this regard: 'China will work hard to turn itself into an innovation driven country, bring in high caliber and innovation-minded professionals from overseas and realize the transformation of *Made in China* to *Created by China*' (Xinhua News Agency, 12 November 2011). But it is still unclear whether these two approaches are compatible in the long term. It will depend not only on the pragmatism of the Chinese direction but also on the capacity of non-Chinese to adapt to China, to its culture, to its rules, and interact in a constructive way with a new and considerable actor, one that is definitely changing the R&D landscape.

Notes

1. I wish to thank my colleague Stéphane Grumbach (INRIA) with whom the original French version of this chapter was published

under the framework of an FMSH Working Paper (*The World Upside Down*): *http://www.msh-paris.fr* (FMSH-WP-2012-07, avril 2012). With this paper I have brought my contribution up to date. Thanks also to Elizabeth Durot-Boucé (University of Le Havre), for her corrections of the English version of a first draft of this chapter.

2. Study of IHS Global Insight (a global information company), cited in *Financial Times*, 13 March 2011.
3. National Bureau of Statistics of China, 27 May 2013 [in Chinese]. Of a total of 262 million migrants, 163 are trans-provincial migrants and 99 million are intra-provincial migrants.
4. *Perspectives Chinoises (China Perspectives)*, 2011 No. 2, dossier : 'Le monde ouvrier chinois en mouvement', CEFC, Hongkong [in French].
5. *OECD Science, Technology and Industry Scoreboard 2011*, *oecd-ilibrary.org*.
6. *Zhongguo keji lunwen tongji jieguo, 2011* (Statistical Data of Chinese S&T Paper 2011) [in Chinese].
7. National Guidelines for the Medium and Long-term Plan for Science and Technology Development (2006–20).
8. *Alternatives économiques: Hors Série n° 94*, Les chiffres de l'économie 2013, octobre 2012, p. 83.
9. *http://www.solarbuzz.com*, 10 October 2011; *Alternatives économiques: Hors Série n° 94*, Les chiffres de l'économie 2013, octobre 2012, pp. 82–3.
10. *Nature Magazine*, special issue, Fall 2004. For a critical approach to the management of science in other countries, see Malrieux (2011).

References

Adams, J. (2012a) *Global Research Report: Leading Research Economies and the New Geography of Knowledge*, Thomson Reuters. Available from: *http://researchanalytics.thomsonreuters.com/grr/*

Adams, J. (2012b) *OECD Science, Technology and Industry Scoreboard, 2011*. OECD Directorate for Science, Technology and Industry, Paris. Available from: *http://www.oecd.org/sti/oecdsciencetechnologyandindustryscoreboard2011innovationandgrowthinknowledgeeconomies.htm*

Anderlini, J. (2010) *Financial Times*, 23 October 2010.

Areddy, J.T. (2011) U.S. firms complain of China's heavy hand. *Wall Street Journal*, 19 January 19 2011.

Artus, P., Mistral, J., et Pagnol, V. (2011) *L'émergence de la Chine: impact économique et implications de politique économique* (Rapport du Conseil d'Analyse Economique). La Documentation Française, Paris [in French].

Bradsher, K. (2010) China drawing high-tech research from US. *New York Times*, 17 March 2010.

Bussey, J. (2011a) Does history say China wins? *Wall Street Journal*, 4 November 2011.

Bussey, J. (2011b) China venture is good for GE but is it good for the U.S? *Wall Street Journal*, 30 September 2011.

Carta IEDI n°482, 26/08/2011, *A transformação da China em economia orientada à inovação, Parte 1*. Available online.

Chandra, N. (2012) Appraising industrial policy of China and India from two perspectives, nationalist and internationalist. In: A.K. Bagchi and A. D'Costa (Eds), *Transformation and Development: The Political Economy of Transition in India and China*. Oxford University Press, Delhi.

Chen Jia (2011) *China Daily*, 18 April 2011.

Dhont-Peltrault, E. and Lallement, R. (2011) *'Investments for the Future' and Industrial Policy in Europe: How to Target and Select Innovative Projects* (La note d'analyse, n°236, september). Centre d'analyse stratégique, Premier Ministre. Available from: *http://www.strategie.gouv.fr*

ECC (2010) *European Business in China* (Position Paper, 2010–11, pp. 353–4). Available from: *http://www.europeanchamber.com.cn/view/static/?sid=7479* [European Chamber of Commerce].

Fabre, G. (2008) China and the black gold of the 21st century: intellectual property, innovation and global competition. In: B. Andreosso-O'Callaghan and B. Zolin (Eds), *Asia and Europe: Connections and Contrasts*. Ed, Cafoscarina, Venice, Italy.

Fabre, G. and Rodwin, V. (2011) Public health and medical care for the world's factory: China's Pearl River Delta region. *BMC Medecine*, **9**, 110. Available from: *http://www.biomedcentral.com*

Gaulier, G., Lemoine, F. and Ünal, D. (2011) *China's Foreign Trade in the Perspective of a More Balanced Economic Growth* (CEPII Working Paper, Paris, march). Centre d'Etudes Prospectives et d'Informations Internationales, Paris.

Gilman, D. (2010) *The New Geography of Global Innovation*. Global Markets Institute, Goldman Sachs, New York.

Glassman, J. (2010) *Is America Suffering an Innovation Gap?'*. Available from: *http://www.itif.org/media/america-suffering-innovation-gap*

Gordon, K., Wong, J.L. and McLain, J.T. (2010) *Out of the Running? How Germany, Spain and China Are Seizing the Energy Opportunity and Why the United States Risks Getting Left Behind*. Center for American Progress, March 2010. Available from: *http://www.americanprogress.org*

Gordon, K., Lyon, S., Paisley, E. and Pool, S. (2011) *Rising to the Challenge: A Progressive U.S. Approach to China's Innovation and Competitiveness Policies*, Center for American Progress. Available from: *http://www.americanprogress.org*

Grueber, M. (2011) Global R&D forecast. *R&D Magazine*, December 2010, p. 3. Available from: *http://www.rdmag.com*

Herrnstadt, O.E. (2010) *China's Emergent Military Aerospace and Commercial Aviation Capabilities*. USCC.gov, U.S-China Economic and Security Review Commission, May 10, 2010. [Testimony of Owen E. Herrnstadt, Director of

Trade and Globalisation, International Association of Machinist and Aerospace Workers.]

Lee, J. (2009) *State-owned Enterprises in China: Reviewing the Evidence*. OECD Working Group on Privatisation and Corporate Governance of State-Owned Assets, 26 January 2009.

Lewis, A. (1954) *Economic Growth with Unlimited Supply of Labor* (Manchester School of Economic and Social Studies No. 22).

Malrieux, J-P. (2011) *La science gouvernée : Essai sur le triangle sciences/techniques/pouvoir*. Librairie Ombres Blanches, Toulouse, France [in French].

McGregor, J. (2011) *China's Drive for 'Indigenous Innovation': A Web of Industrial Policies*. US Chamber of Commerce in China. Available from: *www.amchamchina.org/*

Moody, A. (2011) Research in motion: multinationals moving R&D centers to China as the country aims to become an innovation nation. *China Daily European Weekly*, 11–17 November 2011.

Moran, T.H. (2011) *Foreign Manufacturing Multinationals and the Transformation of the Chinese Economy: New Measurements, New Perspectives* (Working Paper No. 11-11). Peterson Institute of International Economics, Washington, D.C., April 2011.

Morris, R. (2012) Crowded market. *Airline Business*, October 2012, pp. 32–3.

Observatoire des Sciences et Techniques (2010) *Rapport Bi-annuel 2010*. Available from: *www.obs-ost.fr/*

Pisano, G.M. (2009) The U.S. is outsourcing away its competitive edge. *Harvard Business Review*, 1 October 2009. Available from: *http://blogs.harvardbusiness.org/hbr/restoring-american-competitiveness/2009/10/the-us-is-outsourcing-away-its.html*

Rabinovitch, S. (2012) Comac : China offers serious challenge to Boeing and Airbus. *Financial Times*, 7 July 2012.

Rhodes, R. (1986) *The Making of the Atomic Bomb*. Simon & Schuster, New York.

Schaaper, M. (2009) *Measuring China's Innovation System: National Specificities and International Comparisons* (OECD Science, Technology and Industry Working Papers 2009/01). Available online.

Shirouzu, N. (2010) *Wall Street Journal*, 22 November 2010.

Thun, E. (2011) Shaping the new economy: R&D centers in China provide an opportunity for companies to re-think design, innovation. *China Daily European Weekly*, 11–17 November 2011.

WB (2012) *China 2030: Building a Modern, Harmonious, and Creative High-Income Society* (World Bank Report, February 2012). World Bank, Washington, D.C.

WIPO (2011) *World Intellectual Property Indicators* (2011 edition) WIPO. Available online [World Intellectual Property Organization].

WIR (2005) World Investment Report 2005: R&D Internationalization and Development. *China Daily European Weekly*, 11–17 November 2011, p. 1. Available from: *www.unctad.org*

Wu, Y. (2011) China's innovation policy. Paper presented at *Conference at the CEPII, Paris, 12 October 2011*. [Centre d'Etudes Prospectives et d'Informations Internationales].

Wu, Y. (2010) *Indigenous Innovation in China: Implications for Sustainable Growth* (Discussion Paper No. 10.18), University of Western Australia, Crawley, Australia.

Xu Xianjin (2007) Nongmin gong duanque yu nongmin gong shehui baozhan wenti yanjiu (Research on the labor shortage among migrants and the question of social insurance). *Nongye jingji (Agricultural Economics)*, **9**, 44–6 [in Chinese].

Yu Yongding (2009) *China's Policy Responses to the Global Financial Crisis* (Richard Snape Lecture), Productivity Commission, Melbourne, Australia.

Zhongguo keji lunwen tongji jieguo (2011) Statistical data of Chinese S&T. Available from: *www.istic.ac.cn/tabid/640/default.aspx/* [in Chinese].

2

'With a little help from the state': endogenous and exogenous dynamics in China's cluster economy

Valeria Zanier

Abstract: District economics has only recently become an established field of research in China. This chapter aims to help define more precisely the nature of Chinese districts, discover what role they have played in China's dramatic economic growth, and interpret interactions between the Chinese and more mature economies in light of the developments in and interplay between districts. It will do so by analysing the nature and structure of the Wenzhou district economy, concentrating on the role played by endogenous and exogenous factors in the process of globalisation. The chapter will first of all address the role of trade – *per se* an exogenous factor – but an element so closely tied with the structure of the Wenzhou economy to be regarded as endogenous. Second, the study will focus on the role of informal finance, and on its recent impact during the global crisis. In both cases, the analysis will highlight the interplay of local institutions and central government, pointing out how Wenzhou's features as an industrial district do not fit neatly into an already established model. Rather, it can be described as a blend of Asian and Western features, where endogenous and exogenous factors were both responsible for its development.

Key words: district economics, cluster, globalisation, industrial policy, trade, informal finance, financial crisis.

District economics has only recently become an established field of research in China. A systematic study started in the late 1990s as a result of problems in directly retrieving data from earlier years (Christerson and Lever-Tracy, 1997; Oi, 1995). Until now only a moderate amount of both empirical and theoretical research has been completed on the study of Chinese districts. On the empirical side, although the body of real data available is still scant, a number of in-depth analyses of relevant case histories (especially in the more developed coastal provinces of Guangdong, Zhejiang and Jiangsu) have since been produced and there is constant and productive academic exchange on the subject. On the theoretical side, European and US scholars are dominant. Stemming from Marshall's early theories as well as the detailed models produced by scholar G. Becattini, there are now a plethora of models which have been developed mainly from observing conditions in Europe and the United States. Many case studies of extra-European or extra-US district economies exist; thus far, such research has focused predominately on Japan and Korea and has relied on earlier Western theories. With regard to Chinese districts, comparisons with experiences in Western economies have produced varied conclusions. Scholars like Bellandi, Ganne and Lecler and Walcott have found that similar elements appear in both Italian and Chinese industrial clusters (Bellandi, 2007; Ganne and Lecler, 2009; Walcott, 2007); however, other scholars show how difficult it is to assimilate the Chinese experience into existing theories (Walder, 1995; Wang and Tong, 2004). Japanese scholars with direct experience of the phenomenon of district economies and who have been studying it closely for decades have produced interesting seminal works (Sonobe et al., 2002, 2004; Marukawa, 2009).

A preliminary classification of districts in China entails the following: (1) traditional agglomerations of historically integrated industries, more often visible in small towns or in rural areas; (2) high-tech clusters, more often situated in large cities near university centers; (3) clusters resulting from foreign direct investment (FDI), mainly consisting of foreign companies; (4) small and medium enterprise (SME) clusters grouped around large companies (Wang, 2001). Aside from those classifications very few Chinese scholars have applied existing theories to or built new theoretical frameworks for their respective studies of the development of a cluster economy in their country. It seems rather that a fruitful exchange between Chinese and foreign scholars in the theoretical field is yet to come.

This chapter aims to help define more precisely the nature of Chinese districts, discover what role they have played in China's dramatic economic growth, and interpret interactions between the Chinese and more mature economies in light of the developments in and interplay between districts. It will do so by analysing the nature and structure of the Wenzhou district economy, concentrating on the role played by endogenous and exogenous factors in the process of globalisation.

The skeleton of Wenzhou's economy is formed by closely tied networks in the production, commercial and financial sectors. It is a district economy specialising in low-key production, which has successfully expanded abroad. How important is the fact that Wenzhou's economy is district based? Before this question can be answered, it must be considered whether a shared definition of industrial districts in China even exists?

In the evolution of the Wenzhou model during the 1990s and 2000s, which factors enabled the globalisation of the district and which in turn allowed it to play a leading role worldwide? Was it a result of cheap labor production? Or did the strenghtening and expansion of external trade networks have a greater impact?

Finally, the literature on district economies has generally overlooked the role of the state, while emphasizing the role of local institutions. According to significant studies, the key determinants of breaking out of lock-in are often large firms, research institutions and human capital (Martin and Sunley, 2006). When speaking of Asian development models, however, one must remember that in many cases the market is 'governed', particularly in China. Thus, the manner and extent to which the central government has affected the evolution of the Wenzhou cluster economy must also be considered.

The structure of the Wenzhou district economy

Wenzhou is known for having played a crucial role in the development of private entrepreneurship in China's economic reforms. From 1978 to 2010, Wenzhou's GDP increased from ¥2.32 to 292.50 billion, with a 15 per cent growth rate. Very quickly, family micro-businesses popped up in almost every sector of light industry, from footwear and apparel, to zippers, buttons and lighters. Distribution was carried out with the support of local traders, as companies were usually of such small dimensions that they could not afford to have a commercial department.

When explaining the Wenzhou model of development, the following features prove crucial:[1]

(1) The basic unit of production is the rural family. Wenzhou is a rural-based economy; however, economic actitivity is in large part situated in suburban areas. Between 1978 and 1985, an enormous number of peasants (1,400,000) left their farms to work in the newborn companies, taking advantage of the wave of liberalisation.

(2) Wenzhou businesses are most frequently active in agglomerations. This feature allows scholars to investigate the Wenzhou model within the theoretical framework of the industrial district.

(3) Production is consumer oriented (middle to low quality) making use of simple and labor-intensive technology. In the 1980s, neither technology nor big investments were needed to start a new business. Rather, scant amounts of machinery and capital would suffice to guarantee success for those possessing the right entrepreneurial attitude.

(4) Sales are made through selling, purchasing and marketing networks which extend over the whole country thanks to family and village connections. Moreover, during the 1980s people originating from the Wenzhou suburban area migrated to Western Europe, especially to France and Italy, where they often set up small workshops working as subcontractors for local factories.

(5) Operations are largely financed through 'subterranean' or 'shadow' banking. Subterranean banking institutions are the most various, from sweatshops, to rotating credit associations and real – though illegal – banks. Subterranean banking filled a void in a very imperfect banking system, which long provided privileges to state-owned companies, while offering little choice to private businesses.

(6) The specificity of the Wenzhou peasant economy is reflected in the migration pattern: people from suburban areas migrate – not to run away from extreme poverty – but to find better opportunities for acquiring wealth and climbing the social ladder abroad. During the 1990s and 2000s a high number of first-generation immigrants succeeded in transforming themselves from subcontractors into factory owners, clients, distributors and importers.

During the Wenzhou economy's boom years, property rights had not yet been reformed and private enterprise not fully legitimised. Private business operations had the support of local institutions, although often on an unofficial basis.[2] This resulted in a controversial reaction by the central government which only acknowledged Wenzhou as a good example at the end of the 1980s. In the mid and late 1980s many rural family enterprises turned into cooperatives, with the emergence of multiregional enterprises (MREs). Then, in the early and mid-1990s, shareholding enterprises and limited liability companies emerged, eventually including large firms and industrial groups. At this time, factories located on original district sites underwent a process of relocation. This happened in two rounds: first moving to nearby sites, then out of Wenzhou prefecture and out of Zhejiang province (e.g., from Zhejiang's capital city Hangzhou to

Shanghai in Jiangsu province). From 1995 to 2005 the volume of international trade increased 14-fold and Wenzhou's dependency on international trade increased from 20 to 40 per cent, thus proving that the balance had shifted from rural families to traders and that globalisation of the district was complete.

The nature of the Wenzhou economy is moving towards a mixed model, with renewed institutional support, emerging large firms and industrial groups and extended external networks (Wei et al., 2007). Wenzhou is really part of the global economy, sharing the good and the bad. Nowadays the main problem lies in the fact that Wenzhou's economy is quite mature. The territory has been largely exploited both in terms of space and natural resources. In addition, there is a general lack of innovation. Finally, as the global financial crisis hit, the district had to face reduced profit margins and excessive real estate speculation, while informal finance drove many to bankruptcy.

Elements for a typology of China's clusters

Many have written about the characteristics of the Wenzhou district, although only a few have done so using substantial data analysis. There are difficulties in retrieving reliable data, not counting the fact that the government has long avoided providing clear definitions to concepts such as a cluster or a district. The basic data source available to identify industrial clusters in Wenzhou is the survey conducted by the Policy Research Department of Zhejiang Provincial Government. It identified 519, 430 and 360 districts, respectively in 2001, 2003 and 2005 (the number of districts decreased because some disappeared and because the criteria changed). No clear and unique definition of industrial cluster, however, was adopted. Another data source is the National Corporation and Organization Census of 2001, which identified each of the 40,686 business corporations in Wenzhou.[3] Few scholars have conducted field research to verify the number of enterprises. That said, it must be noted that the dimensions of the samples compared with the total remain rather small. Among those scholarly writings are the following: Sonobe et al. (2002) who studied a garment cluster; Sonobe et al. (2004) who researched 112 enterprises in the low-voltage electric appliance industry; and Huang et al. (2005) who did a survey of 140 enterprises active in the footwear industry.

Marukawa (2009) produced a clear definition of a cluster after the 2005 Zhejiang Provincial Government's survey. According to it, a cluster can be identified if the township has more than 15 companies active in the same industry and if they make up more than 5 per cent of all the companies that belong to the same industry in the whole Wenzhou region (Marukawa, 2009). This classification system may seem too generous when compared with others. For example, the scholars Barbieri, Di Tommaso and Rubini follow the classification of the Guangdong provincial government, which accords the status of 'specialised town' to an area which has a minimum of 30 per cent of its manufacturing output concentrated in one sector (Barbieri et al., 2009). Yet, the characteristics of the Wenzhou industrial area are so dense that it can be justified.[4] To get a glimpse of the dimensions of the clusters in the Wenzhou area one only need look at the township of Shatou. There 17 companies engage in rubber shoe production, employing 5000 people from a total population of 16,514. An even more complex issue is to understand the micro-companies (i.e., the cottage industries). Marukawa discovered a cluster of 200 sock manufacturers in Bishan, each with ten employees and a dozen knitting machines. But because only 14 held legal status, they did not fit into the definition of an industrial cluster. This is a very common situation in the Wenzhou district and crucial to understanding the difficulty in classifying Chinese districts.

In all, Marukawa identified 153 industrial clusters as of the 2001 official data. It appears that while some industries are more concentrated, others are more scattered: the apparel cluster spreads over the city centre and the surrounding townships, with the button and zipper clusters of Qiaotou and Puzhou concentrated in those townships. Some districts are new, some were already active during the Republican Era, while others have been there for centuries (e.g., the footwear industry located in the Wenzhou urban centre was active and famous during the Ming Dynasty). That said, the structure of the districts is similar and can be broadly classified as 'traditional', if scholar Wang Jici's perspective is applied.

Western scholarship has long questioned the relevance of the Marshallian industrial district (MID) conceptualisation and empirical validity of the Italian model (Hadjimichalis, 2006; Whitford, 2001). Some scholars have proposed alternative industrial districts and called for 'globalising' regional development (Coe et al., 2004; Yeung, 2005). It was in the 1990s that scholars' views shifted from Becattini's accent on the endogenous local district to Porter's stress on competition and innovation (Becattini, 2000; Porter, 1990). In Porter's reflection, the centre remains the enterprise, but it is an enterprise that develops and stands out among its competitors. Markusen (1996) proposed a wider classification by identifying three more models of the industrial district:

the hub-and-spoke industrial district, the satellite platform and the state-anchored district.

If we want to include the Wenzhou district into European and American scholarship, we can say that during the 1980s Wenzhou operated as a successful MID, resuming its ancient specialisation in footwear and developing other kinds of everyday products, such as buttons, lighters, etc. (see Huang et al., 2007; Liu, A.P.L., 1992; Liu, Y.L., 1992; Ma and Cui, 2002; Parris, 1993; Sonobe et al., 2004). In more recent years, despite the trend of enlarging Wenzhou firms, no singular big group exists that is capable of polarising the agglomeration of smaller companies. For this reason it is not suitable to label Wenzhou either as a *hub-and-spoke* district or a *satellite platform*, let alone a *state-anchored* district. From Marukawa's analysis, we can infer that if we approach the data from a purely economic geography perspective, Wenzhou district still resembles an MID in some respects; however, when we include the dynamics at the centre of the district in the analysis, it appears inappropriate to describe Wenzhou as an MID. If we look at the organization of labor in 1981, soon after resuming its activity, there were 99 footwear factories in the Wenzhou central district. At that time most workshops produced the whole shoe, which obviously required the use of a number of different skills. In the 2000s, however, the ratio of founders having prior shoemaking experience had declined, as the shoemaking industry became increasingly specialised and the technology barrier gradually declined. At the same time, the proportion of marketing specialists rose steadily from an initially low proportion. Sonobe et al. (2004) in their study on the low-voltage electric appliance industry observed that, with the rapid increase in supply in the 1980s, the market underwent a fundamental shift from the demand to the supply side. The result is similar in the findings of Huang et al. (2007): in the mature market, marketing skills became more crucial and individuals with marketing skills began to enjoy comparative advantage in the emerging competitive environment. It seems an evident sign of exogenous dynamics changing the structure of the cluster. Exogenous dynamics can be observed in the actions performed by the economic operators coming from outside and external buyers are certainly actors of exogenous change.

Nevertheless, other studies tell us that private micro-entrepreneurs completely rely on the input received by the local market and upon suggestions received through the network of peddlers and traders. As a result, workshops would quickly modify their production. This is how the 'modern' district economy grew in the suburban areas of Wenzhou (Shi and Ganne, 2009). Marshall's theory can be used to interpret this growth: local entrepreneurs and local traders are part of the 'atmosphere' of the industrial district. Thus, their actions can therefore be ascribed to endogenous dynamics. Sonobe et al. (2002) writes about the development of a garment industry cluster in a small town in Zhejiang, building upon a tradition of low-quality garment production linked to silk weaving. Here again marketplaces and local traders – endogenous actors – are the dynamic force for the creation of industrial clusters. However, the local government has been playing a major role by permitting the liberalisation of marketplaces. They became the driving factor in the reprise of the industry, as they allowed for the free exchange of raw materials and boosted contacts between buyers and sellers.

How are we to classify local government's action? According to Marshall, it is also part of the district atmosphere, although it must be underlined how the literature on the district has generally emphasised local institutions, while neglecting the role played by the central government. According to significant studies, the key determinants of breaking out of lock-in are often large firms, research institutions and human capital (Martin and Sunley, 2006). However, when speaking of Asian development models, one must remember that in many cases the market is 'governed'. In fact, government intervention deliberately facilitated the development of the clusters, and this is contrary to what normally occurs in Europe where no conscious action by the government is the basis of cluster formation. Scholar Ann Markusen's studies on Korean and Japanese industrial clusters show the powerful intervention of those governments (Markusen, 1996). An industrial policy called the 'industrial cluster approach' spread among ASEAN members soon after the 1997 financial crisis (Suehiro, 2009). It involved an important role for the local government, producing laws and giving financial support. The Chinese government has taken inspiration from the well-structured policies carried out in Japan, aimed at building, regulating and promoting local cluster economies. In China, this is typical of the high-tech clusters and of those resulting from FDI-attracting policies enacted by the government (SEZ, ETDZ, industrial parks, etc.). Similar policies were directed at the Wenzhou districts. In 1993 the local government inaugurated special measures to promote economic development, taking on a strategic role, promoting private enterprises and encouraging formal banking institutions to lend out funds to private subjects. Huang et al. (2007) conducted their study in two industrial parks: Footwear Capital of China Industrial Park in the Lucheng District of Wenzhou City and the Shuangyu Industrial Park of Lucheng District.

An important research and policy question raised by any investigation on industrial districts in China is whether agglomerations that begin as governmental projects are able to develop into genuine growth centers with the strong endogenous dynamics of growth (Fan and Scott, 2003). During the 1990s Wenzhou's economic structure underwent a deep transformation: quality improved, production shifted to a more capital-intensive modality and family industry as well as local markets expanded. If we look at the influence that these events had on the area, it appears that the Zhejiang case cannot immediately be classified, as there are totally spontaneous clusters (born from the inputs received by market information) and those which I would call 'semi-spontaneous'. The latter entail clusters which – though driven from an autonomous push to be active – have been influenced/directed by the government as to where to localize and what to produce. The data suggest that these 'semi-spontaneous' clusters tend to go back to being spontaneous, because once the guidelines of production have been set the companies eventually reshuffle their production if a better business opportunity appears. Close proximity of the same sector companies create the perfect conditions. A high level of competition among companies is one of the driving factors. Constant production upgrading is eventually possible thanks to the high division of labor, while the production process is broken into extremely simple phases to which small-sized companies can easily adjust. The flexibility of these operations is possible for two basic reasons: first, the Zhejiang countryside has a long history of intertwined trade and production activities performed on a micro-basis. Here, interpersonal networks are crucial and shape the rules in labor organization. Second, there is recent history of collectively operated companies where the party summons workers to do their job. The local government (collectives) no longer intervenes directly as economic actors, but plays a 'powerful accompanying role' to specialised development (Shi and Ganne, 2009). Finally, the local government facilitates the development of the cluster economy by constructing several local marketplaces. This reinforces the notion that in China it is difficult to draw a neat line between 'natural' endogenous districts, and 'induced' or exogenous districts and also suggests another consideration. Closer to the structure of Zhejiang districts may be the Japanese *sanchi*-type industrial clusters: autonomously developed production and agglomeration, historically rooted in the area, they rely on local-based marketeers and minimum physical and monetary services. Contrary to what happens in European-style clusters, *sanchi*-type clusters do benefit from direct governmental support. For example, they may include fiscal incentives by the government (Suehiro, 2009). In this respect, from this analysis, Zhejiang can be seen as an innovative model of a cluster economy, blending European and Asian characteristics, offering inspiration to the rest of China.

The role of trade in the ascent of the Wenzhou economy in the global value chain

How did such a model react to globalisation? By using their networks in foreign countries, the Wenzhou entrepreneurs succeeded in setting up a successful system composed, on the one hand, of production laboratories and factories and, on the other hand, of distributors and buyers all sharing the same ethnic origin. This system has proved to be very flexible: if it is true that in the early 1980s this system was mainly reliant upon individuals possessing very basic capabilities, during the 1990s it has been enriched by the ever-increasing marketing skills developed by the younger generation.

In the 1990s scholar Gary Gereffi and others developed a theoretical framework, called 'global commodity chains', which tied the concept of the value-added chain directly to the global organisation of industries. By highlighting explicit coordination in disintegrated chains and contrasting them with the relationships contained within vertically integrated, or 'producer driven' chains, the global commodity chains framework drew attention to the role of networks in driving the co-evolution of cross-border industrial organization. The transformation mirrors the theory proposed by Gereffi who highlighted the 'growing importance of new global buyers (mainly retailers and brand marketers) as key drivers in the formation of globally dispersed and organizationally fragmented production and distribution networks' (Gereffi, 1994; Gereffi and Memodovic, 2003). We may as well use the term 'buyer-driven global commodity chain' to depict the global-scale production and distribution system built upon a highly competent supply base (Gereffi, 1994). In their study, Huang et al. show evidence that at the beginning of the 1980s Wenzhou's footwear sector had a predominance of company founders coming from a background in the same sector. They were mainly former state-owned enterprise (SOE) workers in the footwear industry. This fact shows that to succeed in the footwear business a solid technical background was a necessity. Conversely, in the 1990s the majority of company founders had a strong marketing background, mastering the leading skill necessary to become a successful entrepreneur.[5] A keen observer of the district economy and, especially of the situation in Tuscany and in Prato, maintains that 'the development of the Chinese economy in the Italian districts is still more surprising for its recent qualitative transformation, than for the size it has reached' (Dei Ottati, 2009). During the 1990s and 2000s a high number of first-generation immigrants who settled in Italian districts have succeeded in transforming themselves from subcontractors into clients, distributors and importers. The transformation of the Prato district (traditionally an Italian district of excellence in the production and distribution of woollen textiles) had already begun in the 1980s with the establishment of small workshops run by Wenzhou-originated migrants, to whom Italian local factories subcontracted easy phases of labor because of a shortage in the Italian workforce. Such small businesses – often regularly unregistered – were the starting point for many enterprises which, little by little, came to outnumber Italian ones. The district during the 1990s became so intimately connected with the trading network operated by Wenzhou people abroad that it could overcome the crisis of the industry, becoming an example of the new globalised economy. The ascent in the global value chain happened in less than a decade.

How could Chinese ethnic firms make such a qualitative advance in the value chain in such a short amount of time? Scholar Gabi Dei Ottati explains it in this way: the relationships that the Chinese immigrants maintain with economic and political agents in their homeland allow their ethnic firms to benefit from an added type of external economy which is not ordinarily available to district firms; namely, trans-local external economies (Dei Ottati, 2009). Thanks to their relationships with clients and buyers from Italy and the rest of Europe, the Wenzhou entrepreneurs initially learned how to produce according to the standards of developed countries, subsequently learning how to set up a successful trading and distributing transnational network. This explanation shows how Wenzhou-originated companies strategically shifted from labor-intensive production to trading, having seen an opportunity in the latter. Yet it fails to provide an answer as to how Wenzhou entrepreneurs learned to organize a transnational commercial and distribution network so successfully. Dei Ottati admits that there is a contradictory combination of advantages in the foundations of the success of the Prato ethnic economy. Thus, we need more data to understand how these shrewd traders were once the same low-skilled workers who set up workshops and worked under Italian supervision. To this end, a look into the historical background of the Wenzhou economy may prove useful.

Let us consider the historical coexistence of manufacturing clusters and colportage (crafts and small traders) which existed long before the advent of the Communist Regime. Such activities, being private, were banned in the Mao years. During the early 1980s black-market family businesses with a workshop at the front and a shop behind (*qianchang houdian*) began to accumulate capital through trade. They then moved to manufacturing in order to satisfy market demand (Chen and Cao, 2006). This is the endogenous factor which is the basis for the evolution of the Wenzhou district economy from a network of migrant subcontractors into a system of transnational commerce and distribution. This interpretation, however, does not correspond to the classical theories of the district, as Becattini, the 'father' of district theory, described the main feature of a cluster as a network of production units, whereas trade results in playing a less relevant role. Still, this interpretation is very consistent with Becattini's theories, if endogenous/exogenous dynamics are considered: the contact with the outside world may be viewed as a powerful trigger which only puts in motion a pre-existing dynamic. The crucial role was played by local distribution institutions, initially by those 'specialised markets', which form such a peculiar feature of the Chinese district economy. Still this should be looked at conversely. The Wenzhou model of development was first successful because entrepreneurs succeeded in the distribution system. Stemming from a planned economy, this system had many shortcomings and was one of the last to open to private and foreign investment less than ten years ago. Chen and Cao (2006) are among the few who accord trade as opposed to production a much greater role. According to their research, it was the tradition of traders and wandering peddlers which led to implementation of an endogenous cluster (word of a new product spread from village to village, leading to input of new production).

Extremely localised trade areas always emerge in areas close to industrial clusters with which they engage in very tight relationships of mutual benefit. In China's district economy, such a role is played by so-called 'specialised commodity markets', which served the commercial needs of those micro-companies too small to handle supply and sales independently.[6] Did specialised markets become so strong because of the backwardness of Communist China's distributive system? Or were they more intimately embedded in the trading and distribution pattern of such areas of the country characterised by agglomerations of small to medium manufacturers? Actually, markets have traditionally been at the core of peasant life. Skinner describes life in the Chinese countryside in the mid-nineteenth century as cells, with a market town being the nucleus upon which 15–25 villages depended (Skinner, 1971). China's traditional rural economic structure is a web formed by dozens of associations and guilds, which operated through contracts between one another but always referred to the market in order to keep transaction costs low.

Obstacles in the development of Wenzhou's economy

Since the early 1990s, economic development in Wenzhou has faced a problem of lock-ins. According to some scholars, problems arise from the fact that Wenzhou's economic structure is strongly family based, labor intensive, low value added and light manufacturing centered (Shi, 2004; Wei et al., 2007). One crucial aspect is represented by the thick local networks between officials and enterprises depicted by a notable Chinese economist as a network of 'personalized transactions.' These networks are a crucial element, but also a potential obstacle to investment from outside (Shi, 2004).

One of Wenzhou's main problems is the small amount of FDI and outside investment in the local economy. Although in recent years local government has been studying new policies to attract FDIs, the existence of closed social/business/commercial circles prevents people outside Wenzhou from assimilating and discourages foreign investors. Furthermore, Wenzhou manufacturers have introduced very few innovations, keeping low costs as their main competitive advantage.

From the mid-1990s onwards, many local enterprises have taken the initiative to overcome their limitations, adopting four major types of strategies: institutional change (the shift to shareholding enterprises), technological upgrades, industrial diversification and spatial restructuring (Wei et al., 2007). The local government in Wenzhou gave support to enterprises, but both local private enterprises and the local government focused on upgrading industrial technology and structures in an endogenous way. Given this approach, there is limited space and incentives for the inflow of foreign capital and transnational companies (TNCs).

A major problem lies in the fact that Wenzhou's economy is quite mature. The territory has been largely exploited both in terms of space and natural resources. Second, there is a general lack of innovation: Wenzhou missed this opportunity because of a 'generation lock' (Shi, 2004). The generation of the self-made entrepreneurs has not been followed by a generation with the necessary technological and innovative tools. Actually, the self-made entrepreneurs have given way to a generation possessing the right marketing skills. In many sectors of the economy, companies are deeply involved in production for foreign markets. Although this is an evident achievement for China, it does not necessarily lead to innovation. In fact Chinese companies have focused much more on commercial competition, while leaving aside innovation, with the result that 'China may be extensively integrated into global supply chains, yet its integration is shallow' (Steinfeld, 2004). Until the mid-2000s this was not of immediate concern; however, recently it is a problem felt everywhere because of the slump in sales due to the world financial crisis. It is felt probably even more acutely and was visible earlier in Wenzhou which had anticipated many business trends.

During the earliest decade of the twenty-first century, all the abovementioned elements have contributed to the slowing down of Wenzhou's economic growth as well as to a decrease in investments in fixed assets.

As many observers have pointed out, an injection of funds would prove effective in pushing the economy forward. This, however, is not a simple solution. The global financial crisis caused a fall in demand and enhanced the danger from latent problematic aspects of the Wenzhou cluster economy.

The impact of informal finance on Wenzhou's cluster economy

Informal finance can be considered a truly endogenous factor within the Wenzhou district economy. In informal finance, loans are undertaken through private contracts for the launching of new businesses or to fuel business operations when official banks are not avalaible. It works by exploiting social capital. When an entrepreneur takes on a debt with such a structure, he or she pledges his/her commitments to the creditor, giving his/her word and involving relatives and acquaintances. This is not a product of recent industrialization. Rather, the most common informal banking institutions (pawn shops, rotating credit associations, middlemen) go back centuries. The Maoist economy only reinforced those interpersonal links which lied at the basis of informal finance by helping state-owned enterprises and banning private business. Therefore, citizens sought help in interpersonal networks. In 35 years reform has only very slightly altered the situation; instead, the privileges of state companies have almost entirely remained and no effective banking system for the private sector has been established. True liberalisation of the financial sector has not occured in China. RMB is not a freely exchanged currency; thus, the Chinese are not free to invest in foreign stock markets. This has contributed to an inflated real estate bubble which poses a substantial risk to the country's economy.

The attitude to conduct informal banking business inspired a spontaneous experiment during the golden years of the Wenzhou model. In 1984, entrepreneur Fang Peilin opened the first private bank in Cangnan county, challenging a set of norms restricting the activity by private banks which dated back to the early years of the PRC (Parris, 1993; Tsai, 2004). Fang did not succeed in getting his bank approved as a financial institution because local authorities did not dare support him against the central government. He did though achieve a smaller victory by registering his bank as a private enterprise. Fang Peilin's bank operated 24 hours a day, 7 days a week and appealed to those entrepreneurs who were excluded from the circuit of official loans. By using the so-called 'dead money' of those who had large amounts of cash, Fang could satisfy the requests of those who were in need of cash ('live money'), thus acting as a real middleman between the two groups of businessmen. He was able to keep the bank business going solely by relying upon the daily cycle of local tradesmen. At its peak, the bank handled transactions of up to ¥700,000 per day. Quite impressively, Fang's private banking business was useful for everybody. The money was more productive than in official banks: on the one hand, the money invested in the company earned higher interest rates for the investors, on the other hand – according lower interest rates on loans – the money was lent out more easily and thus helped to fuel the economy. The bank operated for five years before financial authorities forced its closure. During that time though more than 27 private banks had opened in the same Wenzhou municipality, thus making small private entrepreneurs radically change their way of doing business. The story of Fang Peiling's bank not only reinforces the notion that the Wenzhou economy is driven by strong endogenous dynamics, relying upon the many resources of a population evidently accustomed to overcoming difficulties through their own determination. This story thoroughly answers the first question that this chapter posed: How important is district modality to the development of a strong Wenzhou (and China's) economy? I would say that it is fundamental: as soon as Fang developed his bank and was successful, his idea was immediately replicated by other entrepreneurs. As observed by a number of researchers, copying is at the core of cluster development (Huang et al., 2007; Sonobe et al. 2002, 2004).

The full force of the global financial crisis hit Wenzhou in the autumn of 2011 when a wave of bankruptcies and suicides among highly-indebted entrepreneurs was hailed by newspapers as a sign of a possible collapse of the Zhejiang economy. Some 230 cases were reported in the entire

Zhejiang Province, 90 in Wenzhou alone, with the majority being local SME owners who left more than 15,000 people without an income overnight. Bankruptcies are the result of the huge debts that many entrepreneurs accrued through 'informal' or 'subterranean' credit structures. The reasons for such a negative outcome as a result of relying on informal finance are surely to be attributed to the financial crisis, but it alone cannot be regarded as the one and only culprit. On the one hand, Wenzhou people saw the possibility of getting rich fast and they invested a lot of money in the Hong Kong Stock Exchange. On the other hand, they lost hope in a revival of their manufacturing businesses which had been so deeply affected by the crisis suffered by US and EU target markets.

Particularly in the Wenzhou area, many moneylenders have set up real businesses, sometimes on a very small scale, even at the level of family. Some sources estimate that as much as 89 per cent of the inhabitants of the Wenzhou district may take part in this network in some manner. Soon after the start of the financial crisis in 2009–10, Wenzhou experienced its greatest real estate boom of all time, with housing prices rising higher than in Shanghai. Many people speculated on the prices of houses by quickly buying and selling apartments. Then, all of a sudden, in 2011, selling became very difficult and prices started to fall.

When the real estate bubble and the debt crisis collided to create a overly heated situation in the area, the central government intervened and established a so-called financial pilot zone.

Establishment of the Wenzhou financial pilot zone as an answer to the private debt crisis?

Far from being an exclusive feature of the Wenzhou economy, informal or 'underground' finance is a very common phenomenon among private companies all over China. In December 2013, *Caijing*, China's most renowned economic magazine, published a thoroughly documented article which estimated the shadow banking system to be about ¥15–17 trillion in size, representing about 12–13 per cent of the formal banking asset, and one third of China's GDP including underground banking, trust products and wealth management products (Liu and Zhou, 2012).

So, when on 28 March 2012 the State Council appointed Wenzhou as a pilot area for the legitimisation of private (black-market) money lending by creating the Wenzhou Experimental Zone for Financial Reform many viewed it as an attempt to 'cure' a much more general 'illness.' The following outline the main measures of the reform:[7]

- improving the local financial system by allowing private investors to invest in local banks and establish loan companies and rural community bank;
- remodeling the financial products and services systems to accommodate the demands of economic development (this measure includes guiding private capital to venture capital and private capital funds);
- improving the private capital market system and the orderly flow of private capital as well as broadening investment channels, by developing local capital markets and opening these for SMEs;
- strengthening the local financial regulatory system to prevent and control financial risks;
- allowing private direct investment to be made overseas.

It is important to note that the experimental policies to be implemented in Wenzhou also include the possibility for Wenzhou residents to make direct overseas investment in RMB. The experiment meets the expectations of the people, as the Zhejiang Provincial Government had already previously asked for the changes. The trial for direct overseas investment, which has already been approved by the State Council, signals a significant step by Beijing to liberalize the country's capital account transactions. Until now Chinese citizens had only been allowed to invest abroad to set up businesses or to buy securities through asset investment programs.

Two core aspects are tested in the project, both representing landmark reforms within the country's financial system. First of all the state banks' credit-lending monopoly is being dismantled. By opening more channels for private capital to flow into the economy and thereby simplifying private enterprise fundraising, Beijing hopes to create a new growth cycle based on non–state sector investment. The result should be an economy less dependent on public spending, which is considered key to sustaining GDP growth.

National and international calls for liberalising China's credit system have grown louder recently, as the country has to prepare for times with lower foreign demand and must focus increasingly on domestic-based growth. As discussed before, one obstacle in achieving this has so far been the reluctance of state banks to sufficiently support the private economy with liquidity. This is a disturbing fact considering the staggering financial figures of the big four state-owned banks. Alone China's largest credit lender, ICBC, earned an incredible US $33 billion in 2011, making it one of the most profitable companies worldwide.

The second remarkable aspect of the pilot reform is the government's intention to further liberalise cross-border capital flows. The Chinese Foreign Exchange Administration lifted the amount foreign institutions can invest in stocks, bonds and bank deposits from US $30 billion to US $80 billion. With this measure, new foreign direct investment ought to be attractive, increasing the business opportunities of promising young enterprises.

That the legalization of private overseas investments is part of the reform can be seen as another reason Wenzhou in particular has been chosen for the pilot project: with a tradition of emigration, the city's entrepreneurs have close international ties, laying a solid foundation for personal cross-border direct investment. An additional advantage of allowing individuals to directly invest overseas is the easing of investment pressure on the Chinese property market. Thus, the reform could turn out to be an effective means of mitigating soaring housing prices – an issue becoming increasingly important for the government as a real estate bubble poses a significant economic danger and has the potential to cause social unrest.

Local institutions have played a leading role in monitoring the effects of reform. Though it went into effect more than a year ago, the reform does not seem to have quickly solved the problems of the local economy. The reform's primary aim was to legalise much of the already flourishing private lending sector. Yet this has not proved as easy as expected. Since April 2012 some companies have experienced severe problems in receiving loans from banks and private lending companies.

During the summer of 2012, businessmen were still lamenting the stalled economy. Although this was probably due to the persistent global financial crisis, they also blamed the slow pace of financial reform. When asked about the improvements brought about by Wenzhou's financial reform over the past 100 days, Zhou Dewen, president of Wenzhou Promotion Association for SMEs answered, 'What are the achievements? What are the real benefits for SMEs and private companies? Honestly, I couldn't answer these questions' (Chen and Ye, 2012).

The problem most likely has a lot to do with the control of the state over new business, an old and well-known problem in the financial sector. Well-developed loan companies are now allowed to become village and township-level banks. Yet, even the loan companies that have become qualified remain rather uninterested in becoming banks. Experimental regulation in the Wenzhou pilot zone requires as a prerequisite that an official (state-owned) financial institution holds shares in the newly established (privately owned) bank. Although the holdings requirement has been reduced from 20 to 15 per cent, this still puts a limitation on the business. If the government allows private capital to enter the financial field, at the same time it should grant a certain degree of independence, otherwise it is a very short-sighted reform.[8] Establishment of the Private Lending Registration Service Center helped to lower monthly interest rates from the 3–4 per cent set by the underground markets to 1.2–1.3 per cent. Yet, very few private financial activities have resulted from the decrease. While more time is needed for such reform to become fully effective, the fact that the regulation is still unclear regarding admission of private enterprises into the lending business seems to be significantly delaying its effectiveness. Indeed, several companies have complained to their business associations about this. The reform has been criticised even by party officials. Chen Derong, secretary of the Wenzhou Municipal Committee of the Communist Party, said, 'Courage is lacking in financial reforms with a slow pace and less significant progress' (Chen and Ye, 2012).

This reform may be seen as an attempt by the central government to change the dynamics of the Wenzhou economy. In the mid-1980s the government finally intervened to halt the escalation of bankruptcies caused by excessive speculation by informal financial institutions (*hui*). On this occasion, the central government also closed down those private banks which had emerged as a spontaneous answer to the needs of local entrepreneurs and had shown an interest in abiding by the law. The strong exogenous push, however, does not seem to have succeeded.

Concluding remarks

This chapter points out that in the Wenzhou district (as well as in many Zhejiang districts), trade always played the central role. This leads to a controversial interpretation: because of its constant exchange with the outside world, trade is to be regarded as an exogenous element. On the other hand, local traders and peddlers and, most importantly, family businesses with a workshop at the front and a shop behind (*qianchang houdian*) – which we can regard as endogenous elements – have traditionally nurtured on-site manufacturing and external networks in the development of the Wenzhou cluster economy locally and abroad.

In the end, it appears that Wenzhou's features as an industrial district do not fit neatly into an already established model. Rather, it can be described as an innovative model which could eventually be extended to the whole Zhejiang area. Endogenous and exogenous factors were both responsible for its development, and we may trace its success back to the ability of its entrepreneurs and politicians to fit themselves into two main power gaps: (1) the weak distribution system; (2) the loose regulatory system for private business. In addressing the question, Beijing leaders held such a controversial attitude that, in the end, the people of Wenzhou benefitted by always finding a way to bypass self-contradictory regulations and making the best of the contrasting relationship between local and central government.

Central government – an exogenous element – interfered many times in the organisation of the Wenzhou district, giving strong orientation and regulation to the local economy. Since 2001 the government has been conducting surveys on local industrial districts, choosing parameters and eventually using this information to actively reshape the economy of the area. On several occasions, it has rearranged the districts and built dedicated industrial parks. This approach has coalesced well with Wenzhou's spontaneous growth, giving birth to what I termed 'semi-spontaneous' clusters, which tend to go back to being spontaneous, eventually reshuffling their production if a better business opportunity appears. Until recently, local forces have always actively reacted, rebalancing the weight of state actions. However, introduction of the financial experiment in March 2012 could result in stronger influence by the state. This may be particularly true given that the local economy has been weakened by the crisis and local businesses might gain an advantage from the easing of limitations in investing abroad, as offered by rules newly introduced by the pilot zone.

Notes

1. The features reported in this chapter are the author's elaboration of two analyses conducted by Zhang Dunfu, who individuated the first three features, which have been listed in the text as (1), (2), (3) (Zhang, 2002) and Kellee S. Tsai, who added and thoroughly analysed the fourth feature, listed in the text as (4) (Tsai, 2007). The features listed as (5) and (6) are the results of the author's personal analysis.
2. Wenzhou had already earned a reputation as a rebellious and

capitalist-oriented area in pre-revolutionary times because of the peculiarity of the area (geographical seclusion, strong family ties, difficult access to resources and an established tendency to rely on local institutions as opposed to central ones). In addition, privately run micro-companies in the Wenzhou area resumed operations even before the start of Deng's Reforms during the last years of the Cultural Revolution (Liu, A.P.L., 1992; Liu, Y.L., 1992; Parris, 1993).

3. The survey does not include micro-companies nor those businesses which had not been officially registered. This is a shortcoming given that they constitute an important feature, especially in the new districts.
4. Wenzhou is a prefecture of 11,784 km^2, administratively subdivided into 11 county-level regions (*xian*) and 299 township-level regions (*xiang* and *zhen*). The latter also include 17 urban sub-districts (*jiedao*) which constitute the city centre. The surveys carried out by the Zhejiang Provincial Government divide the districts according to the *xian* (county) where they are located, but this seems too vast a surface for Wenzhou's industry characteristics, so Marukawa changed the division into townships totalling 283 districts. The township has an average area of 43 km^2. Actually, the fact that technical expertise is what leads an individual to start a business has been further questioned by other authors. In his study on the garment industry, Sonobe notes that most company founders were farmers with no previous working background in that sector (Sonobe et al., 2002).
5. For a detailed description of the specialized commodity markets see Miao (2008).
6. Guowuyuan sheli Wenzhou jinrong gaige shiyanqu. *Xin Jing Bao*, 29 March 2012 [in Chinese].
7. Guowuyuan sheli Wenzhou jinrong gaige shiyanqu. *Xin Jing Bao*, 29 March 2012 [in Chinese].
8. Wenzhou expects substantial financial reforms. *China Daily USA Online*, 1 January 2013. Available from: *http://usa.chinadaily.com.cn/business/2013-01/01/content_16075239.htm*

References

Barbieri, E., Di Tommaso, M. and Rubini, L. (2009) Industrial development policies in southern China: the Specialised Towns Program. *Economia e Politica Industriale*, 3, 179–98.

Becattini, G. (2000) *Il distretto industriale: Un nuovo modo di interpretare il cambiamento economico*. Rosenberg & Sellier, Turin, Italy [in Italian].

Bellandi, M. (2007) Industrial districts and waves of industrialization: a rich and contested terrain. *Scienze Regionali, Italian Journal of Regional Science*, **6**(2).

Chen, L. and Cao, Z. (2006) Zhongguo minying qiye chengzhang: zhidu yu nengli [Development of private enterprises: system and capacity]. In: S. Zhang and X. Jin (Eds), *Zhongguo zhidu bianqian de anli yanjiu [Case studies in China's institutional change]*. China's Economic and Finance Publisher, Hangzhou, China [in Chinese].

Chen, Z. and Ye, J. (2012) Wenzhou jin gai si yue [Four months of reform in Wenzhou]. *Jingji guancha bao*, 4 August 2012 [in Chinese].

Christerson, B. and Lever-Tracy, C. (1997) The Third China? Emerging industrial districts in rural China. *International Journal of Urban and Regional Research*, **21**(4), 569–88.

Coe, N.M., Hess, M., Yeung, H.W., Dicken, P. and Henderson, G. (2004) Globalizing regional development. *Transactions of British Geographers*, **29**, 468–84.

Dei Ottati, G. (2009) Italian industrial districts and the dual Chinese challenge. In: G. Johanson, R. Smyth and R. French (Eds), *Living Outside the Walls: the Chinese in Prato*. Cambridge Scholars Publishing, Newcastle Upon Tyne, UK.

Fan, C.C. and Scott, A.J. (2003) Industrial agglomeration and development: a survey of spatial economic issues in East Asia and a statistical analysis of Chinese regions. *Economic Geography*, **79**(3), 295–319.

Ganne, B. and Lecler, Y. (Eds) (2009) *Asian Industrial Clusters, Global Competitiveness and New Policy Initiatives*. World Scientific Publishing, Singapore.

Gereffi, G. (1994) The organization of buyer-driven global commodity chains: how U.S. retailers shape overseas production networks. In: G. Gereffi and M. Korzeniewicz (Eds), *Commodity Chains and Global Capitalism*. Praeger, Westport, CT, pp. 95–122.

Gereffi, G. and Memodovic, O. (2003) *The Global Apparel Value Chain: What Prospects for Upgrading by Developing Countries?* (Sectoral Studies Series). United Nations Industrial Development Organization (UNIDO). Available from: *http://www.unido.org/doc/12218*

Hadjimichalis, C. (2006) The end of Third Italy as we knew it? *Antipode*, **38**, 82–106.

Huang, Z., Zhang, X. and Zhu, Y. (2007) *The Role of Clustering in Rural Industrialization: A Case Study of the Footwear Industry in Wenzhou* (IFPRI Discussion Paper No. 00705, May 2007). International Food Policy Research Institute, Washington, DC.

Liu, A.P.L. (1992) The 'Wenzhou Model' of development and China's modernization. *Asian Survey*, **32**(8), 696–711.

Liu, L. and Zhou, H. (2012) China's shadow banking revisited: size, implications, risks, and reforms. *Caijing*, English web edition, 5 December 2012. Available from: *http://english.caijing.com.cn/2012-12-05/112336663.htmlg*

Liu, Y.L. (1992) Reform from below: the private economy and local politics in the rural industrialization of Wenzhou. *China Quarterly*, **130**, 293–316.

Ma, L.J.C. and Cui, G.H. (2002) Economic transition at the local level. *Eurasian Geography and Economics*, **43**(2), 79–103.

Markusen, A. (1996) Sticky places in slippery space: a typology of industrial districts. *Economic Geography*, **72**(3), 293–313.

Marshall, A. (1890) *Principles of Economics*. Macmillan, London.

Martin, R. and Sunley, P. (2006) Path dependence and regional economic evolution. *Journal of Economic Geography*, **6**, 395–437.

Marukawa, T. (2009) The emergence of industrial clusters in Wenzhou, China. In: B. Ganne and Y. Lecler (Eds), *Asian Industrial Clusters, Global Competitiveness and New Policy Initiatives*. World Scientific, Singapore, pp. 213–37.

Miao, L. (2008) Wenzhou zhuanye shichang fazhan baogao [The development process and trend of specialized markets in Wenzhou]. *Journal of Shanghai Business School (Shanghai shangxueyuan xuebao)*, **9**(2), 33–7 [in Chinese].

Oi, J.C. (1995) The role of the local state in China's transitional economy. *China Quarterly*, 144, 1132–49.

Parris, K. (1993) Local initiative and national reform. *China Quarterly*, **134**, 242–63.

Porter, M. (1990) *The Competitive Advantage of Nations*. Macmillan, Basingstoke, UK.

Shi, J. (2004) Analysis of the historical system of the Wenzhou model: a view from the perspective of personalized transactions and nonpersonalized transactions. *Chinese Economy*, **37**(2), 47–55.

Shi, L. and Ganne, B. (2009) Understanding the Zhejiang industrial clusters: questions and re-evaluations. In: B. Ganne and Y. Lecler (Eds), *Asian Industrial Clusters, Global Competitiveness and New Policy Initiatives*. World Scientific Publishing, Singapore.

Skinner, G.W. (1971) Chinese peasants and the closed community: an open and shut case. *Comparative Studies in Society and History*, **13**(3), July, 270–81.

Sonobe, T., Hu, D. and Otsuka, K. (2002) Process of cluster formation in China: a case study of a garment town. *Journal of Development Studies*, **39**(1), 118–39.

Sonobe, T., Hu, D. and Otsuka, K. (2004) From inferior to superior products: an inquiry into the Wenzhou model of industrial development in China. *Journal of Comparative Economics*, **32**(3), 542–63.

Steinfeld, E. (2004) China's shallow integration: networked production and the new challenges for late industrialization. *World Development*, **32**(11), 1971–87.

Suehiro, A. (2009) From an industrial policy approach to an industrial cluster approach: Japan, East Asia and Silicon Valley. In: B. Ganne and Y. Lecler (Eds), *Asian Industrial Clusters, Global Competitiveness and New Policy Initiatives*. World Scientific Publishing, Singapore.

Tsai, K., Wang, X., and Li, R. (2004) *Nongcun gongyehua yu minjian jinrong: Wenzhou de jingyan [Rural industrialization and non-governmental finance: insights from Wenzhou's experience]*. Shanxi jingji chubanshe, Taiyuan, China [in Chinese].

Tsai, K.S. (2007) *Capitalism without Democracy: The Private Sector in Contemporary China*. Cornell University Press, Ithaca, NY.

Walcott, S.M. (2007) Wenzhou and the Third Italy: entrepreneurial regions. *Journal of Asia-Pacific Business*, **8**(3), 23–35.

Walder, A.G. (1995) Local governments as industrial firms: an organizational analysis of China's transitional economy. *American Journal of Sociology*, **101**(2), 263–301.

Wang, J. (2001) *Chuangxin de Kongjian: Qiye Jiqun yu Quyu Fazhan [Innovation Spaces: Firm Clusters and Regional Development]*, Peking University Press, Beijing [in Chinese].

Wang, J. and Tong, X. (2004) Industrial clusters in China: embedded or disembedded? In: C. Alystam and E. Schamp (Eds), *Linking Industries across the World: Processes of Global Networking*. Ashgate, Aldershot, UK.

Wei, D.Y-H., Li, W. and Wang, C. (2007) Restructuring industrial districts, scaling up regional development: a study of Wenzhou model, China. *Economic Geography*, **83**, 421–44.

Whitford, J. (2001) The decline of a model? *Economy and Society*, **30**, 38–65.

Yeung, H.W. (2005) Rethinking relational economic geography. *Transactions of the Institute of British Geographers*, **30**, 37–51.

Zhang, D. (2002) *Quyu fazhan moshi de shehuixue fenxi [A Sociological Analysis of Regional Development Models]*. Tianjin Renmin Chubanshe, Tianjin, China.

3

State-owned versus private enterprises in China: adoption of modern HRM practices

Qi Feng, Jacques Jaussaud and Xueming Liu

Abstract: Human resource management (HRM) practices change rapidly in China, at the initiative of both multinational corporations (MNCs) and local enterprises. Differences in the implementation of modern HRM practices by MNCs and local enterprises have been widely investigated. However, differences between Chinese private and state-owned enterprises have not yet been precisely considered. State-owned enterprises, because of strong personal management tradition and institutional pressures, may be slower to introduce some human resource management practices. However, this research finds that, despite some differences, mimetic mechanisms lead to the convergence of practices between state-owned and private Chinese enterprises.

Key words: appraisal, compensation, China, human resource management, mimetism, state-owned enterprises (SOEs), training.

Introduction

Because of the rapid development of the country, human resource management (HRM) practices change permanently and quickly in China. Multinational companies (MNCs) entering the country, on the one hand, introduce management practices that they have developed elsewhere (Cooke, 2004; Lau and Ngo, 2001). Chinese firms, on the other hand, eagerly search out and adopt up-to-date techniques and practices (Ding et al., 2001; Warner, 1996, 1997, 2004; Zhu, 2005). As a consequence, new management practices are currently intensively introduced in China. As emphasised by Jaussaud and Liu (2011), however, these two different modes of introduction of new management practices do not follow the same path and do not necessarily lead to the same result. The main reason is that MNCs have strong experience of introducing into diverse cultural and institutional environments management practices that they have developed elsewhere; thus MNCs are characterised both by their determination and their caution in doing so in China. Chinese firms, on the contrary, lack experience, and seem to be too enthusiastic, underestimating difficulties in introducing some of the practices. As a consequence, for instance, the so-called '360° review' – the staff member appraisal system – was massively adopted by the Chinese firms of Jaussaud and Liu's sample, whereas it was not introduced at all by MNC subsidiaries.

Another question may be raised regarding Chinese firms. Do they all adopt new management practices at the same pace? One may imagine, for instance, that all private firms do not benefit from the same resources in trying to do so, because of size, industry, location and so on. In this chapter we would like to address the criteria of ownership and compare, in particular, Chinese private firms and Chinese state-owned firms. Although Chinese state-owned firms have been radically restructured since the mid-1990s, when not privatised or dissolved they may suffer both stronger personal management tradition and institutional pressures that could reduce their capacity to quickly introduce some management practices, particularly in the field of HRM under investigation in this chapter.

As a consequence, this chapter aims to compare management practices of Chinese private and Chinese state-owned enterprises. Are adopted management practices the same? If so, are they implemented similarly, to the same degree and with the same objectives? We focus on HRM practices, a topic that we have previously investigated in the Chinese context (Jaussaud and Liu, 2005, 2011). We undertake a qualitative comparison of the HRM practices of a few, carefully selected Chinese private and state-owned enterprises.

This chapter is organised as follows. We first detail the theoretical framework of our research and our empirical methodology. We then systematically compare HRM practices by Chinese private and state-owned enterprises.

Theoretical framework: adoption of modern HRM practices

Chinese firms eagerly look for modern managerial practices in all fields, including that of human resource management. Introducing modern management practices helps them to seize opportunities in their rapidly developing environment, and to protect them against aggressive competitors, both Chinese and foreign. Chinese firms often learn from their foreign partners, through joint ventures, licence agreements or buyer–supplier relationships. They also learn from consulting firms, conferences and training programmes, as well as by recruiting former employees of foreign-owned enterprises.

Previous research found significant differences in HRM practices between foreign-owned subsidiaries, whether wholly owned or joint ventures, and Chinese enterprises (Akhtar et al., 2008; Ding et al., 2001; Jaussaud and Liu, 2011; Law et al., 2003; Ngo et al., 2008; Warner, 1997, 2004), but a convergence process also seems to be at work in this rapidly changing context (Jaussaud and Liu, 2011; Warner, 2003).

The import of capital, technology and modern management practices has been among the key concerns of Chinese authorities since the 1980s. In 1978, foreign investment restrictions were eased, allowing first joint ventures with local partners, then wholly foreign-owned subsidiaries from 1986, in a growing number of industries. Chinese enterprises, whether state owned or private, were also strongly encouraged to modernise. As a consequence, two different modes for introducing modern management techniques may be identified in China from the period: by MNCs, on the one hand, and by local independent Chinese firms, on the other. MNCs, with great experience on their side, transfer management practices that they have developed and implemented in other institutional and cultural contexts to their subsidiaries in China. Chinese firms, through various sources such as foreign partners and suppliers, recruitment of staff formerly employed in foreign-owned enterprises, conferences, training programmes, and so on, identify modern management practices that might achieve improvement, and do their best to implement them. As Chinese firms often lack experience, they often expect too much from a given innovative practice, and thus often face tremendous difficulties because of their underestimation of the implementation challenges (Jaussaud and Liu, 2011).

As a consequence, one may consider two different, partly contradictory, processes at work in the implementation of modern management practices in China:

1. Mimetism (DiMaggio and Powell, 1983) should lead to convergence between Chinese and foreign-owned firms.
2. Differentiation in the organisational learning processes between Chinese and foreign-owned firms, as Chinese firms lack the same experience and knowledge as MNCs, whereas MNC subsidiaries experience institutional duality (Kostova and Roth, 2002).

Furthermore, the same may be said regarding Chinese firms themselves. Private firms and state-owned enterprises (SOEs) are certainly not in the same situation as regards adoption of modern management practices, particularly HRM practices. State-owned enterprises are subject to stronger institutional duality than private Chinese firms because, on the one hand, they need to adapt to the rules of competition which have become ever more prevalent from the beginning of the 1980s and, on the other, they are still under strong political and institutional pressure from the state at the national, provincial or even more local level. Although radically restructured since the mid-1990s, Chinese state-owned enterprises may suffer stronger personal management tradition and institutional pressures than private enterprises, and this may reduce the capacity of the former to introduce new management practices, particularly in the field of HRM. Private Chinese firms suffer to a lesser extent such traditions and governmental pressure.

Hypotheses

Keeping these contrasting forces in mind as a means to compare how Chinese private firms and state-owned enterprises adopt modern HRM practices, we derive two hypotheses. First, on the basis of the convergence assumption (DiMaggio and Powell, 1983), we anticipate that firms generally introduce almost similar HRM practices in the same way. We therefore investigate compensation, merit assessments, recruitment and training to gain a rather comprehensive perspective. We predict specifically:

H1 Chinese private and state-owned enterprises implement a wide range of similar HRM practices.

Second, we note differences in the organisational learning processes of the two groups of Chinese firms. State-owned enterprises may have to put up with a stronger personal management tradition and governmental institutional pressures than private enterprises, and this may reduce the capacity of the former to introduce modern HRM practices. Therefore, we predict:

H2 Some significant differences remain in the implementation of HRM practices by Chinese private firms versus state-owned enterprises.

Empirical methodology

As the phenomena that we investigate are subject to rapid change, both in terms of context and implemented mechanisms, we have adopted a qualitative approach. We carefully selected a sample of first-class private and state-owned enterprises in China. We selected only large firms that are widely recognised as modern and efficient, which increases the likelihood that they have introduced modern management practices.

In order to account for recent changes among private and state-owned enterprises in China, we adopted a wide-open perspective. We carried out in-depth interviews with HRM managers in these firms, and asked them to provide us with some operational documents such as assessment forms, anonymous pay-slips, and other work documents. In addition, we collected information from other sources, such as websites and newspapers. The in-depth interviews were conducted in 2010 and 2011 by Q.F. and X.L.

The total sample consisted of 13 state-owned and 7 private enterprises. In a qualitative investigation, sample size matters less than careful selection of appropriate cases (Silverman, 2005; Symon and Cassel, 1998). We interviewed more state-owned firms than private firms because, to the best of our knowledge, state-owned firms have been less investigated in the field of HRM, at least recently. More specifically, when we started this research, we already had a good knowledge base of private Chinese firms among others, because of our own previous research (Jaussaud and Liu, 2005, 2011), but we did not know so much about the HRM of state-owned firms. Thus, we felt sure to have reached saturation point for Chinese private firms when our sample reached 7, in the sense that additional cases would not teach us a lot, while we were not at saturation point until 10 or 11 in our state-owned sample.

Therefore, the Chinese firms in our sample represented industry leaders, such as Haier (a leading household equipment manufacturer), PA (a major hygiene products manufacturer) or PC (a heavy metal equipment manufacturer), as far as private enterprises were concerned; and SA (a port and waterway engineering firm) or SF (a light product manufacturing firm for state-owned enterprises). We mention these cases as these companies did not insist on remaining anonymous. The private firms in our sample are neither foreign owned, wholly owned or joint ventures, in order to avoid any bias; they are all Chinese independent firms.

By including firms from various industries and locations in China (Beijing, Tianjin, Shanghai, Tsingtao, Dalian and Nanchang), we avoided the possibility of the results reflecting any specific sector and local situation. Thus, our sample met the criteria of qualitative representativeness (Mucchieli, 1996; Symon and Cassel, 1998). Specifically, we aimed to select cases that provided the same level of diversity as would be expected in the population, in terms of the main variables that affect HRM practices, such as size, industry and location in China. Table 3.1 contains an overview of our sample, in which we replace company names with codes: PA to PG for private Chinese firms and SA to SM for state-owned ones.

Our interview guide focused on the main dimensions of HRM practices, such as recruitment, compensation, performance and merit appraisal system, training and so on. We invited each interviewee to provide a general description of each of these elements, and then we asked more precise questions. Our aim was to describe management practices actually implemented, as well as to understand why and how they were implemented, and whether any difficulties were encountered. Our interview guide contained 15 main questions and several sub-questions for each.

The interviewees were all human resource managers or held equivalent positions, such as CEOs or general managers. The interviews were conducted in Chinese by Q.F. and X.L. The interviews took from one to three hours. In most cases, we were granted permission to examine various HRM documents, such as appraisal forms, wage bills, and so on. When needed, additional information was collected on the phone and by email, after our visits to the companies.

The interviews were fully transcribed and coded, in order to summarise the whole collected material without losing any significant information.

Table 3.1 Sample description

Case	Private or state owned	Industry	Number of employees in China	Year of establishment under present status
PA	Private	Hygiene products	800	1995
PB	Private	Household appliances, electronic	50,000	1984
PC	Private	Metal equipment	500	2001
PD	Private	Mechanical and electrical equipment	3300	1988
PE	Private	Food industry	10,000	1997
PF	Private	Light consumer goods	30,000	1984
PG	Private	Export–import	120	2002
SA	State owned	Engineering	467	2009
SB	State owned	Consulting	200	1982
SC	State owned	Metal	1000	1969
SD	State owned	Bank	34,589	1987
SEx	State owned	Telecom	3900[a]	1994
SF	State owned	Light consumer goods	6900	1995
SG	State owned	Household appliances	60,000	1969
SH	State owned	Export–import	500	1982
SI	State owned	Pharmaceuticals	3600	1969
SJ	State owned	Electronics	2000[b]	1997[c]
SK	State owned	Household appliances	100	1994
SL	State-owned	Steel products	600	1994
SM	State-owned	Pharmaceuticals	3000	1950

[a] 150,000 for whole group in China.
[b] More than 10,000 for whole group in China.
[c] 1986 for parent company.

From this process, we identified 38 different items. For each of them we summarised the relevant information for each firm in a double-entry table.

State-owned and private enterprise HRM practices compared

We first compare compensation practices and merit assessments, then consider other dimensions, such as hiring, retention, training and so on, which may help to adapt human resources to environmental requirements.

Compensation practices

Wages often consist of fixed and variable parts. The variable part is generally linked to performance. In all our cases of private Chinese firms and most of the state-owned ones, variable elements constitute a significant portion of staff member wages (see Table 3.2). Not surprisingly, the variable portion is higher among sales personnel than other employees and among managerial positions than subordinates. However, variable wages constitute a higher share of total wages for private firms compared with state-owned ones, and in 2 of the 13 state-owned firms in our sample wages had no flexible part.

Both in private and in state-owned firms, the interviewees justify the high share of variable wages as an incentive mechanism, in contrast with China's planned economy until the end of the 1970s. Determination of the variable part is mainly based on individual characteristics and merit, though partly on collective performance.

In addition, all the enterprises in our sample pay for health insurance for their employees. They also contribute to accommodation funds, at rates that vary according to the province and city. Since the mid-1990s, labour and social legislation has been greatly strengthened in China. Firms also subsidise meals during work time, and they provide other allowances.

The Chinese firms in our sample do not pay for all overtime worked by foremen and employees, though they should according to labour legislation. Only factory workers receive pay for all their overtime hours – at least those with contracts, which became compulsory in January 2008 with the enactment of new labour legislation. However, for foremen and employees long working days often translate into higher bonuses.

Table 3.2 Compensation practices

Case	Variable wages	Individual or collective bonuses
PA	50%, differentiated according to categories	Individual
PB	20%, differentiated according to categories	Individual
PC	30%, differentiated according to categories	Individual
PD	50% for sales force, 20% for managers, 10% for others	Mainly collective, but for sales force
PE	30–40% for sales force, 10–20% for others	Mainly individual
PF	30%, differentiated according to categories	Mainly individual
PG	30%, differentiated according to categories	Mainly individual
SA	No variable part	—
SB	10%, differentiated according to categories	Mainly collective
SC	No variable part	—
SD	Variable part for managers	Individual
SE	50% for sales force, 30% for managers, 10% for others	Individual and collective
SF	10%, differentiated according to categories	Individual and collective
SG	10–20%, differentiated according to categories	Individual for around 90% of the bonus; collective for 10%
SH	10%, differentiated according to categories	Individual and collective
SI	40–50% for sales force, 20–30% for others	Collective
SJ	20–30%, or 5–40%, according to the categories	Mainly individual
SK	30%	Individual
SL	30%	Individual and collective
SM	10–20%, differentiated according to categories	Individual and collective

Paid holidays are provided by all the firms in our sample, from 5 to 15 days a year according to the firm and to worker length of service. The private firms in our sample frequently ask their employees not to take all the days they are entitled to, a practice that was common in Japan until recently (Hanami, 1994). Supervisors frequently reject workers' applications for holidays, invoking work overload, for instance. According to our interviewees, top management in private Chinese firms believe that only severe family or personal difficulties make it reasonable for an employee to take his or her full annual holidays. Chinese state-owned enterprises in our sample do not adopt this position: their employees take their full annual holidays in almost all cases.

On the whole, as regards compensation, significant differences remain between Chinese private and state-owned firms, particularly with respect to wages, variable part calculations and management of paid holidays.

Merit appraisal practices

As a significant portion of employees' wages appears to be variable, calculated partly on an individual basis, we should consider how companies assess the merit of employees. The interviews indicate clearly that individual assessments of employees are well developed for all the companies in our sample. Assessments appear more frequent among Chinese private firms, quite often occurring monthly for non-managerial positions ('which is too frequent', according to several interviewees), and quarterly for managers (Table 3.3). Sales forces are assessed more frequently, even weekly in most cases, which is not surprising. The assessments of managers and some employees in specific non-managerial positions include individual interviews with supervisors.

In all cases in our sample, the assessment is multidimensional. It covers the employee's performance based on different performance indicators. In most cases, it also covers competence, behaviour at work and commitment. At PD, for example, the company weighs performance at 60%, actual and potential abilities at 20% and behaviour at work at 20%. Interviewees from both private and state-owned firms often mentioned that supervisors were reluctant to carry out formal assessments, because of the huge administrative work involved and because of workplace tensions that might result from this.

The appraisal system is systematically linked to wage calculation for the variable part in private firms, but not in all state-owned firms (not in SA and

SC). In all cases, however, promotions are based widely on the appraisal system.

The systematic formal assessment of employees may relate to the development of management by objectives (MBO), at both the managerial and other levels in both private and state-owned firms. Yet interviewees underlined the difficulties of implementing MBO (e.g., PB, PE, PD, and most of the state-owned firms in our sample). According to our interviewee in PD, for instance, 'we have difficulties in determining reasonable and realistic objectives'.

In short, appraisal systems have been widely adopted by all the firms in our sample, although apparently they cover all staff members and are more systematically linked to wage calculation system in private firms. In all cases, however, promotion is presented by the interviewees as based widely on appraisal, both in private and state-owned enterprises.

Recruitment and training

Both the private and state-owned firms in our sample encounter rather high staff turnover problems. PB, for instance, mentions a turnover rate of 8–10% for managerial positions and office workers, and 15% for workers; and PD mentions a 20% rate. State-owned firms generally mention lower turnover rates, although SI mentions a rate of 10–20% for managerial positions.

In order to reduce employee turnover, most respondents mention improving recruitment, training, offering job career opportunities and improving the social climate, while pointing out that paying more to reduce turnover is often not an option. Let us specifically consider recruitment and training, two areas where we could gather rather precise information on all the cases in our sample (Table 3.4).

In a rapidly developing economy, firms generally do a lot of hiring, even if employee turnover is low. In all the firms in our sample, internal recruitment seems to have been strongly developed as a way to offer carrier development opportunities, to develop job loyalty and to reduce turnover. State-owned enterprises, more often than private ones, rely on the close relationships they have developed with schools, technological institutes and universities. SE, in addition, mentioned significant mid-carrier recruitment.

When discussing recruitment criteria, it appears that work experience matters a great deal as far as private firms are concerned (PA, PC, PF, PK), both for internal and for external recruitment. By contrast, interviewees

Table 3.3 Appraisal system characteristics

Case	Frequency of appraisal	Main criteria	Variable wage based on appraisal
PA	Annual for managerial positions; monthly for others	Performance and behaviour	Yes
PB	Monthly	Performance and behaviour	Yes
PC	Monthly	Performance	Yes
PD	Annual for managerial positions; monthly for others	Performance (60%), behaviour (20%), competence (20%)	Yes
PE	Monthly, quarterly and annually for managerial positions; monthly for others	Performance, competence, behaviour	Yes
PF	Monthly	Based on a number of key performance Indicators	Yes
PG	Monthly	Performance	Yes
SA	No systematic performance appraisal system	—	No
SB	Monthly	Performance	Yes
SC	Annual	Performance, competence	No
SD	Monthly	Performance	Yes
SE	Annual for managerial positions; quarterly for others	Performance and behaviour	Yes
SF	Biannual	Performance, competence, behaviour	Yes
SG	Biannual	4 criteria on competences; 8 on behaviour	Yes, partially
SH	For managerial staff mainly, annual	Performance, competence	Yes
SI	Quarterly for managers; monthly for others; weekly for sales forces	Competence, behaviour; since 2004, performance (70%), competence and behaviour (30%)	Yes

Case	Frequency of appraisal	Main criteria	Variable wage based on appraisal
SJ	Monthly or quarterly according to categories	Performance, competence, behaviour	Yes
SK	Annual	Performance, competence, behaviour	Yes
SL	Quarterly	Performance, competence, behaviour	Yes
SM	Biannual	Performance, competence, behaviour	Yes

from state-owned firms highlighted the importance of educational achievement (SA, SC, SF, SK, SL and SM, particularly). This may be linked to the strong relationships that state-owned firms maintain with schools, technological institutes and universities.

Training is well developed in almost all the firms in our sample, especially with regard to their industry-related technical domains, and marketing and management techniques. Training is mainly in-house, except for managerial positions. On-the-job training under the guidance of more experienced colleagues is widespread, both in private and state-owned enterprises. No clear difference appears as regards training by private and state-owned enterprises in our sample, but there are differences when it comes to training freshly recruited people. The private firms in our sample scarcely ever organise training at recruitment, before employment, possibly because work experience is one of their preferred criteria when hiring. Only PC and PG do this. By contrast, all the state-owned enterprises in our sample organise such training after recruitment, and before job positions are taken.

Discussion

Having investigated a selected range of HRM practices, including compensation, merit appraisal, hiring, and training, we attempt to

Table 3.4 Recruitment and training policies

Case	Recruitment	Training policy
PA	Internal recruitment, first; external through staff member relationships, next; and widely advertised if needed	Strongly developed, training plan designed and implemented every year
PB	All means of recruitment, both internal and external	Strongly developed; experience in e-learning
PC	Internal recruitment, first; external through staff member relationships, next; and widely advertised if needed	Strongly developed, three levels of training through the year (personal skills, safety and quality)
PD	For managerial positions, internal recruitment, first; external and widely advertised if needed, next; for workers, massive external recruitment	Strongly developed; 10% of the payroll; 8 days a year for managers; 4 days for others
PE	Internal recruitment, first; external through staff member relationships, next; and widely advertised if needed	Strongly developed
PF	For managerial positions, internal recruitment, first; external and widely advertised if needed, next; for workers, massive external recruitment	Not so much developed; emphasis on personal skills and safety
PG	Internal recruitment, first; external through staff member relationships, next; and widely advertised if needed	Strongly developed
SA	Internal recruitment, first; external if needed, next; strong links with schools	Strongly developed; training plan designed and implemented every year
SB	Strong links with schools and universities	Strongly developed
SC	Strong links with professional schools	Strongly developed
SD	Internal recruitment, first; external if needed, next; strong links with schools and universities	Very high; mainly in-house; 40 hours per year per employee
SE	All means of recruitment, both internal and external	Strongly developed; expenses up to 2% of the payroll
SF	Internal recruitment, first; external if needed, next; strong links with universities	Moderately developed

Case	Recruitment	Training policy
SG	Internal recruitment, first; external if needed, next	Strongly developed
SH	Internal recruitment, first; external if needed, next	Strongly developed, particularly for managerial positions
SI	Internal recruitment, first; external if needed, next	Strongly developed, particularly for managerial positions
SJ	Internal recruitment, first; external if needed, next; strong links with schools and universities	In technical domains mainly
SK	Internal recruitment, first; external if needed, next; strong links with schools and universities	Not so much developed; according to needs
SL	Internal recruitment, first; external if needed, next; strong links with schools	Strongly developed; training plan designed and implemented every year
SM	Internal recruitment, first; external if needed, next; strong links with universities	Strongly developed; training plan designed and implemented every year

synthesise our findings within the framework of our set of hypotheses H1 and H2. The hypotheses were formulated as follows.

H1 Chinese private and state-owned enterprises implement a wide range of similar HRM practices.

H2 Some significant differences remain in the implementation of HRM practices by Chinese private firms versus state-owned enterprises.

Specifically, our findings strongly support H1, and to some extent they support H2 too. Of the various types of practices we have investigated, both state-owned and private firms implement sophisticated human resource management practices. In addition, the practices themselves appear to be very similar across both groups of firms. Thus mimetism brought about by strong pressures both from a highly competitive environment and from Chinese authorities seems to be at work, leading all kinds of Chinese firms to implement a wide range of similar modern HRM practices (H1).

However, some differences remain in the way some of these HRM practices are implemented by the private and state-owned firms in our sample. For example, compensation is more strongly linked to performance appraisal in private firms than in state-owned ones, and variable wages constitute a higher share of total wages for the former. In private firms, paid holidays are managed more severely; merit appraisal seems to be carried out more frequently and covers more systematically all categories of staff members. State-owned firms tend to have stronger links with schools, technological institutes and universities than private ones, which may have some influence on recruitment practices and training. Such findings provide some support for H2.

This validation of H1 and H2, despite being partially contradictory, is not surprising. Similarities rather than differences in HRM practices between Chinese private and state-owned enterprises in HRM are underlined in this research. The convergence hypothesis thus seems to hold as a result of strong pressures both from competition and from local authorities leading to isomorphism (DiMaggio and Powell, 1983). However, possibly because of their longer history, traditions and potentially strong pressure from their national or provincial state shareholder, state-owned enterprises still implement some HRM practices (H2) differently. This may also be interpreted as evidence supporting the institutional theory, which states that the institutional environment can affect the development of an enterprise's formal structures more profoundly than market pressure (Di Maggio and Powell, 1983; Kostova and Roth, 2002).

Conclusion

This chapter shows that both Chinese private firms and state-owned enterprises implement sophisticated human resource management practices. In addition, the practices themselves appear to be very similar across both groups of firms. Mimetism (Di Maggio and Powell, 1983) is arguably the result of strong pressures from a highly competitive environment and from Chinese authorities. This process is leading all kinds of Chinese firms to implement a wide range of similar modern HRM practices. However, differences remain in the way some of these HRM practices are implemented by the private and state-owned firms in our sample, possibly because of longer history, traditions and of potentially strong pressure from national or provincial state shareholders. This dual process of convergence can be linked to that between foreign firms in China and Chinese firms (Jaussaud and Liu, 2011). In any event, there is doubt about whether convergent forces will prevail, as the Chinese labour legal framework continues to develop – for instance, the enactment in 2008 of new labour legislation (Anon., 2010; Cooney et al., 2007).

References

Akhtar, S., Ding, D.Z. and Ge, G.L. (2008) Strategic HRM practices and their impact on company performance in Chinese enterprises. *Human Resource Management*, **47**(1), 15–32.

Anon. (2010) Early days for China's labor law. *China Economic Review*, 22 January 2010.

Cooke, F.L. (2004) HRM in China. In: P.S. Budwar (Ed.), *Managing Human Resources in Asia-Pacific*. Routledge, London, pp. 17–34.

Cooney, S., Biddulph, S., Kungang, L. and Zhu, Y. (2007) China's new labour contract law: responding to the growing complexity of labour relations in the PRC. *UNSW Law Journal*, **30**, 788–803.

DiMaggio, P. and Powell, W. (1983) The iron cage revisited: institutional isomorphism and collective rationality in organisational fields. *American Sociological Review*, **48**, 147–60.

Ding, D.Z., Lan, G. and Warner, M. (2001) A new form of Chinese human resource management? Personnel and labor-management relations in Chinese township and village enterprises: a case study approach. *Industrial Relations Journal*, **32**, 328–43.

Hanami, T. (1994) *Managing Japanese Workers*. Japan Institute of Labour, Tokyo.

Jaussaud, J. and Liu, X. (2005) La GRH des personnels locaux dans les entreprises étrangères en Chine, une approche exploratoire. *Revue de Gestion des Ressources Humaines*, **59**, janvier/février/mars, 60–71 [in French].

Jaussaud, J. and Liu, X. (2011) When in China . . . The HRM practices of Chinese and foreign-owned enterprises during a global crisis. *Asia Pacific Business Review*, **17**(4), October, 473–91.

Kostova, T. and Roth, K. (2002) Adoption of an organisational practice by subsidiaries of multinational corporations: institutional and relation effects. *Academy of Management Journal*, **45**(1), 215–33.

Lau, C.M. and Ngo, H.Y. (2001) Organization development and firm performance: a comparison of multinational and local firms. *Journal of International Business Studies*, **32**, 95–114.

Law, K.S., Tse, D.K. and Zhou, N. (2003) Does human resource matter in a transitional economy? China as an example. *Journal of Intenational Business Studies*, **34**, 255–65.

Mucchieli, A (1996) *Dictionnaire des Méthodes Qualitatives en Sciences Humaines et Sociales*. Armand Colin, Paris [in French].

Ngo, H-Y., Lau, C-M. and Foley, S. (2008) Strategic human resource management, firm performance, and employee relations climate in China. *Human Resource Management*, **47**(1), 73–90.

Silverman, D. (2005) *Doing Qualitative Research*. Sage Publications, London.

Symon, G. and Cassel, C. (1998) *Qualitative Methods in Organisational Research*. Sage Publications, London.

Warner, M. (1996) Economic reform, industrial relations and human resources in the People's Republic of China: an overview. *Industrial Relations Journal*, **27**, 195–210.

Warner, M. (1997) China's HRM in transition: towards relative convergence? *Asia Pacific Business Review*, **3**, 19–33.

Warner, M. (2003) China's HRM revisited: a step-wise path to convergence? *Asia Pacific Business Review*, **9**, 15–31.

Warner, M. (2004) Human resource management in China revisited: introduction. *International Journal of Human Resource Management*, **15**, 617–34.

Zhu, C.J. (2005) *Human Resource Management in China: Past, Current and Future HR Practices in the Industrial Sector*. Routledge, New York.

4

The influence of family control on business performance and financial structure: a matched pair investigation of listed companies in China

Bruno Amann, Qianxuan Huang and Jacques Jaussaud

Abstract: Active academic research into family businesses (FBs) consistently indicates that FBs perform better and have sounder financial structures than non-family businesses (NFBs), across time and various nations. However, conventional wisdom once held that these performance benefits did not apply to Japanese FBs, and currently general opinion suggests it is not true in China. This chapter therefore undertakes a precise investigation of Chinese listed companies to compare FBs with NFBs. In China too, FBs perform better than NFBs in terms of profitability and liquidity, though not with regard to long-term indebtedness. Moreover, FBs that fall under strong family control perform better than those with weak levels, in terms of profitability, liquidity and indebtedness.

Key words: China, family businesses, performance, financial structure, listed companies, level of control.

Introduction

Family businesses (FBs) attract widespread research attention, largely because of their prominent roles in most countries throughout the world. In many countries, FBs represent the majority of enterprises, ranging from small to large firms. In addition, academic studies consider FBs in various nations, including Mainland China more recently, as well as developed nations and areas such as North America, Western Europe and Japan.

In the People's Republic of China, FBs emerged in parallel with the development of private firms and businesses, in the course of the open-reform policy that the Chinese government initiated at the end of the 1970s. Thus FBs in China underwent an original period of development, looking for capital, and have since shifted their focus to advanced organizational innovations and management. A survey conducted by *Forbes China* (2012, *http://www.Forbeschina.com*) of listed companies in the Shanghai and Shenzhen Stock Exchanges shows that the nation hosts 1028 state-owned companies and 1394 private companies. Of the latter, 684 represent family-owned firms, or 49% of all private companies. In addition, 182 FBs from Mainland China are registered on the Hong Kong Stock Market.

Many Chinese FBs operate in the manufacturing, information transmission, computer services, software and real estate industries; no FBs appear in the finance or insurance industry; and we find only a few in mining and quarrying, public utility, social services or publishing and culture industries. Similar to the situation in many other Asian countries, FBs in China rarely work in capital-intensive sectors, because they lack the capabilities required to enter such 'highly regulated and state-monopolized industries'.[1] However, unlike in other Asian countries such as Singapore or the Philippines, FBs have a smaller role in Mainland China, due to a high degree of 'government involvement in the mobilization of savings and industrial development'.[2]

Some of these characteristics, as well as some firms' reliance on outdated organizational forms that allow for nepotism, paternalism and autocracy (Tsang, 2001), have prompted negative assessments of FBs in China, among both academics and other practitioners. Moreover, FBs often struggle to obtain long-term loans from financial institutions, compared with other entities, and external investors may resist investing in a family firm. These financing challenges imply that FBs are more likely to face severe constraints when they seek to expand in scale after their initial development (Zhang et al., 2012). Yet in most countries, FBs perform better and enjoy a sounder financial structure than NFBs. This distinction has been established in North America and Europe (Gallo et al., 2004; Smyrnios et al., 1998; Sraer and Thesmar, 2007), as well as in Japan (Allouche et al., 2008; Kurashina, 2003). Is the story different in China?

This chapter investigates the performance of FBs versus NFBs in Mainland China, using a large, paired sample *t*-test. We control for firm size and industry, and we check whether the level of family control affects FBs' performance or financial situation. Briefly, we find that in China, FBs perform better than NFBs, as measured by profitability and liquidity, but not for measures of long-term indebtedness. Moreover, when family control is strong, FBs perform better than if family control is weak, in terms of profitability, liquidity and indebtedness.

After we present our theoretical framework and hypotheses in the next section, we detail our empirical methodology, including the definition of FBs in China, the sample and the data description. Our data analysis leads into a discussion of the main results, before we conclude with a brief summary.

Theoretical framework and hypotheses

Previous academic literature offers several theories and concepts to interpret the impressive performance and financial structure of FBs around the world. For example, Jensen and Meckling (1976) argue that firm value relates positively to the level of managerial ownership due to reduced agency costs; Fama and Jensen (1983) similarly hold that agency problems between top managers and shareholders can be reduced if the residual claimants and decision agents are the same. They predict reduced agency cost in FBs because of the minimal separation between ownership control and managerial decisions. The strategic combination of family and business is thus a primary and influential characteristic of FBs (Habberson and Williams, 1999).

Stewardship theory instead focuses on the capabilities achieved by FBs (e.g., Dibrell, 2010). Because they align personal with firm goals, including non-financial objectives, and establish relational contracts between owners and managers, FBs become sources of stewardship (Christensen, 1997; Davis et al., 1997). From a stewardship perspective, a family manager is motivated to act in a way that maximizes the benefits for the family-owned firm, and the interests of family managers and family owners are aligned (Donaldson and David, 1989, 1991).

Two foundational elements of FB culture and values, altruism and trust (Davis, 1983), can also enhance communication and collaboration efficiency within the firm, with positive influences on work group processes and performance through higher levels of cooperation and joint efforts (Astrachan and Zellweger, 2008; Dirks, 1999). In addition, reciprocal or symmetric altruism leading to mutual trust can reduce agency problems and moral hazards between the principal and agent, leading to lower transaction costs (Bernheim and Stark, 1998; Chami, 2001; Stark, 1989; Tsang, 2001).

The connection between family and business also offers unique advantages for acquiring resources (Aldrich and Cliff, 2003; Haynes et al., 1999; Stewart, 2003). Barney et al. (2002) point out that family ties may facilitate the identification of opportunities, because they increase people's willingness to share information. From a resource-based view, FBs generate a valuable and unique resource or capability that cannot be imitated or purchased by other firms, with positive influences on firm performance (Habberson and Williams, 1999). Similarly, kinship and ethnic ties might further a trust-based relationship, and reliance on these extended, special relationships again can reduce transaction costs (Carney, 2005).

This theoretical foundation strongly supports the prediction of better performance by FBs compared with NFBs, so we anticipate it holds in China as well:

H1 Chinese family businesses enjoy better performance than Chinese non–family businesses.

According to Le Breton-Miller and Miller (2006), FBs adopt a long-term orientation, which may help them avoid myopic behaviour (Stein, 1988, 1989). Their managers also embrace long-term perspectives, so FB strategic decisions should be less restricted by short-term economic circumstances (Harvey, 1999), including optimal investment policies that get implemented in the long run (Allouche et al., 2008). That is, owners prefer to invest in projects from which FBs can benefit in the long run. Yet FBs also adopt cautious attitudes toward debt, because they prefer to avoid the risk of loss of control (Mishra and McConaughy, 1999; McConaughy et al., 2001). As Yeung (2000) points out, Chinese FBs are highly sensitive to cost and financial efficiency concerns. Thus, we predict:

H2 Chinese FBs have stronger financial structures than Chinese NFBs.

In their study of FBs in Japan, Allouche et al. (2008) find that stronger family control leads to better outcomes with regard to both performance and financial structures. Specifically, the interests and goals of shareholders and management are better aligned in strongly controlled FBs. In contrast with weakly controlled FBs, the further reduction in conflicts between owners and managers in strongly controlled FBs can ensure even lower agency costs and better long-term orientation, as these owners seek to maintain family control over the firm. To avoid any loss of control, they likely develop more careful attitudes toward financial management.

Stability in strategic management and orientation might also relate to the level of family control. A more stable strategy, maintained by FBs even in the face of changing circumstances and over time, provides advantages over NFBs with shifting strategies (Van Den Berghe and Carchon, 2003). In particular, a strongly controlled FB confirms the firm's investment planning horizon (Sraer and Thesmar, 2007). However, Gonzalez et al. (2012) argue that the capital structure is an insufficient measure of risk aversion, because debt levels are higher when families take solely ownership roles, whereas they decrease if the families also participate in management duties. In accordance with their findings, strongly controlled FBs should enjoy a better financial structure. Therefore, we hypothesise:

H3 In China, stronger control by the family over the business leads to superior performance.

H4 In China, stronger control by the family over the business leads to a stronger financial structure.

Empirical methodology

Following the method established by Allouche et al. (2008) in the case of Japan, we employ a matched pair design, which ensures that we measure the influence of being a FB on performance, rather than the possible impact of characteristics associated with the firm or industry. That is, we compare FBs and NFBs with similar profiles, sizes and industries. This comparison requires us to build pairs, of one FB and one NFB, as well as pairs of one strongly controlled FB and one weakly controlled FB, in which both firms in each pair represent the same industry and are of the same size.

Other potentially influential variables include firm age and cross-generational involvement, yet most FBs in China are quite young and still controlled by their first-generation owners, considering that private enterprises arose only in the 1980s in response to the open policy adopted by Deng Xiaoping at the end of the 1970s. The capital market in China was established in the middle of the 1990s, and most private firms entered stock markets only after 2000. As of 2012, only 7% of family-owned, listed companies had been taken over by the family's second generation (*Forbes China*, 2012). Thus we did not consider firm age or multi-generational involvement for this research.

Instead, we conducted three comparisons. First, we compared NFBs and strongly controlled FBs, using data from 2007 and 2008. In line with our theoretical foundation and hypotheses, NFBs and strongly controlled FBs should offer the sharpest contrast in terms of performance, so they represent the best choice for testing the hypotheses. Second, we considered NFBs and all FBs, using data from 2007 and 2008 (see Table 4.3), for which the contrast should be somewhat weaker than in the first case. By investigating the results of both these comparisons, we can find the influence of being or not being a FB on performance and financial structures in China, assuming both comparisons support H1 and H2, as well as determine the effect of strong or weak control, as predicted in H3 and H4, if the two comparisons provide distinct results. Third, we directly compare strongly and weakly controlled FBs, again using data from 2007 and 2008 (Table 4.4), as a stronger test of H3 and H4.

Different types of FBs

We relied on an existing summary of listed FBs in Mainland China, which indicates that 421 of all 1591 listed companies were family-controlled firms at the end of 2007 (*Capital Week*, 26 July 2008). These owners can be classified as either entrepreneurs (*qiye jia*) or capitalists (*zibenjia*), according to four criteria. That is, to be an entrepreneur, the ownership family must:

1. Be the founder of the core business. If the company became listed through a backdoor listing, the owner family must be the founder of the core business registered for the rebuilt, listed company.

2. Hold top management positions.

3. Control only firms within a single industry or industrial chain, even if it controls more than one listed company.

4. Have clear and stable main business interests, such that pure financial investors and firms with no clear, main business are excluded.

If the owner family does not satisfy all four criteria, the firm is classified as capitalist. Thus an entrepreneur starts the core business, cares about the norms of the industry, develops the business in that field and participates directly in the management of the listed company. A capitalist instead is more interested in capital operations and pursues its own maximal economic interest by managing capital transactions. Compared with a capitalist, an entrepreneur seeks to develop and strengthen the firm to achieve certain values and interests, with a greater focus on business development (especially long term) and prestige, as well as the family's continuity and reputation.

Because entrepreneurs are not only the largest shareholders but also the top-ranking managers of the firm, whereas capitalists are solely major shareholders, we assume that entrepreneur-owned FBs exhibit greater influence over every step of the business development process than do capitalist-controlled FBs. In turn, we classify FBs owned by entrepreneurs as strongly controlled, whereas FBs owned by capitalists represent weakly controlled FBs. For ease of reference and consistency with prior research (Allouche et al., 2008; Kurashina, 2003), we refer to NFBs as Type A firms, strongly controlled FBs as Type B firms, and weakly controlled FBs as Type C firms. However, it should also be noted that we use different criteria to distinguish Types B and C than did Kurashina (2003) and Allouche et al. (2008), because of the different nations (Japan versus China) and the slightly different kinds of data that are available.

Sample and data

We gathered a sample of companies listed on the Shanghai and Shenzhen Stock Exchanges, the two markets of Mainland China. For the industry classification, we used the codes issued by the China Securities Regulatory Commission (CSRC), which sorts listed companies into 13 general industry sectors, covering 65 industries in second-layer classification and more than 200 sub-industries in third-layer classification (Table 4.1). To compare FBs and NFBs of the same size and industry, we turned to the second-layer classification; we considered the first level insufficiently precise to represent each firm's industry profile, and the third level was overly meticulous, such that many sub-industries contain no or a few cases. For the size criterion, we required that each firm in a pair should earn similar revenues (or sales) or employ approximately the same number of people, as a threshold of 10%.

We thus built 314 matched pairs across the 65 industries; 297 pairs remained valid for our analysis after we cleaned the data by removing pairs featuring companies that were parts of a conglomerate, came from the pure financial industry or offered aberrant data. Among these 297 valid matched pairs, 177 represented the strongly controlled versus NFB comparison (Type B versus Type A), 76 pairs entailed the weakly

Table 4.1 Listed companies in China (Shanghai and Shenzhen Stock Exchanges) and sample

Sector code	Industry sectors	Industry code	Industries	No. of listed companies	No. of family-listed companies	No. of matched pairs
A	Farming, forestry, animal husbandry and fishery	A01	Farming	14	2	1
		A03	Forestry	4	2	0
		A05	Animal husbandry	6	3	1
		A07	Fishery	9	3	2
		A09	Services for farming, forestry, animal husbandry and fishery	1	0	0
B	Mining and quarrying industries	B01	Mining and washing of coal	24	1	0
		B03	Extraction of petroleum and natural gas	3	0	0
		B05	Mining and dressing of ferrous metal ores	2	0	0
		B07	Mining and dressing of nonferrous metal ores	7	1	0
		B09	Mining and dressing of nonmetal ores	0	0	0
		B49	Mining and dressing of other ores	0	0	0
		B50	Services for mining and quarrying	2	1	0

C	Manufacturing	C00	Manufacture of food and beverage	60	15	10
		C01	Manufacture of textile garments, footwear and headgear; feather, furs, down and related products	62	18	16
		C02	Timber processing, bamboo, cane, palm fibre and straw products; manufacture of furniture	6	4	0
		C03	Papermaking and paper products; printing and record medium reproduction; manufacture of cultural, educational and sports goods	31	11	7
		C04	Petroleum processing, coking and nuclear fuel processing; manufacture of raw chemical materials and chemical products; rubber and plastic products	124	32	31
		C05	Electric components, equipment and facilities	68	23	14
		C06	Metal and nonmetal products	139	26	25
		C07	Manufacture of instruments, meters and machinery	243	61	56
		C08	Medical and pharmaceutical products	108	41	24
		C99	Other manufacturing	12	2	0
D	Production and supply of electricity, gas and water	D01	Production and supply of electricity and heating power	57	3	3
		D03	Production and supply of gas	3	1	0
		D05	Production and supply of water	6	0	0

Table 4.1 (continued)

Sector code	Industry sectors	Industry code	Industries	No. of listed companies	No. of family-listed companies	No. of matched pairs
E	Construction	E01	Building and civil engineer work industry	30	6	4
		E05	Architectural decoration industry	2	2	0
F	Traffic, transportation, storage services	F01	Railway transport	2	0	0
		F03	Highway transport	4	1	0
		F05	Pipeline transport	0	0	0
		F07	Waterway transport	12	0	0
		F09	Air transport	9	0	0
		F11	Carrying and other transport services	34	4	4
		F19	Other transportation industries	0	0	0
		F21	Storage industry	2	0	0
G	Information transmission, computer services and software	G81	Communication and related equipment production	41	20	7
		G83	Computer and related equipment production	10	1	0
		G85	Communication service industry	8	3	0
		G87	Computer application service industry	44	17	7

H	Wholesale and retail trade	H01	Food, beverage, tobacco and household goods wholesale trade	4	0	0
		H03	Energy, material, mechanical and electronic equipment wholesale trade	4	0	0
		H09	Other wholesale trade	0	0	0
		H11	Retail trade	56	15	8
		H21	Commercial brokerages and agencies	22	2	1
I	Finance and insurance industry	I01	Banking	14	0	0
		I11	Insurance	2	0	0
		I21	Securities and futures	9	0	0
		I31	Finance and affiance industry	3	0	0
		I41	Fund industry	0	0	0
		I99	Other finance industry	0	0	0
J	Real estate industry	J01	Real estate development and operation	107	41	30
		J05	Real estate management	1	1	0
		J09	Real estate intermediary service	0	0	0

Table 4.1 (continued)

Sector code	Industry sectors	Industry code	Industries	No. of listed companies	No. of family-listed companies	No. of matched pairs
K	Social service industry	K01	Public facilities industry	16	1	1
		K10	Postal services	0	0	0
		K20	Scientific research, technical services	1	0	0
		K30	Catering	26	3	1
		K99	Other social services	2	0	0
L	Publishing and culture industry	L01	Press industry	3	0	0
		L05	Audiovisual industry	0	0	0
		L10	Radio, film and television industry	4	0	0
		L15	Art industry	0	0	0
		L20	Information transmitting services	3	1	0
		L99	Other culture, transmitting services	0	0	0
M	Conglomerate	/	/	69	22	17

controlled versus NFB version (Type C versus Type A) and 44 compared weakly and strongly controlled FBs.

We gathered several financial ratios, including return on assets (ROA), return on equity (ROE), ROE per share and earnings before interest and taxes (EBIT) to gain a complete picture of the relative performance of FBs and NFBs. For the financial structures, from these selected financial indicators we can glean the total debts/total capital, long-term debt/total capital, current ratios and quick ratio. The data came from the well-known Thomson One Banker database.

Data analysis

The comparisons relied on paired sample *t*-tests, frequency tests and Wilcoxon tests, applied to the three comparison sets with various financial indexes for data pertaining to 2007–8. We first compare NFBs (Type A) and strongly controlled FBs (Type B), to test H1. As the results in Table 4.2 show, almost all the profitability-related ratios for 2007 and most of them for 2008 indicate significant differences in favour of FBs. We summarise these comparisons in a separate column in the table, which reveals that nearly all the results are more than 60% favourable toward FBs in 2007, and 55–60% of them are in 2008. The ROA and return on invested capital (ROIC) values show significant differences, at the 1% level for 2007 and 10% for 2008.[3] In support of H1, FBs appear more profitable in terms of using their assets to generate earnings and more efficient at allocating capital to profitable investments.

The ROE per share ratio is important to public shareholders; these outcomes also favour FBs, at significance levels of 1% in 2007 and 10% in 2008. The EBIT and net income measures signal the better performance of FBs too, and the difference is significant at 5% in 2007. The two ratios for 2008 are not significant though. Regarding the profitability earned from sales, we find that net income/sales, EBIT/sales and pretax margins all recommend strongly controlled FBs over NFBs, at significant levels for both years. The ratio of cost of goods sold to sales does not differ significantly, though FBs reveal better value in the majority of pairs (Table 4.2).

All these outcomes match most prior empirical studies in the field: FBs are more profitable and enjoy lower costs with the same sales value, in support of H1. The findings suggest that FBs use their resources very carefully and sparingly, because family members own those resources

Table 4.2 Comparison of performance and financial structure of NFBs and strongly controlled FBs in China

NFBs versus strongly controlled FBs (A versus B)												
Ratios	**2007**						**2008**					
	No.	**Means**			**Significance**	**Pairs in favour of FBs**	**No.**	**Means**			**Significance**	**Pairs in favour of FBs**
		NFB	**FB**	**Difference**	(%)	(%)		**NFB**	**FB**	**Difference**	(%)	(%)
Return on assets	160	5.31%	7.91%	2.60%	<1	65.63	160	4.65%	6.24%	1.60%	<5	56.88
Return on equity per share	153	9.21%	15.39%	6.18%	<1	62.75	155	4.92%	8.69%	3.77%	<10	54.84
Return on invested capital	158	6.50%	10.00%	3.50%	<1	64.56	158	5.92%	7.68%	1.76%	<10	55.70
EBIT	167	15.1	18.19	3.09	<5	62.87	152	27.8	26.19	–1.62	78.80	55.26
Net income	164	7.97	10.08	2.11	<5	60.37	160	15.07	14.4	–0.67	87.30	56.25
Pretax margin	177	9.23%	13.21%	3.98%	<1	59.32	144	8.26%	11.18%	2.93%	<5	54.86
EBIT/Sales	175	12.20%	15.40%	3.20%	<5	60.00	146	9.41%	13.44%	4.03%	<5	58.90
Net income/Sales	177	6.62%	9.93%	3.30%	<1	59.32	149	5.88%	8.02%	2.15%	<10	56.38
Cost of goods/Sales	177	71.91%	70.48%	–1.43%	32.30	57.06	160	71.32%	69.25%	–2.07%	21.40	56.88
Sales per employee	41	1.13	0.22	–0.91	34.90	46.34	157	0.49	0.19	–0.3	37.30	50.96
Total debt/Total capital	154	52.03%	54.34%	2.04%	60.30	47.40	160	54.52%	51.56%	–2.96%	63.90	47.50

Long-term debt/Total capital	176	9.72%	9.95%	0.23%	87.30	35.80	160	10.15%	8.77%	−1.38%	31.20	39.38
Total debt/Total common equity	162	78.62%	75.52%	−3.09%	76.30	47.53	160	316.17%	69.60%	−246.58%	30.10	46.25
Current ratio	163	1.31%	1.67%	0.36%	<1	57.58	154	1.78%	1.64%	−0.14%	51.60	55.19
Quick ratio	170	0.84%	1.15%	0.31%	<1	60.59	138	0.71%	0.81%	0.11%	<10	56.52
Inventory turnover	153	5.32%	6.96%	1.64%	<10	50.98	153	4.30%	5.36%	1.06%	16.00	52.29
Cash and equivalence/ Current assets	171	29.71%	34.34%	4.63%	<5	56.73	154	30.76%	31.96%	1.20%	57.60	50.65
Cashflow/Sales	174	12.67%	14.88%	2.21%	<5	59.77	156	11.30%	14.68%	3.38%	<5	57.69
Capital expenditure/ Total assets	159	6.78%	10.98%	4.21%	<1	57.86	150	5.70%	8.11%	2.42%	<1	66.00
Assets per employee	41	1.79	0.61	−1.18	29	46.34	152	0.38	0.23	−0.15	<5	51.92
R&D/Sales	SD	SD	SD	SD	SD	SD	SD	SD	SD	SD	SD	SD
Foreign assets/Total assets	SD	SD	SD	SD	SD	SD	SD	SD	SD	SD	SD	SD
Foreign sales/Total sales	SD	SD	SD	SD	SD	SD	SD	SD	SD	SD	SD	SD
Dividend payout	SD	SD	SD	SD	SD	SD	SD	SD	SD	SD	SD	SD

SD = shortage of data.

themselves. They also resonate with Carney's (2005) assertion that parsimony is a central governance characteristic of FBs and with Yeung's (2000) view that Chinese FBs tend to be very sensitive to costs and financial efficiency.

With regard to the financial structure, as we predicted in H2, the liquidity ratios for 2007 indicate significant differences in favour of FBs. For example, the current and quick ratios were both significant at 1%; the ratio of cash and cash equivalents to current assets was significant at 5%. Approximately 60% of pairs prefer FBs in terms of these three ratios. The cashflow/sales ratio also suggests a better outcome for FBs at a significant level for both years, which indicates FBs' strong capability to generate cash from their current operations. The ratio of inventory turnover also indicates a preference for FBs at a significant level. Thus, FBs can better face their current liabilities and other short-term demands. These results align with research that suggests FBs can better meet their short-term commitments (Allouche et al., 2008) and manage their current liabilities carefully to avoid any loss of control (Mishra and McConaughy, 1999).

Moreover, the ratio of capital expenditures to total assets reveals a significant difference at 1%, in favour of FBs for both years. Because FBs are more likely to invest in new infrastructure for future development, they appear to have a stronger long-term orientation than NFBs (Le Breton Miller and Miller, 2006). For indebtedness, the ratios of long-term debt/total capital, total debt/total capital and total debt/total common equity do not signal significant differences between FBs and NFBs for either year. In contrast, FBs suffer some loss of favour, which is not consistent with previous empirical studies in other countries (e.g., Allouche et al., 2008; McConaughy et al., 2001; Mishra and McConaughy, 1999). Whereas prior studies suggest that FBs are less dependent on lenders than are NFBs, our conflicting findings in China may reflect its institutional characteristics, as we discuss subsequently.

In Table 4.3 we compare NFBs (Type A) with all FBs (Types B and C) for the two years, with matched pairs *t*-tests and Wilcoxon tests on various financial ratios. Similar to our initial comparison, the results again support H1 in terms of profitability and partially support H2 regarding liquidity, though not for the indebtedness of firms. We do not find substantial differences between the comparisons of NFBs with strongly controlled FBs and of NFBs with all FBs for the same years. At this stage, we cannot determine the actual influence of the strength of family control on performance and financial structures; to test H3 and H4, we instead must rely on direct comparison of the two types of FBs (Table 4.4).

According to Table 4.4, in 2007, ROA and ROIC both favoured strongly controlled FBs, significant at less than 10%. In terms of liquidity, the ratios of inventory turnover, cash and equivalents to current assets and cashflow to sales all encourage strongly controlled FBs, at significant levels; these FBs also enjoy better ratios in the majority of pairs. For indebtedness, we find that strongly controlled FBs have advantages in long-term debt/total capital and total debt/total common equity at significant levels, and again they reveal better ratios in most pairs for these two financial indicators. Finally, strongly controlled FBs offer better capital expenditure/total asset ratios at a significant level, with a high percentage of pairs favouring them. Thus, for 2007, no significant result in any ratio signals a preference for weakly controlled FBs.

For 2008, the results are similar. The profitability ratios of ROA and ROE per share strongly favour controlled FBs, at the 10% significance level. For liquidity, the ratio of cash flow to sales prefers strongly controlled FBs at a 5% significance level, and these FBs enjoy better ratios in most of the pairs. Strongly controlled FBs also have indebtedness advantages, in long-term debt/total capital and total debt/total capital ratios (significant at 5% and 10%, respectively), and demonstrate these better ratios in most pairs. Finally, strongly controlled FBs are better off in their capital expenditures/total assets and sales per employee at the significance level of 5%, across high percentages of the pairs. Again, we find no significant result in any index that favours weakly controlled FBs. The comparisons in Table 4.4 thus support H3 and H4.

Discussion

We find strong support for H1, particularly in 2007, when all related ratios indicate the benefits of FBs over NFBs at significant levels (Tables 4.2 and 4.3). In addition, we find partial support for H2. In terms of liquidity, most relevant ratios for 2007 favour FBs at significant levels, and several relevant ratios for 2008 do so as well. The ratio of capital expenditures to total assets recommends FBs at a significant level in the first comparison for both years (Table 4.2) and in the second comparison for 2007 (Table 4.3). This evidence affirms the stronger long-term orientation of FBs compared with NFBs. That is, FBs have advantages in both liquidity and long-term orientation, which partially supports H2 regarding the sounder financial structure of FBs.

However, FBs do not enjoy advantages, or even suffer from an inferior position, compared with NFBs when it comes to indebtedness (Tables 4.2

Table 4.3 Comparison of performance and financial structure of NFBs and all kinds of FBs in China

NFBs versus all FBs (A versus B and C)											
Ratios	**2007**						**2008**				
	No.	**Means**			**Significance**	**Pairs in favour of FBs**	**No.**	**Means**			**Significance**	**Pairs in favour of FBs**
		NFB	**FB**	**Difference**	(%)	(%)		**NFB**	**FB**	**Difference**	(%)	(%)
Return on assets	229	4.99%	7.42%	2.43%	<1	65.94	230	4.17%	5.73%	1.56%	<5	55.22
Return on equity per share	214	8.06%	12.74%	4.69%	<1	63.08	215	4.84%	6.18%	1.34%	49.10	54.42
Return on invested capital	228	6.03%	9.06%	3.02%	<1	64.91	215	5.37%	7.00%	1.63%	<5	56.74
EBIT	243	19.32	22.69	3.37	<5	62.96	205	16.60	20.16	3.57	<10	55.12
Net income	247	10.14	12.3	2.17	<10	58.30	230	13.56	15.19	1.63	62.50	54.35
Pretax margin	248	9.32%	13.56%	4.24%	<1	59.68	229	5.08%	7.66%	2.58%	14.90	54.59
EBIT/Sales	246	12.40%	16.28%	3.88%	<1	61.38	211	9.70%	12.19%	2.49%	<10	57.35
Net income/Sales	250	6.21%	10.13%	3.92%	<1	59.20	229	3.33%	5.07%	1.74%	28.70	54.59
Cost of goods/Sales	252	71.41%	70.38%	–1.03%	39.00	53.97	229	70.89%	69.11%	–1.78%	19.80	55.02
Sales per employee	58	0.95	0.28	–0.67	32.90	44.83	222	0.16	0.26	0.10	<10	52.25
Total debt/Total capital	253	94.45%	31.58%	–62.87%	17.40	47.83	230	44.24%	44.02%	–1.79%	91.60	48.70

Long-term debt/Total capital	252	11.39%	9.96%	–1.43%	32.60	40.08	230	5.88%	8.66%	2.78%	51.70	40.43
Total debt/Total common equity	252	103.99%	66.98%	–37.01%	38.20	46.43	230	243.41%	76.02%	–167.39%	31.30	48.26
Current ratio	241	1.33%	1.67%	0.34%	<1	57.68	213	1.40%	1.55%	0.16%	11	58.22
Quick ratio	241	0.76%	1.04%	0.28%	<1	60.17	211	0.71%	0.88%	0.17%	<5	57.35
Inventory turnover	223	5.05%	6.31%	1.26%	<10	50.67	220	4.21%	5.34%	1.13%	<10	51.36
Cash and equivalence/ Current assets	242	29.42%	32.82%	3.40%	<5	55.79	222	31.23%	31.62%	0.39%	82.60	50.90
Cashflow/Sales	243	12.73%	13.59%	0.86%	32.80	54.32	230	3.25%	13.24%	9.99%	23.60	56.09
Capital expenditure/ Total assets	232	6.92%	8.84%	1.92%	<5	51.29	230	6.97%	7.13%	0.17%	83.00	55.65
Assets per employee	56	1.01	0.55	–0.46	<10	46.43	223	0.72	0.53	–0.2	48.60	50.22
R&D/Sales	SD	SD	SD	SD	SD	SD	SD	SD	SD	SD	SD	SD
Foreign assets/Total assets	SD	SD	SD	SD	SD	SD	SD	SD	SD	SD	SD	SD
Foreign sales/Total sales	SD	SD	SD	SD	SD	SD	SD	SD	SD	SD	SD	SD
Dividend payout	SD	SD	SD	SD	SD	SD	SD	SD	SD	SD	SD	SD

SD = shortage of data.

Table 4.4 Comparison of performance and financial structure of strongly and weakly controlled FBs in China

Weakly controlled FBs versus strongly controlled FBs (C versus B)													
Ratios	2007						2008						
	No.	Means			Significance	Pairs in favour of FBs	No.	Means			Significance	Pairs in favour of FBs
		NFB	FB	Difference	(%)	(%)		NFB	FB	Difference	(%)	(%)
Return on assets	41	5.89%	7.71%	1.82%	<10	51.22	43	3.42%	6.11%	2.69%	<10	58.14
Return on equity per share	44	11.29%	18.08%	6.79%	<11	56.82	40	5.81%	11.60%	5.79%	<10	55.00
Return on invested capital	44	7.32%	11.93%	4.61%	<10	56.82	44	4.93%	7.91%	2.99%	19.40	56.82
EBIT	42	23.01	20.45	–2.56	50.60	45.24	44	28.98	32.13	3.15	66.40	54.55
Net income	42	10.51	12.23	1.72	50.60	45.24	44	15.47	18.51	3.03	57.20	50.00
Pretax margin	43	10.40%	15.20%	4.80%	10.10	51.16	44	6.63%	9.10%	2.47%	67.20	54.55
EBIT/Sales	40	17.24%	15.62%	–1.62%	48.40	37.50	42	12.23%	14.59%	2.36%	49.70	52.38
Net income/Sales	40	8.95%	11.06%	2.10%	27.30	45.00	44	3.84%	5.77%	1.93%	72.00	52.27
Cost of goods/Sales	43	71.54%	70.26%	–1.28%	66.50	53.49	44	67.40%	61.71%	–5.69%	25.90	56.82
Sales per employee	44	0.15	0.17	0.02	79.80	36.36	42	0.27	0.15	–0.13	<5	30.95
Total debt/Total capital	40	71.64%	44.51%	–27.13%	<5	60.00	38	67.92%	47.14%	–20.77%	<10	52.63

Long-term debt/Total capital	44	10.61%	10.62%	0.01%	99.70	45.45	25	19.33%	7.83%	−11.50%	<5	72.00
Total debt/Total common equity	40	98.17%	62.37%	−35.79%	<10	57.50	44	63.61%	73.73%	10.12%	73.50	50.00
Current ratio	43	1.14%	1.39%	0.25%	10.90	62.79	43	1.39%	1.25%	−0.13%	49.70	53.49
Quick ratio	43	0.60%	0.77%	0.17%	<10	62.79	44	0.77%	0.72%	−0.06%	72.10	47.73
Inventory turnover	44	3.60%	5.34%	1.74%	<10	54.55	44	3.60%	3.62%	0.02%	97.70	47.73
Cash and equivalence/ Current assets	43	27.31%	30.20%	2.89%	41.60	51.16	44	29.66%	26.35%	−3.31%	37.80	45.45
Cashflow/Sales	44	9.12%	15.13%	6.01%	<5	54.55	44	9.15%	15.25%	6.09%	<5	70.45
Capital expenditure/ Total assets	43	4.16%	10.22%	6.06%	<1	69.77	44	4.24%	6.88%	2.64%	<5	61.36
Assets per employee	44	0.34	0.49	0.16	52.60	38.64	44	0.89	0.74	−0.15	69.90	34.99
R&D/Sales	SD	SD	SD	SD	SD	SD	SD	SD	SD	SD	SD	SD
Foreign assets/Total assets	SD	SD	SD	SD	SD	SD	SD	SD	SD	SD	SD	SD
Foreign sales/Total sales	SD	SD	SD	SD	SD	SD	SD	SD	SD	SD	SD	SD
Dividend payout	SD	SD	SD	SD	SD	SD	SD	SD	SD	SD	SD	SD

SD = shortage of data.

and 4.3). We consider two potential causes of the higher debt rate of FBs in China, which conflicts with findings from other countries, by integrating Jin and Chen's (2006) insights. First, most families own very large proportions of total shares in family-controlled, listed companies, to retain strong control over the business. Therefore, FBs in China may be more likely to engage in debt financing, rather than equity financing, to develop their businesses; they are unwilling to dilute their ownership through equity financing. The increasing rates of long-term debt, and then total debt to capital and common equity, thus might reflect these debt financing preferences. This result is consistent with findings by Gonzalez et al. (2012), who show that risk aversion pushes firms to depend less on debts, whereas the need to finance growth without losing family control induces FBs to suffer higher debt levels.

Second, without sufficient compensation for the risk undertaken, outside investors tend to have little interest in FBs in China. Outside investors usually consider these FBs comparatively inferior in terms of their information transparency and protection mechanisms. Furthermore, regulatory and monitoring systems have not achieved maturity in China yet.

We also seek to explain the greater significant differences in outcomes for 2007 compared with 2008. In our first and second comparisons, the significant differences for 2007 are consistently greater than those for 2008. We note that 2008 marked the start of the most recent economic crisis, which had significant negative implications for China's economy, and especially its FBs. The economic growth rate of China began to slow in 2008 (State Statistics Bureau of China), such that the business performance and financial situation of all firms, but especially FBs, may have been particularly affected.

We found no notable differences in the comparisons of NFBs with strongly controlled or all FBs within the same year. Our sample of FBs contains more strongly controlled (177) than weakly controlled (76) firms, so the comparison of all FBs and NFBs remains greatly influenced by strongly controlled FBs. Furthermore, we confirmed H3 and H4 with our direct comparison of strongly and weakly controlled FBs, in line with prior research. Among the 20 financial ratios, 8 indicate significant differences for 2007, and 7 display significant differences for 2008. These significant outcomes all suggest the benefits of strongly controlled FBs, and none of them recommend weakly controlled FBs. In line with H3 and H4, strongly controlled FBs enjoy superior performance and financial structures compared with weakly controlled FBs.

Furthermore, strongly controlled FBs enjoy apparent advantages in terms of their indebtedness for both years. Their more cautious attitude toward debt, compared with weakly controlled FBs in China, may result from their unwillingness to risk bankruptcy or a loss of control (Gilson, 1990; Nam et al., 2003). These findings reinforce Gonzales et al.'s (2012) argument that debt levels decrease when families participate in both ownership and management, rather than just ownership. However, two points are notable in this discussion. First, we had a relatively limited number of valid matched pairs for this third comparison of strongly and weakly controlled FBs. Second, the outcomes in support of H3 and H4 are less strongly valid than those we have provided in support of H1 and H2.

Implications

In China, a widespread assertion holds that FBs need more professional management, such that family leaders of companies should be replaced by professional managers. According to this prevalent but misguided view, to survive for multiple generations, the family's impact on the business should gradually get eliminated from management and operational processes; and an institutionalized, formalized management should take over the FB. In this account, all FBs ultimately should transform into family-owned, rather than family-managed, firms, and a professional, non-family management team should take over governance responsibilities.

The findings of our investigation reject this dominant viewpoint. Instead, we find that in China, as in most of countries of the world, the advantages of FBs derive clearly from the extent and nature of the family's involvement. Reducing the separation between owner and decision maker can limit information asymmetry and agency costs and thus increase the firm's value. Better alignment of the goals and interests of owners and managers also results in long term–oriented strategic decisions and the achievement of non-financial goals. Mutual trust and altruism stemming from kinship relationships help mitigate moral hazard problems and decrease transaction costs. Informal communication structures even can enhance the efficiency of communication and decision-making processes.

Conclusion

Using data from 2007 and 2008, we find that FBs achieve superior performance than NFBs in China. This finding matches similar research conducted in developed economies (Allouche et al., 2008; Kurashina, 2003). We also specify that Chinese FBs enjoy a better financial situation than NFBs in terms of liquidity and long-term orientation, though not with regard to indebtedness. Moreover, FBs even suffer some disadvantages in pairs with better ratios. We suggest some potential explanations for this distinction in China, related to the debt financing preferences of Chinese FBs (Gilson, 1990; Gonzales et al., 2012; Nam et al., 2003) and the risk aversion of outside investors in immature stock markets.

Despite having a limited number of matched pairs, we still find better performance and financial structure among strongly controlled FBs compared with weakly controlled ones, in line with findings from Japan (Allouche et al., 2008). Our study thus offers some evidence that stronger family control leads to better outcomes, for both performance and financial structures.

As its primary contribution, this research offers a rigorous, comparative test of the performance and financial structure of family and non–family businesses in Mainland China by taking a unique sample. Furthermore, we provide some evidence of the specific advantages of FBs, which may be useful for ownership families, the wider public, outside investors and financial institutions. Unfortunately, a strongly negative impression of FBs in China still prevails; we show that it is unwarranted.

For foreign investors or organizations that plan to look for a partner or an investment project in China, family ownership does not need to be a concern. International alliances are far more complicated than domestic ones; concerns about information transparency in capital markets and protection mechanisms for investors remain controversial issues in China, especially considering the weak progress made thus far in developing monitoring systems and relevant regulations. The levels of information asymmetry and differences in institutional environments between Chinese firms and outside investors thus may create complications. Looking for a FB as a partner in China, particularly if the foreign investor is a FB itself, might be a wise strategy, because similar mechanisms are at work in determining FB performance, whatever the country.

Note

1. Credit Suisse (2011) *Asian Family Businesses Report*, October.
2. Credit Suisse (2011) *Asian Family Businesses Report*, October.

3. Significance thresholds generally should reach a maximum of 1 or 5% in social science research that adopts a confirmatory approach. It is also widely accepted to consider a 10% level, with care, in exploratory approaches such as ours.

References

Aldrich, H. and Cliff, J. (2003) The pervasive effects of family on entrepreneurship: toward a family embeddedness perspective. *Journal of Business Venturing*, **18**, 573–96.

Allouche, J., Amann, B., Jaussaud, J. and Kurashina, T. (2008) The impact of family control on the performance and financial characteristics of family versus nonfamily businesses in Japan: a matched-pair investigation. *Family Business Review*, **21**(December), 315–29.

Astrachan, J.H. and Zellweger, T. (2008) Performance of family firms: a literature review and guidance for future research, *ZfKE – Zeitschrift für KMU und Entrepreneurship*, **56**(12), 1–22

Bernheim, B.D. and Stark, O. (1988) Altruism within the family re-considered: Do nice guys finish last? *American Economic Review*, **78**(5), 1034–45.

Barney, J.B., Clark, C. and Alvarez, S. (2002) Where does entrepreneurship come from: network models of opportunity recognition and resource acquisition with application to the family firm. Paper presented at *Second Annual Conference on Theories of the Family Enterprise, Philadelphia, December.*

Carney, M. (2005). Corporate governance and competitive advantage in family-controlled firms. *Entrepreneurship: Theory & Practice*, **29**(3), 249–65.

Chami, R. (2001) *What Is Different about Family Businesses?* International Monetary Fund, Washington, DC.

Christensen, C. (1997) *The Innovator's Dilemma*. Harvard Business School Press, Cambridge, MA.

Davis, P. (1983) Realizing the potential of the family business. *Organizational Dynamics*, Summer, 47–56.

Davis, J.H., Schoorman, F.D., and Donaldson, L. (1997) Toward a stewardship theory of management. *Academy of Management Review*, **22**(1), 1 January, 20–47.

Dibrell, C. (2010) Life settlements from the perspective of institutional, real options, and stewardship theories. *Family Business Review*, **23**, 94–8.

Dirks, K.T. (1999) The effect of interpersonal trust on work group performance. *Journal of Applied Psychology*, **84**, 445–55.

Donaldson, L. and David, J.H. (1989) CEO governance and shareholder returns: agency theory or stewardship theory. Paper presented at *Annual Meeting of the Academy of Management. Washington, DC.*

Donaldson, L. and David, J.H. (1991) Stewardship theory or agency theory: CEO governance and shareholder returns. *Australian Journal of Management*, **16**(1), 49–64.

Fama, E.F. and Jensen M.C. (1983) Separation of ownership and control. *Journal of Law and Economics*, **26**, 301–26.

Gallo, M.A., Tapies, J. and Cappuyns, K. (2004) Comparison of family and nonfamily business: financial logic and personal preferences. *Family Business Review*, **17**(December), 303–18.

Gilson, S.C. (1990) Bankruptcy, boards, banks, and blockholders: evidence on changes in corporate ownership and control when firms default. *Journal of Financial Economics*, **27**, 355–87.

Gonzalez, M., Guzman, A., Pombo, C. and Trujillo, M.A. (2012) Family firms and debt: risk aversion versus risk of losing control. *Journal of Business Research*, (2012.03,014)

Habberson, T.G. and Williams, M.L. (1999) A resource-based framework for assessing the strategic advantages of family firms. *Family Business Review*, **12**(1), 1–25.

Harvey, S.J. (1999) Owner as manager, extended horizons and the family firm. *International Journal of the Economics of Business*, **6**(1), 41–55.

Haynes, G., Walker, R., Rowe, B., and Hong, G. (1999) The intermingling of business and family finances in family-owned businesses. *Family Business Review*, **12**, 225–39.

Jensen, M.C. and Meckling, W.H. (1976) Theory of the firm: managerial behavior, agency costs and ownership structure. *Journal of Financial Economics*, **3**(4), 305–60.

Jin, Yonghong and Chen, Ye. (金永红&陈烨) (2006) Study on corporation governance and performance of family listed companies (我国家族企业上市公司治理与绩效研究), 第三届中国金融学年会, 中国上海.

Kurashina, T. (2003) *Family Kigyô no Keieigaku* (Management Studies on Family Business). Tokyo Keizai Shimbun Sha, Tokyo.

Le Breton-Miller, I. and Miller, D. (2006) Why do some family businesses outcompete? Governance, long-term orientations, and sustainable capability. *Entrepreneurship Theory & Practice*, **30**, 731–46.

McConaughy, D.L., Matthews, C.H. and Fialko, A.S. (2001) Founding family controlled firms: performance, risk and value. *Journal of Small Business Management*, **39**(1), 31–49.

Mishra, C.S. and McConaughy, D.L. (1999) Founding family control and capital structure: the risk of loss of control and the aversion to debt. *Entrepreneurship Theory and Practice*, **23**(4), 53–64.

Nam, J., Ottoo, R.E. and Thornton, J.H. (2003) The effects of managerial incentives to bear risk on corporate capital structure and R&D investment. *Financial Review*, **38**(1), 77–101.

Smyrnios, K., Romano, C. and Tanewski, A. (1998) An exploratory investigation into the financing determinants of family businesses. Paper presented at *Family Business Network Ninth World Conference, Paris.*

Sraer, D. and Thesmar, D. (2007) Performance and behaviour of family firms: evidence from the French stock market. *Journal of the European Economic Association*, **5**(4), 709–51.

Stark, O. (1989) Altruism and the quality of life. *AEA Papers and Proceedings*, **79**, 86–90.

Stein, J.C, (1988) Takeover threats and managerial myopia. *Journal of Political Economy*, **96**, 61–80.
Stein, J.C. (1989) Efficient capital markets, inefficient firms: a model of myopic corporate behavior. *Quarterly Journal of Economics*, November, 655–69.
Stewart, A. (2003) Help one another, use one another: toward an anthropology of family business. *Entrepreneurship Theory & Practice*, **27**(4), 383–96.
Tsang, E.W.K. (2001) Internationalizing the family firm: a case study of a Chinese family business. *Journal of Small Business Management*, **39**(1), 88–94
Van den Berghe, L.A.A. and Carchon, S. (2003) Agency relations within the family business systems: an exploratory approach. *Corporate Governance: An International Review*, **11**(3), 171–9.
Yeung, H.W.C. (2000) Limits to the growth of family-owned business: the case of Chinese transnational corporations from Hong Kong. *Family Business Review*, **10**(3), 209–21.
Zhang, Xian, Venus, J. and Wang, Jong (2012) Family ownership and business expansion of small- and medium-sized Chinese family businesses: the mediating role of financing preference. *Journal of Family Business Strategy*, **3**, 97–105.

5

Internationalisation strategies of medium-size multinational firms: when size matters in Chinese markets

Andrea Pontiggia and Tiziano Vescovi

Abstract: This chapter provides a framework and gives empirical results of an investigation to understand how and why MMNE (medium-size multinational enterprise) internationalisation strategies deviate from the more established strategies of multinational and global companies (MNCs). We study a sample of Italian MMNEs, analysing the strategic and governance models adopted in Chinese businesses and markets and the relationship between the headquarters and overseas branches in China. We investigate two specific factors: 'mirroring effects' and 'acquainted markets'. Mirroring effects relate to adaptation, innovative governance forms of which in our sample are strongly affected by such features as size failing to fit the potential or actual dimension of the market (size factor). Acquainted markets have the effect of decreasing difficulties in accessing countries' institutional externalities and gaining marketing competitive advantages. Our results show that MMNEs tend to replicate their existing business models when they enter 'informed' and 'experienced' markets. Our study explains these differences as an evolutionary path driven by internal capabilities to replicate organisational and business models facilitated by the availability of accustomed and informed markets.

Key words: marketing strategy, organisation design, international management, organisational structures, international business, medium-size enterprises.

Introduction

The strategy of internationalisation has been one of most relevant topics in the managerial literature in the last decade. Although new perspectives are flourishing and new approaches integrate knowledge from and competences of several disciplines there is a sort of 'myopia' caused by the object of analysis: the multinational enterprise (MNE). It's not our intention here to debate the reasons but we need to realize some consequences: there is clearly a lack of deep understanding of small and medium-size enterprise (SME) internationalisation strategies. For example, the literature on international strategy has helped us understand that the optimal MNE strategy achieves cost and differentiation advantages by leveraging the diverse capabilities of constituent subsidiaries (Mudambi and Navarra, 2004). Moreover, there is growing interest in multinational firms from emerging countries entering developed countries. These are further examples of the literature's focus on large companies in the global market. Two consequences stand out: first, theoretical frameworks built on large-size multinationals highlight the limits that need to be adopted when studying medium-size organizations; the second consequence relates to the narrow understanding of the economic impact of medium-size firms in international markets.

The argument to be made in this chapter is quite simple: How do MMNEs innovate when they implement internationalisation strategies in emerging markets? How do differences in scale and size affect internationalisation strategies? How do MMNEs compete in large markets? Is the assumption true that large markets fit (or require) large firms? The results of our exploratory research clearly demonstrate that 'one size does not fit all' and contribute to refreshing interest in the 'size paradigm'.

This chapter provides a framework and gives some preliminary results aimed at comprehending how and why the internationalisation strategies of MMNEs deviate from the more established strategies of MNCs. Our research focusses on MMNEs in China. There are two main reasons for considering Chinese markets: first, the relevance of China's economy in the global competitive arena and the move of the economic center to the East – specifically to China and other emerging markets in Asia. Until now, globalisation has been the domain of developed countries. The second reason for focusing on China's economy and markets is to challenge established perspectives, as some authors underline the fact that differences generate a conflict between the so-called Washington consensus and the Beijing consensus (Luo et al., 2011).

In other words, the massive and complex changes China has experienced illustrates the importance of comprehending how to align international strategies with Chinese institutions, especially political, economic, and enterprise ownership structures. Institutional changes have weakened the constraints and limitations of the old economic systems and led to extensive structural transformations increasing competition in many markets. For example, the number of private firms is flourishing (Zhou and Hui, 2003).

In the next section ('Theoretical background') we present a theoretical background that focusses on the size of international firms. We offer a new definition of medium-size multinational enterprise (MMNE) – this is our research focus. We then turn to the 'Research framework', a section in which we report three main research propositions based on the specificities of MMNE. This is followed by 'Field study: method and evidence' in which we outline the preliminary findings and results of the field study. There then follow sections ('Results and findings') making contributions to theory and research and ('Managerial implications') highlighting managerial implications. The final section ('Further research steps and additional research directions') identifies some key questions for further research on international management.

Theoretical background

The evidence from empirical studies on internationalisation strategies has long been absorbed by the MNCs of developed economies. International business has long been seen as the exclusive domain of large companies. Recent evidence shows that small and medium-size enterprises (SMEs; defined here as firms with 500 or fewer employees, a definition used widely in industrialised countries) are becoming more active internationally. Evidence from Asia, Europe and North America indicates that increasing numbers of SMEs are involved in international trade. Pioneering global startups now account for a substantial portion of the growth in exports in many countries. In recent years, numerous trends have emerged that make exporting and other international involvement a strongly viable alternative for SMEs. As far as we are aware there is little understanding of how international presence can measure the sustainability and feasibility of MMNEs.

The differences between MNCs and MMNEs can be traced both by looking at modes (how) and actions (what) that are implemented internationally. It is basically strategic drivers that reflect the stock of resource availability and the models of exploitation. It follows that in the international competitive arena size matters because it forces the innovation process of governance structures and forms. Size effects can be observed at two levels: first, the stock of resources used to invest and gain access to new, foreign, overseas markets (not limited to marketing and sales but also manufacturing and logistics); second, the organisational capabilities to combine quickly and move faster than MNCs, typical of smaller and entrepreneurial firms.

Evidence from the field (see 'Field study: method and evidence') confirms the challenge and difficulties faced by MMNEs when exploring and implementing new governance forms. Simple imitation of the international modes of MNCs is neither feasible nor sustainable and the data collected seem to confirm a tendency to replicate models and routines and to deploy them from the home organisation to overseas units. Economies of replication and scarce resources suggest and explain these traits in the internationalisation behaviour of MMNEs.

Two sets of firms' characteristics need to be taken into consideration. The first is often mentioned as a marker of small and entrepreneurial firms and refers to flexibility, adaptability, reactiveness and agility (Volberda, 1996). The second is the limited stock of resources available or controlled. Resources in this context cover the full range, from tangible to intangible, from specific and unique to tradable, from financial resources to intellectual property rights (Yiu et al., 2007).

The paradigm of size

Some dimensions – in particular, firm size and market size – are critical when choices are being made about economic and industrial policy, and heavily affect strategic decision making. These two dimensions are important points of connection between macro and industry studies and research that is more micro in nature and focused on individual companies. Today internationalisation strategies, because of the nature of current political and international relations, seem not to be limited to the largest companies; increasingly in the last 20 years subjects which were previously excluded to international markets have come to the fore.

Some studies of internationalisation are strongly rooted in past models, where systems were disconnected and political relations favored larger companies. SMEs have begun to play a critical role in international trade. Statistics from the Organization for Economic Cooperation and Development (OECD) and other sources suggest that SMEs account for a very substantial proportion of exports from most industrialised nations (Knight, 2001).

The size of a firm is indicative of resources available and correlated performance in term of economies or diseconomies of scale and scope.

Large firms do not suffer from the liabilities of smallness, and they are more likely to survive than smaller firms (the 'too big to fail' effect). Foreign economic subjects, such as customers, suppliers, employees and investors, tend to feel more confident interacting with larger firms because size suggests greater reliability and ability to conduct business and to access financial resources.

Entrepreneurship and size

With the increasing globalisation of markets, interest in international entrepreneurship has grown rapidly over the past two decades (Keupp and Gassmann, 2009; Zahra and George, 2002). A major feature of the global economy during this time has been the liberalisation of emerging economies and their integration into the worldwide economy. A common factor of international entrepreneurship development research is the focus on entrepreneurial characteristics such as self-commitment, self-efficacy, dynamism, experience and motivation as mechanisms for overcoming environmental adversities when founding, managing and internationalising firms in emerging countries. The results of this research propose that individual-level characteristics are actually more important than firm and industry-level characteristics in overcoming resource and market constraints. These studies are also important from an economic policy perspective: they underscore the negative perceptions that entrepreneurs in some emerging economies have about the quality and/or accessibility of information provided by governmental agencies regarding various aspects of the entrepreneurial process. Limited availability of or access to information suggests that entrepreneurs often need to rely exclusively on their own abilities to overcome institutional deficiencies and other obstacles.

Much of the literature on SMEs emphasises the role of the entrepreneur as the strategy maker. By doing so, some authors highlight the limits of individual decision-making centralisation and underline the need for a more managerial component to ensure development. Growth seems to suffer from the limits imposed by minor size and from a sort of cognitive blindness to strategic issues. By contrast, the literature on large global companies emphasises the relationship between stockholders and managers or the agency dilemma caused by potential disagreement on strategic goals. The medium-size firm may suffer from the syndrome of being 'stuck in the middle'. However, it also presents the advantage of flexibility of the small firm and the availability of resources needed to be competitive in international markets with high-end products and services. Some advantages come from a lean and less bureaucratic managerial structure; decision making cannot be totally centralised without a long line of command; hierarchies exist without the disadvantages of too complex a structure based on double-reporting and two to three management hierarchies such as matrix structures. Finally, medium-size companies are neither a developed 'small' firm nor a lean 'large' company. These medium-size specificities insinuate that MMNEs seems to fit perfectly with dynamic and hyper-competitive global economic arenas.

Limitations-of-size taxonomy

The EUROSTAT classification of firm size (medium firms having between 50 and 249 employees and large firms having more than 250 employees) as defined and used by the European Union (EU) does not support analysis and negatively affects economic policies. These limitations are evident when we look at internalisation processes. For example, let us consider the EU Small Business Act for Europe, which recognises 'the central role of SMEs in the EU economy' (EU, 2008). It emphasises the role of SMEs to promote growth and job creation. Its definition of an SME is clearly too broad and biased by size limits; it follows that a new definition of size classes is needed, at least in international trade and competition. Moreover, including small and medium enterprises in a common size definition (SMEs) creates confusion and misunderstanding. We emphasise the importance of recognising at least three different classes of companies (small, medium and large) with different characteristics that cannot be ignored, leading to different strategic, international, organisational and marketing behaviours.

There are several definitions of what constitutes a medium-size international company (Ruzzier et al., 2006). We consider a medium-sized multinational enterprise (MMNE) as a firm with the following characteristics: (i) number of employees from 250 to 2500; (ii) branches (trade offices, warehouses) established in extra-European markets; (iii) production plants outside the home country (as well as inside); (iv) a private company.

MMNEs seem to operate in international markets by exploiting the advantage that results from its relative flexibility of governance and routines and by overcoming some of the issues created by insufficient resources. The lack of resources for internationalisation is for many smaller firms an obstacle to the development and implementation of international strategies. The need to join resources with other firms or to enter in new markets using inter-organizational relationships and agreements, or institutional mechanisms of alliances, suffers from many limitations. The so-called 'ambidexterity by size' refers to the capabilities of MMNEs to enter the global competitive arena, using a balanced mix of flexibility and stock of resources.

MMNEs suffer less from bureaucracy or high organisational costs than MNCs . They are often more innovative, more adaptable, and have quicker response times when it comes to implementing new technologies and meeting specific buyer needs. The growing role of direct marketing, global transportation specialists and buyers with specialized needs helps SMEs serve niche market segments (Oviatt and McDougall, 1995). Entrepreneurial firms seem capable of succeeding in the highly competitive environment of international trade. But we recognize some constraints to competing directly in large overseas and emerging markets in many business-to-consumer (B2C) industries since MMNEs may not own or control sufficient resources to develop and operate in large markets. The growing demand for mass products/services or the 'creation' of new markets is sustainable and feasible, at least in terms of resources. Many examples come from the Chinese markets: low performance is caused by early entry of MMNEs. MMNEs operating in international arenas compete against MNCs with their multinational leveraging specialization, agility and flexibility. We expect to see more successful MMNEs in those segments of emerging markets where the demand for specialisation and niche products is stronger, demanding flexibility and adaptability.

The size paradox is drawn from an oversimplified framework based on comparison of assets between large and small firms. The former may follow an innovative path based on resources to invest in innovation. By contrast, small firms are depicted as more effective at innovating because of their entrepreneurial governance. In much the same way, size affects interorganisational strategies or, put another way, the way in which large versus small firms approach relationships with suppliers and customers, and the way in which they establish linkages and cooperate with other external sources of innovation.

In the managerial literature, internationalisation is often considered one of the main drivers of innovation. What is less obvious is the type of innovation required. As far as MMNEs are concerned, we would expect them to balance some advantages of small companies (i.e., flexibility) without the disadvantages (scarcity of resources). In broad terms we expect to see MMNEs emerge as very successful internationally. This line of reasoning has some pitfalls and is partially supported by the evidence. Field observation based on our sample of firms shows two characteristics we define as 'mirroring effects' and 'acquainted markets' which affect the performance and specificities of MMNEs.

Research framework

Our study of MMNEs proceeds on the basis of two research propositions that can be summarised as follows: we refer to the first as 'mirroring and replication economies' and the second as 'informed and acquainted' markets. Mirroring and replication strategies concern methods of internationalisation and, more precisely, how MMNEs exploit internal knowledge and experience in emerging markets. Their business and organisational models are replicated but partially adapted in the target country. The tendency shown by the MMNEs in our sample is to leverage their core competences in term of routines and practices in Chinese markets. Another effect relates to the type of markets MMNEs are concentrated in. Acquainted markets are characterised by demand that is more informed, and customer behavior (and choices) are affected by previous experiences. From a normative perspective, MMNEs tend to have a higher probability of success in informed markets implementing second-mover strategies.

International mirroring and replication of organisational forms

Organisational forms are defined as a configuration of structures, processes and routines. Each form of MMNE can be scrutinised to differentiate the domestic or home organisation (headquarters) from overseas and international units. The implementation and execution of international strategies is largely observable in the organisational forms adopted. We expect to notice some traits of replication in the development of organisational forms in internationalisation actions. We claim the presence of economies of replication, which suggest a tendency to reproduce organisational forms in a mimetic way. The home model is dispersed with some adaptations to new markets and into new competitive environments. Replication can be seen at the organisational level and offers a perspective that is more reliable than simple analysis of strategy statements. Organisational forms are related to the investment of resources and clearly offer insights about entry and competitive modes in international emerging markets. From an organisational point of view there are two main characteristics of replication strategies: the first is modularity, in which replication is based on the advantages of modularity (i.e., interdependence and connections); organisational modules are quite similar, based on the same guidelines, required shared actions and behaviours; each module is an organisational self-contained unit. Second, the cost of replication is lower because it does not involve large amounts of resources for adaptation and no specific learning is required. The successful module is spread and reproduced as a set of guidelines for application in overseas units.

This results in home or domestic forms (structure, processes and routines) being mirrored in international organisations. It allows equilibrium to be achieved between home and subsidiaries and lowers coordination and integration costs. The similarities are also justified by the size and growth of new markets which in many cases have overwhelmed domestic markets. Moreover, international units display some characteristics that make them more susceptible to strong delegation, self-government and autonomy. Finally, the replication path seems to decrease the cost of controlling subsidiaries; it may also lower the coordination costs caused by difficulties establishing and tuning mechanisms to manage interdependences between headquarters and country branches.

The potential pros are countered by some disadvantages: the most relevant is the limit to expansion brought about by the misfit between the home competitive context and the target environment. This gap affects the feasibility and sustainability of business models based on replication. There are two reasons for this: the first relates to the types of markets, which are not yet global or mass markets. The second is that specific niche markets may be too narrow to offer a positive economic return on international investment. In some industries the process of convergence toward a global market is so fast that organisational replication in the subsequent years may become more frequent. In other words we don't expect a 'one size fits all' effect but a repetition of home organisational forms in different markets. The 'nodes' (units) of the network (structure) are kept similar to reduce organisational complexity. Less organisational complexity requires fewer resources to manage processes and similar routines and structures to lower adaptation costs. From this perspective international strategic sustainability has to be verified such that organisational forms match the target competitive environment. Some development strategies of MMNEs, characterized by waiting for acquainted markets to emerge, delay entry and become a clear choice for consideration (as described in the next section).

When 'acquainted' markets drive internationalisation strategy

We consider an 'acquainted market' to be one in which consumer and customer knowledge has reached such a level as to understand and correctly evaluate quality differences in the offerings of competitors (Chang et al., 2010). Acquainted markets normally are developed, differentiated, segmented markets. MMNEs generally do not relate to the mass market because of its large size and basic characteristics, but they are successful in niche markets, where the offer (product features and marketing mix components) they present contains elements of greater complexity, and their value proposition requires customer competence, knowledge and experience. The value perceived by clients depends on the level of knowledge (Grewal et al., 1998) and experience they have about the products and brands; in other words, it depends on their ability to recognise valuable elements of differentiation and higher quality within the offer of the MMNE, compared with the mass market products offered by the MNC, enabling them to adequately perceive the economic value of the MMNE's proposal. Many competences are acquired and learnt by using and consuming products, from simple products to more complex products, in a sort of learning process that normally lasts years by means of a knowledge process that has been formed both individually and collectively called the 'value of social experience' (Sridhar and Srinivasan, 2012). This social–individual process allows evolution from a mass market, based on an offer characterised by strong standardisation, to a niche market, where specificity and differentiation dominate, following a development typical of the history of markets. Internationally, MMNEs need to be able to cope with very different levels of skills spread among customers, due to the different ways national markets have developed, as is so evident in the case of China. MMNEs come from very sophisticated and acquainted home markets, full of market-educated customers, where MMNEs developed their competitive advantage. As part of their internationalisation process they target markets that may appear inexperienced compared with the complexity of their offer.

The availability of an informed and acquainted market affects decisions taken by MMNEs about the timing and the target of entry modes. For many MMNEs this means implementing a second-mover strategy (Carpenter and Nakamoto, 1996), which involves waiting for other companies, usually larger MNCs, to build the basic skills necessary for customers to be able to perceive value in their offering. In B2C industries first-movers are mainly large MNCs. In many cases it requires a huge investment of resources to create and shape emerging markets. When MNCs acquire a presence in these 'new' markets, a learning process affects consumer behaviour. For example, in a country like China, where the consumption of coffee is not traditional and consumers know little about it, the work done by great MNCs like Starbucks allowed the birth and growth of a coffee market. Subsequently, other smaller companies can enter the market, as quality niches become possible, offering higher quality products at understandably higher prices. This is the case with Illy or Lavazza, coming from a sophisticated market like the Italian one. However, they are unable to create basic competence and knowledge about coffee in China because of their small size, which prevents them from having adequate resources to create a value of social experience of coffee. Moreover, the literature of internationalisation underlines the need to acquire the necessary knowledge of foreign markets and points out that the main way of doing this is by gaining experience in operating abroad. But, this is a major problem for MMNEs as their international experience is limited and available resources do not allow them to bear the costs and the time to accomplish that need. This difficulty, which by the way can prompt mirroring and replication seen in the previous section, may be reduced by decreasing the distance between the company and the customer, either through an obvious shift towards the customer by the company (gaining skills on how to operate in a specific international market) or through a shift towards the company by the customer (gaining the ability to understand the company's offer more easily).

Incremental internationalisation has been argued to be the most efficient approach to international expansion for firms without international experience, since it allows them to accumulate international knowledge and experience that can be used to respond to opportunities and deal with foreign market uncertainties. It should be noted that incremental development conflicts with the replication model applied by MMNEs. Foreign market knowledge is classified (Eriksson et al., 1997) in three categories: institutional knowledge, business knowledge and internationalisation knowledge.

The first, institutional knowledge, refers to knowledge of foreign culture, institutions, rules and regulations. Business knowledge is about knowledge of customers, competitors and market conditions (in particular, foreign markets). The last type, internationalisation knowledge, concerns a firm's know-how in terms of adapting resources and capabilities to engage in international operations. While the first two assist firms in being aware of opportunities and problems in the foreign market, the third knowledge component enables the firm to take appropriate action to open up new markets (Zhou, 2007). The MMNEs analysed adopt a strategic posture based on replication because the distances between domestic and overseas markets are perceived low enough to sustain existing business models. The business model used by the company plays an important role and contains characteristics of the market in which that model was born and strengthened (by acquiring competitive advantage and producing profit). MMNEs must collect and elaborate all three types of knowledge to maximise the benefits of mirroring effects.

Customer and consumer behaviour develop increasingly into experiences. This causes a sort of drift toward high-end product and service. The food and beverage industries are good examples of the difficulties MMNEs face in their attempts to gain access to emerging international large markets. The shift of consumers toward high-end products is restricted and narrows culturally, by retailing and distribution structure, and by comparative costs. This is a representative situation in which the value perceptions of final consumers are dependent on persuading them to acquire new consumption and use-of-product behaviour. High-end products require experienced customers and this has clear implications on the economic and strategic feasibility of MNEE entry modes in emerging markets. Customers already operating in these markets is the reason MNEEs decide to enter. This is typical of business-to-business (B2B) industries, where the main driver derives from the demand to keep the same value chain configuration while in other industries the mode of entry is shaped and driven directly by the final markets. For example, our evidence confirms that medium-size companies that are specialist suppliers of larger MNCs are necessarily driven to establish a presence in emergent markets as a direct response to customers who are investing in those markets. Therefore, the decision to enter a new market is neither free nor autonomous, but rather the need to follow big strategic customers wherever they go. In this sense, the acquainted market of the MMNE is relocating to an emergent country. The development process of B2B MMNEs demonstrates the way in which they are led to internationalisation: first by following the customer and then by gaining access to the local market as this becomes acquainted. This explains why MMNEs tend to play the role of second-movers in emerging markets. At the first stage, large B2C companies open and create new markets (supply-side development) and then experienced and acquainted customers breed greater demand in specific high-end niches (demand-side development). In the case of B2B markets, customer companies decide to enter as first-movers and then MMNEs follow them as a sort of second-level decision. In this sense we can define them as second-movers. So the timing-of-entry mode seems to impact deeply on MMNE performances. From this perspective the exploration of new markets for specific high-end niches requires a deep understanding of the speed at which the learning diffusion process of final consumer behaviour and B2B market development accept high-quality, and therefore high-price, products and move from a cost-driven strategy to a performance-driven one.

Performances, strategies and size specificities

The two factors – mirroring effects and acquainted markets – directly address some issues in the theory of firms. The first concerns the firm's growth, the pace of growth and factors enabling development. The second concerns the relationship between size and governance and, consequently, the advantage of specialisation, the effects of economies or diseconomies of scope and scale, and the effects of size on coordination and transaction costs. The third issue concerns the specificities and constraints imposed by size in terms of alternative organisational forms and solutions. The fourth, specular to previous points, concerns the characteristics of the organisation, which are independent of size and contribute to strategy implementation.

Figure 5.1 refers to the research framework we considered when developing our study. Following the dimension paradigm, markets host three archetypical companies: large, medium and small. Definition of the boundaries between the three (turnover, employees, etc.) is still under discussion, but in this context what should be underlined is that large companies rely mainly on resource availability (financial, human, technological, etc.), small companies rely mainly on their agility, while medium-size firms look for an ambidexterity mixture of resources (not as big as that of large companies) and agility (not as flexible as that of small companies). With these preconditions in mind, the internationalisation model of MMNEs should found its strength on two simplifications:

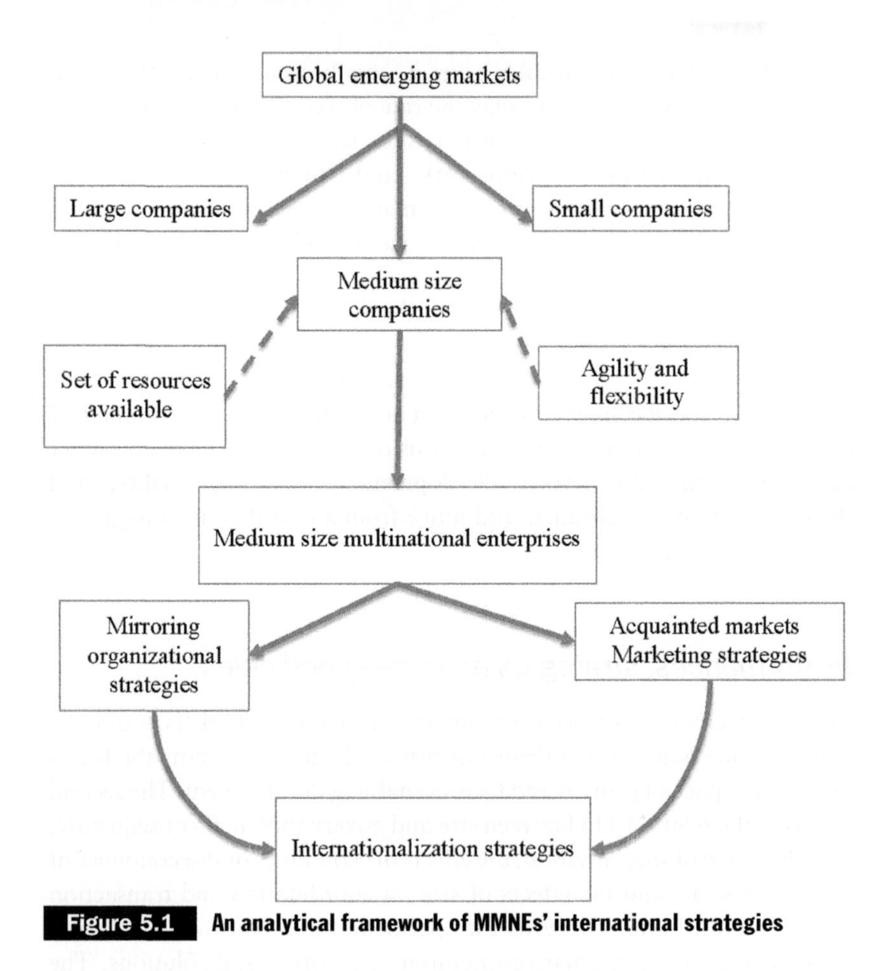

Figure 5.1 **An analytical framework of MMNEs' international strategies**

mirroring of organisational strategies (an internal-based condition), and acquainted markets (an external-based condition). The field study we outline in the next section takes mirroring effects and acquainted markets as its base.

Field study: method and evidence

Our purpose is to shed light on and interpret the size paradigm in the internationalisation strategies of MMNEs in China. Our sample comprises companies that have already decided and taken strategic action to enter the Chinese market. We study firms that are strongly motivated to invest in China at different stages of internationalisation. Our research is designed along the lines of multi-case and multi-level analysis. The evidence was collected in a three-month field study of three of the eight firms that made up our overall analysis. The other five firms were studied by interviewing entrepreneurs and managers and analysing documentation on public sources and, if available, private records. The field study involved collecting information from employees on more than one occasion during case analysis with a view to collecting as much information as possible.

For this study we use qualitative research design, which offers a deeper understanding of the emergent strategies of internalisation. We adopt a multi-case, multi-level study design because it enhances complex and dynamic analysis and facilitates creation of a richer and more grounded framework than a single-case, single-level study (Eisenhardt, 1989; Yin, 2004). The building of theory on the basis of multi-case studies involves replication logic, because each case is a distinct experiment that stands on its own, and researchers search for recurring patterns.

Data collection was based on interviews with top managers, internal documents, meetings with management and information from public sources. At three of the six firms the researchers had the opportunity to use participant observation before interviews and the collection of data. Interviews permitted the collection of both factual information (e.g., dates, events, incidents, policies and the actors involved) and open-ended narrative data.

Documentary research, field interviews and analysis took place between 2011 and 2012. There was a second string to our analysis which consisted of corporate visits, the collection of archival material, and informal and formal interviews. We identified senior and top managers who were knowledgeable about the corporate governance systems and practices of their firms to take part in our field study.

We follow the approach suggested by Schweizer (2005) to address typical concerns about qualitative research design. To improve construct validity, we triangulated data with other sources whenever possible (Yin, 2003). Secondary data dealt with corporate governance (structure and reform measures), firm characteristics (ownership structure, *keiretsu* affiliation, corporate history, industrial environment and exposure to foreign markets). We sourced these data from the academic literature; annual reports of firms; reports from government, banks, research institutes, and industry and professional associations; websites and, when available, newspapers and business journals (Eisenhardt, 1989).

Table 5.1 provides details of the firms in our sample. The firms studied had 500–2500 employees, which corresponds to the medium-size class as defined in the research design phase.

Our investigation focussed on a sample of Italian MMNEs, analysed the strategy choice and governance models adopted by businesses, and looked at the relationship between the headquarters and local branches of firms. Qualitative analysis complied with the research requirement to collect evidence at a precise point in time (2012) and over a more extended period (time of entry in China). Qualitative analysis highlighted both the feasibility and sustainability of governance models (criteria and components) and forms (model of execution and implementation).

As Table 5.2 highlights, the acquainted and informed market proposition is confirmed in all eight cases, both in B2B and in B2C situations. The mirroring proposition is confirmed in five of eight cases and partially in the other three. It is interesting to note that replication affects every practice in the various functional domains (sales, human resource management, operations, logistics, purchasing). Organisational strategies based on replication seem to be consistent with the goal of lowering the investment required to internationalise, on the one hand, and of decreasing the coordination and integration cost among international units and the headquarters, on the other hand. Top managers and entrepreneurs of the firms studied state that duplication of organisational routines is very effective at reducing the time needed to exploit market opportunities and to quickly enter emerging markets. Again, the evidence seems to underline timing as one of the most relevant factors in internationalisation strategies. Despite these advantages, there are questions about whether minor adaptation of routines and practices is sufficient and sustainable in the long term and whether there is a risk of falling into a sort of 'competence trap' and thereby hinder innovative capabilities and efforts. So-called 'ambidexterity by size', which is to be considered one of the advantages of being medium size, can be seriously constrained by the tendency to reproduce or merely adapt routines to different competitive contexts.

Results and findings

This study makes some important contributions to theory and research on international strategies of MMNEs. Our analysis develops an original perspective that focusses the effects of size (in our analysis medium-size firms) on internalisation strategies. Our study further suggests that the evolution of corporate governance is more complex than portrayed by the convergence–divergence debate. Convergence–divergence tends to

Table 5.1 Case description of our sample

Company	Total employees/ revenue (€ m)	Products	Size in China (no. of employees/ revenue)	Year of establish-ment	Objective of entry in China	Entry mode	International presence	% of inter-national revenue
A	750/155	Home appliance components	5/12[a]	1997–2009[b]	Supply big customer	Export – factory project	Brazil, Mexico	80
B	2800/650	Weaving machines	150/40	2003	Entering important market	Assembling and adapting products	Switzerland	75
C	1200/300	Ceramic material–handling systems	80/9	1999–2004[b]	Entering important market	Factory	20 branches and factories	70
D	350/55	Rides and attractions	45/7	2004	Entering growing market	Factory	5 branches, 4 factories	98
E	250/50	Prams and strollers	3/1[a]	2000	High-end growing market	Export	10 branches	50
F	800/180	Tyre changers, balancers	50/10	2010	Supply big customers	Factory	8 factories	80
G	2100/201	Food and beverage – restaurants	70/2.3	2008	Entering important market	Restaurant points of sale	200 PoS in 10 countries	30
H	1280/150	Menswear, clothing – production and retail	90/9	1996	Entering important market	Menswear retail	246 PoS in 70 countries	75

[a] Export. [b] New factory.

Table 5.2 Case evidence

Research question	Evidence from Case A	Evidence from Case B	Evidence from Case C	Evidence from Case D	Evidence from Case E	Evidence from Case F	Evidence from Case G	Evidence from Case G
RQ1: mirroring description	The new factory project in China is finding it difficult to adapt the home model to the new market; the staff are waiting for suitable production conditions	Replication of the home model in manufacturing processes, products and management; expatriates from home country control all the critical processes	Partial replication of the home model (two of the company's three businesses: ceramics and storage systems); partial replication is due to factors about competition	Replication of the home model; commercial strategies in China reflect routines established by minor adaptations	The new factory project in China is a partial replication of the home model when it comes to internal operation and avoids the external network in operation in the home country, which is considered too difficult to replicate quickly	Replication of the home model; pure replication of HRM practices and sales models	Retention of the home model with 13 types of locations such as airports, railway stations and downtown; same product offer (pasta, pizza, coffee); small differences in the service system; same organisation at point of sales	Same homeland retail model for point of sales – layout, communication, atmosphere, shopping experience
RQ1: mirroring comment	Evidence partially confirms the mirroring hypothesis	Evidence confirms the mirroring hypothesis	Evidence partially confirms the mirroring hypothesis	Evidence confirms the mirroring hypothesis	Evidence partially confirms the mirroring hypothesis	Evidence confirms the mirroring hypothesis	Evidence confirms the mirroring hypothesis	Evidence confirms the mirroring hypothesis

RQ2: acquainted market description	The B2B company has followed its previous customers to China	Entered a B2B acquainted market and increased the quality of the offer; local customers moving from cost to performance approach	Entered a B2B acquainted market and moved to a more sophisticated product due to customers moving from cost to performance approach	Entered a B2C acquainted market because the desires of Chinese consumers are aligning themselves with those of Westerners	Entered a B2C acquainted market because the desires of Chinese consumers are aligning themselves with those of Westerners	For the B2B part of the business the company is following its previous customers into the Chinese market; for the B2C part of the business the company is entering the acquainted part of the market	Entered a B2C acquainted market as second-mover after fast food (pizza) and coffee; market development made by the MNCs; offering higher-level quality food and service	Entered a B2C acquainted market as second-mover after the big brands of the high-end fashion industry, targeting second-tier cities as they became acquainted
RQ2: acquainted market comment	Evidence confirms the acquainted market hypothesis	Evidence confirms the acquainted market hypothesis	Evidence confirms the acquainted market hypothesis	Evidence confirms the acquainted market hypothesis	Evidence confirms the acquainted market hypothesis	Evidence confirms the acquainted market hypothesis	Evidence confirms the acquainted market hypothesis	Evidence confirms the acquainted market hypothesis

view the process of governance innovation in a continuous and linear manner: from small to large companies, from domestic to international, from international to global. Our findings underline that changes in governance are discrete and that medium-size companies exploit competitive capacity by leveraging 'ambidexterity by size'; they prefer to replicate existing structures, processes and routines in acquainted markets. Case studies highlight that corporate governance changes can be depicted as fluid and nonlinear in the way they evolve in response to both internal and external pressures despite the need to contain and control the cost of organisational adaptation to international competitive contexts.

Our preliminary findings extend the conventional focus of international strategies research into innovation across MMNEs. In this way we gain a better understanding of the need for economic policies to sustain MMNEs in their international strategies and to show the impact and contribution they make to increasing the competitive capabilities of the different economic systems.

The main findings from the field evidence concerning our three research hypotheses can best be described in term of research statements.

Research Statement 1: mirroring

MMNEs use the mirroring model for organisational design, keeping a flexible approach that follows one of three different paths:

- *(Semi) pure replication of the domestic organisational model* with appropriate minimal modification as a result of the different cultural and institutional contexts. Adaptation concerns HRM policies and marketing strategies. This organisational configuration seems to promote hybrid structures and forms.

- *Pure replication* of the sales, production and operations routines managed by expatriate managers. Employees with several years experience in home firms get the top management and most relevant jobs. In some cases this has been a clearly outlined and communicated strategy since the first attempt to internationalise. The evidence also suggests a strong linkage between domestic and overseas routines concerning business processes (i.e., sales and marketing, accounting, financial reporting, etc.).

- *Waiting for more favourable conditions* before replicating the domestic model in the new international market, preferring to avoid the development of new models that cannot be perfectly managed and controlled. We define such strategic conduct as a 'prudent mirroring approach'.

Research Statement 2: acquainted markets

The field evidence suggests that MMNEs enter acquainted and informed markets in three different ways depending on their specific situation:

- In B2B markets, they follow their existing customers (mainly large companies) and enter new international markets as mass producers. Large companies represent the acquainted and informed market of MMNEs.
- In B2B markets, as potential customers become 'acquainted' (mainly because of modifications to consumer markets, which become 'acquainted' as well) with the value offered by MMNEs, based on sophisticated quality and performance proposals.
- In B2C markets, when consumers perceive the different quality and performance offered by MMNEs they get acquainted and informed about the products and brands as well.

To sum up, our analysis contributes to international management theory in two ways. First, we define the characteristics of and roles played by MMNEs in international competition. The case sample confirms the three-variable model of our research. The three variables refer to: (i) a specificity of MMNEs defined as 'ambidexterity by size'; (ii) organisational strategies based on replication of organisational forms and governance; (iii) the emergence of informed and acquainted markets. We distinguish these variables as structural (size), strategic (replication) and environmental (markets). Second, we provide new insight about how to explore the international context to support strategic decisions about entry to and development of emerging and growing overseas markets. Our 'scouting' activities focus on market opportunities and assess the feasibility of organisational replication. Markets must be explored in terms of customer knowledge and experience and consumer behaviours. Feasibility depends on the fit between the home organisational forms to be duplicated and the international context. Exploration covers institutional, business and international setting information for each target market.

Managerial implications

Our framework strengthens the hypothesis about a future international scenario in which MMNEs will play a more significant role. Some global trends in high-end products will hasten the presence of MMNEs. We also expect to see a shift of attention in economic policies backing the internalisation of MNEEs. The growing awareness of MMNEs as a valuable asset of each country's industrial structure suggests deepening the understanding of medium-size firms and facilitating their internalisation processes.

Evidence confirms the need for acquainted markets to gain entry to a new international market. For managers this means that MMNEs should follow the second-mover strategy and wait for cultural growth of the market. For cultural growth of the market there needs to be widespread knowledge about the product category and about the quality and performance of offers from competitors, thus making it easier for customers to perceive and evaluate differences. This is what happened with the wine and coffee industries in China, for example. MNCs were the firstcomers shaping the market and diffusing knowledge of the product. MMNEs could only enter the competitive arena with their niche high-end offers once consumers had become acquanted. MMNE managers should monitor the international markets they intend to enter, looking for the right market conditions for valuable offers to be acknowledged by customers.

The replication of organisational forms and governance models is another important implication. Case evidence confirms MMNEs cannot rely on the internationalisation framework adopted by MNCs. The most critical reason concerns the availability of resources and the level of investment required to compete in global markets. This fact and the level of flexibility may suggest a different path for international development based on the replication of organisational forms. The replication of organisational forms configurationally emerges as an effective way to enter new markets but it also appears flawed and incomplete. MMNEs reproduce their organisational configuration but the process leaves some space for variation as a result of the availability of resources in different environments. The failure of perfect reproduction can be seen as a source of strategic flexibility. Organisational forms appear to be invariant configurationally (at least in their main components) but leave some autonomy regarding resource choice and allocation. Managers of MMNEs should pay attention to the replication process to assess the sustainability and feasibility of organisational forms as well as to evaluate the fit between organisational configuration and the foreign environment. These findings imply that MMNEs should consider alternative strategic choices to compete in emerging economies, whether by leveraging their global resources or replicating their operations in the particular country. Our results also suggest that MMNEs need to be incisive in their entry timing strategies to facilitate value creation. Timing depends on the emergence of acquainted markets and the replication of existing organisational forms. The first point refers to learning about consumer behaviour under different overseas contexts; the second to the fit between home and foreign environments. Even though our research is still at an early stage, the chapter offers some initial and novel insights into the significant implications that result from analysing international strategies using an inexpensive model based on two sets of variables that refer to

- Use and exploitation of existing resources and models following a replication posture in an attempt to reduce the cost of coordination and adaptation in large markets.
- External factors based on the level of informed and competent markets coherent with a second-mover strategy.

Validation of the model based on the sample suggests size matters for specificities of medium size (ambidexterity by size) expressed by a set of competing goals, the flexibility and adaptability of small firms and the stock of resources available to large companies.

The chapter shows that internationalisation is an effective driver for MMNEs to adapt their business models deeply by replicating organisational forms and governance in new markets. Innovation emerges from the reciprocal interplay among domestic markets and overseas markets, home countries and target countries more than from a mere one-way relationship such as the move from home to other countries.

Finally, there is another important aspect of adaptation that we have not discussed in detail: the cultural distance between the home country and the target countries; this factor often influences the internationalisation decisions and performance of firms. A cross-cultural view is also to be applied in MMNE research. Cross-cultural analysis has its roots and a long tradition in MNCs. The question is whether and how to adapt research methods to match the specific setting of MMNEs.

Further research steps and additional research directions

As this study is based on a small sample of firms, the generalisability of the analytical framework remains to be tested. The focus on a small sample and the research in the field were necessary to explore the complex and dynamic process of internationalisation across firms. Moreover, the advantage of using a small sample of cases to generate theories is increasingly recognised in organisation science (Eisenhardt, 1989). Our research offers some insight into the research approach to be applied for effective study of MMNEs. There is a need to explore hybrid research design in greater depth, a methodology that involves blending and mixing different methods (qualitative, quantitative, simulational, quasi-experimental).

Although this study is limited in scope it can serve as a stepping stone to guide future research. Another limitation is the time span. Our study covers a short time horizon. Strategy implementation was only observed over a two-year period. The depth of our research findings would benefit from using a longitudinal approach and improving the set of measurements, and thereby garner more information about the three main variables of our framework (see 'Research framework').

At times of economic crisis a deeper understanding of the roles and contributions of MMNEs may prove helpful in guiding economic policies. MMNEs seem to play a leading role in the globalisation process offering new organizational and strategic recipes.

References

Carpenter, G.S. and Nakamoto, K. (1996) Impact of consumer preference formation on marketing objectives and second mover strategies. *Journal of Consumer Psychology*, **5**(4).

Chang, T.J., Chen, W.C., Lin, L.Z., and Chiu, J.S.K. (2010) The impact of market orientation on customer knowledge development and NPD success. *International Journal of Innovation & Technology Management*, 7(4).

Eisenhardt, K.M. (1989) Building theories from case study research. *Academy of Management Review*, **14**(4) 532–50.

Eriksson, K., Johanson, J., Majkgard, A. and Sharma, D.D. (1997) Experiential knowledge and cost in the internationalization process. *Journal of International Business Studies*, **28**(2), 337–60.

EU (2008) *Think Small First: A Small Business Act for Europe* (Communication from the Commission to the Council of the European Parliament, COM(2008)

No. 394). European Economic and Social Committee and the Committee of the Regions, Brussels.

Grewal, D., Krishnan, R., Baker, J. and Borin, N. (1998) The effects of store name, brand name and price discounts on consumers' evaluations and purchase intentions. *Journal of Retailing*, Fall, **74**(3).

Keupp, M.M. and Gassmann, O. (2009) The past and future of international entrepreneurship: a review and suggestions for developing the field. *Journal of Management*, **35**(3), June, 600–23.

Knight, G.A. (2001) Entrepreneurship and strategy in the international SME. *Journal of International Management*, **7**, 155–71.

Luo, Y., Sun, J. and Wang, S.L. (2011) Comparative strategic management: an emergent field in international management. *Journal of International Management*, **17**, 190–200.

Mudambi, R. and Navarra, P. (2004) Is knowledge power? Knowledge flows, subsidiary power and rent seeking within MNCs. *Journal of International Business Studies*, **35**, 385–406.

Nachum, L. and Zaheer, S. (2005) The persistence of distance? The impact of technology on MNE motivations for foreign investment. *Strategic Management Journal*, **26**(8), 747–67.

Oviatt, B. and McDougall, P. (1995) Global start-ups: entrepreneurs on a worldwide stage. *Academy of Management Executive*, **9**(2), 30–44.

Ruzzier, M., Hisrich, R.D. and Antoncic, B. (2006) SME internationalization research: past, present, and future. *Journal of Small Business and Enterprise Development*, **13**(4).

Schweizer, L. (2005) Concept and evolution of business models. *Journal of General Management*, **31**(2), 37–56.

Sridhar, S. and Srinivasan, R. (2012) Social influence effects in online product ratings. *Journal of Marketing*, **76**(5).

Volberda, H.W. (1996) Toward the flexible form: how to remain vital in hypercompetitive environments. *Organization Science*, **7**(4), 359–74.

Yin, R. (2003) *Case Study Research: Design and Method*. Sage, Thousand Oaks, CA.

Yin, R. (2004) *Applications of Case Study Research*. Sage, Thousand Oaks, CA.

Yiu, D.W., Lu, Y., Bruton, G.D. and Hoskisson, R.E. (2007) Business groups: an integrated model to direct future research. *Journal of Management Studies*, **44**(8), December, 1551–79.

Zahra, S.A. and George, G. (2002) Absorptive capacity: a review, reconceptualization, and extension. *Academy of Management Review*, **27**, 185–203.

Zhou, L. (2007) The effects of entrepreneurial proclivity and foreign market knowledge in early internationalization. *Journal of World Business*, **42**, 281–93.

Zhou, L. and Hui, M. (2003) Symbolic value of foreign products in the People's Republic of China. *Journal of International Marketing*, **11**(2), 36–58.

6

Transfer of HRM practices in French multinational companies: the case of French subsidiaries in China

Cuiling Jiang

Abstract: Our research investigates the transfer of home country human resource management (HRM) practices to their overseas subsidiaries. We seek to figure out how three levels of factors (country, organisation and individual) from a host country affect the international transfer process. We identify the effects of culture, institutional interactions, entry modes and expatriates on this transfer. Based on a detailed case study of eight French multinational companies in China, we explain how the transfer of HRM practices is realised. Our empirical findings indicate that French subsidiaries tend to adopt the parent company's HRM practices to a considerable extent. Instead of focussing on cultural differences, the main contraints to the successful transfer of HRM practices are institutional interactions and entry modes. Additionally, we identify the role of expatriates in the transfer process.

Key words: international transfer of practices, human resource management, French multinational companies, China, culture, institutional interaction, entry mode, expatriates.

Introduction

With ongoing globalisation, more and more companies are engaging in international business. One of the key issues regarding international business is the transfer of management practices within multinational companies (MNCs), which enables newly established subsidiaries to benefit from successful expertise developed in a company's headquarters and other subsidiaries (Dunning, 1981).

International transfer is a process that transfers management practices within MNCs in three directions (Kostova, 1999). The first is forward transfer of practices from a parent company to its overseas subsidiaries. This kind of transfer is widely used in MNCs. The second direction is reverse transfer, which starts from foreign subsidiaries and flows back to the parent company (Edwards and Ferner, 2004). The third direction is horizontal transfer of practices among various overseas subsidiaries. In our research, we focus mainly on forward transfers of HRM practices from French parent companies to their Chinese subsidiaries.

Transferring practices can help to build coherence within an MNC. However, some difficulties can arise from foreign adaptation. For instance, foreign companies may have problems accessing information from the entry market, which, in return, may complicate the transfer process. Successful transfer of management practices still remains a crucial goal (Kogut and Singh, 1988). Hence, companies question whether MNCs should transfer the whole management practice or apply only one part to the subsidiaries. What adaptation should be put in place in order to ensure the transfer and, if practices cannot be transferred, should MNCs adopt local practices or create new ones? On the basis of these questions, we found that there exists a significant gap between theory and practice. Therefore, we are particularly interested in subsidiary-level explanations of the transfer of management practices. We extend previous work by describing how managers in subsidiaries reproduce and adapt the best practices to the host country so as to keep internal consistency while taking appropriate local structures and practices into consideration.

HRM practices have strategic importance for MNCs. They are part of corporate strategy and HRM specialists use them to integrate employees and boost their competences. Bartlett and Ghoshal (1989) emphasise that HRM policies and practices can contribute to coordination and control within MNCs. Studies show that successful forward transfer of HRM practices can promote more professional types of management and enhance company performance, which contributes to a dynamic HRM balance between headquarters and subsidiaries (Alcazar et al., 2005; Boxall and Purcell, 2011; Child and Tse, 2001; Thory, 2008). Hence, MNCs invariably want to transfer their HRM practices abroad.

There were two reasons for our study of French MNCs in China. First, extant research has focussed mainly on Japanese or American MNCs (Becker-Ritterspach, 2005). A possible reason is that since the 1980s, the United States and Japan have been among the largest economies in the world. They are the major foreign direct investment (FDI) contributors. For instance, there is an extensive literature on Japanese company internationalisation (Abo, 1994; Smith and Elger, 2000). Within

Europe, researchers focus more on MNCs from Germany or the United Kingdom (Ferner and Varul, 2000; Rosenzweig and Nohria, 1994). Research on French MNC internationalisation – in particular, their Chinese sites – has received little empirical attention. Second, China is an important emerging market in the world. The Chinese context is challenging for foreign companies because it is considered to be profoundly different from Western countries in terms of culture, legal systems, labor markets and so forth. As a main FDI contributor to China among the European member states, there are many French MNCs with operations in China. However, little research has reviewed French MNC internationalisation and their Chinese subsidiaries.

Consequently, we wanted to investigate the transfer of HRM practices in French MNCs to figure out how subsidiaries interpret the HRM policies and practices of their headquarters, and to fill the gap in the literature on forward transfer in French MNCs. We hope to arrive at conclusions and recommendations that will benefit the transfer process for French MNCs and other similar companies.

In our research, we adopt a multilevel approach to study such a complex organisational phenomenon. This approach is supported by three levels of theories: country level (cultural distance), organization level (institutional interactions and entry mode choice), and individual level (expatriates). In light of this, our research explores the following questions: (1) Which HRM practices are more likely to be transferred? (2) How do factors originating from different cultures, institutional interactions, entry modes and expatriates affect the transfer of HRM practices? (3) What adaptations may be needed in order to transfer HRM practices from French headquarters to their Chinese subsidiaries?

We organize the remainder of this chapter as follows: we review related literature and discuss the core contributions from cultural, institutional, entry mode and expatriate viewpoints. We then describe our methodology. We begin our findings by presenting an overview of the sample. Then, we detail the transfer process by discussing the reproduction of HRM practices in China and various adaptations. We conclude by pointing out the implications for managers from the international transfer of HRM practices, addressing the limitations of the study as well as further research.

Transfer of HRM practices at three levels

The context of our research is cross border within French multinational companies. According to Myloni et al. (2004), using a common set of specific HRM practices can provide a broad basis of comparison. Hence, we limit our research to the four basic HRM practices: recruitment, training, annual performance review, and compensation and benefits. These practices are widely used in French companies and they have explicit and tacit characteristics. The explicit aspects are generally codified and usually documented. The tacit ones are to some extent difficult to transfer because they are informal in some ways.

Our framework is informed by Kostova's work. Instead of analysing international transfer through social, organisational and relational factors (Kostova, 1999), we examine country-level, organization-level and individual-level factors. For the country level, we adopt Hofstede's cultural model to analyse national differences between France and China. Core theory starts at the organisational level. Institutionalism and entry mode theory are therefore presented. Finally, regarding the individual level, expatriate roles in the international transfer of HRM practices are discussed. Through such a multilevel framework, we hope to combine micro and macro-factors, and capture a wide range of influences on the international transfer of HRM practices.

Cultural distance

According to Menipaz and Menipaz (2011), culture is the set of values, symbols, beliefs, languages and norms that guide human behavior within the workplace, region or country. In their work, Stone et al. (2007) highlight that companies must understand the expectations of each employee well, because many cultures and subcultures have different preferences regarding work-scripts and role conceptions. Schneider and Barsoux (1997) argue that cultural difference has become one of the main reasons the same HRM policies are not producing the same effects in different subsidiaries. Hence, we consider a cultural approach that can provide us with a starting point to understand constraints in the international transfer of HRM practices.

Up to now, there has been substantial research on cultural distance. Hofstede's cultural model (power distance, individualism versus collectivism, uncertainty avoidance, masculinity versus femininity and long-term orientation) is perhaps the most widely cited in the literature on international business. In his work, Hofstede (2004) indicates that both France and China respect authority and accept hierarchy. However, China tends to value long-term relationships, collective activities, change and a culture of masculinity. Whereas France is more characterized by its short-term orientation, individualism, risk avoidance and culture of femininity. Through Hofstede's research, we can develop an initial understanding of the cultural differences between France and China. But a number of researchers have challenged Hofstede's theory (Kitayama et al., 2000; Schwartz, 2004; Trompenaars, 1994).

One of the limitations of Hofstede's model is the breadth of the data, which was drawn only from IBM employees. The second limitation is that Hofstede's 'dimensions are not directly accessible to observation but inferable from verbal statements and other behavior' (Abdellatif et al., 2010). Hence, Schwartz (2004) developed an alternative theory to identify cultural distance, which covers conservatism, intellectual autonomy, affective autonomy, hierarchy, egalitarian commitment, mastery and harmony. In this chapter, we adopt Hofstede's approach because it still holds value as a general framework to view culture (Kogut and Singh, 1988). However, we keep in mind the limitations of Hofstede's model.

Institutional interactions

Organisations are subject to pressures from the local environment and the international isomorphic process (DiMaggio and Powell, 1991). Subsidiaries, on the one hand, must conform to headquarters' expectations in realizing internal consistency and legitimacy. On the other hand, subsidiaries should adapt themselves to the local institutional context (e.g., structure of labor market, labor laws and regulations, training and educational systems, etc.) by adopting the perceived appropriate structures and practices (Kostova, 1999; Kostova and Roth, 2002).

In their research, Rosenzweig and Singh (1991) highlight seven factors that affect the international transfer of HRM practices: legal constraints, shared technology, parent country culture, cultural distance, composition of workforce, entry mode (acquired versus greenfield subsidiaries) and MNC dependence on the host country. Similar arguments have been proposed by Scott (2007), who shows that 'institutional environments are characterized by the elaboration of rules and requirements to which individuals must conform in order to receive legitimacy and support.' More recently, through detailed case studies on four automobile MNCs in India, Becker-Ritterspach (2005) states that 'institutional distance has a distinct explanatory value for hybridization outcomes of production systems.'

A number of researchers (Becker-Ritterspach, 2005; DiMaggio and Powell, 1991; Kostova, 1999; Kostova and Roth, 2002; Rosenzweig and Singh, 1991; Scott, 2007) have adopted an institutional approach to studying the international transfer of management practices. Therefore, we extend these previous works by identifying the effects of institutional factors in Chinese contexts. Some key points are employment contracts, the five work-related benefits, the housing fund in China's revised labour law, 'face' issues, *guanxi*, *hukou* and so forth.

Entry mode choice

All MNCs must make decisions on their entry mode when they plan business operations in foreign countries. In our research, we focus only on the transfer of HRM practices to French wholly owned subsidiaries and joint ventures in China.

Scholars state that it is more difficult to transfer management practices in a joint venture than in a wholly owned subsidiary (Bresman et al., 1999; Meyer, 2001). Put simply, a joint venture is established when two or more existing companies, which have their own organisational practices, come together. In such a case, the MNC has to share power with a local partner. In addition, protection of ownership may become a barrier to knowledge transfer. By contrast, wholly owned subsidiaries have few problems with this issue. Hence, in this chapter we attempt to clarify the real situation for transfer of HRM practices in French wholly owned subsidiaries as well as joint ventures.

Expatriates

Expatriates are employees sent on long-term assignments (in our case by French MNCs to their Chinese subsidiaries). They are the practice carriers who bring direct personal experience and knowledge to business units in China. In the meantime they take on the roles of commander, conductor, coach and connector (Cerdin, 2003). Previous research on international business has frequently addressed the contributions of expatriates to the process of MNC internationalisation, which can be categorised into three areas.

For forward transfer of management practices, the presence of expatriates and their constant communication with the parent company can significantly affect the degree of similarity between local HRM practices and those at headquarters (Rosenzweig and Nohria, 1994), help transfer general knowledge as well as firm-specific knowledge (Tan and Mahoney, 2003, 2006), and carry and implement the business strategies of headquarters (Björkman and Lu, 1999, 2001; Gupta and Govindarajan, 2000). For the reverse transfer of management practices, expatriates are responsible for acquiring local knowledge and communicating local business updates to headquarters (Heenan and Perlmutter, 1979). The third contribution made by expatriates is that they act as a link between headquarters and subsidiaries (Cerdin, 2003). Such a link can help a parent company control subsidiaries (Jaussaud and Schaaper, 2006) and enhance subsidiary performance (Wang et al., 2009). Based on the literature and our own research, we believe the presence of expatriates does in fact ease the transfer process of HRM practices.

Methodology and research design

Understanding the nature of the transfer process can be achieved by observing qualitative changes in the forms and meanings of practices, getting updated knowledge to the local institutional environment and gaining insight into the current situation by reporting interviewee experiences (Miles and Huberman, 1994). To do this we consider a qualitative methodology is best suited for our research. Furthermore, case studies are embraced as the appropriate approach because 'they are the preferred strategy when "how" and "why" questions are being posed, when the investigator has little control over events and when the focus is on a contemporary phenomenon within some real life context' (Yin, 2008).

In order to meet the criteria of qualitative representations and increase the reliability of results, we contacted French subsidiaries in China randomly. In total, we conducted interviews at 16 French multinational companies in June 2011 in China. In this chapter we chose to focus solely on eight companies as we found this number of case studies gave us enough data to discover the major factors (Symon and Cassell, 1998). These eight companies are from a wide range of industries: aviation, aerospace and defense, food, insurance, energy, chemistry, transportation and electricity. They are well known in their respective sectors both in France and in China. Five companies are located in Beijing and the rest are in Shanghai.

We prepared two questionnaires. One targetted general managers, and the other was aimed at HR directors. Both questionnaires were pilot-tested through experts and practitioners in the area of international business. Furthermore, each questionnaire had three versions: English, French and Chinese. The translated versions were reviewed by native speakers. The interviewees were asked general and specific research questions relating to the transfer of HRM practices. In particular, we gathered information about the following six areas: general information about headquarters and Chinese subsidiary sites, recruitment, training, annual performance review, compensation and benefits, and the expatriate role in the international transfer of HRM practices.

We sent the questions to the interviewees two weeks before the interviews. The main purpose of collecting data in this way was to ensure that the interviewees had time to think about the answers and come up with meaningful examples from their daily operations before the interviews. The language used in the interviews was primarily English. We also conducted interviews in French and Chinese. Each interview lasted between one and two hours. Given the confidential nature of the information and the promises of confidentiality given to the interviewees, the real company and interviewee names will not appear in our chapter. The companies are therefore identified by codes as C1, C2, C3, C4, C5, C6, C7, and C8. This constraint greatly encouraged interviewees to discuss the subjects at greater depth and without hesitation.

Besides collecting the data through semi-structured interviews, we also used participant observations, storyboards, annual reports, websites and internal documents to support our findings. Because of the richness of data collected, we were able to reduce the amount of data and structure the information by writing summaries about each interview, highlighting the critical phrases and identifying key words. Then, we set up the analysis categories as reproductions and adaptations of HRM practices to identify the international transfer process.

Findings and discussion

We focused our analysis on the reproduction and adaptation of HRM practices in eight French MNCs in eight different industries. Each company has been in China for a long time,[1] except C4, which is an insurance company. China opened up its insurance market only in 2005. In fact, C4 is a pioneer among foreign companies in the Chinese insurance market. All the participating companies are wholly owned subsidiaries, except C4. The insurance industry is a highly regulated market in China. Any foreign insurance investor can hold no more than 50% of the shares in the joint

Table 6.1 Cases

Case	Industry	EP/EM/LC	GM	HR	First entry
C1	Aviation	90/1200 Beijing	French	French[a]	1994
C2	Aerospace and defence	60/800 Beijing	French[a]	French[a]	1996
C3	Food	7/6000 Shanghai	Chinese	Chinese[a]	1987
C4	Insurance	3/40 Beijing	French[a]	Chinese	2005
C5	Energy	85/458 Beijing	French	Chinese[a]	1980
C6	Chemistry	N/A/2500 Shanghai	French	French[a]	1991
C7	Transportation	123/5500 Shanghai	French	Chinese[a]	1989
C8	Electricity	100/22000 Beijing	Chinese	Chinese[a]	1989

Note: Interviewees are anonymous. EP = number of expatriates in China; EM = number of employees in China; LC = location; GM = general manager; HR = human resource director. First entry as wholly owned subsidiary or joint venture in China. [a]Interviewees.

venture. Table 6.1 gives details about the companies participating in our research.

The reproduction of HRM practices in a foreign market

We investigated the transfer process of each HRM practice for each focal company. Then, we detailed what adaptations were needed for HRM practices to be transferred from the French headquarters to the Chinese subsidiaries.

Generally speaking, each French MNC introduced four types of HRM practices to Chinese subsidiaries. However, HRM practices are subject to different transfer levels. The main transfer modes are documents, training, e-campus,[2] frequent communication between HR team members within the group and expatriates.

Recruitment

Our findings show there is a high level of involvement of French parent companies in the transfer of recruitment practices. Seven cases indicate that it is the parent companies that decide the annual recruitment budget for subsidiaries, provide the selection criteria and standardised job descriptions, and propose the recruitment tools (internal recruitment is by means of employee referral and self-recommendation through the company intranet; external recruitment mainly concentrates on campus staffing).

Specifically, the top managerial staff of the eight companies (e.g., CEO and general managers) and expatriates were recruited by headquarters. These employees are treated no differently from those in France or at other subsidiaries, especially regarding compensation and regular benefits. For other managerial staff, seven cases indicated that their parent companies needed to verify and approve staffing proposals (the exception being C4). As for the recruitment of employees, the parent companies in all eight cases provided the recruitment framework and authorised each subsidiary to do its own staffing. Subsidiaries needed to explain to headquarters how they recruited candidates and documented procedures. Six cases emphasized their preference to recruit undergraduates from Chinese and/or foreign universities as well as candidates with Francophile sentiments. 'These employees are relatively easier to teach and appreciate our company culture,' says the French HR director of C1 in the aviation industry.

Two major differences were identified when we compared local recruitment practices with those at parent companies. First, contract terms are obliged to adapt to Chinese labor laws (e.g., 40-hour working week, minimum salary variation from city to city, contracts in Chinese, and so forth). Second, all eight companies made use of casual labour. These employees work in Chinese wholly owned subsidiaries (or joint ventures, as with C4) and have contracts but their employers are dispatching companies.[3] Casual labour is allowed in China as long as the workers perform services in temporary, substitute or auxiliary positions in companies. Many MNCs have a contract in place with a FESCO (Foreign Enterprise Service Company) for labour, dispatching, payroll and/or additional services for some job functions in China. This is usual and typical in China.

There are two reasons MNCs use casual labour. First, China is developing so fast that MNCs have difficulty estimating the annual recruitment quota adequately. When this happens, especially during the peak season, additional labour (including casual labour) is paid through operational expenses. Second, in the event of a labour dispute, FESCO is responsible for negotiation, arbitration and/or litigation. Many FESCOs are state-owned companies. They are familiar with local arbitration and litigation processes. They know how to handle the relationship with the central government and local institutions. To some extent, FESCOs can lower risks for MNCs. Hence, using casual labour is widely accepted by MNCs.

Overall, recruitment practices in seven of our eight companies followed the parent companies closely but they were not reproduced identically in China. Adaptation was necessary because of the different institutional contexts and entry modes. For example, C4 was obliged to set up a joint venture with a government-recommended partner on a 50/50 basis. The Chinese shareholder is a strong state-owned company in terms of its national marketing network. However, it is characterized by bureaucracy, hierarchy, and a *guanxi* (network) orientation. The Chinese shareholder was charged with carrying out HRM practices. The recruitment practices of managerial staff at C4 focussed less on objective criteria and more on mutual relationships. A similar situation exists in the seven other cases regarding their joint ventures. For instance, C1 has a joint venture with a state-owned company in Harbin (C1 owns 20% of the company). C1 has equal input to HRM policies and documentation. Despite C1 providing training to HR team members in Harbin, there still remain concerns about learning capacity and learning willingness.

Besides the issue of entry modes, which are found to limit the transfer of HRM practices, our case study also reveals that joint venture partners can affect the transfer process. For example, when the partners are state-owned companies, they face relatively fewer direct pressures of market competition because they enjoy preferential policies from the Chinese government. As a consequence, they may not be incentivised to take on board foreign management's know-how.

Training

Nine interviewees confirmed that training plays an important role in building a single community within the group and promoting a knowledge-sharing organizational culture. Furthermore, Chinese employees prefer standardized training programs, which make them feel they belong to one big family. They place high value on training and they are eager to become more competent.

In general, each company has some specific training tools, which are closely in line with the ones at headquarters. For instance, the common training tools used by the eight companies include handbooks, videos, internal magazines, telepresence, training abroad (except C4) and e-campus. In order to improve training, interviewees mentioned that some training is carried out in Chinese, too. While this is going on, companies make use of local examples to make the training more easily understood. In particular, each company has some interesting tools to transfer training and get knowledge shared.

A case in hand is C3, which is a food company. The parent company organizes a practice marketplace each year in a different country. Subsidiaries thus get a chance to introduce their own projects and get fresh ideas from external colleagues to improve themselves. In the marketplace, all subsidiaries are given the opportunity to take the lead to deliver their experience of good practice. At the same time, subsidiaries can learn from the experience of others. Each year, around 9000 managers from the C3 group participate in this practice marketplace. Employees therefore are getting used to sharing good practices, building solutions together and motivating themselves to develop new tools. Transfer of practices has become a cultural attitude in the group. Interestingly, C3 also provides courses in French at its Chinese subsidiaries.

Another example is C2 (aerospace and defence). Each year, C2's headquarters organizes a special group-wide forum, called 'the Discovery Days'. This training is for all newly promoted management staff. Employees have the opportunity to learn everything they need to know about the group: its businesses, professions, HR policy strategy, and so forth. When we look at C4 (insurance), both shareholders participate in organized training but the forms and focus of the training are different. The French shareholder provides training on the basis of performance review. The Chinese shareholder prefers to organize less formal training, such as training plus entertainment (e.g., lunch, dinner, karaoke) in a hotel during a weekend.

At C8 (electricity), an individualised training and development plan for the next 12-month period is set after the career and competency review. At C7 (transportation), employees can enjoy training in seven areas: sales, design, engineering, technique, process advancement, quality and marketing. At C6 (chemical), headquarters use key performance indicators to manage training performance within the group, which includes a training plan, a number of days of training (total and per employee), percentage of employees who had training per year, training costs and audit results of training effectiveness (documented evaluation of all the trainees). C5 has a talent-building program. In addition to sending engineers to Europe for short-term training, C1 offers Chinese employees the opportunity to work at other subsidiaries in other countries for 18 months to three years.

Compensation and benefits

All the interviewees confirmed that compensation and benefits are localized. Parent company involvement is restricted to proposing percentages for bonus and profit sharing, deciding the annual budget and the compensation and benefits package for top managers and expatriates. The eight cases reveal that their compensation and benefits package ranks in the medium to upper level in the Chinese market. Differences are found regarding the components of compensation and benefits. For example, Chinese subsidiaries mainly make the following three adjustments:

1. Chinese subsidiaries increase the fixed salary portion and lower the variable payment. Salary is linked more to realization of team objectives and seniority than individual contributions. This may reflect MNCs' marketing learning about Chinese cultural affinities, which value collectivism and age hierarchy.

2. Chinese subsidiaries provide five work-related benefits (pension, medical, injury, unemployment and maternity) as well as a housing fund. The housing fund is specifically a uniquely Chinese benefit and employees do not have to contribute to it. When companies are able to pay a higher amount toward housing, they become more attractive to candidates and employees. Buying houses on credit is still a fairly recent phenomenon in China. However, housing prices have grown out of control since the new millennium. Even the Chinese government has made efforts to cool the market but most young people still have difficulty affording a house. Hence, the housing fund is warmly welcomed by Chinese employees. According to our analysis, the amount provided for housing varies among the interviewed companies but it usually equates to between 7 and 13% of an employee's salary. There are other benefits that too are exclusive to China: a heating subsidy; free breakfast, lunch and dinner; a *hukou* handling fee; and a pension plan for employees' parents. The *hukou* handling fee is an example of a special benefit peculiar to China. Required by Chinese law, *hukou* is a household registration system which identifies a person as a resident of a given area. Each family needs to pay an extra fee in order to let their child study in areas other than their origin of *hukou*. In order to attract and retain talent, Chinese subsidiaries take care not only of employees but also their families. Hence, interviewees take *hukou* into consideration and pay a *hukou*

handling fee, which allows their children to benefit from studying in cities to which the company locates.

3. The shares are not widely offered among the eight companies. Some companies offer shares but only to a few top managers. C1 offered ten shares per employee to celebrate its ten-year presence in China. But it was not easy to bring about such a transfer of fringe benefits. According to Chinese labour law, foreign companies should first get approval from the Chinese government regarding any offer of shares. Then and only then are employees given a certificate allowing them to own shares. Note that casual labour are not entitled to such fringe benefits because they are recruited by the dispatching company. Hence, transferring such fringe benefits to Chinese subsidiaries involved a couple of complex issues for C1, which made use of casual labour. On the one hand, it had to explain this delicate situation to its headquarters to see whether it could provide casual labour with other benefits instead of shares. On the other hand, C1 had to figure out what benefits could replace the value of shares. Hence, the French HR director from C1 stated, 'I am not strong enough to refuse implementing this practice but there is no point to transfer this fringe benefit for it is in contrast to the Chinese labor law.'

Annual performance reviews

Results show that annual performance reviews are widely used at eight companies. However, such practices as 360° performance reviews are rarely used. The same result was found by Jaussaud and Liu (2011).

When this practice was first introduced to Chinese subsidiaries, there was strong resistance and hesitation on the part of employees. They were sensitive to any comment, let alone negative ones. HR team members and top executives had to introduce this practice progressively through meetings and documents. HR team members were specifically given the remit to emphasize the importance of annual performance reviews, the way in which they could identify current working capacity and how they are linked to more concrete career development. Furthermore, successful examples from other subsidiaries were introduced. Employees began to realize that this practice could provide them with an opportunity to express their willingness and expectations. In short, the transfer of annual performance reviews is progressive and takes time for Chinese employees to accept and get used to.

As shown in the previous discussion, the extent to which French MNCs transfer HRM practices to Chinese subsidiaries is considerable. Let us attempt to answer the first research question posed in the 'Introduction': Which HRM practices are more likely to be transferred? We find it is possible to transfer HRM practices from French parent companies to Chinese subsidiaries but there are different levels of transfer. This result is in line with previous research by Myloni et al. (2004). For instance, annual performance reviews can be introduced to Chinese workers progressively. Training practices meet with few difficulties when implemented in China. Some practices, such as the determination of compensation and benefits, need to be localized. Chinese subsidiaries need to offer a salary package in line with Chinese labour regulations and cultural norms. It is possible to transfer recruitment practices but Chinese subsidiaries are under institutional pressures to adopt perceived good practice, such as making use of casual labour.

Parent company HRM practices in foreign market adaptation

In this section we elaborate the ways of adapting HRM practices in a foreign market. Continuing from the previous discussion, we emphasize that the adaptation of HRM practices is a market-learning process. Instead of cultural differences, institutional interactions and entry modes affect the transfer process. Additionally, we identify the role of expatriates in the transfer process.

Cultural differences

Interviewees frequently mentioned their awareness of the cultural differences between France and China. For instance, the work culture in China values high power distance and there are clear authority structures. Chinese employees pay attention to job titles in a company, which reflects their concern with 'face' (self-dignity). Respecting elders and seniors still matters a lot in China. In the workplace, employees will not openly argue with superiors. Chinese employees prefer collective decisions and group harmony. They value the sense of group affiliation. Considering these cultural differences, we cannot help asking whether cultural differences affect the transfer of HRM practices or not.

Empirical analysis of the eight cases shows that each of the eight companies has accumulated a certain experience in dealing with Chinese culture. Their long presence in China and constant organisational learning of Chinese culture combine to ease the transfer of HRM practices. For instance, during the annual performance review, C2 avoids telling Chinese employees about any weak points but concentrates instead on coming up with suggestions to achieve better performance. This adaptation hints that C2 pays attention to the face issue by simply avoiding directly communicating negative aspects. C2's HR team has gradually become localised. Five of the eight companies have Chinese HR directors. Local personnel can offer solutions to cultural conflicts. The HR team plays the role of cultural teacher for MNCs.

For Chinese employees, foreign management practices are the 'selling points' for MNCs. Chinese employees look up to self-progress and development. They are keen to learn international standards. They believe working in MNCs can enrich their CVs and advance their careers. Furthermore, China's culture still looks up to collectivism and high power distance. Chinese employees are relatively comfortable with accepting transferred practices without questioning. 'Chinese employees tend to consider their supervisors and managers as the reference,' says the Chinese HR director of C5 in the energy industry.

Despite the existence of cultural differences, their impacts are diminishing or giving way to a range of other institutional forces as a result of constant organisational learning.

Institutional interactions

A revised labour law came into effect on 1 January 2008. One of the major changes regards the length of probationary periods. The new law sets a limited probation period to prevent employers from using long-term or multi-probationary periods. The new law also regulates salaries during probationary periods, which should not be less than 80% of fixed salaries or lower than the minimum salary for the same post. A second major change relates to employment contracts. All employees must sign a written employment contract, and only the Chinese version is valid. If an employee works without a contract, the employer is subject to paying twice the monthly salary for the entire duration that the employee worked without a legal contract.

The interviews revealed institutional factors about Chinese regulations are mainly considered barriers to the HRM transfer process. While each

MNC understands the need to adapt labour contracts to local regulations, in China 'the same regulation will be implemented in a different way at different levels of government and in different regions,' says the Chinese HR directory of C3 in the food industry. All the interviewees expressed their confusion about the Chinese labour system, notably regarding transparency and the various exceptions that run counter to the regulations. For instance, workers from acquired companies have no labour contracts (such problems exist at C3, C5, C6 and C8). This means companies must first establish a contract system for these employees and then integrate them into the groups. 'This is a time-consuming process. We need a lot of communications with workers themselves, with labor unions and the institutions which are in charge of five mandatory welfare systems,' says the Chinese HR director of C8 in the electricity industry.

Our findings reveal that institutional misfits have the effect of holding back HR transfer. Adaptations are necessary. This evidence is in line with previous research by Becker-Ritterspach (2005), DiMaggio and Powell (1991), Kostova (1999) and Scott (2007). In order to lessen the number of misfits, 'we should work closely with local HR team members. And it is important to hire Chinese specialists who are capable of handling the relationships with different institutions,' says the French HR director of C2 in the aerospace and defence industry.

The question about how institutional factors affect the international transfer process is simply answered by our research, which confirms that institutional interactions have substantial impacts on transfer output. Chinese regulations are by far the most influential factors pushing MNCs to adapt their HRM practices to local contexts. MNCs should enhance organisational learning in order to keep abreast of environmental complexities and differences in China.

Entry mode

Seven of the eight companies comprising our study make use of both entry modes (joint ventures and wholly owned subsidiaries), whereas C4 is a joint venture only. Being either a joint venture or a wholly owned subsidiary has its own advantages. For instance, forming joint ventures can help MNCs get local market information and conform to government regulations. However, according to our findings, being a joint venture is not an ideal means of transferring HRM practices to Chinese subsidiaries.

There are several reasons for this. Both parties, for instance, have different company profiles, such as management practices, corporate culture and values, stage of internationalisation, level of maturity and so forth. These differences shape constraints on transfer. By contrast, our findings show that wholly owned subsidiaries are better able to transfer home country templates. This is also found by Bresman et al. (1999) and Meyer (2001). Seven of the eight cases have established standardised HRM systems in their Chinese wholly owned subsidiaries. All our information providers emphasised that they avoided setting up joint ventures. Inevitably, wholly owned subsidiaries are generally simpler and better to control. This is also confirmed by Jaussaud and Schaaper (2006), who demonstrate that the development of MNCs in China avoids joint ventures and strives to develop new activities only through wholly owned subsidiaries.

The question about how entry modes impact transfer output is simply answered by our research, which confirms that wholly owned subsidiaries perform better than joint ventures in transferring home country HRM practices. Note that whenever the general manager in the joint venture is French or the French partner holds more shares or the French partner is in charge of HRM, this will help French MNCs standardise practices in an efficient way. If the general manager is Chinese and uses a third language (e.g., English) to discuss business this will easily cause misunderstanding and misinterpretation. Lastly, if the establishment of a joint venture is required by Chinese regulations (e.g., in sectors like insurance and mining), it is important to cooperate with an appropriate partner.

Expatriates

Our study shows that French MNCs employ a considerable number of expatriates in their overseas operations in China. Six of the eight companies have French general managers. This result reveals 'expatriates, especially the general managers, play a role of sharing headquarter knowledge to the subsidiary. Their knowledge towards headquarter's operation can guide and ensure the implementation of home-country HRM practices in the Chinese subsidiaries,' says the Chinese HR directory from C7 (which is in transportation sector). This is in line with research by Amann et al. (2013), Cerdin (2003), Rosenzweig and Nohria (1994).

Despite the potential advantages of expatriates, it should be noted that employing expatriates is relatively expensive. Moreover, sometimes it is difficult to get competent expatriates to work in overseas operations. Therefore, there is a tendency for French MNCs to use Chinese HR directors. For instance, C6's parent company organizes a program called "Knowing C6', which lasts nine months. Potential Chinese employees are selected to work at headquaters or at well-developed subsidiaries in other countries. The parent company expects these potential employees to spread their knowledge once they return to China. This is what they call 'C6's way of dissemination', according to the French HR director. Overall, five out of eight subsidiaries have Chinese HR directors. They not only implement parent company HRM practices in Chinese operations but also adapt them to comply with local employment regulations and cultural norms. Apart from C4, all the Chinese HR directors receive training at headquarters. Hence, Chinese HR directors are considered practice trainers, culture teachers and coordinators in the subsidiaries.

Conclusion

Our analysis investigates the transfer of HRM practices in French MNCs. We explain how factors originating from culture, institutional interactions, entry modes, and expatriates affect international transfer. Based on our findings, we can make foreign companies aware of the following managerial implications:

1. Multinational companies need to engage in organisational learning in their international transfer activities (i.e., recognizing local, cultural and institutional contexts, learning about entry modes and Chinese partners).

2. Global HR teams and local HR players need to work closely through constant communication and meetings. In this way they can better identify potential areas of incompatibility and figure out their adaptation strategies together. Moreover, instead of sending expatriates to Chinese subsidiaries, MNCs can train HR inpatriates. This is a long-term consideration for learning global and acting local.

3. Note that successful transfer relies on progressive steps. It takes time for Chinese employees to learn about, recognize and accept new practices. Furthermore, transfer mechanisms should be diversified. For instance, organizing a practice marketplace or a forum like

'Discovery Days' can facilitate the transfer. Let the transfer of practices be fun and become a cultural attitude within the group.

4. We encourage MNCs to continue working with dispatching companies. These companies have the expertise and experience in handling relationships with central government and various institutions.

Our research is limited insofar as our sample reviews only eight French MNCs, a relatively small sample size. This chapter has produced visible results but it would be interesting to start with our results and further test the various factors. This work is also limited by restricting its focus to interviews with general managers and HR directors. We have made the assumption that general managers and HR directors have the knowledge and experience to provide us with expert information. However, discussions with other employees at the subsidiaries may enrich the findings. Our unit of analysis is limited to China. It would be interesting to compare the transfer of HRM practices in French MNCs among other Asian emerging markets as a follow-on research project.

Notes

1. Seven of the eight companies established their first wholly owned subsidiary and/or joint venture in China more than 17 years previously.
2. An e-campus is a virtual campus, a web-based learning system for faculty and students.
3. Dispatching companies specialise in handling relationships with central government and governmental institutions.

References

Abdellatif, M., Amann, B. and Jaussaud, J. (2010) International firm strategies: is cultural distance a main determinant? *Transit Study Review*, **17**, 611–23, doi: 10.1007/s11300-010-0177-8.

Abo, T. (1994) *Hybrid Factory: The Japanese Production System in the United States*. Oxford University Press, Oxford, UK.

Alcazar, F.M., Fernandez, P.M.R. and Gardey, G.S. (2005) Researching on SHRM: an analysis of the debate over the role played by human resources in firm success. *Management Revue*, **16**(2), 213–41.

Amann, B., Jaussaud, J. and Schaaper, J. (2013) The complementary and alternative roles of expatriates and flexpatriates: a qualitative study of 47 French MNCs in

Asia. Paper presented at *18th International Euro-Asia Research Conference, Venice, Italy, 31 January–1 February.*

Bartlett, C. and Ghoshal, S. (1989) *Managing across Borders and the Transnational Solution.* Harvard Business School Press, Boston, MA.

Becker-Ritterspach, F. (2005) Transfer, intercultural friction and hybridization: empirical evidence from a German automobile subsidiary in India. *Asian Business & Management*, **4**(4), 365–87, doi: 10.1057/palgrave.abm.9200139.

Björkman, I. and Lu, Y. (1999) The management of human resources in Chinese–Western joint ventures. *Journal of World Business*, **34**(3), 306–24, doi: 10.1016/S1090-9516(99)00021-8.

Björkman, I. and Lu, Y. (2001) Institutionalization and bargaining power explanations of HRM practices in international joint ventures: the case of Chinese–Western joint ventures. *Organization Studies*, **22**(3), 491–512, doi: 10.1177/0170840601223005.

Boxall, P. and Purcell, J. (2011) *Strategy and Human Resource Management.* Palgrave Macmillan, Basingstoke, UK.

Bresman, H., Birkinshaw, J. and Nobel, R. (1999) Knowledge transfer in international acquisitions. *Journal of International Business Studies*, **30**(3), 439–62. Available from: *http://www.jstor.org/stable/155460*

Cerdin, J.L. (2003) International diffusion of HRM practices: the role of expatriates. *Beta Scandinavian Journal of Business Research*, **17**(1), 48–58.

Child, J. and Tse, D. (2001) China's transition and its implications for international business. *Journal of International Business Studies*, **32**(1), 5–21. Available from: *http://www.jstor.org/stable/3069507*

DiMaggio, P. and Powell, W. (1991) *The New Institutionalism in Organizational Analysis.* University of Chicago Press, Chicago, IL.

Dunning, J.H. (1981) *International Production and the Multinational Enterprise.* George Allen & Unwin, London.

Edwards, T. and Ferner, A. (2004) Multinationals, reverse diffusion and national business systems. *Management International Review*, **44**(1), 49–79. Available from: *http://www.jstor.org/stable/40836011*

Ferner, A. and Varul, M. (2000) 'Vanguard' subsidiaries and the diffusion of new practices: a case study of German multinationals. *British Journal of Industrial Relations*, **38**(1), 115–40, doi: 10.1111/1467-8543.00154.

Gupta, A.K. and Govindarajan, V. (2000) Knowledge flows within multinational corporations. *Strategic Management Journal*, **21**(4), 473–96. Available from: *http://www.jstor.org/stable/3094239.*

Heenan, D.A. and Perlmutter, H.V. (1979) *Multinational Organization Development.* Addison Wesley Longman Publishing, Boston, MA.

Hofstede, G. (2004) *Culture and Organizations: Software of the Mind.* McGraw-Hill, London.

Jaussaud, J. and Liu, X.M. (2011) When in China . . .: the HRM practices of Chinese and foreign-owned enterprises during a global crisis. *Asia Pacific Business Review*, **17**(4), 473–91.

Jaussaud, J. and Schaaper, J. (2006) Control mechanisms of their subsidiaries by multinational firms: a multidimensional perspective. *Journal of International Management*, **12**(1), 23–45.

Kitayama, S., Markus, H.R. and Kurokawa, M. (2000) Culture, emotion, and well-being: good feelings in Japan and the United States. *Cognition and Emotion*, **14**(1), 93–124, doi: 10.1080/026999300379003.

Kogut, B. and Singh, H. (1988) The effect of national culture on the choice of entry mode. *Journal of International Business Study*, **19**(3), 411–32, doi: 10.1057/palgrave.jibs.8490394.

Kostova, T. (1999) Transnational transfer of strategic organizational practices: a contextual perspective. *Academy of Management Review*, **24**(2), 308–24. Available from: *http://www.jstor.org/stable/259084*

Kostova, T. and Roth, K. (2002) Adoption of an organizational practice by subsidiaries of multinational corporations: institutional and relational effects. *Academy of Management Journal*, **45**(1), 215–33. Available from: *http://www.jstor.org/stable/3069293*

Menipaz, E. and Menipaz, A. (2011) *International Business: Theory and Practice*. Sage Publications, London.

Meyer, K.E. (2001) Institutions, transaction costs and entry mode choice in Eastern Europe. *Journal of International Business Studies*, **32**(2), 357–67, doi: 10.1057/palgrave.jibs.8490957.

Miles, M.B. and Huberman, A.M. (1994) *Qualitative Data Analysis*. Sage Publications, Thousand Oaks, CA.

Myloni, B., Harzing, A.W. and Mirza, H. (2004) Host country specific factors and the transfer of human resource management practices in multinational companies. *International Journal of Manpower*, **25**(6), 518–34, doi: 10.1108/01437720410560424.

Rosenzweig, P. and Nohria, N. (1994) Influences on human resource management practices in multinational corporations. *Journal of International Business Studies*, **25**(2), 229–51. Available from: *http://www.jstor.org/stable/155388*

Rosenzweig, P. and Singh, J. (1991) Organizational environments and the multinational enterprise. *Academy of Management Review*, **16**(2), 340–61. Available from: *http://www.jstor.org/stable/258865*

Schneider, S. and Barsoux, J.L. (1997) *Managing across Cultures*. Financial Times/Prentice Hall, London.

Schwartz, S.H. (2004) Mapping and interpreting cultural differences around the world. In: H. Vinken, J. Soeters and P. Ester (Eds.), *Comparing Cultures: Dimensions of Culture in a Comparative Perspective* (International Studies in Sociology and Social Anthropology). Brill Academic Publishers, Leiden, The Netherlands.

Scott, W.R. (2007) *Institutions and Organizations: Ideas and Interests*. Sage Publications, London.

Smith, C. and Elger, T. (2000) The societal effects school and transnational transfer: the case of Japanese investment in Britain. In: M. Maurice and A. Sorge (Eds.), *Embedding Organizations: Societal Analysis of Actors, Organizations and Socio-economic Context*. John Benjamin Publishing Company, Amsterdam, The Netherlands.

Stone, D.L., Stone-Romero, E.F. and Lukaszewski, K.M. (2007) The impact of cultural values on the acceptance and effectiveness of human resource management policies and practices. *Human Resource Management Review*, **17**(2), 152–65.

Symon, G. and Cassell, C. (1998) *Qualitative Methods and Analysis in Organizational Research*. Sage Publications, London.
Tan, D. and Mahoney, J.T. (2003) Explaining the utilization of managerial expatriates from the perspectives of resource-based, agency, and transaction-costs theories. *Advances in International Management*, **15**, 179–205, doi: 10.1016/S0747-7929(03)15009-3.
Tan, D. and Mahoney, J.T. (2006) Why a multinational firm chooses expatriates: integrating resource-based, agency and transaction costs perspectives. *Journal of Management Studies*, **43**(3), 457–84, doi: 10.1111/j.1467-6486.2006.00598.x.
Thory, K. (2008) The internationalization of HRM through reverse transfer: two case studies of French multinationals in Scotland. *Human Resource Management Journal*, **18**(1), 54–71.
Trompenaars, H. C. (1994) *Culture and Social Behavior*. McGraw-Hill, New York.
Wang, S., Tong, T.W., Chen, G.L. and Kim, H. (2009) Expatriate utilization and foreign direct investment performance: the mediating role of knowledge transfer. *Journal of Management*, **35**(5), 1181–206, doi: 10.1177/0149206308328511.
Yin, R.K. (2008) *Case Study Research: Design and Methods (Applied Social Research Methods)*. Sage Publications, London.

Part 2
China's growing services sector

How risky is China's red capitalism? Restructuring in the Chinese financial services sector

Bernadette Andreosso-O'Callaghan and Joern Gottwald

Abstract: With the rise of China as a new global economic player, several authors have attempted to qualify the evolving Chinese capitalist system. In spite of the different theoretical frameworks used and results obtained, these approaches tend to highlight, in the main, the pivotal role of the Chinese state. China's red, or party-driven, capitalism is highly concerned with the risks inherent in current economic growth. The concept of 'sustainable economic growth' thus becomes paramount in today's official political discourse and refers to change in the type of reform (see 'Conceptualising the sustainability of the Chinese capitalist system'). Because of its core role in modern economic growth, the financial services sector is analysed in this chapter by means of (i) statistical analysis ('Statistical analysis of the financial services sector in China') and (ii) policy elements and political implications ('Reforms and control of the banking sector and of financial services'). The concluding section ('Concluding analysis') presents an analysis of the risks inherent in this sector and in modern Chinese capitalism as a whole; it also highlights the weaknesses of the system. The chapter argues that issues of political control and vested interests in the Chinese system create serious challenges for further reform and internationalisation. While China's financial sector as a whole seems to be reasonably stable, the issues of how to pursue the objective of further internationalisation puts the central leadership at odds with strong inner-party opposition.

Key words: China, red capitalism, financial reforms, banking regulation, shadow finance.

Introduction

With the rise of China as a new global economic player, several authors have attempted to qualify the evolving Chinese capitalist system (Ahrens and Jünemann, 2007; Breslin, 2009; Huang, 2008; Nee and Opper, 2012; Pearson, 2010; Ten Brink, 2012; and Witt, 2010). In spite of the different theoretical frameworks used and results obtained, these approaches tend to highlight, in the main, the pivotal role of the Chinese state. The export-led growth model based on underpriced factors of production is a model of the past (Fabre, 2013), for contemporary Chinese growth has tended to rest increasingly on the development of the real estate and financial sectors. Persistently low–efficiency levels in the manufacturing sector (especially in state-owned enterprises) and a tendency towards 'financialisation' of the economy are the new characteristics of contemporary growth in China. The risks inherent in this contemporary growth model have therefore led China's red, or party-driven, capitalist system to embark upon a new path of 'sustainable economic growth'. This concept thus becomes paramount in today's official political discourse.

Because of its growing role in modern economic growth and in contemporary Chinese development, the financial services sector lies at the heart of this chapter. The first section of this chapter ('Conceptualizing the sustainability of the Chinese capitalist system') will therefore clarify this concept by re-placing it in a brief discussion of the evolving Chinese capitalist system. The second section ('Statistical analysis of the financial services sector in China') will provide a statistical analysis aimed at unveiling the potential risks inherent in this sector whereas the third section ('Reforms and control of the banking sector and of financial services') will discuss policy reform elements aimed at strengthening the financial sector; in this section, the issue of a party-permeated banking and financial sector will be expored. A concluding section will discuss the risks inherent in this sector and in modern Chinese capitalism as a whole, and will highlight the weaknesses of the system.

The chapter argues that issues of political control and vested interests in the Chinese system create serious challenges for further reform and internationalisation. While China's financial and banking sector as a whole looks *prima facie* as being reasonably stable, the issues of how to pursue the objective of further internationalisation puts the central leadership at odds with strong inner-party opposition.

Conceptualising the sustainability of the Chinese capitalist system

This section suggests, first, a brief summary of the recent literature related to analysis of the evolving Chinese capitalist system; it then tries to throw some light on the concept of 'sustainable economic growth' in general and in the Chinese contemporary context.

The Chinese capitalist system

Since the rise of China as a new global economic player, much has been written about the emerging type of capitalism in that country (Ahrens and Jünemann, 2007; Andreosso-O'Callaghan and Gottwald, 2013; Breslin, 2009; Huang, 2008; Noelke, 2013; Walter and Zhang, 2012; Witt, 2010). Starting with the Marxian definition of a capitalist system, which entails a system where capital is being accumulated for the purpose of allowing transactions to take place in the areas of production and consumption, and where power relations stem from the division between the two groups, the Chinese capitalist system has been analysed on the basis of various theoretical strands embracing the fields of political science, economics and management. For example, Ahrens and Jünemann (2007) and Witt (2010) apply the 'varieties of capitalism' (VoC) framework – as one of the most popular approaches to studying capitalist systems – to the Chinese case, and these authors arrive at diverging conclusions when it comes to labelling the Chinese capitalist system either as a 'coordinated market economy' or a 'liberal market economy'. Several shortcomings of the VoC approach (e.g., the fact that the role of political institutions is underestimated) – in contrast with the work of Wang (2003) who puts political institutions at the top of all actors in the Chinese system – show that the VoC approach is inadequate in explaining the type of modern capitalism that has emerged in China since the beginning of economic reforms. Given the strong involvement of the state, as is typical for East Asian and Asian countries, other authors such as Ten Brink (2012) refer to the Chinese system as a 'state-permeated capitalist' system. This view follows the 'developmental state' (DS) approach which sees the state largely as a substitute for market coordination (Pearson, 2010). But, since the state is normally viewed in the DS discourse as being a coercive and yet 'friendly' actor, this approach may therefore not be suitable to the case of authoritarian states such as the Chinese state, although it might suit the case of post–World War 2 Japan, for example. Convenient expressions such as 'socialist market economy' or 'capitalism with Chinese characteristics' (Huang, 2008) show the difficulty in categorizing the Chinese capitalist system along the lines drawn by different existing theoretical frameworks. As we have shown in earlier work (Andreosso-O'Callaghan and Gottwald, 2013, p. 447), the Chinese capitalist system can be 'best understood via the state-centered approach' and the fact that the Leninist basis of formal institutions is still intact allows us to qualify the Chinese capitalist system as a 'state capitalist system'. Continuity in a statist tradition cemented by a stable Leninist basis of formal institutions is achieved through self-preservation of the Communist Party of China (CPC). This implies that a paramount objective of the Chinese Communist State or of China's red capitalist system is to preserve social harmony. In return, this entails sustainable economic growth and better income distribution, both spatially and across income groups.

Sustainable economic growth

Sustainable economic growth can be understood to refer to relatively high growth rates in the short term that do not undermine long-term growth. Policies geared towards ensuring sustainable economic growth are ultimately aimed at minimising risk or at minimising the economic vulnerability of countries (Andreosso-O'Callaghan, 2007).

By the turn of the new millennium, it had become evident that the economic reforms of the 1980s and 1990s had led to a great deal of both structural change and fast economic growth, but, as noted by Chen et al. (2011), this had been at the expense of productive efficiency. In addition, the global financial crisis has radically raised doubts about the traditional engines of economic growth in China (namely investment-led and export-led growth). Consequently, the Chinese growth model had to be reassessed and the theme of sustainable economic growth became embedded in official political discourse.[1] In this discourse, sustainable economic growth is defined as promoting reform of the Chinese economy, particularly by allowing a shift from an investment-led to a domestic demand-led growth pattern (*kuoda neixu*). The key role that domestic (as opposed to foreign) demand can play in Chinese economic growth was again formulated in China's Twelfth Five-Year Plan spanning the years 2011 to 2015. This shift away from the traditional export-led growth model follows econometric evidence which shows that the new millennium has been critical in changing the type of demand as an explanatory variable of growth stimulated mostly by inward investment. For example, Wei (2006) shows how provincial GDP (as a proxy for domestic demand at the regional level) and revealed comparative advantage exports (as a proxy for foreign demand) together explain inward foreign direct investment from EU firms between 1996 and 2002.

The necessity to implement policies aimed at boosting domestic consumption (such as increasing the threshold for personal income tax) and at switching away from foreign demand-based growth is only one of a few priority areas for the future. As specified in the Chinese business press,[2] the PRC's economic reforms also need to rely increasingly on services for growth. It is thus clear how, according to current Chinese official discourse, sustainable economic growth refers to: (i) a change in the type of economic reforms and, for the purpose of our analysis, to (ii) accelerating structural change by focussing on the services sector. One key issue still to be resolved is the balance between increased economic liberalisation and the preservation of one-party stability. This conflict is highlighted in the rapid publication of two documents after the Third Plenum of the 18th Central Committee of the CPC in November 2013. The first, a short summary of the decisions, resembled an uneasy combination – apparently drafted under serious political and time pressures – between reform ideas and more conservative ideological concerns. The official announcement regarding the deepening of reforms (*Xinhua News Agency*, 15 November 2013)[3] which followed within days outlined ambitious policy objectives in various fields including financial services. The announcement confirmed, among others, the idea to use the recently established (earlier in 2013) China Shanghai Pilot Free Trade Zone as part of a new drive to further liberalise financial services.

Given the pivotal role of financial services in modern economic growth, as will be discussed in our section on 'Reforms and control of the banking sector and of financial services', and given their ability to either preserve or jeopardise the sustainability of economic growth in a typical capitalist system, the ensuing section ('Statistical analysis of the financial services sector in China') will focus on financial services as the main laboratory case of a potentially risky and red capitalist system. As the Chinese leadership pointed out in the official announcement following the Third Plenum of the 18th Central Committee of the CPC, 'finance is the basis and an important pillar of national governance, scientific financial and fiscal structures are an institutional guarantee to optimize resource allocation, safeguard market unity, stimulate social fairness and realize a long period of peace and order for the country' (CPC CC, 2013).

Statistical analysis of the financial services sector in China

Before presenting a number of characteristics and performance indicators of the financial services sector in China, this section will start with a brief discussion on the link between economic growth and the development of the financial services sector.

Financial services and economic growth in China

In spite of its relatively underdeveloped state, the Chinese financial services sector has been the subject of several empirical studies (using mostly econometric analysis) testing the finance-led growth hypothesis. For example, Hao (2006) analysed the way financial intermediation influenced economic growth in China during the period 1985–99 and showed how financial services have contributed to economic growth, by capturing household savings, in particular. The positive impact of 'deeper financial markets', together with such developments as a legal basis in the area of property rights protection, on economic growth up to the late 2000s is also found by Hasan et al. (2009). The study by Guillaumont-Jeanneney et al. (2006) also finds evidence of the finance-led growth hypothesis for the period 1993–2001. Of particular note in this study is the importance of financial development to productivity growth during this period. The provincial-level work of Guariglia and Poncet (2008) also concludes that there is a positive relationship between the development of the financial sector and economic growth, as well as total factor productivity (TFP), for the period 1989–2003 in China. This study suggests an interesting decomposition between indicators such as those measuring the degree of state intervention in the financial sector, which are negatively associated with economic growth, whereas the indicators measuring market-driven financing show a positive association with growth. However, other studies disprove the finance-led growth hypothesis. For example, using a VAR (vector autoregressive) model in the case of China over a 20-year time span from the mid-1980s, Shan and Qi (2006) find that financial development is only second to labour input in explaining economic growth. This study also shows two-way causality (growth leading to financial development). Using a much longer period than most studies (1952–2001), the VAR-based study by Liang and Teng (2006) concludes that there is only unidirectional causality running from economic growth to financial development.

The two-way causality highlighted in the literature is clearly an important finding substantiating the Chinese government's view that sustainable economic growth rests partly on the development of services and, in particular, on financial services. It also suggests that financial development can stimulate, or on the contrary, undermine economic growth.

Characteristics of the Chinese financial system[4]

Path dependency and the legacy of the command economy explain the characteristics of the Chinese banking and financial system today: a high savings rate; the existence of captive deposits and biased allocation of savings; the use of capital controls; controlled and distorted interest rates that allow state-owned enterprises (SOEs) and the government to obtain interest rates that are below the base rate; low incidence of interbank lending; the preponderance of traditional banking although, as will be discussed later, this is changing rapidly; and low foreign penetration. An additional feature, political protection of the biggest banks by the central government is increasingly under pressure. For once, the need to rebalance China's overall growth patterns requires dismantling the oligopolistic dominance of the biggest banks secured through centrally defined ceilings and floors for interest rates on credit and savings. A second driving force for substantial changes in the Chinese banking system is the increased global integration of the Chinese economy. While a certain level of state protection against the fluidity of global capital movements has proved valuable in protecting China against fallout from the global financial crisis, the issue of liberalising the exchange rate and developing the yuan into a global currency requires decisive policies in weaning the biggest banks, and SOEs, off centrally administered interest rates and lending policies.

In this regard, China's reform path promises to continue to follow the specific logic of political negotiations and compromises rather than a new comprehensive blueprint. This is underscored by the decision to use the new Shanghai Free Trade Zone to function as a pilot for financial reforms.

Structure and performance of China's banking system

Economic reforms turned the monobank system (represented by the People's Bank of China, PBOC) into a two-tier system with the foundation of four state-owned banks (the so-called 'Big Four'). These are the Bank of China (BoC), China Construction Bank (CCB), the Agricultural Bank of China (ABC) and the Industrial and Commercial Bank of China (ICBC). They form the core of a multi-tiered banking system that includes specialist policy banks both at the central level – China Development Bank, Agricultural Development Bank of China and China Export–Import Bank (Hui, 2010; Zheng and Zhu, 2008) – and at the provincial and local level, as well as a large number of banks at provincial and local levels (Martin, 2012). With the creation of special economic zones, new actors were able to enter the market in the coastal regions of China. Consequently, a number of local and regional banks partly owned by local governments, such as Shanghai Pudong Development Bank, as well as rural credit corporations and urban credit corporations mushroomed whereas non-bank financial actors (trust and investment corporations) multiplied. With China's entry into the World Trade Organisation (WTO), foreign banks (in particular, asset management institutions) have entered the Chinese market but their market share in terms of total assets was still below 2 per cent in 2012 (CBRC, 2013).

Although the banking system is now a multi-tier system consisting of wholly state-owned policy banks, equitized banks (the Big Four plus China Communications Bank), local banks, private commercial banks and a growing underground banking system (Martin, 2012), the system is far from being efficient. Managers of the top banks are nominated by the state, the PBOC is far from aspiring to become an independent central bank and market concentration is relatively high (as shown in Table 7.1). The table depicts the evolution of the CR3 concentration ratio in China compared with Japan and the USA; as can be seen, and despite the reforms facilitating market entry into China, recent evidence does not seem to show increased competition. The sector is still rather opaque with the Big Four allocating 60 per cent of total credit to SOEs, which in turn get more than half of all bank loans although they account for less than 30 per cent of all industrial output (Fabre, 2013).

In terms of the performance of the sector, official data from the China Banking Regulatory Commission (CBRC) show a loan-to-deposit ratio of 70.38 per cent in 2011, down from 77.01 per cent in 2003 (Table 7.2). This suggests that banking institutions in China perform increasingly better in that they tend to be less leveraged. Moreover, with the creation of the four asset management corporations (AMCs) to tackle the problem of non-performing loans (NPLs) granted by the Big Four in 1999, official figures from the CBRC (2013) show an impressive decline in the NPL-to-gross-loan ratio (from 30 per cent in 2001 to about 1 per cent in 2012), implying again improvement in overall performance. Yet, since stress-testing in June 2013, financial stability has become an overriding priority of the Chinese government (Fabre, 2013). Zhang and Chen (2013) argue that the apparently low NPLs of banks are connected with the ability of wealth management funds and other trust institutions to provide new loans to the increasingly indebted local governments through a number of local government financial vehicles (LGFVs).

Table 7.1 Concentration in the banking industry – comparative analysis (CR3)

Year	US (%)	China (%)	Japan (%)
2000	21.4	55.4	35.0
2001	23.1	57.2	38.5
2002	23.4	42.2	36.5
2003	23.3	60.8	37.0
2004	28.0	65.8	37.2
2005	29.8	64.1	40.0
2006	32.7	70.1	38.3
2007	34.0	57.2	45.0
2008	35.4	58.3	44.7
2009	31.9	55.7	44.2
2010	31.6	50.9	44.2
2011	35.4	51.5	44.6

Source: Federal Reserve Bank of St Louis.
Note: the calculation of CR3 is based on the assets of the three largest commercial banks as a share of total commercial banking assets.[5]

These new loans are then used to pay off the outstanding debts. High debts at local government level are in turn explained by unprecedented speculation on land, a new factor driving contemporary growth in China. Fabre (2013, p. 11) argues how the sale of land use rights has gradually become a 'part [...] of the operating budgets of local governments' as a response to the need to finance the stimulus package launched at the end of 2008.[6]

Another aspect that mitigates against the improvement of China's banking performance is the impressive increase in shadow banking (Allen et al., 2012).[7] Shadow banking refers to the complex intermediation of credit by banks and financial institutions who engage in maturity, liquidity and credit transformation with far less transparency and regulation than in traditional banks or in a traditional financial

Table 7.2 Total deposits and loans of banking institutions in China (2003–11)

Year / items	2003 (¥100m)	2004 (¥100m)	2005 (¥100m)	2006 (¥100m)	2007 (¥100m)	2008 (¥100m)	2009 (¥100m)	2010 (¥100m)	2011 (¥100m)
Total deposits	220,364	253,188	300,209	348,016	401,051	478,444	612,006	733,382	826,701
Savings deposits	110,695	126,196	147,054	166,616	176,213	221,503	264,761	307,166	347,401
Total loans	169,771	188,566	206,839	238,280	277,747	320,129	425,597	509,226	581,893
Short-term loans	87,398	90,808	91,158	101,698	118,898	128,609	151,353	171,237	217,480
Medium and long-term loans	67,252	81,010	92,941	113,010	138,581	164,195	235,579	305,128	333,747
Bill financing	9,234	11,618	16,319	17,333	12,884	19,314	23,879	14,845	15,154

Note: data include the People's Bank of China and are from the PBoC.
Source: China Banking Regulatory Commission Annual Report, 2011.

intermediation system. Due to regulatory restrictions, a huge shadow banking system has emerged in China over the years and has added further complexity to the banking system (Orlik, 2013) and allowed for creative dealings between public authority, bank and investment vehicles behind the backs of central authorities (Frangos, 2013). According to Li (2013), trust companies, brokers, small lenders and financial guarantors are all part of the growing shadow banking system in China. Estimates of shadow banking assets, as a proportion of all assets, vary between 15 per cent (BofA Merrill Lynch) to 31 per cent (GFS Securities) (Li, 2013). What is most worrisome is the increase in shadow banking, particularly since the global financial crisis and the ensuing stimulus package. According to some estimates, about half of all new credit in 2013 came from shadow banking (Fabre, 2013). This implies that when all off-balance-sheet activity in China is accounted for, including loans to property developers and through LGFVs, this represents a third of GDP (Sheng and Geng, 2013). Although NGAM (2013) believes it is dubious whether the development of shadow banking has made the Chinese financial system more efficient and therefore allowed SMEs, for example, to access credit more easily, a direct consequence of this rapid change is an increase in credit risk and, therefore, systemic risk in the entire Chinese banking and financial sector.

Reforms and control of the banking sector and of financial services

China is in the process of establishing a socialist market economy as part of its socialism with Chinese characteristics. It combines one-party rule by the Communist Party of China, which still enshrines the principle of democratic centralism (*People's Daily Online*, 29 March 2013) and the CPC's mass line (*Xinhua News Agency*, 15 July 2013), with various institutional and regulatory structures emulating established market economies (Gottwald and Collins, 2011; Naughton, 2007). In spite of a high degree of centralisation in its political structures, China's policy making has always incorporated an element of bottom up even before the reform period of Deng Xiaoping starting in the late 1970s. The discretionary powers of local and provincial authorities and their control of substantial parts of SOEs made them important driving forces in the process of economic reform. The spread of all sorts of special economic zones has further contributed to the emergence of an economic order described by one prominent observer of the 1990s as a patchwork of different economic areas (Herrmann-Pillath, 1994). The difficulties of the central leadership to supervise and reign in local authorities have recently gained prominence in the context of excess investment and bad debt issues in the wake of the 2008 stimulus program.

The strong influence of local authorities and the rise of vested interests within the party state make China's economic control structures increasingly differentiated between sectors. In the case of banking, some observers argue that the existence of rival functions has had a major impact on institutional change and evolving policies, with different factions at various levels of the political system pursuing their own interests (Shih, 2007).

These structural elements have affected the reform policies for financial services by defining mutually contradictory objectives: to establish viable, open and stable markets and, at the same time, solve the financial issues of China's SOEs (Heilmann, 2002) and allow in enough foreign funding and know-how to improve overall performance but without giving away too much party state control.

Today, China's largest commercial banks (the Big Four) are traded on international stock exchanges yet remain under the control of the central government. The introduction of two stock exchanges in Shenzhen and Shanghai in 1990/91 and the introduction of various other markets for bonds were originally closely linked with efforts to modernise SOEs. Right up to today, issues relating to financial reforms are still strongly influenced by the situation of the remaining 117 enterprises under the central control of the State Assets Supervision and Administration Commission, SASAC (SASAC, 2013). Notwithstanding the various rounds of reforms, small and medium-sized companies and the private sector, in general, have found it difficult to access credit through the official banking sector or acquire permission for an initial public offering. More recent attempts to improve access to credit for private enterprises have raised new doubt regarding the stability of the banks involved as many doubt their ability to manage the risks involved (Kazer, 2013). Substantial underground banking played a major role in financing China's industrial modernisation. Private and/or illegal provision of credit are a major source of funding, particularly for the very competitive private sector which finds itself at a strategic disadvantage against companies run by the state. In some areas, like Wenzhou, underground banking gained a significance that led to various efforts to bring illegal operations into the official banking sector.

In summary, this process of banking reforms through Leninist means

(Heilmann, 2005) created a unique blend of, on the surface, state-of-the-art regulatory and supervisory structures with more traditional organisations of party state policies like the National Development and Reform Commission or the new committee announced to be set up in 2014 to oversee the implementation of comprehensive new reforms (*The Economist*, 16 November 2013). China followed Western best practice in establishing a regulatory system built around independent regulatory bodies and the central bank. At the same time, it needed to address top-level decision making on financial reform conducted through leading small groups and central work conferences (Gottwald and Collins, 2011; Pearson, 2007).

Following a top-level reshuffle, the CCP has appointed two new leaders, Xi Jinping, the Secretary General, and Li Keqiang, the new No. 2. in the official hierarchy and new Prime Minister. Following the dual structure of the Chinese party state where party organisations lead and supervise the state apparatus, core political issues are decided in joint decision-making bodies. At the very top, the Leading Small Group on Finance and Economics brings together top representatives of the state apparatus, supervising bodies and party leadership (Miller, 2008). The number of conferences and working groups involved in defining the main direction of regulation has been criticised within China. The large scope of the State Council with its numerous ministries, powerful commissions, State Information Bureau and sectoral watchdogs for banking, securities and insurance, has become a playing field for intense turf wars. This might explain the reason for setting up a new committee to push through comprehensive reforms in 2013.

In the area of financial markets, both the Ministry of Finance and the Central Bank have their own asset and investment vehicles (Huijin Investments and the China Investment Corporation). These in turn vie for control of China's banks. Walter and Howie (2011) depict how various efforts to deal with NPLs in Chinese banks resembled a merry-go-around of cross-cutting mutual investments and masking liabilities. The Central Bank has preserved the responsibility for prudential regulation. Specialised regulatory commissions for securities, banking and insurance have taken on sector-specific supervisory functions. Their official 'independence' cannot conceal their deep integration into the party state apparatus (Gottwald and Collins, 2011). Leading cadres continue to stay within the human resources domain of the Organisation Department of the Central Committee, and often have to deal with higher ranking cadres in the enterprises that fall under their supervision. Following the fallout from the global financial crisis, the PBOC seems to have gained further traction with the party leadership and has emerged as the most influential and powerful organisation with the regulatory setup even providing key input into China's role in the G20 and the Financial Stability Board (FSB) rivalling the Ministry of Foreign Affairs duties in coordinating China's policies there.

The regulatory authorities are charged with prudential regulation as well as code-of-conduct supervision. In established market economies, regulatory agencies are complemented with independent self-regulatory bodies. In China, however, a rising number of business organisations and sectoral bodies are still part of the party state–led complementation of markets through social organisations following the principle of building a big society to allow for small government from the 1980s. Regulatory bodies control the governing bodies of these organisations and, thereby, blur the lines between regulatory agencies and self-regulatory bodies (Hui, 2010). Other important elements which are considered a prerequisite to the US–European model of regulation – an independent judiciary, free press and unfettered representation of consumer interests – are also absent (Gottwald and Collins, 2011).

As all leading positions are filled through the nomenklatura system, the issue of individual ranking of leading representatives of the regulatory bodies and the big enterprises including the banks creates issues for the implementation of regulation. Deputy governors of the Central Bank, for example, are simply appointed by the Premier of the State Council (PBOC Law, Article 10). Here, a new ministerial-level super-regulator might clarify the superiority of its leading cadres over the regulatees. The issue of authority is aggravated by the business interests of relatives of leading cadres – including the families of Xi Jingping or Wen Jiabao – who are increasingly active in financial conglomerates, banks or private equity. These well-networked princelings are able to mobilise substantial political clout. Thus, even the most powerful weapon in the arsenal of the party state, cadre control, has lost some of its effectiveness (Cheng, 2012).

Overall, the CPC has allowed a quasi-private market to emerge in financial services while preserving substantial influence in all areas of the market through cadre management of the party, control of substantial funds and integration of regulatory authorities into the party state apparatus. It appoints and assesses the top managers of the biggest banks, exchanges, intermediaries, regulators, the media and the judiciary. It also owns substantial shares in all major financial service companies, directs credit and decides about venues for recapitalisation. In addition, it sets funding requirements and options and controls foreign access to the market as well as outward investments. The party sets and enforces the scope for investigative journalism and reporting. Therefore, the CPC wears many hats and has many faces in the context of financial services. The CPC, however, has huge problems acting coherently. Thus, the future course of economic reforms including the planned liberalisation of China's capital account depends heavily on finding compromises between vested interests within the party.

Concluding analysis: How risky is China's capitalist system judging by its financial services industry?

China's financial system has proved surprisingly resilient in the face of the global financial crisis. While a number of prominent doomsayers have strong arguments regarding the amount of NPLs and the opaque entanglement of local authorities and creatively arranged financing vehicles, a high savings rate, massive foreign exchange reserves and strong state protection against the more disastrous new financial market products, which played a crucial role in triggering the global financial crisis in the US and Europe, seem to more than balance the negative developments.

One major often underestimated element is the increasing involvement of leading CPC families. The regulatory and supervisory structures in China's socialist market economy, in general, and in the financial sector, in particular, rest with the ability of the party state to control access to funds and personnel. Being able to use party channels to complement or even replace government policies has proved to be an important element of economic governance, particularly at times of crisis. Red families combining political clout with business interests in an increasingly mature economy is a direct threat to a key pillar of the economic and political order.

Even the fundamental pattern of China's reform policies might be history. Gradual reforms – famously 'crossing the river by groping for stones' – have proved extremely successful in China between 1978 and 2013. Even if they provided space for vested interests to claim their share of China's economic and political order, they allowed for careful experiments of specific measures before they were turned into official general policy. The Third Plenum of the 18th Central Committee of the CPC seems to have broken with this tradition. The attempt to instigate comprehensive new reforms through a detailed reform program and a push for recentralisation of authority in the hands of new committees signals a potential departure from well-established reform patterns.

These changes in China's overall economic reforms happen at a time when the central government finds itself under substantial domestic and external pressure to deal with the global financial crisis and fallout from the massive stimulus of 2008. Massive public spending and government-induced cheap credit has increased overcapacity, has led to numerous 'white elephant' infrastructure projects, has inflated an already significant property bubble and has led to all sorts of new financing vehicles between banks and local authorities. Land sales have become one of the most important ways for the local state to finance itself. This promises serious future issues for macroeconomic rebalancing.

Notes

1. The 16th Party Congress in 2002 proposed for the first time a sustainable development strategy.
2. The interested reader is referred, for example, to the article by Hu Yuyue in *The Financial Times* (Chinese edition), 'Investment shall not be the only determinant for China's economic growth,' 18 September 2013, and to Chi Fulin's article in the People.com.cn 'A transforming reform towards a justified and sustainable economic growth', 11 November 2013.
3. *Xinhua News Agency* (2013) *Zhonguo zhnogyang guanyu quanmian shenhua gaige ruogan zhongyao wenti de jueding*, 15 November 2013. Available from: *http://news.xinhuanet.com/politics/2013-11/15/c_118164235.htm* [accessed 10 December 2013].
4. For more on this, see Andreosso-O'Callaghan and Gottwald (2013).
5. Total assets include earning assets, cash and due from banks, foreclosed real estate, fixed assets, goodwill, other intangibles, current tax assets, deferred tax, discontinued operations and other assets.
6. Private debt is another mounting issue. According to Charlene Chu, private sector debt in China rose from '129% of the size of the national economy to 214% at the end of June 2013' (Frangos, 2013, ch. 1).
7. Shadow banking refers to lending outside the regular or official banking system and it is problematic in that it does not appear on banks' balance sheets.

References

Ahrens, J. and Jünemann, P. (2007) *Transitional Institutions, Institutional Complementarities and Economic Performance in China: A 'Varieties of Capitalism' Approach* (Department of Economics Papers). European Business School, Oestrich-Winkel, Germany.

Allen, F., Qian, Q.J., Zhang, C. and Zhao, M. (2012) *China's Financial System: Opportunities and Challenges* (NBER Working Paper 17828). National Bureau of Economic Research, Cambridge, MA. Available from: *http://www.nber.org/papers/w17828*

Andreosso-O'Callaghan, B. (2007) From linkages to dependency and vulnerability: the case of China, the EU and the USA. Paper presented at *Workshop on Global Economic Security and the EU–US–China Triangle, European Institute for Asian Studies, Brussels, 21–22 June.*

Andreosso-O'Callaghan, B. and Gottwald, J. (2013) How red is China's red capitalism? Continuity and change in China's financial services sector during the global crisis. *Asia Pacific Business Review*, **19**(4), 444–60, October, Special Issue: 'Demystifying Chinese Management: Issues and Challenges'.

Breslin, S. (2009) *China and the Global Political Economy*. Palgrave, London.

CBRC (2013) *Annual Report*. China Banking Regulatory Commission, Beijing.

Chen, S., Jefferson, G.H. and Zhang, J. (2011) Structural change, productivity growth and industrial transformation in China. *China Economic Review*, **22**, 133–50.

Cheng, L. (2012) The battle for China's Top Nine leadership posts. *Washington Quarterly*, **35**(1), 131–45.

CPC CC (2013) Communique of the Third Plenum of the 18th Party Congress (unofficial English translation). Available from: *http://chinacopyrightandmedia.wordpress.com/2013/11/12/communique-of-the-3rd-plenum-of-the-18th-party-congress/* [accessed 5 December 2013].

Fabre, G. (2013) The lion's share: What's behind China's economic slowdown? Paper presented at *Séminaire BRICs*. Fondation Maison des Sciences de l'Homme, No. 53, Octobre, Paris.

Frangos, A. (2013) Charlene Chu is the 'rock star' of Chinese debt analysis. *Wall Street Journal*, 22 August 2013.

Gottwald, J.-C. (2011) Cadre capitalism goes global: financial market reforms and the new role of the People's Republic of China in world markets. In: L. Brennan (Ed.), *The Emergence of Southern Multinationals and Their Impact on Europe*. Palgrave Macmillan, Basingstoke, UK, pp. 283–300.

Gottwald, J.-C. and Collins, N. (2011) The Chinese model of a regulatory state. In: D. Levy-Faur (Ed.), *Handbook on the Politics of Regulation*. E. Elgar, Cheltenham, UK, pp. 142–55.

Guariglia, A. and Poncet, S. (2008) Could financial distortions be no impediment to economic growth after all? Evidence from China. *Journal of Comparative Economics*, **36**(4), December, 633–57.

Guillaumont Jeanneney, S., Hua, P. and Liang, Z. (2006) Financial development, economic efficiency and productivity growth: evidence from China. *The Developing Economies*, **44**(1), March, 27–52.

Hao, C. (2006) Development of financial intermediation and economic growth: the Chinese experience. *China Economic Review*, **17**(4), 347–62.

Hasan, I., Wachtel, P. and Zhou, M. (2009) Institutional development, financial deepening and economic growth: evidence from China. *Journal of Banking & Finance*, **33**(1), January, 157–70.

Heilmann, S. (2002) The Chinese Stock Market: pitfalls of a policy-driven market. *China Analysis*, No. 15 (September). Available from: *www.chinapolitik.de*

Heilmann, S. (2005) Regulatory innovation by Leninist means: Communist Party supervision in China's financial industry. *China Quarterly*, **181**, March, 1–21.

Herrmann-Pillath, C. (1994) *Soziale Marktwirtschaft in China*. Leske + Budrich Verlag, Opladen, Germany [in German].

Huang, Y. (2008) *Capitalism with Chinese Characteristics: Entrepreneurship and the State*. Cambridge University Press, London.

Hui, H. (2010) Institutional structure of financial regulation in China: lessons from the global financial crisis. *Journal of Corporate Law Studies*, **10**(1), 219–54.

Kazer, W. (2013) China Minsheng Banking turns to small-business loans. *Wall Street Journal*, 29 August 2013.

Li, C. (2013) *Shadow Banking in China: Expanding Scale, Evolving Structure*. Federal Reserve Bank of San Francisco, San Francisco, CA.

Liang, Q. and Teng, J.-Z. (2006) Financial development and economic growth: evidence from China. *China Economic Review*, **17**(4), 395–411.

Martin, M.F. (2012) *China's Banking System: Issues for Congress*. Congress Research Service, Washington, DC.

Miller, A. (2008) The CCP Central Committee's leading small groups. *China Leadership Monitor*, **26**.

Naughton, B. (2007) *The Chinese Economy: Transition and Growth*. MIT Press, London.

Nee, V. and Opper, S. (2012) *Capitalism from Below: Markets and Institutional Change in China*. Harvard University Press, Cambridge, MA.

NGAM (2013) *Asie émergente – Chine: comment est financée l'économie chinoise?* (Note Mensuelle, Janvier, No. 1, Recherche Economique). Natixis Global Asset Management, Paris.

Noelke, A. (2013) International regulation and domestic coalitions in state-permeated capitalism: China and global banking regulation. Paper presented at *Annual Meeting of the SASE Annual Conference 2012*. MIT Press, Cambridge, MA.

Orlik, T. (2013) Debt drags on China's growth. *Wall Street Journal*, 26 August 2013.

Pearson, M.M. (2007) Governing the Chinese economy: regulatory reform in the service of the state. *Public Administration Review*, **67**(4), July/August, 718–30.

Pearson, M.M. (2010) The impact of the PRC's economic crisis response on regulatory institutions. *China Analysis*, **78**, February. Available from: *http://www.chinapolitik.de*.

People's Daily Online (2013) Organizational status of the CPC, 29 March 2013. Available from: *http://english.cpc.people.com.cn/206972/206981/8188126.html* [accessed 10 December 2013].

SASAC (2013) Central SOEs. Available from: *http://www.sasac.gov.cn/n2963340/n2971121/n4956567/4956583.html* [accessed 10 December 2013] [State Assets Supervision and Administration Commission].

Shan, J. and Qi, J. (2006) Does financial development 'lead' economic growth? The case of China. *Annals of Economics and Finance*, **1**, 197–216.

Sheng, A. and Geng, X. (2013) Lending in the dark. *Project Syndicate*, 22 April.

Shih, V. (2007) *Factions and Finance in China: Elite Conflict and Inflation*. Cambridge University Press, Cambridge, UK.

Ten Brink, T. (2012) Kapitalistische Entwicklung in China Entstehungskontexte, Verlaufsformen und Paradoxien eines eigentümlichen Modernisierungsprozesses. Habilitationsschrift, Goethe Universität, Frankfurt am Main, Germany [in German].

The Economist (2013) Reform in China: the party's new blueprint (Economist online, 16 November 2013). Available from: *http://www.economist.com/blogs/analects/2013/11/reform-china* [accessed 7 December 2013].

Walter, C.E. and Howie, F.J.T. (2011) *Red Capitalism: The Fragile Financial Foundation of China's Extraordinary Rise*. John Wiley & Sons, Singapore.

Walter, A. and Zhang Xiaoke (2012) *East Asian Capitalism: Diversity, Continuity, and Change*. Oxford University Press, London.

Wang, Y. (2003) *China's Economic Development and Democratization*. Ashgate, Aldershot, UK.

Wei, X. (2006) EU FDI to China: locational determinants and lessons from an enlarged European Union. Unpublished PhD thesis, University of Limerick, Ireland.

Witt, M.A. (2010) *China: What Variety of Capitalism?* (INSEAD Working Paper No. 2010/88/EPS). INSEAD, Fontainebleau, France.

Xinhua News Agency (2013) CPC's 'mass line' campaign not a short-term movement, 15 July 2013. Available from: *http://english.cpc.people.com.cn/206972/206976/8325279.html* [accessed 10 December 2013].

Zhang, Z. and Chen, W. (2013) *China: Rising Risks of Financial Crisis* (Asia Special Report). Nomura Global Economics, Hongkong, China, 15 March.

Zheng Tianyong and Zhu Lianyu (2008) Wo guo jinrong tizhi gaige yu shichang fazhan 30 nian. Zhongguo gaige kaifang 30 nian. *Fazhan he gaige lanpishu*, Vol. 8. CASS, Beijing [in Chinese].

8

The effects of the global financial crisis on the Shanghai stock market

Su Qian Kong, Lucía Morales and Joseph Coughlan

Abstract: Since the 1990s the Chinese financial market has experienced dramatic changes by virtue of the aim to consolidate the country's transition from a central planned economy towards a market-oriented one. China was able to create a respectable stock market from scratch in the early 1990s, and its performance has been characterised by better behaviour, when compared with other transition economies, regarding market fundraising capacity, liquidity and capitalisation levels. China's stock market capitalisation has become the second largest in the Asian region, after Japan. Due to the prominent role of the Chinese economy and the continuous development of both its stock market and financial system, this study focuses on understanding the effects of the global financial crisis on China's mainland stock market. Our analysis looks at contagion and/or spillover effects originating in the US stock market to understand how they impacted on the Shanghai Stock Exchange. We look to identify whether the Shanghai Stock Exchange is affected by global shocks or whether it is more prone to regional shock waves emanating from major local markets. Regional analysis focuses its attention on the Hong Kong and Singapore stock exchanges, well-established markets in the region with strong connections to the Shanghai Stock Exchange. Using the extended Forbes and Rigobon (2002) contagion methodology, this research finds significant evidence supporting the existence of spillover effects in the Asian stock market derived from the US. Nevertheless, our findings do not justify the existence of contagion effects running from the US or from the regional markets. Instead, the Hong Kong and Singapore stock markets appeared to be the ones affected by regional contagion effects. We also found that the Chinese stock market made a quick recovery after the global financial crisis, which could have contributed to the enhancement of contagion effects in the regional markets.

Key words: Shanghai Composite, Hang Seng Index, Straits Times Index, market contagion, spillover effects and global financial crisis.

Introduction

The US financial crisis rapidly spread to the rest of the world's economies due to the interconnectedness of international financial systems, an interconnectedness that is enhanced by increased levels of market globalisation. In the case of China, these effects are more visible, as the country is transitioning from a centralised economy towards a market one through the implementation of fiscal and financial policies that have their origins in the early 1980s. In September 2008 – at the time of Lehman Brothers' collapse – the Shanghai market index was about 70 per cent below its registered level in October 2007 (Lai and Yang, 2009). This low position was short lived, as the Chinese stock market reacted in a positive manner when Beijing responded decisively to the initial effects of the financial crisis on trading performance. On 9 November 2008, the government announced a fiscal stimulus of ¥4 trillion ($586 billion). This announcement was followed by strong market behaviour that led towards stabilisation and recovery (Overholt, 2010, p. 28). Looking back to the 1997/98 Asian crisis, strong evidence was found in relation to the Chinese stock market being also less affected by the chain of events than other financial markets (like, for example, Thailand, Indonesia, Philippines and Malaysia) in South Asia (Arestis et al., 2005; Cartapanis et al., 2002; Chia Siow, 1998; Dungey et al., 2004). At the time, although the Chinese economy suffered a loss in demand and confidence in the financial markets, the pace of recovery was faster because of the speedy reaction of the government to regulate its financial market. For example, growth-oriented policies were changed from export led to domestic consumption led. In addition, capital controls during the Asian financial crisis helped the Chinese economy to escape from attacks by international speculators (Chin, 2010; Lardy, 1998). Therefore, it is of great interest to examine the downturn, relating to the current international financial crisis, in the Chinese mainland stock market, and to investigate whether there is sufficient evidence demonstrating the existence of contagion effects emanating from the US stock market or whether China managed, once more, to emerge relatively unscathed by a major global shock.

The Chinese financial market is becoming more mature and integrated with the domestic economy and with international financial markets after years of effort and development. On the Chinese mainland, financial regulation has been relaxed since the introduction of reform policies in 2003. The new policies aimed to create incentives that attracted foreign direct investment into the country. Formerly, foreigners were not allowed to buy and sell shares in China's stock exchanges due to tight capital controls exercised by the government. Foreign investors were, from 2003 onwards, permitted to trade Class A shares under the QFII (Qualified Foreign Institutional Investors) program that licensed investors to buy and sell yuan-denominated shares. Moreover, the Hong Kong stock market has been considered the most globally integrated stock market in the region (Ding, 2010). This market acts as an intermediary between China's mainland stock market and international financial markets due to its economic interdependence and its close historical, and political, relationship with mainland China. As a result, a substantial amount of capital flows into the Chinese mainland financial market from the Hong Kong stock market. Most large Chinese state-owned companies' shares are also traded on the Hong Kong stock market.

The Hong Kong stock market has a multilateral relationship with mainland Chin and the world's financial market, which has contributed to enhancing the interaction and transmission of information between the Chinese mainland, Hong Kong and world stock markets. He et al. (2009) suggest that the Hong Kong stock market is more aligned with the US stock market during turbulent times, while it appears to be more integrated with the mainland Chinese market during times of normality. Substantial capital flows into the Chinese mainland financial system from the Hong Kong stock market (Yang and Lim, 2004), as most large Chinese state-owned companies' shares are traded on the Hong Kong stock market, which provides another channel for global investors to diversify their investment in China.

It is also worth considering the Singapore stock market, as this market shares some similarities with the Hong Kong stock market. Both are considered developed equity markets in the Asian region, and they share a strong positive correlation and strong connection with the Chinese stock market (Ding, 2010). The Chinese economy plays an important role in the Asian region, owing to intra-regional trade and mainland Chinese companies being cross-listed both on the Hong Kong and Singapore stock markets (Johansson, 2012). Accordingly, cross-listing could be considered as a source of instability through the region. Looking into the potential transmission of shocks from the US financial system might not only be subject to a direct effect from the US, as the main regional markets may also act as a channel for volatility between the US financial market and the Chinese stock market. In addition, we have identified a clear lack of research looking into integration relationships between the Chinese mainland stock market and the Singapore stock market. Therefore, our study aims to contribute to the field by considering the role of the Singapore stock market in the measurement of regional contagion.

The main purpose of this chapter is to gain a better understanding of Chinese stock market behaviour during times of financial turmoil and its implications for multinational corporations when designing their diversification and investment strategies. The analysis aims to extend the Forbes and Rigobon (2002) contagion methodology to distinguish whether the US financial crisis generated contagion effects in the Shanghai stock market or whether the Hong Kong or Singapore financial markets could be considered as sources of China's financial instability. Being able to identify how China might be exposed to global financial events will help investors to identify diversification strategies that are more efficient and that take into consideration not only global but also regional risks. We argue that China seems to be more integrated with its regional markets and, consequently, investors need to be aware of the need to integrate regional strategies that allows them to hedge more specific risks if they wish to protect their investments in the Asian region.

The remainder of the chapter is organised as follows: in the next section ('Literature review') a general review of the literature in this area is presented and critically discussed. This is followed by a section on the data and methodology adopted to support this study. There then follows a section ('Research findings and analysis') which deals with the discussions of our main research outcomes and a 'Conclusions' section.

Literature review

Until now academics and practitioners have not been able to agree on a single definition of what actually constitutes contagion. The complexity of defining contagion limits the ability of researchers to investigate the full impact and damage that financial crises could cause to countries' economies and poses extraordinary limits on their predictive capacity and ability to design fiscal and monetary policies that counteract market shocks in an effective manner. The research developed by Forbes and Rigobon (2002) used a basic definition to deal with contagion in the financial context. The authors referred to contagion as: 'a significant increase in cross-market linkages after a shock to the country' (p. 2223). This definition states that contagion is evident when co-movement increases dramatically following a shock. The authors also use the term 'shift-contagion'. This makes sense because it not only clarifies that contagion arises from a shift in cross-market linkages, but it also avoids taking a stance on how this shift occurs (Forbes and Rigobon, 2002). If co-movement is not significant enough to affect market correlations, the authors indicate that it should then be known as market interdependence because of its macro-fundamental linkages such as trading behaviour. Therefore, we should consider with care how stock market correlations are impacted by shocks with the aim of identifying a major shift in their behaviour. Otherwise, there would not be evidence of market contagion effects and they should be categorised as normal spillover effects. This definition of contagion is adopted in this chapter, because it is very clear and allows us to develop a well-defined framework for testing contagion effects. In our analysis, the linkage between stock markets in a stable period is treated as the expected correlation level. Consequently, the excess of correlation between these markets will be deemed as evidence confirming the existence of contagion between these markets having its main origins in the US subprime crisis. In addition, we test contagion effects in a regional manner through the introduction of the Hong Kong and Singapore stock market indices in our econometric model. In this manner, we are able to differentiate between global and regional effects offering greater clarity on how the Chinese stock market reacted to the global financial crisis.

Three main channels of contagion can be identified: (i) financial, (ii) trade and (iii) competitiveness. Contagion is associated with a high degree of volatility in capital movements, where large reversals occur in short-term capital flows. This chapter focuses on the financial channel of contagion, because the trade and competitive channels can be treated as normal due to countries' macroeconomic linkages.

Contagion research examining the Asian crisis

Since 1997, a vast literature dedicated to analysing the Asian crisis has emerged. This has given rise to interest being shown in understanding how shocks propagate at regional and international levels by financial and economic analysts – not only academics. Yang et al. (2003) used a vector autoregressive (VAR) approach to examine long-run and short-run dynamic causal linkages among ten Asian emerging stock markets (Hong Kong, Singapore, Korea, Taiwan, India, Indonesia, Malaysia, Pakistan,

Philippines and Thailand) and two developed markets (Japan and the US). Comparative analyses of the pre-crisis, crisis and post-crisis periods were conducted by the authors with the aim of understanding market behaviour during times of stability, turmoil and recovery. The authors found that the Hong Kong stock market became a more influential market in the Asian region after the crisis, as Asian markets became significantly more responsive to innovations implemented in the Hong Kong market during the crisis. At the time, the Singapore stock market was identified as the most integrated and influential market in the region in that during the crisis it became a 'victim' of its exposure to the other markets. According to Yang et al. (2003) 'the crisis caused the victim markets to be more responsive to external shocks from non-victim markets' (p. 485). In this regard, we expect that the Hong Kong and Singapore stock markets would be the most integrated markets in the region, and as a result they should be more responsive to shocks originating from the US stock market than other developing stock markets in the Asian region. Hence, our initial hypothesis explores the belief that the Chinese stock market should display a strong reaction to market volatility in the region rather being driven by direct exposure to global shocks.

Another study analysing the information transmitted among the Chinese, Hong Kong and Singapore stock markets was carried out by Cajueiro and Tabak (2004). Their study investigated long-range dependence phenomena in these markets. The authors' main findings suggest that these markets present long-memory dependence, implying that shocks affecting these markets will persist over time. These findings indicate that their market behaviour is not independent and precaution needs to be taken, as shocks will be transmitted and would persist in the markets. Furthermore, the authors identified Hong Kong as the most efficient stock market followed by Chinese Class A shares and the Singapore stock market, while Chinese Class B shares were highlighted as exhibiting more inefficient behaviour. These results indicate that this market dependency hinges on market liquidity levels and any capital restrictions that might be imposed by national governments.

Contagion effects in a sample of East Asian stock markets were studied by Yang and Lim (2004). The authors explored the importance of linkages between stock markets as a transmission channel during the currency crisis. The VAR approach was employed, and the authors found that shocks or impacts due to market innovations were short lived. After the 1997 currency crisis, a substantial increase in the degree of interdependence was recorded and latent evidence on the existence of contagion effects in the region was found. Evidence of contagion effects was also found by Chen and Poon (2007) during the Asian crisis. They used copula modelling and risk appetite analysis to look for the existence of contagion effects. After controlling for heteroskedasticity, they found clear evidence suggesting the existence of contagion effects during the Asian crisis. They suggested that developed financial markets were more prone to financial crises and contagion effects than developing financial markets. Their findings were supported by the use of the same research method to examine five other extreme events: two terrorist attacks, corporate scandals in the US (Enron, WorldCom), the LTCM (Long Term Capital Management fund) default and the Internet bubble burst; all events that took place in the last decade. In line with their initial findings in former studies, they corroborated the existence of contagion effects among the Asian stock markets during the Asian crisis. The stock markets in this region are characterised by being more integrated due to their strong trade linkages and geographical closeness, a feature that helps to support initial findings of contagion effects among Asian stock markets.

Contagion research on the 2007 financial crisis

More recent research papers have focused their attention on the global financial crisis. They have tried to understand its origins, effects and general implications for the world economy. Researchers have used various models to investigate whether or not contagion effects exist between the US stock market and emerging stock markets. They have tried to understand how the financial crisis might spread to the world economy, and comparative analyses looking at the Asian Crisis have been developed. Cheung et al. (2008) employed the Forbes and Rigobon (2002) method to test for financial contagion and they did not find significant evidence of contagion between equity markets in the US and the EMEA (Europe, Middle East and Africa) region. However, the authors were unable to assess whether contagion took place after the collapse of the US investment bank Lehman Brothers in September 2008, due to the limited data available at the time of their research. In addition, their analysis did not take into consideration the Asian region and the issues being addressed in this chapter.

Another study on financial contagion was conducted by Ogum (2010). In this case there was only limited evidence of contagion effects in conditional correlations, even though the US stock market influenced conditional variances of emerging market economies during the period January 2005 to June 2009. However, his research assumed the occurrence of a structural breakpoint on 1 March 2007 because of the

Black Tuesday stock market crash, but there was no formal test to support this assumption. Morales and Andreosso-O'Callaghan (2010) used the Forbes and Rigobon (2002) contagion approach and two other research methodologies; they also included an extra variable to measure for regional effects to investigate the existence of contagion in a broad sample consisting of the stock markets of 58 countries. The authors used three different models to test for contagion effects and found that two of their models showed little evidence of contagion effects from the US stock market affecting the countries under study. However, a significant result that is relevant to our study is evidence suggesting that the contagion effects, as per the results of the classical Forbes and Rigobon method, that affected the Shanghai stock market did come from the US. However, after the addition of an extra variable controlling for regional effects, the results changed suggesting that the Shanghai Stock Exchange did not have contagion effects from the US and that regional effects were more appropriate to explain market instability in China.

The vulnerability of countries to financial crises was analysed by Frankel and Saravelos (2010). They reviewed more than 80 previous papers on early-warning indicators in order to investigate the leading indicators for cross-country incidence of the 2008/09 financial crisis. The authors stated that 'a country is considered more vulnerable if it experienced larger output drops, bigger stock market falls, greater currency weakness, larger losses in reserves, or the need for access to IMF funds' (p. 2). In their study, they included six variables: drops in GDP and industrial production, currency depreciation, stock market performance, reserve losses, or participation in an IMF programme to measure the 2008/09 crisis incidence. They found that the lower the level of reserves and the existence of currency devaluations in the market appeared as leading indicators of the current crisis.

From the above literature, it is clear that most studies suggested there was evidence supporting the existence of regional contagion during the Asian crisis, but there is no clear suggestion that contagion exists between the US and Chinese stock market during the current crisis. However, there is also a gap in the research in terms of regional contagion derived from the subprime crisis. The Chinese stock market is found to be more integrated with regional financial markets than with the world financial market, when it comes to Chinese stock market liquidity and regulation restrictions. Therefore, this research focusses not only on the US and mainland Chinese stock markets, but also includes the Hong Kong and Singapore stock markets as intermediaries to spillover shocks running from the US stock market to mainland Chinese stock markets.

Data and methodology

The data used in this study include daily prices from the following indices: the Shanghai Composite index (SH), the Standard and Poor's 500 (SP), the Hang Seng Index (HS), and the Straits Times Index (ST). All data were taken from Datastream, covering the period from January 2006 to June 2012. Daily observations were used as this frequency was identified as appropriate at capturing relevant information due to price movements. As the markets under study were located in different regions, time zone effects were considered by applying relevant VAR techniques that helped identify the appropriate number of lags for use in our time series modelling. We looked at stock indices from the perspective of the same currency, as estimations could then be deemed to provide more accurate results. Therefore, all the stock indices in this study are valued in US dollars.

The Shanghai Composite index is China's main stock market index. Since 2009 many investors have considered the trend of the Shanghai Composite as a potential leading indicator for the US stock market. The reason behind this is that the Shanghai Composite peaked just prior to the US market in 2007 and troughed ahead of the US in 2009. The S&P 500 is a leading indicator of US equities and one of the most commonly used benchmarks for the overall US stock market; consequently, we considered it appropriate to use this index as our main indicator to measure the performance of the US stock market during the global financial crisis. The Hang Seng Index is the leading index for shares traded on the Hong Kong Stock Exchange; it also tracks the performance of Chinese state-owned enterprises listed on the Hong Kong stock market. The Straits Times Index allows 24-hour trading, tracks the performance of large companies based in Singapore and also observes and captures changes in international stock markets.

To get a better picture of the change in trading behaviour during the global financial crisis and its potential transmission effects towards the Chinese stock market, a dummy variable is created to ensure that a clear division is made between the crisis and normality periods that would be determined by the identified breakpoint. The rest of this section provides a general discussion on the basic econometric tests that are implemented to ensure our results are neither biased nor spurious.

Stationary series

The initial econometric test used to analyse the properties of our series was the traditional Dickey–Fuller test. The analysis of stationarity in our series is core to ensuring our model outcomes are valid and that we do not end up developing an analysis that could be considered spurious. This research relies on the well-known Augmented Dickey-Fuller (ADF) test (Dickey and Fuller, 1979, 1981) which is used to determine the order of integration of our series, such that the number of unit roots present in each of the variables can be inferred.

Series stability

The long-run relationship between financial time series can be affected or changed by the existence of structural breaks due to a sudden/unexpected change in behaviour of the series, such as financial market crises. To take this issue into account Gregory Chow introduced the Chow test in 1960 (Chow, 1960) for a linear model with one known single break in mean. In this research, we were interested in identifying a common breakpoint that affected all four of our series. Therefore, the Chow text would be used in support of the Quandt–Andrews (Andrews, 1993; Quandt, 1960) approach that would help us understand how we could break down our series to determine the common starting point of the global financial crisis.

In order to find a common breakpoint for our four variables, the residuals of the ordinary least squares (OLS) equation were used. The residuals were estimated based on the following equation:

$$Y_t = \alpha_0 + \beta_1 X_t + \delta_1 Z_t + \gamma_1 W_t + \varepsilon_t \tag{8.1}$$

where Y_t = the Shanghai Composite index; X_t = the S&P 500 index; Z_t = the Hang Seng Index; and W_t = the Straits Times Index.

A common structural breakpoint can be achieved by conducting the Chow test on the residuals obtained from the above regression. However, when there is more than one known breakpoint, the Chow test needs to test each possible breakpoint. In order to simplify the process and improve the accuracy of our estimation, the Quandt–Andrews breakpoint test (Andrews, 1993) was adopted in combination with the Chow test. However, the distribution of this statistic is non-standard, and therefore we verified the consistency of our result by running an individual Chow test to confirm that a structural change in the relationship occurred in the identified period. Afterwards, a dummy variable was created to count the identified breakpoint, which helped us progress our contagion analysis.

The Forbes and Rigobon (2002) contagion approach

Contagion occurs when financial shocks experienced in one country are transferred to another country's financial system. The initial test introduced to measure contagion effects can be linked to the methodology developed by Forbes and Rigobon in 2002. Their research approach considered the use of correlations and covariance analysis to determine whether the correlation between two stock indices is affected by a dramatic increase during a market shock, also termed a crisis period. In order to test for changes in correlation we transformed our variables into returns as follows:

$$R(y_t) = \ln(y_t) - \ln(y_{t-1}) \qquad (8.2)$$

All four variables were transformed into returns as shown in Eq. 8.2 for the specific case of China. Afterwards, we identified all pre-crisis index returns, which allowed us to estimate their respective standard deviations for the 'normality' period that would then be used to correct our series for abnormal behaviour.

Pre-crisis regression using scaled returns is defined as follows:

$$\left(\frac{x_{2,t}}{\sigma_{x,2}}\right) = \alpha_0 + \alpha_1\left(\frac{x_{1,t}}{\sigma_{x,1}}\right) + \eta_{x,t} \qquad (8.3)$$

All variables have zero mean and α is a regression parameter, which is related to the pre-crisis correlation coefficient as $\alpha_1 = \rho_x$. The dependent variable is the country that is being analysed for contagion effects, the returns from which are scaled to correct for abnormal behaviour. The independent variable accounts for the scaled returns of the country in which the contagion effects are deemed to originate. This equation is applied to all of our four variables.

Regression during the crisis period regression is given as follows (with crisis returns scaled by respective pre-crisis standard deviations):

$$\left(\frac{y_{2,t}}{\sigma_{x,2}}\right) = \beta_0 + \beta_1\left(\frac{y_{1,t}}{\sigma_{x,1}}\right) + \eta_{y,t} \qquad (8.4)$$

where β_1 is a regression parameter that is related to the Forbes–Rigobon adjusted correlation coefficient $\beta_1 = \nu_y$.

The above standard deviation is calculated by assuming that volatility during a stable period is constant and stable over time. We deem this approach as inappropriate, as the market environment is often subject to considerable changes. Therefore, we consider that it is unreasonable to assume that asset risk would be constant during a stable period. A common technique to assess the constancy of parameters is to compute parameter estimates over a rolling window approach of fixed size through the sample under study. The rolling window approach is used to capture changes in market returns during a stable period (Harris and Jian, 2003). Therefore, our estimation is based on a standard deviation calculated from a rolling window approach which is expected to be more accurate, as it considers any potential changes in market volatility.

Another way of implementing the Forbes–Rigobon adjusted correlation method is by running an OLS regression on the two pooled regressions and testing their parameters for significance.

The overall pooled equation is presented as follows:

$$\left(\frac{z_{2,t}}{\sigma_{x,2}}\right) = \gamma_0 + \gamma_1 d_t + \gamma_2\left(\frac{z_{1,t}}{\sigma_{x,1}}\right) + \gamma_3\left(\frac{z_{1,t}}{\sigma_{x,1}}\right)d_t + \eta_t \qquad (8.5)$$

where $z_i = (x_{i,j}, x_{i,2}, \ldots, x_{i,T_x}; y_{i,j}, y_{i,2}, \ldots, y_{i,T_y})$, $i = 1, 2, \ldots$, d_t is a dummy variable with a value of 1 if $t > T_x$ (which is based on the stability test) and 0 otherwise.

The effect of contagion is given by the parameter $\gamma_3 = \beta_1 - \alpha_1$, which represents the additional contribution made by information on stock index returns in our variables to pre-crisis regression. If there is no change in the relationship, the dummy variable provides no new additional information during the crisis period, resulting in $\gamma_3 = 0$. In this study, the Forbes–Rigobon method is implemented by estimating pooled regression, and carrying out a one-sided t-test on γ_3 using the following hypothesis:

Null hypothesis H_0: $\gamma_3 = 0$ (equivalent to $\beta_1 = \alpha_1$)

Alternative hypothesis $H_A : \gamma_3 > 0$

If the null hypothesis is rejected, we can conclude that there is sufficient evidence to support the existence of contagion from shocks between the variables under study. Let us put this into context: this implies that we are considering, as our main research issue, contagion effects running from the US stock market to the Chinese stock market as well as to two other regional markets. The researchers are aware that the Forbes and Rigobon test for contagion is a simple and basic contagion approach with weaknesses that affect model estimation. For example, the model uses a constant pre-crisis standard deviation to scale stock market returns with the aim of correcting for heteroskedasticity, but these issues are minimised throughout by using a rolling window approach.

Using the above methods, we have been able to identify seven contagion equations, which are summarised in this chapter's 'Appendix'. These equations were mainly used to test for contagion effects from the US stock market to the Chinese stock market. In addition, we complemented our analysis by studying regional contagion effects, where we introduced the Hang Seng and the Straits Times indices as key variables to understanding whether China reacted to the US crisis as a direct effect of contagion or whether the country was reacting to instability in the regional markets. Our main findings are discussed and examined in the next section.

Research findings and analysis

This research starts with a discussion of our stationary analysis. We find that the raw financial data are non-stationary, whereas our returns are stationary. This suggests our series are integrated at level one. These initial outcomes allow us to proceed with our econometric analysis and thereby avoid the spurious regression problem.

After 2006, markets were affected by substantial instability. The origins of this instability could be traced back to the US market. However, there is no agreement with regard to a specific breakpoint indicating when market instability was at its highest, and this makes it difficult to identify when the global financial crisis actually started and, consequently, how it spread to the other world economies. Difficulties in estimating the breakpoint are highlighted by the different approaches that have been followed by studies and by the variety of data, frequencies, models, approaches and theories employed, all of which makes estimation of a clear breakpoint difficult. For example, George (2010) assumes that the crisis started on 1 March 2007 (Black Tuesday); Morales and Andreosso (2010) consider the initial stock market downturn to be 15 October 2007 after they carried out a Chow test on the US stock markets (Dow Jones Industrial and S&P 500). A common approach is to take the collapse of Lehman Brothers as the main reference point. Of the different approaches that could be taken, we considered it appropriate to base our breakpoint identification on the results of our Eq. 8.1. The results are presented in Table 8.1.

The results show a discrepancy with regard to the starting point of market instability. By conducting an analysis on the series residuals as indicated in Eq. 8.1, we identify the breakpoint guiding our research as

Table 8.1 Series breakpoint

	Shanghai Composite	S&P 500 Composite	Hang Seng Composite	Straits Times Index	OLS residual
Breakpoint[a]	10/17/2007	10/02/2008	10/31/2007	10/03/2008	08/20/2007

[a]The breakpoints identified were significant at 1 per cent.

20 August 2007. This result is consistent with the results of Frankel and Saravelos (2010) who used a similar approach.

The structural breakpoint in the Shanghai Composite Index is identified as 17 October 2007. It is earlier than the breakpoint of the Hang Seng Index (31 October 2007) and far earlier than that of the S&P 500 (2 October 2008) and that of the Straits Times Index (3 October 2008). These results clearly show that the Hong Kong stock market seems to be more aligned with the behaviour of the Chinese mainland stock market, while the Singapore stock market is more in line with the US stock market. The Singapore stock market is considered one of the most integrated markets in the region, and as a result it appears to be more responsive to shocks coming from the US stock market than is the case with Hong Kong or China. The trading conditions of each market could be the reason for this. The Straits Times is operated on a continuous basis (24-hour period) allowing it to reflect movements in the international stock market immediately. Consequently, the Hong Kong stock market can react quickly to any changes in the Singapore stock market and act as an intermediary that transfers a signal and/or information to the Chinese financial market. This could justify the argument that the Chinese stock market is more exposed to regional instability than to global shocks.

Market volatility can be initially measured by its standard deviation. In Table 8.2 we present computed standard deviations (SD) following both a static and a rolling window approach. Rolling window outcomes provide a smoother measure of volatility and are more appropriate when measuring for contagion. The Shanghai stock market appears to be the most volatile market, while the S&P 500 seems to be the more stable during periods of normality (before the identified breakpoint). Initial results indicate that the Shanghai stock market, as a developing market, is subject to higher levels of risk than developed and well-established markets. However, this outcome is not entirely reflective of the country's economic behaviour or the measures taken by the government to ensure stability through strong regulation and capital restrictions.

Table 8.2 Standard deviations[a] for periods of normality

Stock indices	SD without rolling window	SD with rolling window
Shanghai Composite	0.0174	0.0147
Straits Times	0.0111	0.0098
Hang Seng	0.0107	0.0096
S&P 500	0.0072	0.0064

[a]Estimated standard deviations for periods of normality. Sample period before the breakpoint estimated as 20 August 2007.

Estimated results measuring contagion effects derived from the S&P 500 or developed regional stock markets (Hang Seng or Straits Times) in the Shanghai stock market are depicted in Table 8.3.

The results show no evidence of contagion affecting the Shanghai stock market from the S&P 500. This result is in line with previous research (Cheung et al., 2008; Morales and Andreosso-O'Callaghan, 2010) in which the Chinese stock market did not appear to react to shocks from the US and a regional effect was found to be more relevant. The Chinese

Table 8.3 Contagion results

	Returns scaled by standard deviation	Returns scaled by adjusted standard deviation	
Equations	Coefficient	Coefficient	p-value
SH c SP	−0.0738	−0.0771	0.1589
SH c HS	0.0614	0.0651	0.1885
SH c ST	0.0755	0.0786	0.1421
HS c SP	0.0777	0.0766	0.3423
ST c SP	0.0933	0.0937	0.1544
HS c ST	0.1883[a]	0.1849[a]	0.0007
ST c HS	−0.1519[a]	−0.1547[a]	0.0006

Note: [a]statistical significance at 1 per cent level. SH = Shanghai; SP = Standard & Poor's 500; HS = Hang Seng; ST = Straits Times; c = contagion.

stock market downturn could be characterised as a spillover effect rather than as 'shift-contagion', as per the definition offered by Forbes and Rigobon (2002). The inevitable economic depression that then affected the US, one of China's major trading partners, has had an impact on Chinese exports and industries that have clear connections with the US consumer market. However, the incompletely open capital market and the high levels of savings that characterise the domestic economy allowed the Chinese government to reverse the decline in exports quickly by expanding domestic demand and stimulating national investment. Consequently, the Chinese stock market did not seem to react to the US financial meltdown as did other world economies, because the government was able to introduce macroeconomic and financial policies that helped minimise and limit the depth of the stock market decline.

The next issue to consider is the role played by regional economies: whether the Hong Kong and/or Singapore stock markets are acting as a propagation mechanism between the Chinese stock market and international financial markets. Looking at our results, we did not find significant evidence of contagion effects between the Shanghai Composite index and the Hang Seng Index nor between the Shanghai Composite and the Straits Times Index. Furthermore, there is no evidence to suggest the existence of contagion effects from the S&P 500 to the Hang Seng Index or Straits Times Index. These results suggest that the financial market decline experienced in the Asian region matches a spillover effect from the US stock market and that contagion did not take place during the global financial crisis. The damage in the Asian region appears to be relatively less severe than the situation in the US stock market during the financial crisis, as Asian markets were able to recover faster. An interesting finding from our study is the contagion relationship that exists between the Hang Seng and Straits Times indices, which indicates strong co-movement between the Hong Kong and Singapore stock markets, which seemed to increase in a significant manner after the global financial crisis. Our findings are similar to those of Ding (2010) indicating that the Chinese stock market has low correlations with other Asian markets and the US market. On the other hand, Hong Kong and Singapore show stronger correlations with regional stock markets than international ones. Ding (2010) believes that the degree of correlation depends on the degree of openness of each country. For example, the country openness number for the US is 111 (rank 1), Hong Kong 532 (rank 81), Singapore 576 (rank 91), China 924 (rank 165). Hong Kong and Singapore are aligned at a similar level of country openness, indicating that these two markets work closely and are more reactive to global shocks like the financial crisis, a result that agrees with our own findings.

Conclusions

This study examines whether there is evidence of contagion effects on the Shanghai Composite, Hang Seng and Straits Times indices from the US. Stock index returns experienced a significant decline that had spillover effects on Asian countries rather than contagion effects. Stock markets in the Asian region emerge as being able to recover more quickly than the US stock market. For example, the Chinese stock market was able to react quicker to market instability, as the Chinese authorities were able to introduce stimulus measures to enhance national investment combined with policies that aimed to encourage domestic demand due to high levels of savings. This innovation in the Chinese stock market created a positive effect in the region, helping the Chinese economy to achieve high and stable growth rates that attracted the attention of regional and global investors. However, the Chinese financial market is still considered to be developing and its stock market is not entirely reflective of its economy nor, in turn, of the economies that have strong trade connections with China like the US. Therefore, we think that future research into contagion effects needs to consider alternative variables, because looking at stock market performance in isolation prevents understanding how the country could be better prepared to react to and correct negative shocks affecting its economic performance. For example, when considering the level of exchange rate pressure suffered by the country, the level of inflation and the level of foreign currency reserves held in China, it would be useful to further explore how these variables might define market independence and contagion relationships. This is important as it would likely facilitate future research into how the market reacted after the crisis period, and the way in which investors perceived the country's financial system.

Appendix

Stock market indices

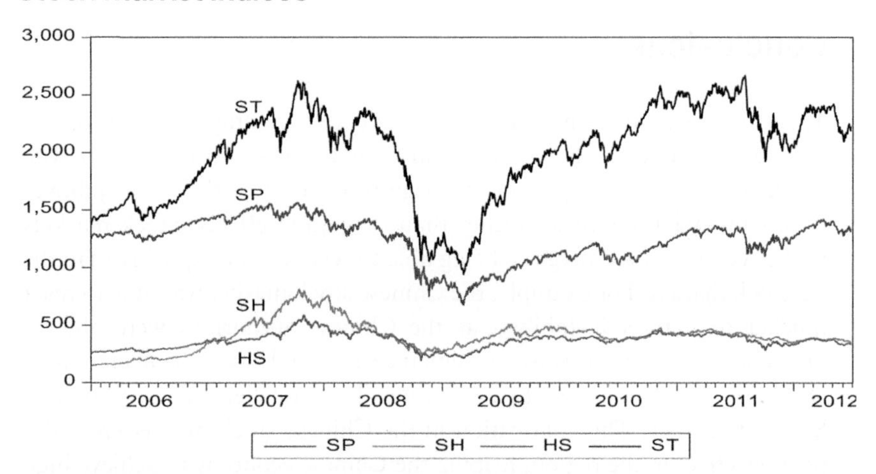

SP = Standard & Poor's 500; SH = Shanghai Composite index; HS = Hang Seng Index; ST = Strait Times Index.

Seven contagion equations

Contagion form	Equation No.	Equations
SH c SP 500	1	$\left(\frac{R_{sh,t}}{\sigma_{sh}}\right) = \gamma_0 + \gamma_1 d_t + \gamma_2\left(\frac{R_{sp,t}}{\sigma_{sp}}\right) + \gamma_3\left(\frac{R_{sp,t}}{\sigma_{sp}}\right)d_t + \eta_t$
SH c HS	2	$\left(\frac{R_{sh,t}}{\sigma_{sh}}\right) = \gamma_0 + \gamma_1 d_t + \gamma_2\left(\frac{R_{hs,t}}{\sigma_{hs}}\right) + \gamma_3\left(\frac{R_{hs,t}}{\sigma_{hs}}\right)d_t + \eta_t$
SH c ST	3	$\left(\frac{R_{sh,t}}{\sigma_{sh}}\right) = \gamma_0 + \gamma_1 d_t + \gamma_2\left(\frac{R_{st,t}}{\sigma_{st}}\right) + \gamma_3\left(\frac{R_{st,t}}{\sigma_{st}}\right)d_t + \eta_t$
HS c SP 500	4	$\left(\frac{R_{hs,t}}{\sigma_{hs}}\right) = \gamma_0 + \gamma_1 d_t + \gamma_2\left(\frac{R_{sp,t}}{\sigma_{sp}}\right) + \gamma_3\left(\frac{R_{sp,t}}{\sigma_{sp}}\right)d_t + \eta_t$
ST c SP 500	5	$\left(\frac{R_{st,t}}{\sigma_{st}}\right) = \gamma_0 + \gamma_1 d_t + \gamma_2\left(\frac{R_{sp,t}}{\sigma_{sp}}\right) + \gamma_3\left(\frac{R_{sp,t}}{\sigma_{sp}}\right)d_t + \eta_t$
HS c ST	6	$\left(\frac{R_{hs,t}}{\sigma_{hs}}\right) = \gamma_0 + \gamma_1 d_t + \gamma_2\left(\frac{R_{st,t}}{\sigma_{st}}\right) + \gamma_3\left(\frac{R_{st,t}}{\sigma_{st}}\right)d_t + \eta_t$
ST c HS	7	$\left(\frac{R_{st,t}}{\sigma_{st}}\right) = \gamma_0 + \gamma_1 d_t + \gamma_2\left(\frac{R_{hs,t}}{\sigma_{hs}}\right) + \gamma_3\left(\frac{R_{hs,t}}{\sigma_{hs}}\right)d_t + \eta_t$

R = returns; σ = pre-crisis standard deviation; d = dummy variable; SH = Shanghai Composite index; SP = S&P 500 index; HS = Hang Seng Index; ST = Straits Times Index.

References

Andrews, D.W.K. (1993) Tests for parameter instability and structural change with unknown change point. *Econometrica*, **61**(4), 821–56.

Arestis, P., Caporale, G.M., Cipollini, A. and Spagnolo, N. (2005) Testing for financial contagion between developed and emerging markets during the 1997 East Asian Crisis. *International Journal of Finance & Economics*, **10**(4), 359–67.

Cajueiro, D.O. and Tabak, B.M. (2004) Evidence of long range dependence in Asian equity markets: the role of liquidity and market restrictions. *Physica A*, **342**, 656–64.

Cartapanis, A., Dropsy, V. and Mametz, S. (2002) The Asian currency crises: vulnerability, contagion, or unsustainability. *Review of International Economics*, **10**(1), 79.

Chen, S. and Poon, S. (2007) *Modelling International Stock Market Contagion Using Copula and Risk Appetite*. University of Manchester, Manchester, UK.

Cheung, L., Fung, L. and Chi-Sang, T. (2008) *Measuring Financial Market Interdependence and Assessing Possible Contagion Risk in the EMEAP Region*. Hong Kong Monetary Authority, Hong Kong, China.

Chia Siow, Y. (1998) The Asian financial crisis. *ASEAN Economic Bulletin*, **15**(3), 297.

Chin, G.T. (2010) Remaking the architecture: the emerging powers, self-insuring and regional insulation. *International Affairs*, **86**(3), 693–715.

Chow, G.C. (1960) Tests of equality between sets of coefficients in two linear regressions. *Econometrica*, **28**(3), 591–605.

Dickey, D.A. and Fuller, W.A. (1979) Distribution of the estimators for autoregressive time series with a unit root. *Journal of the American Statistical Association*, **366**(74), 427–31.

Dickey, D.A. and Fuller, W.A. (1981) Likelihood ratio statistics for autoregressive time series with a unit root. *Econometrica*, **49**(4), 1057–72.

Ding, L. (2010) U.S. and Asia Pacific equity markets causality test. *International Journal of Business and Management*, **5**(9), 38–45.

Dungey, M., Fry, R. and Martin, V.L. (2004) Currency market contagion in the Asia-Pacific Region. *Australian Economic Papers*, **43**(4), 379–95.

Forbes, K.J. and Rigobon, R. (2002) No contagion, only interdependence: measuring stock market comovements. *Journal of Finance*, **57**(5), 2223–61.

Frankel, J.A. and Saravelos, G. (2010) *Are Leading Indicators of Financial Crises Useful for Assessing Country Vulnerability? Evidence from the 2008–09 Global Crisis* (NBER Working Paper). National Bureau of Economic Research, Cambridge, MA.

George, O. (2010) *Equity Volatility Transmission and Contagion between the US and Emerging Stock Markets: The Role of the US Subprime Crisis* (working paper). School of Business, La Sierra University, TX.

Harris, R.D.F. and Jian, S. (2003) Robust estimation of the optimal hedge ratio. *Journal of Futures Markets*, **23**(8), 799–816.

He, D., Zhang, Z. and Wang, H. (2009) *Hong Kong's Financial Market Interactions with the US and Mainland China in Crisis and Tranquil Times*. Research Department, Hong Kong Monetary Authority, Hong Kong, China.

Johansson, A.C. (2012) China's growing influence in Southeast Asia: monetary policy and equity markets. *World Economy*, **35**(7), 816–37.

Lai, S.W.M. and Yang, Y. (2009) From scorned to loved? The political economy of the development of the stock market in China. *Global Economic Review: Perspectives on East Asian Economies and Industries*, **38**(4), 409–29.

Lardy, N.R. (1998) China and the Asian contagion. *Foreign Affairs*, **77**(4), 78–88.

Morales, L. and Andreosso-O'Callaghan, B. (2010) The global financial crisis: world market or regional contagion effects? Paper presented at *MFA (Midwest Finance Association) Annual Meeting, Las Vegas, NV.*

Ogum, G. (2010) Equity volatility transmission and contagion between the US and emerging stock markets: the role of the US subprime crisis. Paper presented at *The Southwestern Finance Association, 49th Annual Meeting. Dallas, TX.*

Overholt, W.H. (2010) China in the global financial crisis: rising influence, rising challenges. *Washington Quarterly*, **33**(1), 21–34.

Quandt, R. (1960) Test of the hypothesis that a linear regression obeys two separate regimes. *Journal of the American Statistical Association*, **55**, 324–30.

Yang, J., Kolari, J.W. and Min, I. (2003) Stock market integration and financial crises: the case of Asia. *Applied Financial Economics*, **13**(7), 477.

Yang, T. and Lim, J.J. (2004) Crisis, contagion, and East Asian stock markets. *Review of Pacific Basin Financial Markets and Policies*, **7**(1), 119–51.

9

Chinese healthcare system reforms and household saving patterns: some stylised facts

Vincenzo Atella, Agar Brugiavini, Hao Chen and Noemi Pace

Abstract: This chapter aims to evaluate the relationship between one of the recent healthcare reforms in the People's Republic of China and household decisions both in terms of out-of-pocket expenditure and saving. Evidence on the results achieved by reforms of the health insurance sector in terms of reducing out-of-pocket medical expenditure is still uncertain and contradictory, and very little is known about the effect of these measures on the consumption and saving behaviour of the Chinese population. To shed light on this issue we use data collected by Chinese Household Income Project surveys (CHIPs), through a series of questionnaire-based interviews conducted in urban areas in 1995 and 2002. Our descriptive analysis suggests that there is a positive relationship between public health insurance coverage and household saving. This empirical evidence suggests that public insurance coverage is ineffective as a source of protection against income losses and might induce households to save more.

Key words: China, health insurance, healthcare system reform, household saving, out-of-pocket expenditure, public health.

Introduction

Given the increasing importance of China in the world economy and the importance of the household sector, considerable effort has recently been made to understand Chinese household saving decisions. Almost all studies find that Chinese households have had higher saving rates than those of developed nations since the 1970s. Since the end of the 1970s, China has launched several reforms affecting the economic sector and the social security system. The main objective of these reforms was to transform

China's stagnant, impoverished and centrally planned economic system into a more flexible and decentralized system capable of generating sustained economic growth and increasing the well-being of citizens.

Economic reform began in 1978 and occurred in two stages. The first stage, between the late 1970s and the early 1980s, involved the de-collectivisation of agriculture, the opening up of the country to foreign investments, and the permission for entrepreneurs to start up businesses. However, most industries remained state owned. The second stage of the reform, between the late 1980s and the 1990s, involved the privatisation and contracting out of many state-owned enterprises (SOEs) and the lifting of price controls, protectionist policies, and redundant regulations, although state monopolies in sectors such as banking and petroleum remained state owned. Following these changes, the private sector grew remarkably, accounting for as much as 70 per cent of China's GDP by 2005, a figure larger than that of many Western nations. Along with economic reform, the period between the end of the 1980s and the middle of the 1990s was characterized by high inflation and low real interest rates, which might have induced an increase in saving rates (Aaberge and Zhu, 2001; Modigliani and Cao, 2004; Nabar, 2011).

Over the same period, the Chinese government implemented a series of reforms in the social security sector, including the pension system. Before the reforms, the saving rate of urban Chinese households was flat whereas from 1978 it started to increase reaching at the beginning of the 1990s as much as 35 per cent of GDP (Modigliani and Cao, 2004). The average saving rate of urban households relative to their disposable income rose from 17 per cent in 1995 to 24 per cent in 2005 (Chamon and Prasad, 2011; Yang et al., 2010). Moreover, empirical studies have provided evidence of increased uncertainty related to income and consumption brought on by economic sector reforms and, as a consequence, an increase in precautionary savings (Kraay, 2000; Ma and Yi, 2010).

In this chapter we focus on reforms in the health sector and on their potential impact on household saving rates. In particular, we look at the healthcare system reform undertaken in 1998 and at its effect on household saving rates and out-of-pocket expenses. Little research has examined these effects. What we know today is that following this reform the population covered by the Labor Insurance Scheme (LIS) and the Government Insurance Scheme (GIS) declined significantly between 1993 and 1998. Out-of-pocket expenses increased from 28 per cent in 1993 to 44 per cent in 1998. The lowest income group was reluctant to seek medical treatment, and the main reason was financial. The health service has worsened and become more inequitable since the early 1990s (Gao et al., 2001).

Some studies show that public health insurance coverage positively affects out-of-pocket expenses. People covered by public insurance are more likely to move up the medical provider 'ladder' by making use of hospitals. Hospitals are prepared to deliver more costly tests, drugs and medical interventions to people who have public insurance coverage (Wagstaff and Lindelow, 2008). Little research has examined the relation between household health risks and saving rates. Chamon and Prasad (2011) find that older households allocate 5 per cent more of their income than do younger households for health insurance.

We will present and discuss such evidence in the remainder of this chapter, which is organized as follows. The next section ('Healthcare sector reform in urban China') reviews the institutional background of the healthcare system. There then follows a section 'Literature review on saving behavior in China'. 'Data and empirical analysis' describes the data and provides some stylised facts. Finally, there is a 'Conclusion'.

Healthcare sector reform in urban China

Reforms of China's health insurance system in urban areas have come about by socioeconomic changes and the need to correct healthcare system deficiencies. The urban health insurance system consisted mainly of two insurance schemes: (i) the Labor Insurance Scheme (LIS), which bore all costs of medical treatment, medicine and hospitalisation for workers and, often, for their dependants; (ii) the Government Insurance Scheme (GIS) under which medical costs for civil servants were covered by government budgetary allocation. While the GIS and LIS have played important roles in providing China's urban working population with health protection (Liu, 2002), several aspects of the original schemes contributed to China's rapid healthcare cost inflation and inefficient resource allocation in the 1990s. First, the GIS and LIS are third-party health insurance schemes, providing comprehensive benefits with minimal cost sharing to constrain beneficiaries from excessively consuming medical services. Without any or limited consumer financial responsibility for the use of health services, the urban insured have no incentive to seek the most cost-effective healthcare. Second, except for employees in large enterprises with their own hospitals and clinics, both GIS and LIS beneficiaries seek medical services from public hospitals, which are usually reimbursed on a fee-for-service basis according to a government-set fee schedule, which gives providers incentives to overprovide services.

To address these problems, during the 1980s China implemented a whole series of reforms in the urban health insurance system and did so in three major stages. The first lasted from the early 1980s to 1991, the second from 1992 to 1998 with city-wide pilot reforms, and the third was announced at the end of 1998. During the first stage the primary objective of the reform was cost containment; major reform measures included the introduction of demand-side and supply-side cost sharing. During the second stage, health sector reforms addressed the issue of inadequate risk pooling. Two cities in the provinces of Jiangxi and Jiangsu began pilot reforms that used a combination of individual savings accounts and social risk-pooling funds to finance medical expenditure. Before an individual could access the social risk-pooling fund, however, he or she had first to pay deductibles (excess) from a first tier of his or her individual medical savings account and a second tier of direct deductibles equal to 5 per cent of annual income. At the end of 1998, the Chinese government announced a major decision to establish a social insurance program for urban workers that replaced the existing LIS and GIS in the two cities, known as the Basic Insurance Scheme (BIS).

Compared with the old GIS and LIS, the new program expanded coverage to private enterprises and smaller public enterprises. Self-employed workers were allowed to enter the program. Workers' dependants were not covered. The program was financed by premium contributions from employers (6 per cent of the employee's wage) and employees (2 per cent of their wage).[1] Retired workers were exempt from premium contributions and the cost of their contributions was to be borne by their former employers.

Total contributions (on average 8 per cent of the employee's wage) were divided into two accounts: 3.8 per cent went into the individual's Medical Saving Account (MSA) (each contributor could only use his or her MSA for healthcare expenses); the remaining 4.2 percent went into the Social Risk Pooling (SRP) fund, which was used to cover large medical expenses. At the city level local government had the right to decide whether SRP had to cover just inpatient expenses or catastrophic expenses as well, defined as expenditure exceeding a certain large deductible. In a typical BIS benefit structure, the contributor was expected to pay all of his or her outpatient medical expenses using his or her annual MSA until the funds were exhausted. Unused MSA funds at the end of the year were carried over to the next year, and unused funds at the end of a person's life became a part of his or her bequest. When the MSA was exhausted, the contributor had to pay outpatient expenses out of pocket. In case of any inpatient expense, the contributor had to pay a deductible set equal to 10 per cent of his or her annual wage. Expenses exceeding the deductible were paid by the SRP, which limited the payment for each contributor to four times the annual average wage of employees in that city.

Inpatient expenses exceeding this ceiling had either to be covered by other supplementary insurance schemes, or had to be paid by the patient out of pocket. However, local governments in the two cities provided other supplementary insurance schemes for their employees. The employees could also purchase supplementary private insurance individually. Each local government at the city level had to establish a Social Insurance Bureau (SIB), which was responsible for collecting the premium and contracting out the payment for services. SIB, working with health authorities, accredited and contracted with a set of healthcare providers, including outpatient clinics, pharmacies and hospitals. The central government did not specify the exact payment method to be used by SIBs to pay healthcare providers, but it required risks to be pooled at the city level and local governments to be responsible for any shortfalls.

The new benefit structure under the current system has two major gaps in coverage. First, the dependants of urban workers, who used to receive partial coverage, are no longer covered. Second, the new system has a ceiling on the amount of medical expenditure allocated to an indivisual (equivalent to four times the annual average wage in the region). Imposition of this ceiling had two main reasons – budget constraints and political emphasis on wide coverage – but it left most catastrophic illnesses uncovered. It is estimated that a premium contribution based on 8 per cent of the current wage could only cover about 70 per cent of the total outlay under the old GIS and LIS systems (MLSS, 1999). Moreover, Gao et al. (2007) show that the proportion of elderly covered by health insurance in urban China declined over the period 1998–2007. This may be partially attributed to the reform of state-owned enterprises, which has resulted in many enterprises being closed and a substantial number of workers laid off (Gao et al., 2001). As the Chinese government has only guaranteed the minimum living allowance, the elderly or people laid off as a consequence of enterprises closing (as a result of ongoing economic reforms) may have lost such entitlements as health insurance.

Literature review on saving behaviour in China

The enormous importance that China has gained over recent decades at the international level has prompted many researchers to study the socioeconomic effects of ongoing reforms in several economic sectors. In particular, the determinants of household savings have received a lot of attention from both Chinese and international researchers. Brugiavini et al. (2013), Chamon and Prasad (2011) and Feng et al. (2011), among others, use household-level data to explain the high saving rates rather than rapid income growth. Chamon and Prasad (2011) use household-level data from the Urban Household Survey over the period 1990–2005. They estimate how saving rates vary with time, age and cohort of the household head. They find a U-shaped pattern of saving over the life cycle, wherein younger and older households have the highest saving rates. They also investigate the determinants of increasing saving rates in the period under consideration. They find: (i) home ownership is an important determinant of saving rate; (ii) the private burdens imposed by education and health expenditure seem to be prime candidates for explaining the increase in saving rates. Chamon and Prasad (2011) consider, among other relevant factors, the effect of health risk on saving but they do not specifically consider the effect of healthcare coverage on saving (which we do). Brugiavini et al. (2013) use the same data to study the effect of pension reforms on saving rates. They find that a number of factors can explain changes over time and in age profiles. In particular, households that migrated to urban areas tend to save more. Moreover, homeowners who recently bought on the open market save more than tenants; they also save more than homeowners who acquired their property long ago or at the time of the housing reform. Feng et al. (2011) attempt to answer the similar research question that focusses on the effect the pension reform of 1995–1997 had on household savings rates in urban China. They use the Chinese Household Income Project data (the same data we use in this chapter). Their estimates show that pension reform boosted household saving rates by about 6–9 percentage points for cohorts aged 25–29 and by about 2–3 percentage points for cohorts aged 50–59. Our chapter shares with the last three works the main objective (understanding the determinants of household saving) even though we focus on the potential relationship between the healthcare sector reform undertaken in 1998 and household saving rates.

To the best of our knowledge, to date there are no contributions that make use of microdata to study the relationship between healthcare reforms and household saving and consumption rates.

The only two studies that focus on the relationship between reforms in the healthcare sector and savings are Baldacci et al. (2010) and Barnett and Brooks (2010), but they use macrodata. Barnett and Brooks (2010) pool provincial data in China from 1994 to 2008 to exploit variations in provincial spending on health and differences in saving rates. Their results suggest a statistically significant negative relationship between government health spending and savings in urban areas. The estimated coefficient is around −2, which suggests that each additional 1 yuan of government health spending results in a 2-yuan increase in consumption. They argue that this is a strong impact, as it would imply that a 1 per cent of GDP increase in government health spending would boost private consumption by 2 per cent of GDP, and yield a total demand effect of 3 per cent of GDP for every 1 per cent of GDP increase in health spending. Baldacci et al. (2010) examine the impact of expanding social programs on household consumption/savings in China. They simulate the effects of alternative government social expenditure reforms on aggregate consumption using estimates of age-specific marginal propensities to consume for different income groups and estimates of the lifetime amount of resources available to each cohort (these estimates are obtained from CHIPs). They find that the resulting total consumption impacts range from 1.6 per cent of GDP for pensions, 0.8 per cent for education and 1.3 per cent for health. This result implies that a 1 percentage point GDP increase in social expenditure allocated across pension, education and health would result in a permanent increase in household consumption of 1.2 per cent of GDP.

Data and empirical analysis

To explore the statistical relationship between Chinese household saving behaviour and healthcare system reforms, we exploit cross-sectional data from the Chinese Household Income Project surveys (CHIPs) conducted by the Chinese Academy of Social Science (CASS) in 1988, 1995 and 2002. The surveys use sub-samples from the main nationally representative household survey programme conducted by the Chinese National Bureau of Statistics in urban and rural areas. The surveys by CASS are reasonably large and designed to be representative of urban China. For the scope of our analysis, we only focus on the 1995 and 2002 surveys that represent the pre-reform and post-reform periods, respectively. We exclude from the analysis the 1988 survey because there was incomplete information on income and expenditure. Furthermore, we do not consider the rural sample because the Basic Insurance Scheme (BIS) was introduced only in urban areas.

The urban sample includes individuals and households from 11 provinces and municipalities.[2] The purpose of CHIPs urban data collection was to measure the distribution of personal income. Moreover, the data provide a lot of information on each household member concerning his/her social and economic status, including employment characteristics, wage, tax and source of income, as well as demographic variables such as, age, gender, marital status and relationship to the household head. Information is also gathered on household expenditure and on general living conditions.[3]

Summary statistics

Empirical analysis was performed at household level, using information collected at head-of-household level (sociodemographic and employment characteristics) and at household level (income, expenditure and savings). We restricted the sample to household heads aged 25–65.[4] Moreover, to avoid potential measurement errors, we trimmed saving rates (dropping the values of saving rates below the first percentile and above the 99th percentile). This resulted in our getting a sample of 6496 households in 1995 and 6252 households in 2002. However, after eliminating households where the value of the income variable and that of some employment characteristics variables were missing, the sample size reduces to 5337 households in 1995 and to 4551 in 2002.

Table 9.1 reports summary statistics for household disposable income, consumption expenditure, resulting saving rates and out-of-pocket expenses.

The measure of disposable income that we focus on includes labour income, property income, transfers and income from household sideline production minus income tax. The consumption expenditure variable covers a broad range of categories.[5] All flow variables are expressed in 2011 US dollars, PPP adjusted, and nominal variables in 2002 are deflated using the national CPI (base year 1995 = 100). Furthermore, we measure savings as the difference between disposable income and consumption expenditure and define the saving rate as the ratio between saving and disposable income. On average, we observe that household total income and household disposable income increased significantly from 1995 to 2002. Moreover, household expenditure increased significantly, even though the rate of growth of expenditure was lower than observed for the other two variables.

Out-of-pocket medical expense is defined as the difference between total household healthcare expenditure and the amount of reimbursement by any kind of health insurance. We observe that average out-of-pocket

Table 9.1 Household income, saving rate and OOP expenses

Variable	1995	2002	[t-stat]
Total household disposable income	5099.23	7306.24	35.40
Total household expenditure	4260.42	5439.25	26.35
Saving rate	13.20%	21.8%	16.79
Out-of-pocket expenses	127.22	345.11	17.48

Notes: total household disposable income and household expenditure are reported in 2011 US dollar. The fourth column shows the absolute *t*-value of a standard test of mean difference. OOP = out of pocket.

expenses increased significantly from 1995 to 2002, which is consistent with the findings of Gao et al. (2001) and Wagstaff and Linderlow (2008). There may be two main reasons for this. First, in 1995 the healthcare costs of dependants of LIS and BIS beneficiaries could be partially reimbursed, whereas in 2002 BIS no longer reimbursed their healthcare costs. Second, the cost of healthcare escalated, which led to higher household expenses. Moreover, public insurance coverage significantly decreased from 1995 to 2002. This result is not surprising, since the Ministry of Labor and Social Security (1999) reported that BIS could only cover 70 per cent of the total outlay under GIS and LIS. This may be attributed to the reform of SOEs which has resulted in many enterprises being closed and a substantial number of workers laid off (Gao et al., 2001).

Changes in household saving rates

Since our main objective is to explore the relationship between healthcare reforms and savings, we deepen our analysis of these variables by exploring age group patterns and a number of other relevant variables. Table 9.2 and Figure 9.1 provide information on average saving rates by age group. For all age groups saving rates are significantly higher in 2002. Moreover, in both surveys, saving rates have a U-shape pattern. The lowest saving rates are registered among the 30–44 age group in 1995 and among the 35–49 age group in 2002. This empirical evidence is consistent with previous findings of Brugiavini at al. (2013), Chamon and Prasad (2011) and Yang et al. (2010).

Table 9.2 Saving rates by survey year and age groups

Saving rates by age group	All samples	1995	2002	[t-stat]
25–29	17.10	15.24	21.25	2.20
30–34	16.80	11.87	23.79	8.66
35–39	15.75	12.43	19.27	5.96
40–44	15.09	11.09	20.08	8.05
45–49	17.23	12.82	20.53	6.40
50–54	21.19	15.91	25.88	6.65
55–59	20.65	16.35	27.46	5.62
60–65	16.07	15.17	21.93	1.81

Note: the fifth column shows the absolute *t*-statistic of a standard test of mean difference.

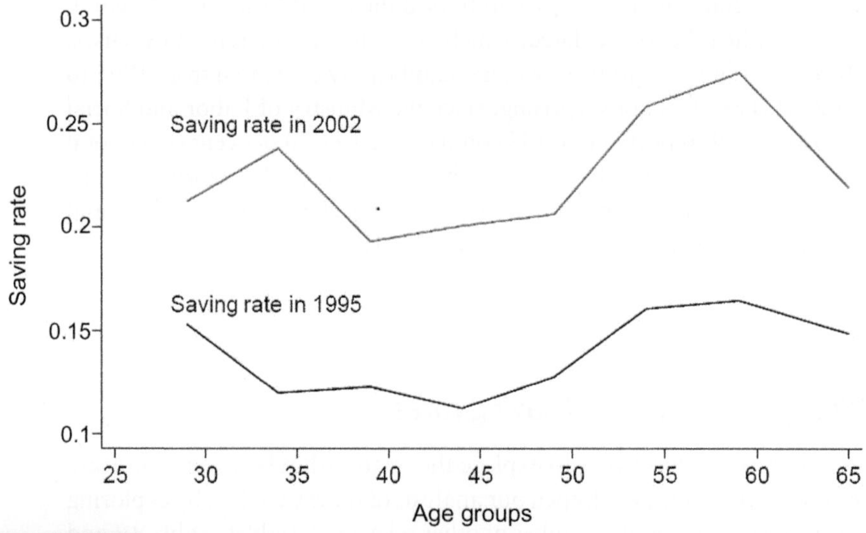

Figure 9.1 **Saving rates by age groups and survey year**

Another interesting aspect is the way in which saving rates by type of insurance coverage have evolved. In China, the household head can be covered either by public insurance, private insurance or can remain uninsured. According to the data collected, in the 1995 survey public insurance was provided by either the LIS or GIS, whereas in the 2002 survey it was provided only by the BIS. In 1995, 70.58 per cent of household heads were covered by the LIS or GIS, 17.23 per cent were covered by private health insurance while the remaining 12.19 per cent of household heads were not covered by any kind of health insurance. In 2002, 68.79 per cent of household heads were covered by the BIS, 5.31 per cent were covered by private health insurance while the remaining 25.9 per cent of household heads were not covered by any kind of health insurance.

Table 9.3 and Figure 9.2 provide this information by showing average saving rates by survey, public health insurance coverage and age groups. What stands out is that saving rates in 2002 were significantly higher for households where household heads were covered by public health insurance and in the 40–54 age group. No significant differences can be found in 1995 with the only exception of the 30–34 age group.

As for geographical heterogeneity, in Table 9.4 we present household saving rates by province, survey year and public insurance (PI) coverage. Household saving rates in 1995 ranged between 7.5 in Sichuan and Chongqing provinces and 18.7 in Shanxi province. In 2002 they ranged between 14.4 in Beijing and 28.9 in Henan. In all provinces, saving rates

Table 9.3 Saving rates by health insurance coverage, survey year and age groups

Saving rates	1995			2002		
	Coverage	No coverage	[t-stat]	Coverage	No coverage	[t-stat]
All age groups	13.0	13.6	0.75	23.2	18.7	5.25
25–29	14.3	16.9	0.89	22.6	19.7	0.58
30–34	10.4	14.9	2.47	23.9	23.5	0.22
35–39	12.2	12.5	0.18	20.3	17.4	1.53
40–44	11.8	10.9	0.34	21.1	17.6	1.85
45–49	12.6	13.1	0.26	22.6	16.2	3.64
50–54	15.9	16.4	0.20	27.5	20.6	2.77
55–59	16.6	16.1	0.18	28.7	23.9	1.30
60–65	15.7	12.7	1.04	24.1	17.4	0.76

Note: the fourth and the seventh columns show the absolute *t*-statistic of a standard test of mean difference.

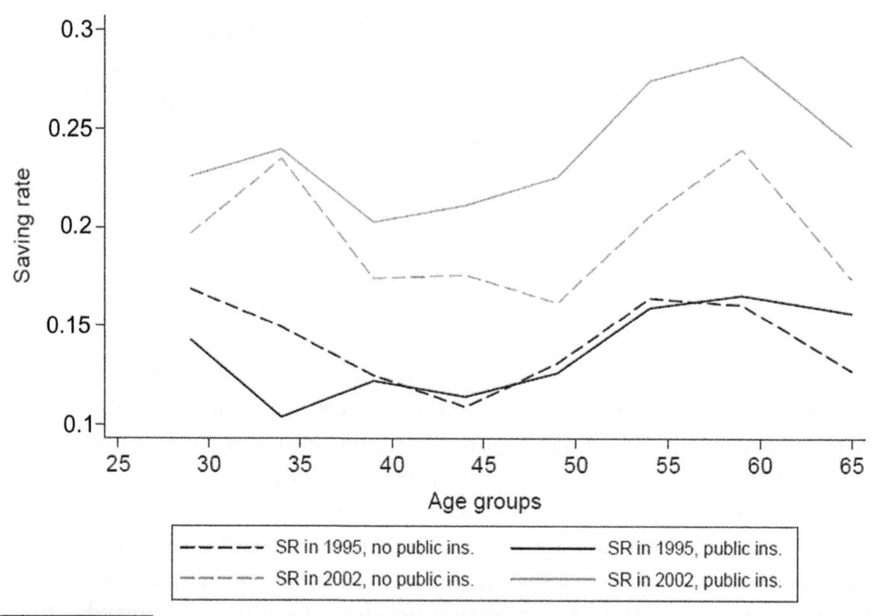

Figure 9.2 **Saving rates by age group, health insurance coverage and survey year**

increased significantly between 1995 and 2002, with the only exception of Beijing where they decreased, although not significantly. Looking at the last three columns in Table 9.4, we have a clear picture of differences in saving rates by public insurance coverage after the healthcare reforms. In the provinces of Beijing, Shanxi, Henan, Hubei and Gansu the saving rates of household heads covered by public health insurance (BIS) were not statistically different from uninsured households, while in all other provinces saving rates were significantly higher for household heads covered by public health insurance.

Another interesting aspect is whether household saving rates changed according to job characteristics. In particular, Table 9.5 provides descriptive statistics of saving rates by employment contract (permanent versus temporary), occupation (director of government agency, institution or enterprise, owner of private firm, self-employed or professional, skilled worker, unskilled worker), survey year and public health insurance coverage (PI).

Household heads in permanent employment saved significantly more than household heads with temporary contracts, both in 1995 and 2002. Directors of government agencies, institutions or enterprises saved more than all the other job occupations, both in 1995 and in 2002. We can deepen our analysis of employment characteristics by looking at public

Table 9.4 Saving rates by province, survey year and public health insurance coverage

	1995	2002	1995			2002		
Province			**PI**	**No PI**	**[t-stat]**	**PI**	**No PI**	**[t-stat]**
Beijing	16.9	14.4	18.19	9.72	2.47	14.84	9.97	0.91
Shanxi	18.7	24.8	15.74	20.41	2.15	22.42	27.03	1.46
Liaoning	9.7	20.1	9.11	11.52	1.11	21.78	16.54	2.11
Jiangsu	15.2	26.8	15.10	14.19	0.37	30.65	21.83	3.21
Anhui	12.3	22.1	12.93	11.05	0.86	24.64	15.30	3.40
Henan	14.7	28.9	15.04	13.80	0.51	30.08	26.83	1.38
Hubei	12.4	19.4	12.15	13.15	0.44	20.40	17.60	1.12
Guangdong	11.8	23.9	12.67	10.89	0.68	26.40	19.07	3.25
Sichuan and Chongqing	7.5	16.7	7.47	7.69	0.09	20.58	7.95	5.16
Yunnan	14.9	24.1	14.81	10.38	0.82	25.56	19.16	2.02
Gansu	13.7	19.9	14.56	9.28	1.39	20.94	17.44	0.96

Note: the sixth and ninth columns show the absolute *t*-statistic of a standard test of mean difference. PI = public insurance.

health insurance coverage in 1995 and 2002. A clear picture emerges from Table 9.5. In 1995, before the healthcare reforms, in all categories (type of contract and occupation) the saving rates of household heads covered by health insurance were not significantly different from uninsured household heads. In contrast, after the healthcare reforms saving rates in 2002 were significantly higher for household heads covered by public health insurance with temporary contracts, irrespective of whether they were employed in occupations that required particular skills or not.

Conclusion

Healthcare reform is an important component of China's social security reform process. In this chapter we focus on the third stage of healthcare

Table 9.5 Saving rates by employment characteristics, survey year and public health insurance coverage

	1995	2002	1995			2002		
Type of contract			**PI**	**No PI**	**[t-stat]**	**PI**	**No PI**	**[t-stat]**
Permanent	13.52	23.98	13.39	13.87	0.59	24.31	22.55	1.36
Temporary	11.32	18.89	10.74	12.27	0.87	20.88	16.79	3.25
Occupation			**PI**	**No PI**	**[t-stat]**	**PI**	**No PI**	**[t-stat]**
Directors of government agencies, institutions or enterprises	15.37	25.14	14.70	17.63	1.43	25.01	25.76	0.26
Owner of private firm, professional	14.14	23.65	13.47	16.51	1.90	24.57	21.80	1.67
Skilled worker	12.16	22.03	12.22	12.01	0.19	22.86	19.63	2.33
Unskilled worker	12.13	16.44	12.37	11.81	0.34	19.69	13.24	3.59

Note: the sixth and ninth columns show the absolute *t*-statistic of a standard test of mean difference. PI = public insurance.

system reform, which occurred in 1998 when the Chinese government established nationwide a new public insurance scheme called the Basic Insurance Scheme (BIS). The BIS is financed by premium contributions from both the employer and the employee. Differently from previous public insurance schemes in urban areas – the Labor Insurance Scheme (LIS) and the Government Insurance Scheme (GIS) – the BIS does not reimburse contributors' healthcare costs entirely. Indeed, it only reimburses contributors' outpatient expenses if they are less than the amount accumulated in medical saving accounts, and their inpatient expenses are paid out of pocket if they exceed the fixed ceiling determined by each local government.

Using data from the 1995 and 2002 Chinese Household Income Project surveys for urban households, we performed a descriptive analysis to explore the relationship between reform in the healthcare sector in 1998 and household saving rates. The results show that the saving rates of household heads covered by public health insurance was higher after the reform than those of uninsured household heads. This finding suggests that public health insurance seems to be ineffective as a source of protection against income loss and forces households to save more for precautionary reasons.

To conclude, although China's healthcare reform in 1998 established a nationwide risk-pooling mechanism at the city level and alleviated the burden on employers, it cannot be denied that this reform resulted in urban households being less protected and obliged them to save more to deal with potential future healthcare expenditure due to negative health shocks.

Notes

1. Employers' contributions differed across provinces and cities. The average level was 6 per cent of an employee's wage.
2. In the 1995 survey, the 11 provinces and municipalities were Anhui, Beijing, Gansu, Guangdong, Henan, Hubei, Jiangsu, Liaoning, Shanxi, Sichuan and Yunnan. In the 2002 survey, the municipality of Chongqing was also included. Since it was a city in Sichuan province and became a municipality in 1997, we combine Chongqing and Sichuan in the 2002 survey. These 11 provinces and municipalities cover all six geographical areas and reflect the economic situation in China. In 2002, Guangdong ranked first for GDP and the municipality of Beijing ranked first for per-capita GDP, whereas Gansu ranked 25th for GDP out of China's total 31 provinces and had one of the lowest per-capita GDPs in the country; Liaoning was the most productive heavy-industry center with its petrochemical, machinery manufacturing and metallurgy industries representing 70 per cent of total Liaoning gross industrial output value; Henan was the most important agriculture province with its cultivated area ranking first for productivity in the country (*Statistical Yearbook*, 2003).
3. In the 2002 survey, CHIPs provide two special data sets which investigate rural-to-urban migrant information covering both individuals and households. However, such data do not exist in the 1995 survey. Therefore, we do not take rural-to-urban migrant households into account in our analysis.
4. We only take into account the working age population because health insurance coverage is strictly linked to employer and employee contributions.
5. Consumption expenditure includes food; clothing and footwear; household appliances, goods and services; medical care and health;

transport and communications; and recreational, educational and cultural services and housing.

References

Aaberge, R. and Zhu, Y. (2001) The pattern of household savings during a hyperinflation: the case of urban China in the late 1980s. *Review of Income and Wealth*, **47**, 181–202.

Baldacci, E., Callegari, G., Coady, D., Ding, D., Kumar, M. et al. (2010) *Public Expenditures on Social Programs and Household Consumption in China* (IMF Working Paper 10/69). International Monetary Fund, Washington, DC.

Barnett, S. and Brooks, R. (2010) *China: Does Government Health and Education Spending Boost Consumption?* (IMF Working Paper 10/16). International Monetary Fund, Washington, DC.

Brugiavini, A., Weber, G. and Wu, B. (2013) Saving rates of urban households in China. In: G. Gomel, D. Marconi, I. Musu and B. Quintieri (Eds), *The Chinese Economy*. Springer-Verlag, Berlin.

Chamon, M.D. and Prasad, E.S. (2011) Why are saving rates of urban households in China rising? *American Economic Journal: Macroeconomics*, **2**(1), 93–130.

Feng, J., He, L. and Sato, H. (2011) Public pension and household saving: evidence from urban China. *Journal of Comparative Economics*, **39**(4), 470–85.

Gao, J., Tang, S., Tolhurst, R. and Rao, K. (2001) Changing access to health services in urban China: implications for equity. *Health Policy and Planning*, **16**(3), 302–12.

Gao, J., Raven, J. and Tang, S. (2007) Hospitalization among elderly in urban China. *Health Policy*, **84**, 210–19.

Kraay, A. (2000) Household saving in China. *World Bank Economic Review*, **14**(3), 545–70.

Liu, Y. (2002) Reforming China's urban health insurance system. *Health Policy*, **60**, 133–50.

Ma, G. and Yi, W. (2010) *China's High Saving Rate: Myth and Reality* (BIS Working Paper 312). Bank for International Settlements, Cambridge, UK.

MLSS (1999) The policy options for supplementary medical insurance in China (mimeo). Ministry of Labor and Social Security, Beijing.

Modigliani, F. and Cao, S.L. (2004) The Chinese saving puzzle and the life-cycle hypothesis. *Journal of Economic Literature*, **42**(1), 145–70.

Nabar, M. (2011) *Targets, Interest Rates, and Household Saving in Urban China* (IMF Working Paper 11/223). International Monetary Fund, Washington, DC.

Statistical Yearbook (2003) Various provinces. China Statistics Press, Beijing.

Wagstaff, A. and Lindelow, M. (2008) Can insurance increase financial risk? The curious case of health insurance in China. *Journal of Health Economics*, **27**(4), 990–1005.

Yang, D.T., Zhang, J. and Zhou, S. (2010) *Why Are Saving Rates So High in China?* (Working Paper 16771). National Bureau of Economic Research, Cambridge, MA.

10

China's growing consumer culture: implications for marketing strategy

Robert Taylor

Abstract: China's phenomenal economic growth in recent decades has led to an emerging consumer culture and, additionally, in the wake of a global recession currently affecting the country's trading partners in Western countries, the Chinese leaders in the 12th Five Year Plan (2011–15) have sought to encourage domestic consumption of goods and services. Economic development, however, has entailed social costs, witness urban–rural inequalities.

The emergence of a vocal middle class in China's coastal cities and the consequent emergence of a civil society, facilitated by social media, have brought greater awareness of consumer rights and discernment in branded product purchasing. While these trends tend still to be an urban phenomenon, they are becoming more widespread, as government seeks to coordinate city and village markets, a process nevertheless still inhibited by poor infrastructure and low rural purchasing power due to income differentials.

Consequently, this chapter will focus on increasing consumer discernment in purchasing of products. Chinese government emphasis on moves towards high-tech value-added products, prompted at least in part by the need to circumvent import barriers overseas, but as importantly by domestic brand diversification in China increasingly demanded by consumers, has accelerated competition, with implications for marketing strategy.

Such demands for competitive innovation and market targeting bring into sharp relief a number of legal issues like trade descriptions and intellectual property. A raft of legislation is applicable to goods and services but is subject to local enforcement. A special concern of this chapter is food safety, consciousness of which may determine consumer purchasing behaviour. Greater urban consumer spending power has focused on diversified choice of food products. In the context of food safety, factors like age, sex, marital status, educational level and number of household members, which impact upon purchasing of, for example, green and genetically modified categories, are examined.

In summary, greater Chinese consumer choice and discernment will necessarily influence marketing strategy by domestic and foreign firms alike.

Key words: consumer culture, domestic consumption, urban–rural inequality, marketing strategy.

Introduction

In recent decades China's consumer culture has emerged in the context of the country's growing foreign trade and domestic inward investment. China's economic development model, in its rapid expansion of exports, has followed the experience of other East Asian countries like South Korea and Singapore but there is now a consensus among Chinese and foreign experts that growth has been unbalanced, with the share of domestic consumption in the country's gross domestic product (GDP) being too low. There are signs, however, that China is moving from an economy driven by foreign trade and inward investment to one in which personal consumption plays a greater role. Thus, while in the first half of 2011 the country's trade surplus fell, retail sales of consumer goods grew (Zhang, 2012). Demand for economic restructuring has also been intensified by a decline in Chinese exports to Western countries in the wake of the ongoing global recession, with a potential increase in barriers against Chinese trade, a scenario which has already resulted in the closure of factories and growing unemployment along China's southeastern coast (APCO, 2010).

Response to these trends has been reflected in the priorities of the current 12th Five Year Plan (2011–15) which extends the previous plan's focus on the creation of a harmonious society (*hexie shehui*) based on balanced growth, the implication being that China's economic success had its costs in terms of an increasing urban–rural divide, increasing social and income inequality and environmental degradation.

Accordingly, the 12th Five Year Plan seeks to give the general population a greater share in the country's wealth by shifting emphasis from investment to personal consumption (*China Daily*, 2010).

There have nevertheless been barriers to an increase in individual spending power, among them domestic interest rates, a high rate of personal savings and an as yet nascent social security system. A large differential between deposit and lending rates set by the central bank has stimulated investment in the urban housing sector inhibiting spending in other areas (Lardy, 2012). The caveat must, however, be added that expenditure on residences may stimulate purchasing of such household items as furniture and whiteware. Additionally, the absence of a fully comprehensive national social security system, especially for rural inhabitants, has placed limits on consumer spending.

As will be discussed in the later sections, diversified consumption is still largely an urban phenomenon but the 12th Five Year Plan priorities are intended to increase the spending power of rural residents. One indicator of discretionary spending is expenditure on food; in 2009 while rural households spent 40.7 per cent of their total on food, the equivalent figure for their urban counterparts was 29.4 per cent, statistics being taken from China's 2010 Statistical Yearbook (Anon., 2011).

While the priority of increasingly moving from labour-intensive manufacturing towards more high-tech value-added industries and innovation will impact most upon the cities, particularly those on the southeastern seaboard, the task of reducing the urban–rural divide necessitates also rebalancing of the economy in the countryside, in the interests of maintaining social stability.

Thus, since agriculture employs 40 per cent of Chinese labour but only represents 10 per cent of China's GDP, one key to reducing the urban–rural income gap is restructuring employment in the countryside. Another need is to control immigration to the cities. Migration, however, is only a partial answer; urbanisation has tended not to narrow urban–rural inequality since peasant migrants, while remitting funds back to the countryside, earn low wages from the unskilled industrial and service sectors and, given the *hukou* system, are not considered permanent urban residents and thus ineligible for social welfare provision (Zhang, 2012). In addition, central government's objective is to focus on high-tech strategic industries rather than labour-intensive processing. While there may still be opportunities for rural migrants in low-tech industries, it remains to be seen whether the estimated 45 million rural migrants during the course of the 12th Five Year Plan period can be successfully absorbed into the urban labour force.

In a macroeconomic sense, however, the problem of low rural consumption can be best addressed by raising income levels in the countryside itself, given that in 2010 rural residents, over 50 per cent of China's population, only took 23 per cent of the country's total consumption, according to China's National Bureau of Statistics. Since the turn of the century a number of measures have been taken to boost rural income: the elimination of agricultural taxes in 2004 as well as increased subsidies. There are, nevertheless, countervailing forces. As there is no private land ownership as such, local governments, with the connivance of village leaders, have requisitioned land for development rather than farming. Once again local government action may be seen in conflict with central government policy. There are cases, however, in which local government initiatives may provide new sources of peasant income (e.g., the development of rural industries). In fact, such extra wages for farmers have actually exceeded their agriculturally derived income in some places.

One trend which may help to enhance rural income is crop diversification. This, in effect, means regional specialisation in non-grain crops but movement of, for example, fruit and vegetables across provisional boundaries has been impeded by local protectionism as well as deficient infrastructure. There have been resulting effects on food quality. Improvement in infrastructure is significantly a target of the 12th Five Year Plan. Additionally, observers have noted that logistics costs are higher than in developed countries. If such barriers can be overcome it will facilitate specialisation in agricultural production which itself partially reflects diversification of taste in foodstuffs, especially in the cities, since, with rising income, the role of grain in the diet has decreased, and there is also a greater consciousness of food quality and safety (Zhang, 2012).

An increase in food diversity is in part at least a reflection of the growth of China's middle class. One source quoted Master Card Worldwide Asia Pacific as stating that China's middle class will number 340 million by 2016 (Cui and Song, 2009). With a growing middle class has emerged the beginnings of a civil society which is likely to engender a greater consciousness of civil liberties and human rights. Accordingly, this chapter takes knowledge of and concern with food quality as a case study of consumer culture. Its main hypothesis is that an emerging civil society is heightening consciousness of consumer rights and that the laws governing food safety are both a reflection of and an impetus to that concern. Attempts to increase consumption through the integration of urban and rural commerce and trade form the subject of the next section.

Bridging the urban–rural divide

The emergence of a nationwide market in China is impeded by both the wealth differentials discussed above and a deficient physical infrastructure; market strategists must thus target a series of regional markets. In general, it could be said that living standards follow governmental and administrative structures in descending order: the wealthiest are the Tier 1 cities at the top like Beijing, Chongqing, Tianjin and Guangzhou, while provincial capitals make up the second tier.

Provinces are divided into prefectural-level cities which in turn are above county-level cities and counties at Levels 4 and 5. At the lowest levels, six and seven, stand townships and villages. For the purpose of understanding distribution and consumption, these levels are, however, not as rigid as they might appear. Some food and drink manufacturers have focussed their attention on smaller cities before targeting bigger markets, an example being Xiao Piao Piao Food Company Limited (XPP). As a successful powdered beverage brand it entered the market in 2005. When attempting to distribute its milk tea product in smaller cities where few modern trade channels exist, it took advantage of traditional media like small supermarkets and other small retailers which accounted for most of the company's sales. In fact, more and more retailers are introducing brands to their stores in lower tier cities (Bassolino and Smith, 2010). Furthermore, while the greatest concentration of wealth is found in the major cities of the seaboard, increasingly rich consumers are being found outside those cities and their number will undoubtedly increase with the growth of the middle class. Similarly, there seems little doubt that supermarkets like Linhua of the Shanghai Bailian Group, which already has over 5000 retail outlets, will successfully expand into smaller cities (Sinclair, 2010).

In spite, however, of the growing presence of wealthy and well-educated people in the countryside, backward facilities still adversely impact on consumption in the villages. Nevertheless, this is gradually being ameliorated by use of the Internet and concomitant social media, even if their penetration still varies greatly across the country (Xi, 2010). In fact, online shoppers in China numbered 142 million by June 2010, representing nearly 34 per cent of netizens (Michael and Zhou, 2011). Thus the Internet is an effective way to reach consumers, especially where physical retail outlets are absent (e.g., western China). A wide range of bulletin boards and e-commerce platforms are excellent reconnaissance tools, enabling retailers to access consumer demographics and feedback from customers regarding a whole range of products, thereby facilitating marketing strategy (Crampton, 2011). With the growth of an affluent middle class the demand for domestic delivery of, for instance, foods through e-commerce can only accelerate (Baden, 2012).

But precisely because e-commerce will depend on domestic delivery, particularly to remote areas, a premium is placed on physical infrastructure and logistics. To date most high-tech industrial activity has been concentrated in coastal areas but, in order to reduce regional and income inequality, the 12th Five Year Plan is targetting spending on infrastructure, especially in relation to Tier 2 cities. Additionally, development of western China is a priority; in fact, because of rising wage costs in eastern China and a growing potential market in the hinterland, manufacturers are already moving to the centre and the west of the country, necessitating efficient express services to Tier 2 and 3 cities (Craig and Qiang, 2010).

There are, in fact, two aspects of infrastructure, hardware and software, both of which are currently being addressed by central and, importantly, given the example that follows, provincial government. Central government is enhancing hardware like airports, roads and railways and this is facilitating the migration of manufacturers referred to earlier. In turn, efficient logistics is an element of software, including government legislation, regulations and procedures which govern the movement of goods (Baden, 2012).

An example of promoting the better distribution of goods to the villages is provided by the Ten Million Project in Zhejiang province which was designed to coordinate urban–rural trade and commerce. A survey of the project, conducted through interviewing representatives drawn from commercial enterprises and village consumers, indicated the extent to which objectives are being achieved. In order to improve distribution to and in the village with its convenience consumers, in 2005 the Ministries of Commerce and Finance, in cooperation with the provincial government, helped to launch the Ten Million Project, providing finance and subsidies, in order to further the development of the so-called socialist new village as part of the harmonious society. Under the scheme city retailers and distributors were given financial incentives to use their large-scale retail outlets as a basis for the establishment of village shops to satisfy local consumer demand. In addition, to improve distribution, attempts have been made to concentrate scattered agricultural wholesale markets. The project has been seen to succeed on a number of fronts, distribution being enhanced and living standards raised. In 2010 average per-capita GDP in Zhejiang was ¥51,711, an increase of ¥7070 over the figure for 2009, while per-capita financial income for the province was ¥5512, an increase of ¥958 compared with 2009. The differential between the respective incomes of city and village inhabitants was 2.42 times, in favour of the former, in 2010, as opposed to a multiple of 2.46 times in 2009. Given, for instance, the substantial increase in networked convenience stores in the villages, employment in the latter has benefitted from commercial enterprises engaging surplus labour. Spin-off effects for village commerce have included employment in food and drink manufacturing enterprises, warehousing, transport and computer services (Yi, 2011).

Thus, one of the keys to reducing urban–rural inequality is to provide employment opportunities in the villages. While services, like those listed immediately above, are often more labour intensive than manufacturing, increasingly, in Zhejiang and elsewhere, there is emerging a division of labour between the villages, as sources of raw materials and early-stage processing, and the cities, as centres of later-stage production. Village employment is thus furthered. In a national context, however, where future industry in China will be high tech, employability of village inhabitants will depend on the expansion of technical education both for those leaving the countryside for the cities and those remaining in the villages, with an emphasis on advanced agricultural technology for the latter category, as suggested by the above survey. Given the frequent inability of villagers to afford education, provincial government subsidies are necessary for primary and middle-school students from indigent families (Yi, 2011).

In summary, the fact that China is not yet a nationwide market is partly a reflection of the urban–rural divide and also due to deficient physical infrastructure. The software element, logistics, is equally important and shown by the success of the Ten Million Project. The next section focuses on the growing diversification of taste and consumer discernment which are still largely urban phenomena.

The diversification of taste and consumer discernment

Increased personal wealth and exposure to foreign products have brought diversification of taste and consumer discernment, especially among China's urban middle class. The Chinese Academy of Social Sciences reported in 2010 that China's middle class, defined on the basis of income, occupation and educational level, make up 23 per cent of the country's urban population (Kan, 2010). One source states that, as urban per-capita disposable income rose during the years from 2000 to 2009, retail sales volume actually tripled (Zhang, 2011). It could be said that a more diversified diet is following economic and social change in China. As their wealth increases, consumers will spend a lower proportion of their income on food but their diet may nevertheless become more diversified. In addition, retired consumers could spend more on groceries as government pension provision increases in line with inflation. Younger consumers with families are likely to favour quality and convenience foods and spend more on groceries than previous generations (Qiu, 2011). These trends have led to growth in the food-processing industry, as consumers replace fresh foods bought in traditional markets with packaged products sold in modern supermarkets (Craig and Qiang, 2010). This was borne out by a recent survey which found that those in their twenties and younger were more likely to buy packaged and convenience foods, a reflection of a wider diversity of packaged products (Qiu, 2011). A recognition of the growing quality of such products was demonstrated by the China Food Industry Association granting the top brand food accolade to Wahaha, Jianlibao and Yili, in addition to 17 other food brands (CFIA, 2012).

To indicate greater consumer choice and discernment this section will include three case studies, focussing on food safety and nutrition labelling. In the last two decades the Chinese government has begun to give priority to food safety and in 2002, for instance, required products to be labelled regarding content (Zhang et al., 2004). The first case study relates to a survey, conducted by questionnaire, of food safety in Tianjin vegetable markets. Consumers were asked about food safety in relation to pork, beef, chicken, fish, fresh meat and vegetables. Questions covered levels of nutrition, fat content, disease carried by bacteria, insecticide residue and incidence of the use of hormones, and were designed to assess whether levels of consumer anxiety regarding such issues impacted on buying decisions. Consumer responses varied, depending on the food in question. In relation to pork the concern was with harmful bacteria. Regarding fish, information about nutritive value was sought. Vegetables were assessed according to quality and the presence of insecticide residues. On the basis of such responses the study found that 70 and 73 per cent of those questioned had very real concerns about the quality of milk and vegetables, respectively, while only 40 per cent were extremely anxious about chicken and fish. Anxiety about the safety of beef and pork fell in the middle range of concern, accounting respectively for 54 and 64 per cent of the responses (Zhang et al., 2004).

A salient feature in this quest for quality, as shown in the survey, was consumer knowledge of environmentally friendly, organic and genetically modified (GM) foods and unpolluted vegetables. In fact, less than half of those questioned knew about organic and GM products. Those responses were reflected in purchasing decisions, especially in relation to green food products, recognisable through the official logo. When asked whether they would be prepared to pay more for green foods, 262 out of 298 respondents expressed a willingness to do so but few expressed an interest in GM varieties. Not surprisingly, the survey found that, being more concerned with quality, the highly educated were likely to be aware and willing to buy GM foods. Since such foods do not seem to meet the resistance present in Western countries, more people in China may be prepared to buy, as the middle class expands (Zhang et al., 2004).

The second study, similarly focussed on vegetable markets, this time in Nanjing, examined in more depth the relationship between the declared intention of consumers and their actual purchasing behaviour regarding safe foods. The questionnaire given to consumers was divided into four parts. The first was designed to ascertain the level of concern about food safety among consumers on the basis of a sliding scale. The second examined consumers' general knowledge of food safety. The third, seeking to investigate stated intention and actual purchasing, focussed on consumer assessment of the safety of vegetables, including ordinary, environmentally polluted, green and organic categories. The fourth covered information about individuals and households: sex, age, marital status, average monthly income, number of residents, presence or absence of elderly people and children. The first finding of the survey suggested high consumer concern with food safety. Not surprisingly, consumers with high incomes were more likely to carry out their intention of purchasing safe foods. There was nevertheless a countervailing tendency, where it was shown that those with a high level of education and income and consequently greater knowledge of food safety issues were in some cases likely not to follow up a stated buying intention with actual purchasing. This apparent contradiction was explained by the fact that the highly educated were inclined to think in abstract terms and take a moral position. In addition, there may have been a built-in bias, not unknown in other surveys, where respondents select the reply they think is expected of them in terms of conventional wisdom. There were, of course, other reasons some educated respondents' actions were at variance with their responses: higher prices for safe foods, occasions where the perceived quality of other vegetables was similar, lack of trust in government-directed food labelling regarding organic, green and unpolluted categories as well as convenience of purchasing venues. Similarly, as in the case of the educated, households with elderly people and children tried in their responses to conform to expectations in their expressed concern with food safety but this did not necessarily follow through to purchasing (Zhang and Yi, 2010). In summary, the above survey indicates variance between stated preference and actual purchase of safe foods.

Consumer recognition of safe foods is closely linked to the perceived credibility of nutrition labelling. The United States and Western European countries have been the pacesetters in establishing standards regarding nutrition labelling, and the Chinese authorities have only latterly followed suit in the wake of the greater diversity of food products available. There has been a call for the education of consumers, even though public awareness is in any case growing, given increasing cognisance of individual rights. China's Health Ministry set down standards for the management of food nutrition labelling, with implementation beginning in 2008, its special targets being false claims and counterfeiting. The latter are referred to in regulations issued by the government of Jiangsu province. The measures are designed to reduce food poisoning–induced illness and its attendant cost to the individual and society. Accordingly, to conduct research concerning knowledge and attitude towards nutrition labelling, the following survey targeted a sample of 1200 consumers in four streets in the Lu Yi district of Shanghai. Of the distributed questionnaires 95 per cent were returned, 56.9 per cent were from women and 43.1 per cent from men. There was a fairly even spread of age groups but a bias in favour of the more educated, those with higher middle-school and university education representing 72.8 per cent of the total. Those having a monthly income of less than ¥1000 numbered 5.4 per cent, those earning from ¥1000 and above 39.2 per cent and those with ¥3000 and above 34.9 per cent, while people in the top income bracket of ¥5000 represented 20.7 per cent.

Occupational structure was as follows: officials and administrators numbered 27.5 per cent, workers 19.5 per cent, the retired 15.1 per cent, students 6.8 per cent, teachers 4.9 per cent, personnel in services 3.7 per cent and other categories – including the unemployed, those waiting to take up work and the self-employed – 22.5 per cent. Consumers were tested concerning their knowledge and understanding of nutrition and as to whether standards in nutrition labelling were necessary. In terms of knowledge of nutrition labelling, educational level was statistically significant. In terms of awareness, women scored higher than men, the younger were better informed than the older and the highly educated were more knowledgeable. There was, however, some misunderstanding regarding detail in labelling itself, with a sizeable proportion of consumers seeing it as merely a list of ingredients contained in the product (JG, 2010; Liu et al., 2012). Not only did consumers gain knowledge of nutrition from food labelling itself but from media, including newspapers, television broadcasts and the

Internet as well as through relations, work colleagues and fellow students (Liu et al., 2012).

Levels of knowledge were necessarily reflected in consumers' assessments of health-enhancing properties and purchasing decisions. Consumers were shown to be more concerned with nutrition labelling when buying staples like bread and milk products; in the latter case the presence of children in a household was an important criterion. Significantly, those interviewed showed great concern with energy-giving properties and core nutritional value but paid less attention to the presence of sodium and vitamins in food. Concern with the food safety aspect was also high. There was also some awareness of the connection between nutrition or the lack of it and chronic illness. Additionally, however, buying was determined by consumer trust in the credibility of nutrition labelling. Only a small minority had scant regard for nutrition labelling; some did not wish to change their habit of purchasing certain brands, while others thought the stated claims regarding nutrition were fictitious. Knowledge of and faith in nutrition labelling was more common among the highly educated.

In summary, while the Chinese government has only recently begun to legislate concerning the nutrition labelling of food products, the above research demonstrates that concern is growing in its influence on purchasing decisions. The above has focussed on consumer attitudes to food safety. State laws are both driven by and in turn influence such public concern and form the topic of the next section.

China's Food Safety Law and Tort Law

In the years immediately following their accession to power in 1949 the priority of Chinese Communist Party (CCP) leaders, like that of their current counterparts in developing countries, was supply of goods, especially grain reserves, in the face of scarcity and a growing population. In the decades since the initiation of the open-door policy, however, there has been greater consumer awareness of food quality and safety. Greater discretionary income has brought more commercial opportunities but simultaneously increased the incidence of fraud (Xu, 2011; Zhang et al., 2004).

Recent instances of malpractice by producers and distributors have added impetus to the initiation of more comprehensive food safety legislation. Such offences fall into two main categories, the first being the use of additives like those used to enhance the texture of *mantou* or steamed bread and others designed to produce a leaner appearance in meat. A second and connected issue relates to exaggerated claims for additives in, for example, powdered milk (JG, 2010; *The Economist*, 2012). In fact, the most infamous cases have concerned the consumption by infants of milk contaminated with melamine, a chemical used in plastic which can make protein content appear artificially high. In a case headlined in 2008 six infants died. The enterprise responsible, a partially state-owned and leading dairy company, the Sanlu Group, was at the heart of the scandal, even though partial responsibility rested with suppliers who were not adequately monitored. Significantly, in 2011 central government ordered the closure of 50 per cent of the country's dairies because they did not adhere to sufficient control standards (Ramzy, 2009; Rein, 2011). As might be expected, the greatest dangers have appeared on the mass market as, for instance, especially, counterfeit brands are targeted at lower income consumers. This is also indicated by a growing aversion to traditional Chinese snacks like roasted sunflower seeds and dried sweet potatoes, produced in a large number of local factories. Consequently, there is evidence that the market for foreign-style foods like potato chips and chocolate is growing, particularly among the young, leading to a mistrust among consumers of local producers and distributors alike (Qiu, 2011).

Accordingly, in February 2009 the Chinese government passed the Food Safety Law which came into effect in June of that year, superseding the 1995 Food Hygiene Law. The new law, designed to oversee the operations of producers, distributors, exporters and importers and strengthen national authorities' supervisory powers, unified food safety standards and increased penalties for lawbreakers. At the heart of the administration stands the State Council's Food Safety Commission and its secretariat as the highest overseer in China. The purpose of the commission is to coordinate the activities of those bodies responsible for implementation, namely the General Administration of Quality Supervision, Inspection and Quarantine, the State Food and Drug Administration and the Ministries of Health, Agriculture and Commerce. Hitherto, division of responsibility between bureaux had been a disadvantage since they vied for control in 'turf wars' and extraction of revenue from penalty fines. The objective of the Food Safety Law is to unify the large number of disparate regulations which govern the industry, an example being the use of clearer certification. The Food Distribution Certificate, the Catering Service Certificate and the Food Production Certificate replace the old food hygiene document. In

July 2009, for example, the State Administration for Industry and Commerce (SAIC) initiated measures regarding food distribution. One target was strengthening control over food additives, with type, usage and amount regulated, with no other chemicals allowed to be added during the production process. Food additives not on the approved government list may not be used. Clear record keeping and registration are demanded of foreign food producers and distributors. In addition, prepackaged food imports require appropriate Chinese labels. As much fraud has been facilitated by dishonest advertising, claims regarding the prophylactic and diagnostic functions of products are not permitted in food advertising. By implication, advertisers share joint liability with food producers and distributors. Additionally, the government may order the recall of unsafe foods. It is stated that the Food Safety Inspection Department must not exempt food manufacturers from inspection, and audits on food samples must be undertaken without charging fees from producers, an attempt to eliminate corruption (CSRN, 2009; Ramzy, 2009; Winston and Strawn, 2009).

China's Tort Liability Law was passed in December 2009 to take effect the following year. It was designed to protect consumers against defective products and stated the punitive damages which could be sought by litigants. The new law, unlike previous laws, does not place a limit on damages that may be awarded and, significantly, it extends protection to as well as imposing penalties on producers and distributors who may claim compensation from third-party transportation and service providers. The Tort Law framework when read in conjunction with the Food Safety Law increases the scope for consumers to take action against injury-causing food standard violations by producers and distributors. In short, the government is seeking to protect consumers through insisting, for instance, on the recall of defective food products and the barring of food safety violators for five years. There are, however, still impediments to the pursuit of litigation by consumers, given cost and the belated development of modern civil law in China (CSRN, 2009; Neumann and Ding, 2010).

In addition, while earlier sections of this chapter have suggested that awareness of rights among consumers is growing, especially among those residents of southeastern coastal provinces, there is a need for greater publicity regarding safety over the whole production and distribution process. To this end, in 2011, the State Council Food Safety Commission Secretariat issued the Food Safety Educational Work Outline, designed to make production managers aware of relevant regulations and further training in both technical knowledge and professional ethics. At the same time central government stated the need to make the public more aware of risk by utilizing all manner of mass and social media (Liu, 2011; Xu, 2011).

In spite, however, of the raft of food safety measures and central government–initiated policy enforcement, as in other legislation such as that relating to intellectual property, actual implementation is under the jurisdiction of provincial and local authorities. There are two major impediments to effective local implementation. First, producers face intense competition and will use, for instance, illegal additives to enhance their products. Because local authorities wish to maintain employment, close relationships with employers will encourage venality. The second barrier is the fragmentation of production and distribution. The latter impediment may be seen in the nature of China's husbandry: while in the United States four large-scale meat enterprises take 90 per cent of the market, the share of China's Top 10 equivalent producers does not reach 10 per cent. Farmers and fishermen number more than 200 million and there are 500,000 food production companies. In fact, it is said that almost anyone in China can become a dairy farmer or milk station collection agent without having received quality assurance training. The small scale of many food producers and distributors makes safety supervision by authorities that much more difficult (de Laurentis, 2009; Harris, 2009; Ramzy, 2009; Wang, 2011; Xu, 2011).

Two brief case studies relating to the provinces of Guangdong and Jiangsu will be cited to illustrate the progress of food safety supervision. The population of Guangdong exceeds 100 million and the province's consumption of food and drink is the highest in China. Its food-processing and import and export trade are similarly prominent in a national context. Nevertheless, supervision needs to address such deep-seated problems as polluted agricultural products and illegal food additives. The Provincial Food Safety Commission has set up a secretariat responsible for the daily supervision of food safety, its main duties being assessing current issues, deploying research personnel and implementing policy. The aim is to coordinate supervision of food safety 'from the field to the table', involving inspection of agriculture and fisheries, manufacturers of food and drugs as well as border control and quarantine, given Guangdong's coastal location. An important priority in 2011 was the testing and evaluation of staple food products like grain, bread, meat, vegetables and meat products. Additionally, market entry was to be controlled by tracing to source oil and other additives used in foods, health foods, fresh meat and meat products and wine, at the same time perfecting risk assessment. While the provincial People's Procuratorate is responsible for bringing offenders and officials accused of dereliction of duty before the courts, a main focus is on participation by the mass of consumers, with publicity given to cases reflecting consumer concern (Wu et al., 2011).

Similar emphases inform implementation in Jiangsu under State Council guidelines and the overall direction of the province's Food Safety Commission Secretariat. Once again all the parties (i.e., the government inspectorate, producers, distributors and consumers) are said to be involved in promoting food safety. Local authorities control the licensing of producers and are responsible for tracing illegal food additives back to their sources in the rural areas. This applies especially to residues of illegal drugs and pesticides found in milk, vegetables, fruit and tea; grain, as it is transferred to warehouses, is particularly subject to scrutiny. Likewise, the management of slaughter houses should seek to prevent the input of toxic matter into husbandry and the storage of sick or dying animals. At the next stage stand food processing and production where specialist personnel are to be trained in ethical and legal standards by trade associations. In the event of defective products reaching the market the law insists on recall but the ideal is where distributors themselves insist on immediate withdrawal (i.e., self-regulation). Finally, in Jiangsu, as elsewhere in China, food safety policy exhorts the force of public opinion as a preventative measure, and ultimately the most effective means of enforcement is the threat of litigation by consumers, even though the latter, while growing, is still in its infancy. Here the role of mass and, increasingly social, media is key (JG, 2010).

Traditionally, however, in post-1949 China law has been conceived of as an instrument of policy, even if in recent decades greater domestic and foreign trade has necessitated adherence to global commercial norms and the passing of legislation like the Food Safety Law. Consequently, there are still vestiges of rule by law, the *Rechtsstaat*, rather than the Anglo-American conception of rule of law. Law enforcement in China may also be uneven across the country. Moreover, given signs of a rise in national confidence, inspired in part by China's growing global economic power, there is a stronger possibility of the Food Safety Law being wielded against foreign manufacturers and distributors. Authorities in Jiangsu, for instance, have issued regulations to increase inspection procedures at customs for imported foods (JG, 2010).

A case where discrimination was in evidence concerned the penalty inflicted on the American retailer, Walmart, in Chongqing for mislabelling ordinary pork as an organic product. Some of its stores were closed, the company fined US$575,000 and employees arrested.

Walmart was a daunting target; with 350 stores and 100,000 employees it has been a tough adversary for Chinese competitors. This action followed a number of penalties for offences allegedly committed by Walmart since 2006, ranging from false advertising to selling out-of-date food (*The Economist*, 2012).

While, as indicated by the earlier melamine scandal, China's producers and distributors have not been immune to draconian penalties, including expropriation, imprisonment and the death sentence, at the disposal of the judiciary, the Walmart case highlights the vulnerability to prosecution of selected targets (Hua, 2010).

In summary, this section has examined food safety legislation and procedures for its enforcement. It was noted, however, that there are barriers to implementation: official venality, and fragmented production and distribution. Supervision of food safety was discussed with reference to the two provinces of Guangdong and Jiangsu, involving participation by local government authorities, distributors, producers and consumers. Finally, it was stressed that the traditional CCP conception of law as a policy instrument leaves the way open for discriminate enforcement, especially against foreign producers and distributors. It was concluded that potentially the most effective instrument in ensuring food safety in China is consumer awareness and action. Attention is now turned to the implications of China's food safety laws and greater consumer awareness for marketing strategy.

Implications for marketing strategy

China's food safety legislation and Tort Law, together with greater consciousness of consumer rights and increased choice of goods, place a premium on effectively targetted marketing as well as raising the cost of conducting business in China for both foreign and domestic companies alike. The caveat, however, must be entered that the effectiveness of these laws will depend on consumers' access to the courts and successful claims through the legal system. As yet there is no certainty on these counts. As precautionary measures, however, foreign companies active in the Chinese market must focus on quality control and allow recall of goods. Additionally, scrutiny of partners and suppliers as well as review of current insurance policies are advised. Thus, the factors of consumer rights and associated legislation must be successfully addressed (Neumann and Ding, 2010).

Chinese consumers with discretionary income reflect the American scholar Maslow's hierarchy of needs; once basic subsistence demands have been met, quality and safety (e.g., of food products) become paramount (Yuan et al., 2010).

Consequently, producers and retailers must satisfy these emerging needs. If, for example, only one item is defective, this will adversely affect consumers' perceptions of the rest of the product range, with resulting damage to the manufacturer's reputation, as in the additives to milk scandal (Lu and Wang, 2011).

One means by which manufacturers may enhance consumers' perception of quality is through brand strategy and reputation. There was reference earlier to the vulnerability of foreign companies to prosecution under the food safety laws in the midst of a nationalist tide potentially favouring domestic companies. While since the 1990s foreign manufacturers have favoured wholly owned rather than joint ventures as a means of entering China's markets, there could, in the wake of the above legislation, be strong arguments for alliances with domestic players. Such joint ventures could take the form of brand alliances, especially where a domestic brand has a large share of the market, since the Chinese partner can bring customer goodwill. Brands are intended to be distinctive and Western companies are in general more familiar with differentials in consumer taste than their Chinese counterparts who, only in the last two decades, have adjusted to a buyer's market. An awareness of brand value has nevertheless been growing, particularly since the adoption in Beijing in 1995 of evaluation methods, pioneered originally by the globally known institution, Interbrand. The conception of branding is necessarily associated with quality and for an alliance to be successful the two parties involved must have complementary strengths in order to gain positive consumer response. If one side's product brand is regarded as deficient, this will necessarily impact upon the alliance's image. As an alliance is established, a well-known trademark from one partner may assist in creating an image of reliability in the eyes of consumers (Han, 2011; Lu and Wang, 2011; Zhang and Mao, 2011; Yuan et al., 2010).

Taking food products as an example, once a successful brand has been launched, retailing comes into focus. In this context, as China's economy matures, services become increasingly important. Under the command economy there was a seller's market; Western strategists, however, have long been cognisant of the need for high-quality presentation and ambience in a sales environment (Lu and Wang, 2011). A contribution to better presentation by a foreign alliance with a Chinese retailer may help avoid the danger of discrimination by local authorities, at the same time updating services in line with consumer demand. Marketing strategy is a relatively new concept in post-reform China and, since its task is to anticipate trends, foreign parties with such skills will be advantaged, as laws governing food safety in Western countries predate legislation in China.

The foregoing has suggested ways in which foreign companies may address the impact of China's food safety and tort legislation. Such measures include joint venture partnerships, brand alliances and attention to services. Greater familiarity with the marketing concept is also an asset.

Summary and conclusions

In the wake of increased foreign trade and inward investment, a consumer culture has begun to emerge in China, especially in the cities of the wealthier southeastern seaboard. Given the global recession and barriers against Chinese exports, China's economic growth cannot depend on foreign trade alone. An alternative motor of development is domestic consumption and this is reflected in the priorities of China's 12th Five Year Plan which seeks to give China's population, particularly the poorer rural people, a greater share in the nation's wealth. Currently, discretionary income and diversification of consumption are urban phenomena but central government is taking steps to increase rural income, including tax concessions and crop specialisation, the latter assisting food choice for consumers. It was suggested that awareness of consumer rights may emerge in the villages in the context of increased wealth, e-commerce and the relocation of industry. The Ten Million Project in Zhejiang, in improving the logistics of distribution and employment opportunities, is designed to increase rural wealth.

Even though China is not yet a nationwide market, increased urban income has led to the diversification of taste and consumer discernment, especially in relation to food safety. Thus, China's food safety and tort laws, passed in 2009, have both responded to and in turn mould consumer awareness. Consumer discretionary income and choice of goods have heightened consumer awareness but also provided opportunities for fraud by producers and distributors. An example of this is the use of illegal additives and dishonest nutrition labelling. While a raft of legislation mandates heavy penalties for violation, enforcement is in the hands of local authorities, a situation where official venality has proved a barrier to effectiveness. The Guangdong and Jiangsu cases cited indicate attempts to monitor food safety 'from field to the table', with publicity intended to unleash the initiative of consumers. A further barrier to implementation, however, is fragmented production and distribution.

Nevertheless, the CCP legal tradition has been rule by law, the *Rechtsstaat*, and civil litigation is in its infancy. This, in conjunction with a growing national self-confidence, has facilitated discrimination against foreign retailers like Walmart. Accordingly, ways have been suggested by which marketing strategy may counter the danger of discrimination against foreign companies. Such means include joint venture and brand alliances with Chinese partners as well as attention to Western-style ambience in retail outlets. Finally, the hypothesis that an emerging civil society has heightened consciousness of consumer rights and that the food safety and tort laws both reflect and help further that concern are proven.

References

Anon. (2011) China data: economy. *China Business Review*, **38**(2), 37.

APCO (2010) China's economic restructuring: role of agriculture. APCO Worldwide Inc. Available from: *http://www.rsispublication@ntu.edu.sg* [accessed 7 June 2012].

Baden, B. (2012) Interview with David L. Cunningham Jnr, FedEx delivers in China. *China Business Review*, **39**(2), 22–5.

Bassolino, F. and Smith, M. (2010) Find first-tier consumers – in hundreds of cities. *China Business Review*, **37**(6), 16-19, 42.

CFIA (2001) Top 20 brands to China's food industry made debut. Available from: *http://english.people.com.cn/200112/03/eng20011203_85860.shtml* [accessed 7 June 2012] [China Food Industry Association].

China Daily (2010) China's 12th Five Year Plan signifies a new phase in growth, quoting Professor Kay Shimizu. Available from: *http://www.chinadaily.com.cn/bizchina/2010-10/27/content_11463985.htm* [accessed 7 June 2012].

Craig, R. and Qiang, J. (2010) China's emerging tier 2 cities: opportunities for US companies. *China Business Review*, **37**(6), 20–3.

Crampton, T. (2011) Social media in China: the same but different. *China Business Review*, **38**(1), 28–31.

CSRN (2009) China to initiate two-year campaign on food safety. Available from: *http://www.chinacsr.com/cn/2009/05/13/5224* [accessed 27 June 2012] [Corporate Social Responsibility Newsletter].

Cui, A. and Song, K.C. (2009) Understanding China's middle class. *China Business Review*, **36**(1), 38–41, 54.

de Laurentis, T. (2009) Ethical supply chain management. *China Business Review*, **36**(3), 38–41.

Han, Z.Y. (2011) Analysis on the function of technical trademark for building high-tech brand. *Keji he chanye (Science, Technology and Industry)*, **11**(12), 93–5.

Harris, D. (2009) China's new Food Safety Law: an early report, 16 December 2009. Harris Moure, PLLC. Available from: *http://www. chinalawblog.com/2009/12/china's%20_new_food_safety_law_an.html* [accessed 26 June 2012].

Hua, J. (2010) Chinese central government departments: the death penalty for food products safety violations must not be suspended. *Laodong Zhi Zhiyou*, **11**, 19.

JG (2010) Notification regarding the issuing of Jiangsu Province 2010 Food Safety Management Work Plan: the Jiangsu Government Order, Number 38, 6 April 2010. *Jiangsu Sheng Renmin Zhengfu Gongbao*, **38**, 61–6 [Jiangsu Government].

Kan, J. (2010) Environmentally friendly consumers emerge. *China Business Review*, **37**(3), 42–5.

Lardy, N. (2012) Sustaining economic growth in China. Available from: *http://www.eastasiaforum.org/2012/02/05/* [accessed 7 June 2012].

Liu, P. (2011) Protecting the safety of food products must be publicized more while avoiding inaction. *China Food*, **11**, 38.

Liu, Z.Y., Dan, C.D., Lu, J., Wu, J.H., Hu, G.Q. et al. (2012) Investigation and research into the factors influencing consumers' use of nutrition labelling. *Zhonghua Jibing Kongzhi Zazhi*, **16**(1), 60–3.

Lu, L.X. and Wang, Y.X. (2011) Enlightenment concerning how consumers' wrong decisions affect marketing. *Shangye Jingji*, **12**, 32–4.

Michael, D.C. and Zhou, Y. (2011) Understand and tap into China's digital generation. *China Business Review*, **38**(1), 22–6.

Neumann, P. and Ding, C. (2010) China's new Tort Law: dawn of the product liability era. *China Business Review*, **37**(2), 28–30.

Qiu, Y.T. (2011) Understanding Chinese consumers. *China Business Review*, **38**(3), 18–23, 58.

Ramzy, A. (2009) Will China's new safety laws work?, 3 March 2009. Available from: *http://www.time.com/time/world/article/0,8599,1882711,00.html* [accessed 26 June 2012].

Rein, S. (2011) Why Western fast food brands are winning in China, 3 August 2011. Available from: *http://webcache.googleusercontent.com/search?q=cache:2vXk720PvugJ:seekingalph* [accessed 7 June 2012].

Sinclair, J.A.C. (2010) Reaching China's next 600 cities. *China Business Review*, **37**(6), 12–15.

The Economist (2012) In the gutter: an American firm is punished but China's food safety problems run much deeper, 8 June 2012. Available from: *http:www.economist.com/node/21534812* [accessed 8 June 2012).

Wang, X. (2011) Food safety and media guidance. *China Food*, **3**, 70.

Winston & Strawn (2009) Greater China Law Update: PRC Food Safety Law and its impacts on Chinese food industry. Winston & Strawn, LLP. Available from: *http://www.winston.com* [accessed 7 June 2012].

Wu, C.Y., Ding, X.F. and Jin, N. (2011) Five provincial leaders order a directive to ensure food safety for the masses. *China Food*, **14**, 22–3.

Xi, H.X. (2010) The blue sea of change in city consumer demand. *China Marketing*, **10**, 20–1 [in Chinese].

Xu, X.L. (2011) We must use publicity and education as an important means of increasing the safety of food products. *China Food*, **14**, 10–11.

Yi, K.G. (2011) The plan for and broad analysis of the overall development of city-village commerce and trade: a case study of the results of Zhejiang Province's Ten Million Project. *Jingji Dili (Economic Geography)*, **31**(12), 2070–5.

Yuan, Z.M., Liu, S.S. and Chen, G.Q. (2010) Promoting the management of brand value: assessment theory and method for creating brands. *Xiandai Huiji*, **3**, 40–3.

Zhang, F.N. and Yi, X.P. (2010) Analysis of variance between levels of consumer concern with food safety and purchasing behaviour: Nanjing vegetable market as a case study. *Journal of Nanjing Agricultural University (Social Science Edition)*, **10**(2), 19–26.

Zhang, H.Z. (2012) China's economic restructuring: role of agriculture. Available from: *http://www.rsispublication@ntu.sg* [accessed 7 June 2012].

Zhang, L. (2011) Advertising in a new age of media. *China Business Review*, **38**(1), 16–20.

Zhang, X.R. and Mao, G.Q. (2011) Study on influential factors and effects of brand alliance: taking the mobile-phone industry as an example. *Jiangsu Shanglun*, **12**, 84–7.

Zhang, X.Y., Li, G. and Zhang, L. (2004) China's consumers' deep concern with food safety: an analysis of consumers in Tianjin. *Zhongguo Nongcun Guancha*, **1**, 14–20.

11

Country-of-origin effects on Chinese consumption of branded foreign products

Lingfang Fayol-Song

Abstract: Despite the global recession, international prestige brands continue to build on their success in the Chinese market. In order to sustain long-term achievement in this market, it is critical to have a profound understanding of local customers' attitudes towards branded foreign products. Consciously or subconsciously, consumers tend to use country-of-origin (COO) products as one of the selection criteria they keep in mind when purchasing. Our present research intends to disocver how and to what extent the COO effect influences Chinese consumer perception, preference and selection of branded foreign products. In order to have a better understanding of consumers' innermost opinions of COO effects, qualitative research was deemed the order of the day. Semi-directive interviews were carried out in the mainland of China. In order to make the research results more representative, the interviewees selected were of different sex, age, educational background, income and occupation. Research results on COO effects on Chinese consumers may help companies better understand how to communicate with and serve Chinese consumers in a more effective way.

Key words: China, consumer behaviour, COO, branded foreign products.

Introduction

Despite the global recession, internationally branded products continue to build on their success in the Chinese market. In 2010, the market registered growth of more than 10 per cent, representing 15 per cent of the world market share (Hu, 2011). China is currently the second largest luxury market (it overtook the USA in 2008), and is expected to overtake Japan to become the largest luxury market in the near future (CLSA, 2011).

The Chinese market, which is full of potential and dynamism, presents not only great opportunities but also significant challenges. Even though many international prestige brands like Nike and Intel are currently experiencing great success in the market, it does not guarantee that will be the case long term. Moreover, there are many cases of failure. Many global brands have failed to live up to expectations. According to the latest information released by Australia–China Business Week, 48 per cent of foreign businesses fail in China within 2 years of entering the market (Jones, 2013). Best Buy and Home Depot quit the market in 2011. eBay and Amazon lost competition to local Chinese companies. Walmart faces a dwindling market share (Rein, 2013). The intensifying levels of competition, fast-evolving market situation and cultural particularities of the market are the main obstacles influencing company performance. Foreign prestige brands face pressure to increase their commitment to the market or risk losing ground to their rivals (KPMG, 2007). Thus, a profound knowledge of the target market is indispensable to achieve competitive advantage and sustain long-term success.

Among the many issues related to Chinese consumption, consumer brand awareness and selection criteria represent particular interest for both academic researchers and business practitioners because they are the first step in the decision-making process involved in making a purchase. Numerous previous studies have revealed that the country of origin (COO) of prestige products has a great impact on customer perception and purchase intentions of brands especially in relation to international prestige brands (Aiello et al., 2010; Haubl and Elrod, 1999; Maheswaran, 2006; Schooler, 1965).

Some studies have been carried out regarding COO influence on the selection criteria of Chinese customers, in general (Gong et al., 2004; Kwok et al., 2005; Schmitt, 1997; Zhang, 1996), as well as other studies on the Chinese luxury market such as purchasing motives (Bian and Forsythe, 2012; Wang et al., 2010; Zhu, 2006) and general consumer behaviour (Qi and Li, 2009; Tang, 2009). There have been a number of surveys and investigations carried out mainly by consulting groups on the foreign premium branded product sector. These studies show sector information by means of numbers, figures and graphics. However, limited rigorous academic research has studied the issue in a systematic way. Few marketing concepts and frameworks have been tested in this context. Even less academic research has focussed on the COO effect on Chinese consumption of branded foreign products. This is because the presence of these products is a relatively recent phenomenon in China, and its rapid evolution exceeds expectations. Thus, there exists a real need to explore the subject and increase our understanding of the COO in Chinese consumption. One objective of our present research is to discover how and to what extent the COO effect influences Chinese consumer perception, preference and selection of branded foreign products. Another is to provide some practical insights for companies into the development of business and communication strategies.

Literature review

Today's luxury business is a matter of brands. When a consumer has a preference for a brand stemming from its cultural background, heritage or image, they are willing to spend more for this brand than for another. 'There is always a strong emotional value attached to a strong brand for reasons that are historical, and social as well as emotional' (Chevalier and Mazzalovo, 2008).

While consumers are supposed to make rational choices about products by comparing product features, functions and performance objectively, they are very often driven by emotion when deciding to purchase products. Favourable or unfavourable feelings towards a product determine the decision to purchase or reject it regardless of its quality or other attributes (Gürhan-Canli and Maheswaran, 2000; Klein et al., 1998; Maheswaran, 2006; Usunier and Lee, 2009). Consumers tend to use the COO of the product as a principal reference for choosing it.

Ever since the concept of COO was first broached (Schooler, 1965), numerous studies have revealed that customer perception of a product is greatly influenced by the COO of the product. Products, identical in every respect except for their COO, are perceived differently by consumers. The COO has an effect not only on consumer perceptions but also on their preferences and purchase intentions. Nowadays, business globalisation allows customers to have access to products that originate from many different countries, and their choice is often driven by the COO of the product (Maheswaran, 2006).

Many factors moderate the influence of COO on consumer evaluation including customer awareness of COO (such as knowledge of and familiarity with the product), ethnocentric tendencies, product category and risk perception (Usunier and Lee, 2009). When customers are unfamiliar with and lack knowledge of the products, or they don't want to spend time on research to improve their knowledge, they may use COO as a shortcut to accelerate the decision-making process (Usunier and Lee, 2009).

The notion of COO is evolving constantly. Originally, it referred to the country of manufacture, where the product is designed and made. Nowadays, with business globalisation and the practice of outsourcing, where the brand is created and designed and where the product is manufactured and assembled may be in different countries. Finally, the meaning of COO is no longer specific enough. As a result, new terms like country of brand (COB), country of manufacture (COM) and country of design (COD) have come into being (Aiello et al., 2010). Consumers tend to have a more favourable perception of the product's quality if there is coherence between the brand and the country of production (Haubl and Elrod, 1999).

In spite of the recognized influence of COO, the research of Aiello et al. (2010) carried out in three European countries – Italy, France and Germany – shows that, of the various factors influencing purchase intention, design is the most important, followed by brand name and that COO is almost the last factor on the list of considerations.

As far as general influences of COO on Chinese consumers are concerned, research reveals mixed evidence on consumer preference between foreign and local brands (see the review of Kwok et al., 2005). Some studies show a strong preference in China for foreign brands (Cui, 1999; Li et al., 1997; Schmitt, 1997; Zhou and Hui, 2003) while other research results do not support this contention (Cui and Liu, 2001; Li and Gallup, 1995). Others reveal that the COO effect varies according to product types (Kwok et al., 2005; Lin et al., 2003; Zhang, 1996). Consumer durables tend to be more influenced by COO (Cui et al., 2004). By contrast, the survey of Kwok et al. (2005) shows that about 50 per cent of respondents do not really know the COO of brands. So the COO effect is limited.

According to Verlegh and Steenkamp (1999), the COO effect on consumer behaviour is based on a wider connotation, including emotional dimensions (the COO has a symbolic and emotional value to the consumer) and normative dimensions (consumers have social norms and personal links to the COO). Consumers in developing countries perceive the COO as a factor indicating not only quality but also social symbolic values (Batra et al., 2000).

Research method

Instead of producing statistics and figures indicating the general situation and tendencies of the COO effect on Chinese consumers, the objective of the present research is to understand why and how Chinese consumers are influenced by the COO of luxury brands. We chose the qualitative method of using semi-structured interviews to achieve this objective. Soliciting interviewees' opinions as to their perception and selection criteria, we sought to acquire an intimate knowledge of consumer mentality and behaviour that transcends factual statistics.

Twelve in-depth interviews were carried out. The average time of each interview was an hour and a half. The interviews made use of carefully designed open questions. It was agreed before beginning the interview that the research results would be presented anonymously so that the interviewees could feel free to express themselves openly. In order to make the research results more representative, the interviewees selected were of different sex, age, educational background, income and occupation. Of the 12 interviewees, 6 were men and 6 women. The youngest respondent was 25 years old and the oldest 51. Monthly net income varied from ¥3000 to ¥20,000. None had the same occupation. The lowest education level was a middle-school diploma and the highest a master's degree. Table 11.1 shows the main characteristics of the participants.

Research results and discussions

The participants were asked in the interviews to mention one to five categories of branded foreign products (not services) they had bought in the past three years as well as one to five categories of products they intended to buy in the coming three years. If they had bought or intended to purchase more than five categories, we asked them to mention the ones that were most important for them either financially or emotionally or both. Eight main product categories were revealed: clothes including shoes; cellphones; wine including whisky, brandy and cognac; cars; handbags; watches; cosmetics including make-up and perfume; home appliances including TVs, air conditioners and furniture.

The interviews revealed that all our respondents were consumers of branded foreign products. However, the products they bought and intended to buy were quite different from each other. Income was the main reason there were differences. The most bought products were clothes and cellphones. Eleven bought foreign branded clothes and/or shoes. Nine bought a foreign brand cellphone. For the female interviewees, cosmetics and handbags were must haves. Table 11.2

Table 11.1 Profile of the interviewees

Participant	Sex	Age	Income (¥/month)	Education	Occupation
Interviewee 1	Male	25	3 000	High school	Restaurant employee
Interviewee 2	Female	32	6,500	College	Nurse
Interviewee 3	Male	43	12,000	Master	Doctor
Interviewee 4	Female	46	4,000	Middle school	Shop salesperson
Interviewee 5	Male	51	20,000	Master	Company manager
Interviewee 6	Male	42	15,000	Bachelor	Small-shop owner
Interviewee 7	Male	50	5,000	Middle school	Hotel employee
Interviewee 8	Female	28	6,000	Bachelor	Office clerk
Interviewee 9	Female	38	10,000	Bachelor	Company accountant
Interviewee 10	Female	35	9,000	Bachelor	Middle-school teacher
Interviewee 11	Female	37	8,000	College	Freelancer
Interviewee 12	Male	45	6,000	High school	Taxi driver

summarizes the consumption and intended consumption of foreign branded products.

During the interviews, the respondents were also asked to cite the three most important criteria they considered when purchasing different products. At the same time, they were asked to explain the reasons for their criteria. Table 11.3 represents a summary of the three most popular criteria given by way of response, applied to each of the products listed in Table 11.2.

Our research reveals that the COO plays an important role in persuading the Chinese consumer to purchase a foreign branded product. Of all the criteria put forward, COO was the most cited. It was also the only criterion cited for each of the seven product categories; brand name and product design were the next most cited. Our respondents clearly demonstrated how they associated product categories and preferred product COOs (Table 11.5).

When asked why COO was considered important, 8 of the 12 respondents felt COO added value to the product. The country image

Table 11.2 Branded foreign products already purchased and to be purchased

Participant	Branded foreign products already purchased	Branded foreign products to be purchased in the future
Interviewee 1 (restaurant employee)	Clothes, TV	Cellphone, clothes
Interviewee 2 (nurse)	Cellphone, clothes, cosmetics, handbag	Cosmetics, clothes
Interviewee 3 (doctor)	Cellphone, clothes, wine, watch, handbag	Clothes, car, TV
Interviewee 4 (shop assistant)	Clothes, cosmetics, handbag	Cosmetics, clothes, cellphone
Interviewee 5 (company manager)	Car, cellphone, wine, clothes	Wine, watch, clothes, cellphone
Interviewee 6 (small-shop owner)	Cosmetics, clothes, cellphone, car, handbag	Watch, clothes, air conditioner, cellphone
Interviewee 7 (hotel employee)	Clothes, wine, cellphone	Wine, TV, washing machine
Interviewee 8 (company assistant)	Handbag, cellphone, cosmetics, clothes	Cosmetics, clothes, watch, handbag
Interviewee 9 (company accountant)	TV, air conditioner, cellphone, clothes	Refrigerator
Interviewee 10 (middle-school teacher)	Cellphone, cosmetics, clothes	Cosmetics, handbag
Interviewee 11 (freelancer)	Clothes, watch, cosmetics, cellphone	Cellphone, cosmetics, handbag
Interviewee 12 (taxi driver)	TV, washing machine, wine	Cellphone

was deeply rooted in people's minds. Consciously or subconsciously, people felt more comfortable and secure in choosing a brand from a country known for the quality of the product, such as Germany for cars; France for handbags, cosmetics and wine; South Korea for cellphones, clothes and cosmetics (Table 11.4). Here are a few comments made by the interviewees: 'I know the country of origin is

Table 11.3 Selection criteria for purchase

Product	No. 1 criterion	No. 2 criterion	No. 3 criterion
Car	Brand name	Design	Country of origin
Cellphone	Brand name	Design	Country of origin
Clothes	Place of purchase	Country of origin	Design
Cosmetics	Brand name	Country of origin	Effects
Handbag	Brand name	Country of origin	Design
Watch	Brand name	Country of origin	Design
Wine	Country of origin	Brand name	Taste
Home appliances	Brand name	Design	Country of origin

Table 11.4 Relation between product category and COO

Product	COO preferred
Car	Germany, USA, Japan
Cellphone	USA, South Korea
Clothes	South Korea, Japan, Italy, France
Cosmetics	France, Japan, USA, South Korea
Handbag	France, USA, UK
Watch	Switzerland, France, UK
Wine	France, Italy
Home appliance	Korea, Japan, Germany

not 100% reliable in judging the quality and the performance of the product but it helps in making purchasing decisions. I can save a lot of time in making the choice. For example, between a French perfume and a German one, I won't hesitate to choose the first . . . French cars don't sell well in China. The main reason is that people don't associate France with car manufacturer . . . I always buy wine imported from France, and will buy definitely a German car. Why a German car? I don't mean the cars of other countries are no good but a German car is much better recognized.'

The interviewees felt COO was also a guarantee of high quality and performance, as shown by comments like 'Western products are usually better in quality than China-made ones. When I have the choice and if I can afford it, I prefer to buy international branded products especially for durables.' For some of our respondents, group affiliation was important when selecting a brand: 'When I needed to change my cellphone last year, I thought at first of buying a Nokia because my previous one was a Nokia, and it worked well. But finally I bought a Samsung because I saw all my friends used either Apple or Samsung. If I buy a Nokia, I will feel somewhat uncomfortable for I'm afraid they would think I made a wrong choice.'

All of our respondents had very clear ideas about the brand origin of the products they had bought and those they intended to purchase in the future. They spent a lot of time researching the brand such as COO, prices, designs, etc.: 'I won't buy a branded foreign product if I don't know from which country it comes. Otherwise, there is no difference from buying a Chinese product ... Of course, I know the country of origin of the products I have bought. Before I make the purchase, I'll discuss with my friends and my relatives. They always give me plenty of useful information. I also surf in the internet to get more information.'

Despite unanimity about the importance of COO, our research reveals that COO is not cited as the No. 1 criterion for the selection of most products. Its effect is less important than brand name: 'We usually know the brand name first, and if we like it, we'll try to find out which country it is from ... It is not interesting to buy a Korean cellphone if it is not Samsung ... Brand name plus its country of origin is a double guarantee for me to choose a product.'

The importance of COO also varies according to the product category. Of the different products listed, wine would appear to be the most sensitive to COO for it is ranked as the No. 1 criterion considered for selection. Indeed, our research concludes that our interviewees' knowledge of this product area was quite limited. Currently, most Chinese consumers still prefer to drink Chinese alcohol. Consumption of Western wine is a recent phenomenon. People drink it because it is fashionable and representative of the Western way of life and high social status, rather than because of its taste. Few people can really tell the difference between the various types of wine. The country of origin in such circumstances is often used as a reliable shortcut to choosing good wine without losing face.

Our research results indicate some interesting details about COO effects on Chinese consumption. First of all, the coherence between a brand's COO and its country of manufacture is highly sought after. It is considered to be a guarantee of prestige and quality. When examining the product at the moment of purchase, consumers systematically check the 'made in' label. They are ready to pay a higher price for the product if it is manufactured in the COO of the brand: 'I bought a Lacoste polo shirt for my son in France. It was made in France. Even if it is more expensive that those made in China, it is worthwhile. My son appreciates it more ... My friend in USA gave me a Raphael Laurent wallet as a gift. It was made in China. I would prefer it made in US but he told me it didn't exist. I don't know whether it is true or not.'

Surprisingly, place of purchase was nominated as a selection criterion, especially for clothing and shoes. It was also mentioned in relation to the other products. It is not shown in the table because the number of responses for these criteria were fewer than for other criteria. But its influence on the decision to purchase does exist, nonetheless. Consumers prefer to make their purchase in the COO of the brand in question, such as Louis Vinton handbags and wine in France, cosmetics in South Korea and France, clothing in famous shopping areas abroad like the Champs-Élysées, Fifth Avenue, and Oxford Street. Duty-free shops are also considered good places to go shopping. It is not uncommon for consumers to travel to Hong Kong once or twice a year specifically to go shopping. If overseas travel is not affordable or possible, consumers prefer to make purchases in well-known domestic luxury shopping malls. Such behaviour is because shopping location is seen as an extension of COO. Location can also add value to the product. Another reason for consumer preference in relation to location has to do with the fake product phenomenon in China. The act of shopping in the abovementioned locations is a sure way of protecting oneself from fake products. Moreover, shopping abroad or at duty-free shops has a financial dimension for the prices are much lower than in Chinese shops.

In recent years South Korea has emerged as the COO of choice for numerous product categories, especially clothing and cosmetics. This is due to cultural similarities between the two countries and the physical resemblance between Chinese and Korean people. Chinese consumers buy Western brands of cosmetics and clothes more for the prestige and brand names, but buy Korean brands more for the effect and design.

Managerial implications and conclusion

For historical, cultural and economic reasons, Chinese consumers have developed particular attitudes and behaviours in the way they purchase branded foreign products. Their consumption values and patterns differ significantly from their Western counterparts. The present research on COO effects on Chinese consumers may help companies better understand how to target and communicate with Chinese consumers in a more effective way. Here are some practical recommendations:

- As COO plays such a significant role in the selection process, companies need to target customers by emphasizing the COO of the brand especially when there is a positive relation between the brand and the country image. For example, when selling French wine it is important to emphasise the origin.
- When there is coherence between country of brand (COB) and country of manufacture (COM) there are opportunities for companies to charge a premium.
- Chinese consumer preference for shopping abroad suggests a need for companies to differentiate offers made in the Chinese market and those made outside. Additional services should be provided in Chinese shops to compensate for the high prices currently charged there.
- South Korea's predominance as a COO should incentivise Western companies to benchmark against Korean brands and better adapt to the special conditions encountered in the Chinese market.

In conclusion, our findings have hopefully met the objective of this chapter and provided a better understanding of COO effects on Chinese consumers regarding their consumption of branded foreign products. We intend our future research to involve a larger number of participants with as many different profiles as possible. By doing so we hope to discover whether there is a relationship between participant characteristics and COO effects.

References

Aiello, G., Donvito, R., Godey, B., Pederzoli, D., Wiedmann, K.P. et al. (2010) Luxury brand and country of origin effect: results of an international empirical study. *Journal of Marketing Trends*, **1**, January, 67–75

Batra, R., Ramaswamy, V., Alden, D., Steenkamp, J.B.E.M. and Ramachander, S. (2000) Effects of brand local and non local origin on consumer attitudes in developing countries. *Journal of Consumer Psychology*, **9**(2), 83–95.

Bian, Q. and Forsythe, S. (2012) Purchase intention for luxury brands: a cross cultural comparison. *Journal of Business Research*, **65**(10), October, 1443–51.

Chevalier, M. and Mazzalovo, G. (2008) *Luxury Brand Management: A World of Privilege*. Wiley-Blackwell, Hoboken, NJ, p. 81.

CLSA (2011) China to become the world's largest market for luxury goods over the next decade. Available from: *https://www.clsa.com/about-clsa/media-centre/2011-media-releases.php?start=10* [accessed: 2 February, 2012] [Crédit Lyonnais Securities Asia].

Cui, G. (1999) Segmenting China's consumer market: a hybrid approach. *Journal of International Consumer Marketing*, **11**(1), 55–76.

Cui, G. and Liu, Q. (2001) Executive insights: emerging market segments in a transitional economy: a study of urban consumers in China. *Journal of International Marketing*, **9**(1), 84–106.

Cui, G., Wang, Y. and Zhou, N. (2004) Backlash of global brands? Consumer purchases of foreign and domestic products in an emerging market. *Proceedings of the AIB Southeast Asia Regional Conference, Macau.*

Gong, W., Li, Z. and Li, T. (2004) Youth consumption behaviour in China: cultural changes and marketing opportunities. *Proceedings of the AIB Southeast Asia Regional Conference, Macau.*

Gürhan-Canli, Z. and Maheswaran, D. (2000) Cultural variations in country of origin effects. *Journal of Marketing Research*, **37**(3), 309–17

Haubl, G. and Elrod, T. (1999) The impact of congruity between brand name and country of production on consumers product quality judgments. *International Journal of Research in Marketing*, **16**(3), 199–215.

Hu, Z.F. (2011) Luxuries and sadness. *Xinmin Weekly*, Issue 5, p. 25.

Jones, A. (2013) Business failure in China – why? (19 June 2013). Available from: *http://www.lexology.com/library/detail.aspx?g=96f57998-5a62-4c59-af1e-f41b4114d96c* [accessed 20 July 2013].

Klein, J.G., Ettenson, R. and Morris, M.D. (1998) The animosity model of foreign product purchase: an empirical test in the People's Republic of China. *Journal of Marketing*, **62**, January, 89–100.

KPMG (2007) Luxury brands in China. Available from: *http://www.kpmg.com/CN/en/IssuesAndInsights/ArticlesPublications/Documents/Luxury-brands-China-200703.pdf* [accessed 16 March 2012].

Kwok, S., Uncles, M. and Huang, Y. (2005) Country-of-origin effects in China: an investigation of urban Chinese consumers. Paper presented at *ANZMAC 2005 Conference: Marketing Issues in Asia*. Available from: *http://smib.vuw.ac.nz:8081/www/anzmac2005/cd-site/pdfs/21-Mktg-Asia/21-Kwok.pdf* [accessed 21 May 2013].

Li, D. and Gallup, A.M. (1995) In search of the Chinese consumer. *China Business Review*, September/October, 19–22.

Li, Z.G., Fu, S. and Murray, L.W. (1997) Country and product images: the perceptions of consumers in the People's Republic of China. *Journal of International Consumer Marketing*, **10**(1/2), 115–39.

Lin, Z., Wang, S. and Lu, X. (2003) Research on Chinese and foreign brand preferences in urban areas. *Management World*, September [in Mandarin].

Maheswaran, D. (2006) *Country of Origin Effects: Consumer Perceptions of Japan in South East Asia* (Working Paper N-006, December). Available from: *http://w4.stern.nyu.edu/emplibrary/mahesh006.pdf* [accessed 10 December 2010].

Qi, Y. and Li, W. (2009) Empirical study on relationship between self-concept attribution and conspicuous consumption behavior. *Technology Economics*, **4**.

Rein, S. (2013) Why global brands fail in China? CNBC. Available from: *http://www.cnbc.com/id/46009614* [accessed 14 November 2012].

Schmitt, B. (1997) Who is the Chinese consumer? Segmentation in the People's Republic of China. *European Management Journal*, **15**(2), 191–4.

Schooler, R.D. (1965) Product bias in Central American Common Market. *Journal of Marketing Research*, **2**(4), 394–7.

Tang, L. (2009) Please reasoningly [*sic*] consume luxury: the discussion of luxury consumption behavior in China. *Journal of Hunan University of Science and Engineering*, **3**. Available from: *http://en.cnki.com.cn/Article_en/CJFDTOTAL-JMLK200903038.htm* [accessed 13 November 2010].

Usunier, J-C. and Lee, J.A. (2009) *Marketing across Culture* (Fifth Edition). Pearson Education, London.

Verlegh, P. and Steenkamp, J-B. (1999) A review and meta-analysis of country-of-origin research. *Journal of Economic Psychology*, **20**, 521–46.

Wang, Y, Sun, S. and Song, Y. (2010) Motivation for luxury consumption: evidence from a metropolitan city in China. In: R.W. Belk (Ed.), *Research in Consumer Behavior*, Vol. 12. Emerald Group Publishing, Bingley, UK, pp. 161–81

Zhang, Y. (1996) Chinese consumers' evaluation of foreign products: the influence of culture, product types and product presentation format. *European Journal of Marketing*, **30**(12), 50–68.

Zhou, L. and Hui, M.K. (2003) Symbolic value of foreign products in the People's Republic of China. *Journal of International Marketing*, **11**(2), 36–58.

Zhu, X. (2006) An empirical research on luxury consumption motives of Chinese consumers. *Journal of Business Economics*, **7**, 42–8.

12

Advertising in the luxury sector in China: standardisation or adaptation? A comparison between China and Italy

Francesca Checchinato, Cinzia Colapinto and Alice Giusto

Abstract: In the general framework of internationalisation, this chapter focusses on the advertising strategies adopted by top companies in the luxury sector. The chapter reports some of the findings of a study to determine the importance of local culture in advertising content by comparing Chinese and Italian ads. In particular, after an overview of the advertising market in China and in Italy, the content of ads from *Vogue*, one of the most popular and influential fashion and beauty magazines in both China and Italy, are analysed. The focus is on three industries: clothing, cosmetics and jewellery. This chapter contributes to the standardisation–adaptation discussion and shows that strategies are affected by both country and product category.

Key words: brand communication, cross-cultural marketing, advertising strategies, China, Italy.

Introduction

Recent popular and academic discourses have speculated much on China's rise and its implications for the future global order. Indeed, the Chinese economy has increased more than tenfold since the start of reform and opening up in 1978, when a new era in contemporary Chinese history began. In the last decade we have been witnessing East Asia shifting position from periphery to prominence: China is the last 'miracle' and the world's most dynamic centre of economic and commercial expansion (Arrighi, 2008). China has transitioned from a planned and centralised economy to a market economy, and this transition has been accompanied by unprecedented social change and reform in different industries (Zhao, 2008). In particular, not only are media affected by this economic transformation they are also agents and drivers of this shift: they sustain marketing, advertising and consumerism (mass market). The dual and mutual relationship between the economy and media can be explained through the role of advertising. Advertising and media contents are agents of change: on the one hand, they reflect culture and the increasing desires of consumers and new consumption aspirations; on the other hand, they influence behaviour and beliefs.

Since China opened its door to the world, many foreign brands have flocked in and local brands have developed rapidly in response to competition (Yifan, 2007). Economic reforms and development are evident in increasing per-capita income – from €345 in 2000 to €695 in 2006 (NBS, 2008)[1] – and as a result advertisers are increasingly becoming interested in capturing the attention of recipients (Rochet and Tirole, 2002): brand awareness in China is growing; branded products are produced because of demand from both the business and the buyer side (Yifan, 2007). Even though per-capita GDP in China is low, the structure of social consumption is moving towards enjoyment and is taking on a commercial-oriented pattern, resulting in increasing numbers of people moving beyond the basics: as often the rise of consumerism is strictly linked to mass media development.

There has been growing interest in consumer behaviour in China as a result of the growing significance of the Chinese market and seemingly paradoxical consumer purchasing patterns (Wang and Lin, 2009). Culture is often considered as all pervasive and clearly affects Chinese consumers; moreover, conceptualisations of Chinese cultural values are numerous (Fan, 2010; Wang and Lin, 2009).

Chinese consumers are increasingly looking beyond the basic functional attributes of products at various other dimensions in line with the more sophisticated consumer habits commonly found in developed economies. They are increasingly able to use personal choice in their spending and purchase independently and intelligently as opposed to dictatorially (EI, 2010).

Studies have shown how Chinese people endorse both traditional and modern values. They also show that these values co-exist in contemporary Chinese advertising (Zhang and Shavitt, 2003). This leads naturally to investigating in greater depth how Chinese people overcome conflict values in magazine advertising and how international marketeers identify appropriate ads for firms' brand strategies in China.

Since advertising is at the forefront of international marketing and communication strategies and at the same time reflects the cultural values of consumers, many studies have analysed the appeal of Chinese advertising compared with that of other countries (Ji and McNeal, 2001; Nelson and Paek, 2007).

This chapter contributes to the standardisation–adaptation discussion by providing an empirical analysis that compares findings from print ads in the same magazine (*Vogue*) in two countries: China and Italy. Italy has been chosen as it is well known for fashion and luxury products and is investing a lot in that sector in China.

Cross-cultural research in advertising

National cultural differences can influence advertising practices and this influence can be observable at the component level of individual ads (Cutler et al., 1992). On the one hand, some Western advertising conventions have been transferred to Asia through international versions of global magazines (Cheng and Frith, 2006). On the other hand, especially in China, a glocal advertising approach has been pursued: a mix of standardisation and specialisation (Mueller, 2004). Yin (1999) pointed out that some local elements, such as culture, language, product attributes and models are relevant.

According to research on print ads by Cutler et al. (1992) the visual elements of ads include size, frequency of black and white versus colour pictures, photographic effects (illustrations versus photographs), size and frequency of product portrayal and mention of price in the ad. Moreover, the appeal of the visual process (e.g., description, association, metaphor and storytelling approaches) is considered an advertising element and has been analysed (Javalgi et al., 1995) from a cross-cultural perspective.

Other research concerns the visual elements of advertising and compares, for example, the characteristics of models involved in the pictures. In particular, in cross-cultural studies differences in the way women are portrayed across cultures have been analysed (Maynard and Taylor, 1999). There are interesting studies about Asian ads, in which the race of models used in each culture did not reflect the radical mix of that country's population (Frith et al., 2004).

Some studies look at the informative content of advertising by making use of specific categories such as packaging, taste, nutrition, warranties and the presence of independent research information (Abemethy and Franke,

1996). Elements can also be specifically related to the textual part of the message such as what the ad claims, analysed for example in Javalgi et al. (1995), and the language used, which varies according to the extent to which it is localised (Nelson and Paek, 2007). Other elements that have been analysed in current Chinese advertising include cultural values such as modernity, tradition, individualism and collectivism (Zhang and Shavitt, 2003).

Some other studies compare ads in terms of their emotional appeal, information content, and use of humour and sex (Biswas et al., 1992). Cross-cultural differences in the use of intrinsic and extrinsic product cues, such as physical quality, design, brand name and price have been analysed as well (Forsythe et al., 1999). Cross-cultural research not only analyses a lot of different advertising elements but also involves many different countries.

Many studies compare US ads with those of other countries such as the UK and India (Frith and Sengupta, 1991), France (Biswas et al., 1992), Japan (Belk and Pollay, 1995; Javalgi et al., 1995; Maynard and Taylor, 1999) and China (Wang and Chan, 2001). But there are also studies between European countries – such as the research by Nelson and Paek (2007) that compares British and French TV commercials and reveals differences in customisation between the two countries – or between Asian countries. Fam and Grohs (2007) have compared cultural values in ads between China and other Asian countries, such as Indonesia, Thailand, India and Hong Kong.

Advertising: a comparison between China and Italy

In the current crisis (2007–13) investments have collapsed and GDP has declined: obviously this setting affects advertising and marketing strategies pursued by companies all over the world. According to Warc Advertising expenditure growth is expected to increase despite the fragility of the global economy; Warc's Consensus Advertising Forecast[2] predicts adspend will rise by 4 per cent in 2013 and 5.5 per cent in 2014, ahead of the 3.9 per cent uptick estimated for 2012. The US, the world's biggest advertising market, is in line to enjoy expansions of 2.2 per cent in 2013 and 4 per cent in 2014. Russia is likely to be the fastest-growing market in 2013 thanks to a 12.3 per cent leap, followed by China on 10.9 per cent and Brazil on 9.8 per cent. Spain is set to log the worst performance in 2013, with adspend down

2.8 per cent. Brazil is expected to assume the top spot in growth terms in 2014, up by 12.1 per cent, ahead of India on 12 per cent, China on 11.2 per cent and Russia on 11 per cent.

According to media channel, the Internet is predicted to increase demand in excess of 13 per cent annually going forward, although this marks a moderation of the estimated 14.4 per cent expansion recorded in 2012. Television will also prove robust, as revenues rise by 3.2 per cent in 2013 and 6.4 per cent in 2014. Newspapers are due to see growth in both 2013 and 2014, but only in three nations: Brazil, India and Russia. China joins this group for magazines, showing that fast-growth markets are vital for publishers. Worldwide, though, newspaper ad sales are pegged to contract at 2.7 per cent in 2013 and 1.6 per cent in 2014, the figures hitting 2.5 per cent and 1.7 per cent for magazines, indicating broader structural issues facing the print sector. It is important to remember that the world of media remains in continuous flux, and the Internet has broken all the rules of communications. Moreover, luxury brands believe that digital media is more effective at raising online and offline sales; however, fashion magazines still play a relevant role.

With the Eurozone crisis dragging on and the US recovery lacking momentum, the world economy entered a new phase of adjustment in 2012, which is expected to suppress the rate of global recovery further in the coming years. With this in mind we analyse two countries in depth: China and Italy.

China's GDP growth rate in 2012 was 7.8 per cent. This year marked the first time the annual GDP growth rate was lower than 8 per cent since 1999, and the annual growth rate became the lowest since 1998 (CTR, 2013), but it still presented a positive trend considering the world situation. According to the latest CTR publication on Chinese adspend data, traditional advertising annual growth in the Chinese market in 2012 was only 4.5 per cent, the lowest in the last 5 years. Influenced by the economic environment, the forecast of depression in the Chinese advertising market at the beginning of 2012 eventually materialised at the year end. From the perspective of the China media market, the landscape is quite complex and constantly evolving, as attitudes and policies continue to change.

As the world's third largest ad market, traditional media in China continued to play an important role in theburgeoning media landscape of 2012. Despite considerable general growth in online news sources and communities, they remained the most trusted sources of information and the predominant media channel; therefore, the importance of television to the Chinese cannot be underestimated.

According to Nielsen Analysts[3] recent research, TV adspend grew 1.87 per cent over the previous year, whereas advertising duration on China Central Television (CCTV) dropped 8.9 per cent compared with 2011. Under political influence, the advertising capacity of TV drama on various channels dropped substantially. At the same time, the advertising capacity of news/current affair programs grew.

In 2012 newspaper rate card adspend fell 6.88 per cent over the previous year. In the Top 10 ranking on newspaper advertising, only pharmaceuticals and personal items were growing. Industries with the fastest magazine advertising growth were personal items (31.0 per cent), computer and office automation products (14.7 per cent) and alcohol (66.2 per cent).

Let us look at this in greater detail (see Table 12.1 and Figure 12.1). If we break Nielsen adspend data down into the different media channels there is a −6.88 per cent drop for magazines and a −9.44 per cent drop for the Internet' whereas there is a positive growth of, respectively, +1.87 per cent for TV, +8.12 per cent for magazines and +7.61 per cent for radio, which represented a sharp fall after 32.05 per cent of accelerating growth in the previous year. Note that, despite new media variations throughout 2012, overall growth slowed down.

As far as industrial adspend is concerned, growth in all industrial advertising in 2012 decelerated and there was even negative growth. Only adspend on beverage and alcohol overtook their levels in 2011 (by 12.4 and 31.9 per cent, respectively). Alcohol led the market contribution to adspend in all industries by 33.0 per cent. Alcohol brands were increasingly keen to develop their brand images, and advertising was the obvious way to do so.

As far as the Italian media landscape is concerned, it is characterised by being particularly strongly concentrated in both broadcasting and print sectors. TV is notoriously highly concentrated and politicised: since the mid-1980s it has been dominated by a duopoly consisting of public broadcaster RAI and commercial broadcaster Mediaset (Colapinto, 2010). The Italian media landscape is peculiar and characterised by the predominance of TV when it comes to advertising expenditure: most of the adspend on media is absorbed by the broadcasting sector (53 per cent, see Figure 12.1), which is the more than double the figure in the UK (26 per cent) and Germany (24 per cent).

Adspend in 2012 was once again negative falling by 14.3 per cent on average, the worst performance in the last 20 years. The overall drop from 2012 to 2011 of 14.3 per cent can be further broken down by media channel as −17.6 per cent for newspapers, −18.4 per cent for

Table 12.1 Chinese and Italian advertising market performance (in millions)

	China (¥ and (€))			**Italy** (€)		
Media	**2011**	**2012**	**Year-on-year growth** (%)	**2011**	**2012**	**Year-on-year growth** (%)
Newspapers	111.355 (14.476)	103.698 (13.481)	−6.88	1.357	1.118	−17.6
Magazines	19.13 (2.487)	20.683 (2.689)	8.12	0.853	0.695	−18.4
TV	647.609 (84.189)	659.74 (85.766)	1.87	4.624	3.918	−15.3
Radio	14.504 (1.886)	15.608 (2.029)	7.61	0.433	0.389	−10.2
Internet	23.469 (3.051)	21.254 (2.763)	−9.44	0.631	0.665	5.3

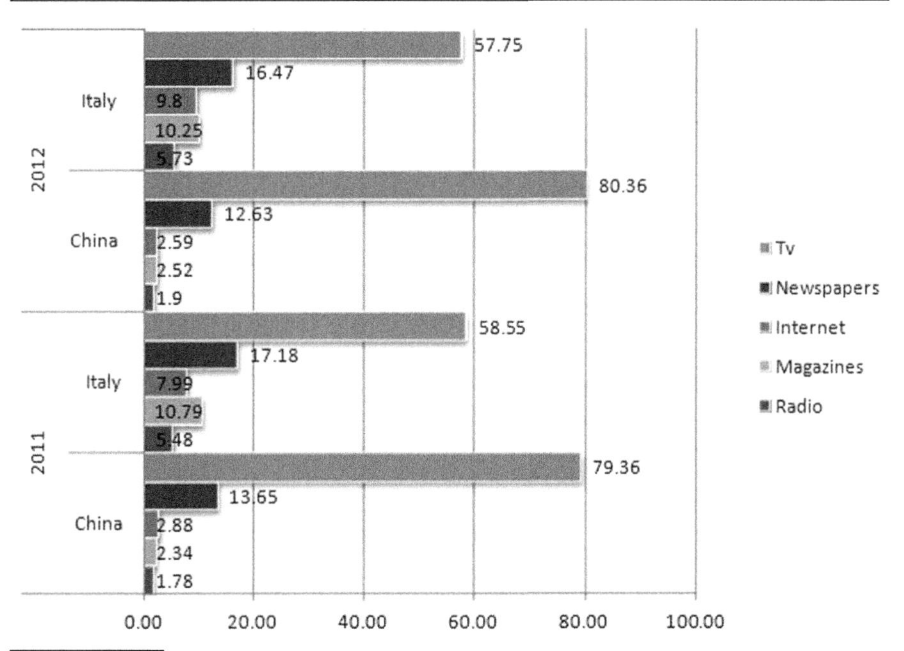

Figure 12.1 **Comparison between the Italian and Chinese communication mix**

Source: authors' elaboration of data from the Nielsen China Office, June 2013 and Nielsen Media Research, 2013.[4]

magazines and −15.3 per cent for TV, followed by −10.2 per cent for radio. Interestingly, the 5.3 per cent increase of the Internet sector, which on the surface was positive, was in reality little more than a strong sign of the crisis and felt even online.

Industries generally reduced their advertising budgets, positive signs indicated that the number of advertisers remained stable despite the market collapse (−2.4 per cent overall, −0.4 per cent on TV and +20 per cent on the Internet). On the one hand, this signalled a decrease in the average price of advertising; on the other hand, it expressed some confidence in the communication mix, despite the difficult economic times.

Luxury fashion advertising: a comparative analysis

More than three decades of cross-cultural comparative research results suggest that advertising content varies between countries that are culturally dissimilar (Albers-Miller, 1996) such as China and Italy. In the luxury industries, in particular, advertisers promote the beauty ideal[5] (Greer, 1999) which can vary across cultures and time (Frith et al., 2005).

The purpose of this study is to compare the way in which luxury brands choose to be portrayed in Chinese and Italian ads in *Vogue*. We seek to discern and investigate in much greater depth two main areas:

- the degree of standardisation of touchpoints, language and models used locally in advertising between the two editions of the magazine – one Chinese and one Italian;
- the extent to which the degree of standardisation is affected by product category (i.e., clothing, cosmetics, and jewellery).

Based on a literature review and available market data, we feel able in particular to answer the following questions:

(1) Are the visual and textual contents of Chinese ads different from Italian ones? As for the visual content (images), we compare (a) the models used by the brand and analyse a number of their attributes like race, type, colour, and length of hair; and (b) photographic characteristics (colour versus black and white). As for the textual

content, we compare the language used in the claim and in the body copy.[6]

(2) Does the Chinese market need different information and touchpoints for brands and products?

The Italian market is both mature and capillary (i.e., with many points of sale) and has a higher awareness of luxury brands and products; hence, it does not need so much information. By contrast, the Chinese are the new big spenders in the luxury sector and do not have enough information about these kinds of products. As each country has its own values (Hofstede, 1997) and each culture has a set of general beliefs about beauty (Frith et al., 2005), we would expect information and touchpoints to be more numerous in Chinese ads than in Italian ones.

A comparison between Chinese and Italian ads

Methodology

Like previous research our study is based only on magazine advertising because this vehicle is one of the main media for fashion, even though it is not the principal tool used by firms generally in the entire advertising market. Considering the magazines in the industry under analysis, *Vogue* is the leading one[7] and it is distributed both in Italy (since 1964) and in China (since 2005). Hence, it was chosen for the study. As Hartley and Montgomery (2009) pointed out, the launch of *Vogue China* in 2005 also reflected the growth of fashion and luxury brand consumption in the country. It was an important catalyst for further development of fashion values and the consumer culture linked to global trends. *Vogue* deals exclusively in 'fashion, beauty, art and the fashionable lifestyle' (Cheung, 2005), which makes it the ideal setting for our research, focussed as it is on luxury products.

The contents of each ad relating to a selected sample of brands found in four issues of *Vogue* for each country, which were chosen from the seven-month period January 2012 to September 2012 (i.e., January, March, May and July 2012), were codified to trace their appeal and Italian samples were compared with Chinese ones to ascertain whether messages and cultural values were different.

We defined our sample by first listing all the brands that appeared in ads in the selected issues; we then chose for our present research only those brands that had at least one ad that appeared in both countries. We decided to restrict our analysis to full-page ads, and ignored half-page ads or other kinds of communication made by brands. The unit we used for analysis was twofold: (1) the advertising slot of a brand, which could comprise one or more advertising subjects or pictures; (2) a single advertising subject/picture.

To answer our questions we first need to examine each ad analytically in order to code single elements (i.e., number of models, race, hairstyle, etc.) and compare the result of the Italian sample with the Chinese one; second, we need to make an overall comparison of the advertising of each brand, in which each Italian ad is compared with its Chinese counterpart, in order to define the standardisation strategy.

Visual elements, textual elements and touchpoints in Italian versus Chinese advertising

As regards codifying single elements, the variables of our analysis allow elements of ads to be compared concerning the three aspects we identify above: visual, textual and touchpoints. The main aspects analysed are visual ones such as models' characteristics (number, race, type, length and colour of hair), price and photographic characteristics (black and white versus colour). Textual analysis regards claims and language. Finally, we look at relational aspects, identifying which touchpoints have been chosen by the brand in question.

Results

We collected data from 191 advertising slots, almost equally distributed (53 per cent in China and 47 per cent in Italy). As shown in Figure 12.2 most relate to clothing, then cosmetics and a few to jewellery. The Chinese edition clearly contains many ads for cosmetics and facial beauty products whereas the Italian is clearly dominated by clothing. Moreover, we can see from Figure 12.2 that slot size between the two countries is basically opposite: more space for single brands in clothing ads in Italy, whereas more space for cosmetics in China.

The first area of analysis concerns advertising content. At the visual level, we pay attention to the characteristics of the models chosen. Generally, ads show only one model and a female one at that; clothing ads use only one model in 58.82 per cent of analysed subjects in China and 62.86 per cent in Italy; models are less frequent in cosmetics ads; however, the presence of

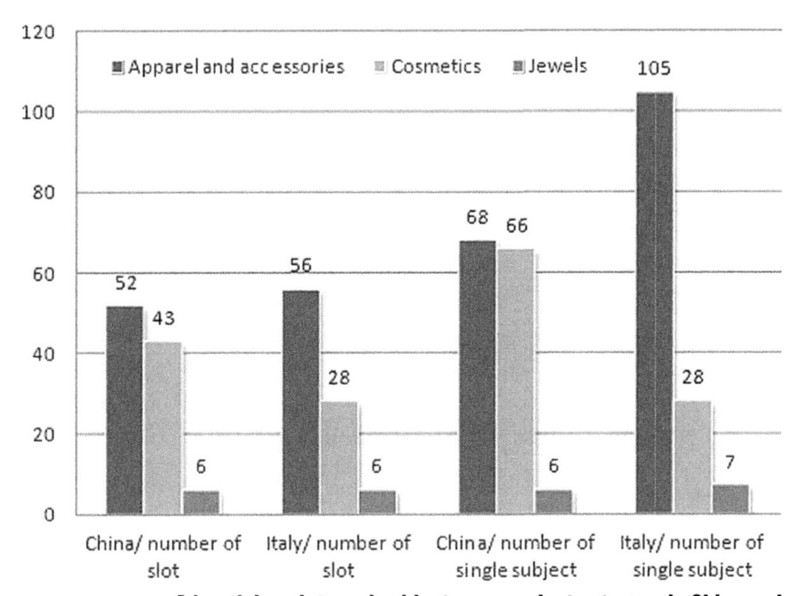

Figure 12.2 **Advertising slots and subjects per product category in China and Italy**

a single model is the preferred choice (36.36 per cent in China and 50.0 per cent in Italy). Regarding jewellery ads, the model is always a solitary female in both countries.

As illustrated in Figure 12.3, female models are far more frequently portrayed in ads and this is consistent with the gender orientation of the

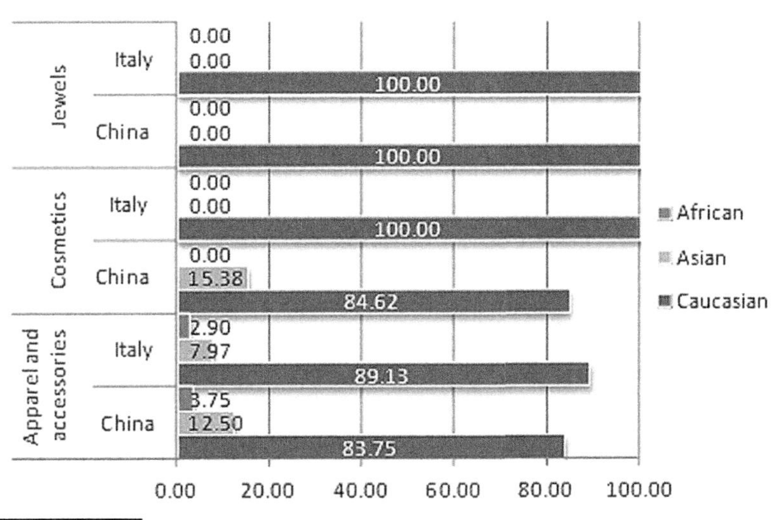

Figure 12.3 **Race of female models (in %)**

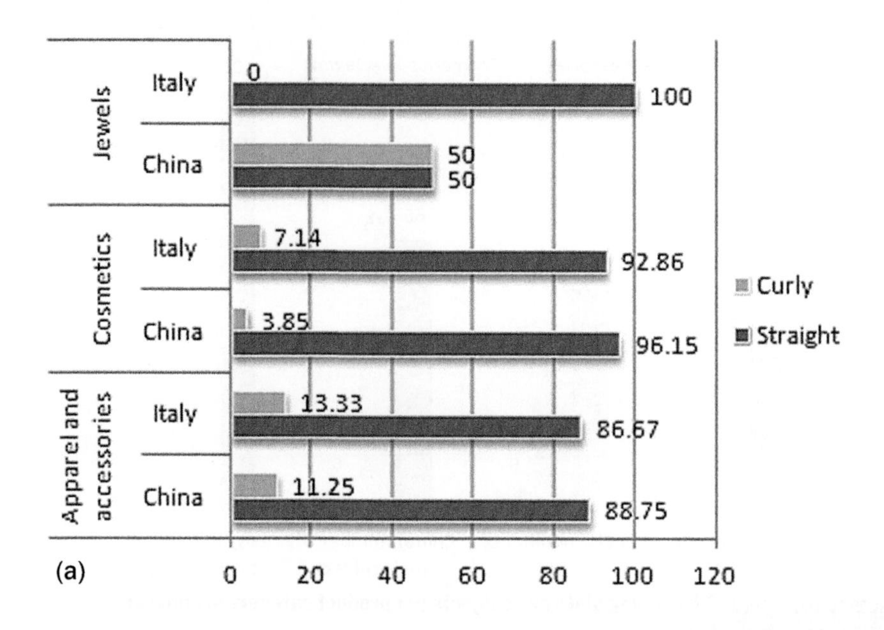

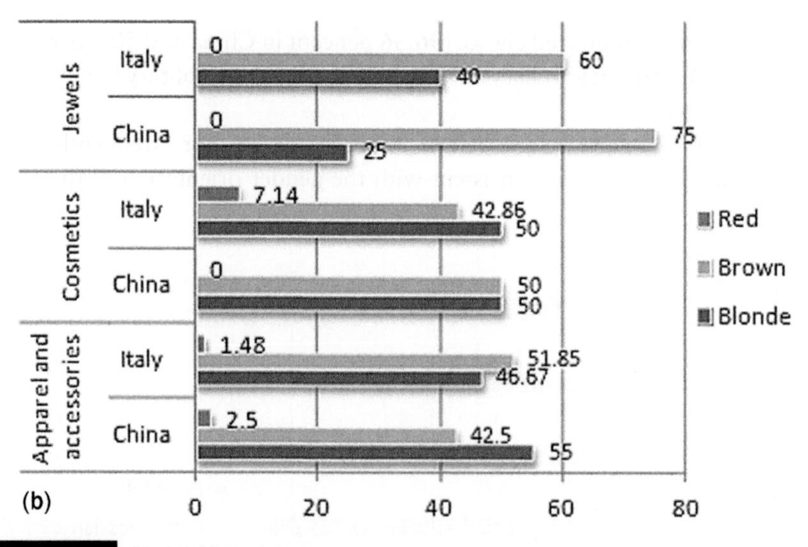

Figure 12.4 **Models' hairstyle**

magazine. Caucasian models make up the majority in all industries in both countries. Moreover, the majority of male models portrayed in clothing ads are Caucasian, 100 per cent in Italian ads versus 87.50 per cent in Chinese ads. The other 12.50 per cent are African. We were surprised to notice such

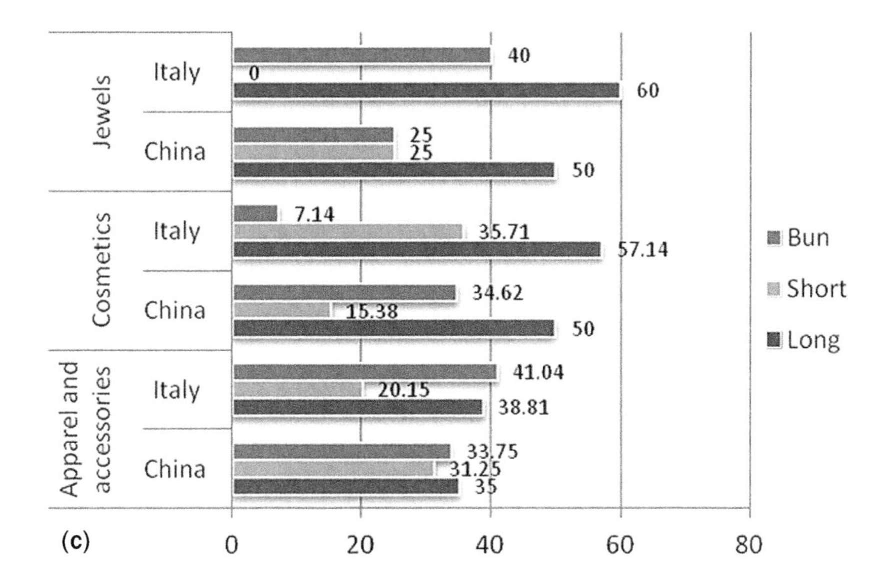

a high percentage of African models, since this is neither the target race nor the brand origin race. No male models were used for cosmetics or jewellery ads.

Figure 12.4(a, b and c) presents data on the hairstyles of female models. In this case it is not possible to identify a preferred style. Results show that all types are present in both countries but to varying degrees with a general preference for straight and long hair in both countries.

The names of models are credited more in China than in Italy: 11.63 per cent of Chinese cosmetics ads mention the name of the model in the picture versus only 3.57 per cent of Italian ones. In clothing ads the difference is not so high (7.69 versus 5.36 per cent). No credits appear in jewellery ads.

Coloured pictures predominate overall throughout the magazine. Jewellery ads are exclusively coloured because of the characteristics of the product; black and white pictures are rare for cosmetics ads and for clothing make up 31.75 per cent in China and 29.52 per cent in Italy.

The second area we analysed concerns how the brand prefers to communicate and the channels used to contact readers (see Table 12.2). This can range from physical places to virtual reality in light of the options offered by new and social media. Price information is rare. Fewer than 2.0 per cent of ads in the clothing sector in both Italy and China and fewer than 4.0 per cent of ads in the cosmetics sector show prices. Claims and textual information are used much more in cosmetics ads than in the other categories.

Table 12.2 Touchpoints (in %)

	Apparel and accessories		Cosmetics		Jewellery	
	China	Italy	China	Italy	China	Italy
Point of sale	34.62	1.79	9.30	0.00	50.00	14.29
Website	92.31	64.29	83.72	67.86	83.33	57.14
E-commerce website	11.54	12.50	23.26	14.29	0.00	0.00
Applications	0.00	1.79	2.33	0.00	0.00	0.00
QR code	5.77	1.79	2.33	0.00	0.00	0.00
Social media	1.92	0.00	2.33	10.71	0.00	0.00
Telephone number	25.00	21.43	16.28	57.14	50.00	14.29

Note: each ad can have more than one piece of information. Information refers to the advertising slot – not to a single subject. QR = Quick Response code (a type of matrix barcode).

The message: language, claim and body copy

When it comes to the message portrayed by ads, we now analyse the language used in the claims and in the body copy and describe how it is generally put together.

As far as language is concerned, it is interesting to note that brand names are not translated into Chinese in clothing, while in cosmetics only about 70 per cent of brands are translated. Intriguingly, brands that advertise in both categories are inconsistent in their behaviour. For example, Chanel appears only as 'Chanel' in clothing, while in cosmetics it appears both as Chanel and '香奈儿' (read *xiang nai'er*, the phonetic translation of the brand name).

We found only a few cases in Chinese ads of the use of claims in clothing. In such cases the language was English, although we did find one case where it was Italian, but then it referred to an Italian brand. Additional information was present in only three cases: two were in the claim language and one in Chinese. Claims were present in almost all the cosmetics ads. Claims were frequently made for cosmetics in Italy and were mostly in Italian (75 per cent). In contrast, they were rare for clothing and in such instances they were in English. No claims were made in jewellery ads.

Considering the small number of texts found for apparel, we could only compare messages in the cosmetic sector. In Italy the claims made for body or face cream refer to youth and most body-copy texts highlight the fact that youth fades, but thanks to the cream advertised women can control it in some way. Makeup and beauty messages are more to do with women being perceived as stars who thanks to the branded product can 'be iconic' – as a Dior claim stated. Other messages highlight the vividness of their makeup and the beauty that comes from having a glowing tan, with the body copy extolling some virtue of the product such as it enhancing confidence, making you feel good or getting you noticed.

The cosmetic sector in China generally encompasses creams, skin serums, makeup products and perfumes. Body-copy messages for cream products in China focus mainly on the whiteness of skin. The purity and beautifulness of a white skin is often associated metaphorically with an eternal spring. The importance of maintaining and taking care of one's own health is often emphasised and use of the product advertised is promoted as helping to achieve that goal. Negative attributes like 'half beauty' and 'prematurely aged' are associated with a dark and a yellow-spotted skin.

The body copy for serum products usually exalts the repair effects the product has. This kind of product is addressed at middle-aged women and the message contains information about the high technology used by the brand to develop the product and the product's long-term effects, from slowing down the aging process, brightening the skin (returning to 'spring' and starting a 'new life'), cleaning the skin to removing dark spots, one of the main cosmetic issues for Chinese women. The positive characteristics that are associated with the women who purchase these products are emphasised by the body copy and words such as 'respect' and 'deep love' for their skin are often used.

When it comes to cream and serum, the body copy often likens the effects of the product to the perfection of oriental flowers (paeonies and orchids) and how the woman's skin should take on the glow of a flower after using the product.

Many brands decide to display both types of products in the same slot. When this happens the body-copy explains how the set of products complement each other. Chinese body copy sometimes makes use of testimonials from Asian celebrities who describe their own experience of using the product. While the body copy for makeup products waxes lyrical about the smoothness of the skin thanks to the product usage, the body copy for perfumes in China consists of a few words and sometimes just the brand's 'iconic' name, similar to the Italian ads.

Overall comparison: standardisation or adaptations?

The last area we observed was the degree of standardisation between the two countries regarding ads by the same brand in the Italian and Chinese editions of *Vogue*. We compare ads promoting Valentino in both countries to see whether the same visual and textual elements are used, and thus define standardisation of communication.

Two different levels of standardisation were identified. The first we called 'absolute standardisation'. It included the same ads published in the same issue of each country's edition of the magazine (i.e., March China and March Italy). The second we called 'lag standardisation'. It included the same ads but published in two different issues of each country's edition of the magazine (i.e., March China and July Italy). By breaking standardisation down in this way, we are able to investigate adaptation–standardisation strategies differently, since previous research always focused on single elements, without caring about which brands were involved in the magazine being analyzed.

We noted that of the 56 clothing sector ads analysed in *Vogue Italia*, only 15 (26.7 per cent) appear to fit our definition of absolute standardisation when compared with the Chinese *Vogue*, showing the same product in the same issue of each country's edition. Analysing the ads that fit lag standardisation in the same sector, only 11 of the 56 Italian ads (19.6 per cent) appear with the same content in the Chinese edition, but always in two issues of each country's edition.

It was interesting to note that in the clothing sector one brand appeared with slight differences in each country's edition. The same internationally known model (Naomi Campbell) was chosen for the two countries, but different poses were adopted (Pinko) in each country's issue. Absent knowledge of the entire advertising campaign, we can explain this difference both as an adaptation to culture, but also to image size, which is different (one page in China, two pages in Italy). In both cases there is clearly different behaviour in terms of brand management, in the former related to willingness to fit the culture, in the latter related to the advertising investment/pressure, which is lower in China.

When compared with other sectors, the cosmetics sector presents itself as being much more variable. With an absolute standardisation level of 0 per cent and a lag standardisation level of only 7.1 per cent (2 of the 28 Italian ads analysed in this category), it shows itself with little margin for standardisation. This might be the result of several factors, such as the different product typologies presented in each country's edition and the systems of values in each country, which differ both in terms of product/brand knowledge and the personal preferences of customers.

One cosmetic brand (Helena Rubinstein) adopted the same technique used by the clothing brand Pinko and decided to modify slightly its ads in each country's edition: the product displayed remained the same, used the same background (laboratory setting with round-bottom flask and radiant light courtesy of Prodigy behind the product) and changed only some small details (different model of flask and more extensive body copy in the Italian edition, two pages instead of one page in the Chinese edition).

The jewellery sector is the sector with the lowest level of standardisation. Of the six Italian ads compared, none used the same subjects as the Chinese edition in either the same issue or a different one. Even this sector throws up an interesting case. The brand Chaumet Paris decided to display a similar ad in the May issue (Italian and Chinese) using the same model, but changed the content of the ads which promoted the same category (rings) by adding another product. We can thus see three rings in both ads (gold, bronze and white) but displayed in different positions (on the right side of the page for the Italian issue and on the left side of the page, after the *Vogue* indexes, for the Chinese one) and the same model, who wears the ring in the Italian issue, but a silver coronet in the Chinese one. Coronets are often used in Asian ads, since it makes the person wearing it look more regal. Chaumet Paris likely decided to use an ad and product that was more appropriate to Chinese culture.

Despite absolute and lag standardisation being generally low in all three product categories analysed, we note that the highest level of standardisation between both countries' *Vogue* editions was achieved by clothing, with 26.78 per cent of absolute standardisation in the ads compared.

Discussion

As far as visual and textual content is concerned, findings differ between single elements analysed and between sectors. In general, brands do not use a standard advertising strategy. Only 16.6 per cent of Italian ads present absolute standardisation in the Chinese version, but they are all in the clothing industry. The same occurs for lag standardisation, which appears in 14.4 per cent of cases, 84.6 per cent of them being in the clothing industry.

Analysing the visual content of single elements concerning hairstyles we find little differences between models' hair. Results on visual content in all sectors reveal that Caucasian models are portrayed the most in Italy and in China and this confirms the findings of Frith et al. (2005): 'Caucasian models are used more often across cultures than models of other ethnic groups in women's beauty and fashion magazine advertising.'

When it comes to considering the way brands want to be contacted, we can state that the touchpoints used in the two countries are different. It is evident that Chinese ads in all sectors invite their target to get in touch with them using more than one point. Chinese ads refer to brands' points of sale (likely flagship stores) much more than is the case with Italian ads. There are a couple of reasons for this: first, in Italy there are too many points of sale for each brand (capillary distribution) to be listed in ads, whereas in China the limited number of stores allows brands to highlight them; second, as stores communicate the brand image, absent interference by other brands or spokespersons, and represent tangible evidence of brand strength, these communication tools could be more important for luxury brands in markets where the brand is not already known rather than in a mature market. This is consistent with the findings of Moore et al. (2010, p. 154): luxury companies use flagship stores 'as a signal of the strength of their brand to prospective consumers and as a means of assuring partner companies of their commitment to China.' This is also consistent with the differences we found relating to the three sectors analysed: points-of-sale citations were lowest in cosmetics as a result of retailing formats being used other than those of flagship stores.

Our analysis shows the Internet to be the favourite communication channel for all industries in both countries; however, its use as a selling platform is more limited; there is no e-commerce for jewellery. The Internet is widely used in China and in Italy[8] and represents an easy and cheap way to interact with customers (Efendioglu and Yip, 2004) and provide them with more product information (Guo et al., 2011).

Social networks are seldom referred to in China and Italy. Few brands promote their YouTube and Facebook pages in Italy. However, it is not a standardized decision. For example, in Chinese cosmetic ads, Elizabeth Arden is the only brand to mention social media, but the social media it refers to is the Chinese microblog Sina Weibo (*www.sina.com.cn*), which was launched in 2009 and the popularity of which is now similar to that of Twitter in the rest of the world (Deans and Miles, 2011). However, Elizabeth Arden does not promote Sina Weibo in Italy.

As far as jewellery is concerned, the preferred communication channel in both countries is the telephone because companies privilege direct contact in order to provide a better pre-sales and after-sales customer service.

Much of the literature on the representation of women in advertising is built on the feminist argument that media are patriarchal and that, in patriarchal societies, men watch women and women watch men watching women (Berger, 1972). Yet, as Frith et al. (2005) suggested, in Western societies women may think it is mainly their bodies that get noticed by men, whereas in Asia women think it is their faces that are most important. The beauty products aimed at improving women's appearance in *Vogue China* are represented by Asian models, with clear white skin. More than 20 per cent of body/face cream and skin serum ads were related to products that whiten the skin.

Advertisers often make a concerted effort to select credible and attractive celebrities, who are well suited to particular products and are popular with the target audience (Miciak and Shanklin, 1994). The practice of using well-known Chinese celebrities as spokespeople and to make testimonials is simply an attempt to enhance the popularity of the brands being advertised and has become increasingly popular as companies recognize the added value and increased sales that such a practice bring to their products, irrespective of the fact that some products may not have a clear link with the celebrities concerned (Leung, 2003).

Language tacitly reflects a particular culture since the spoken language manifests beliefs and attitudes. The language used for brand names has been widely discussed in international advertising literature (Terpstra and Sarathy, 1997). Moreover, language is one of the most important factors influencing international advertising in China (Hite and Fraser, 1988), but the language used in global advertising varies according to the extent to which it is localized (Nelson and Paek, 2007). When it comes to China, Dong and Helms (2001) astutely pointed out that, because Chinese customers purchase these products not only for personal consumption but also as mementoes of holidays and special occasions, the symbolic meaning of a brand name and a brand ad may greatly influence their purchase decision. We will leave investigation of the most effective way to translate the content of brands or ads to another study, but it is worthy of note that English is by and large restricted to headlines and slogans, whereas the body copy of ads is almost always written in the local language.

Looking at the usage of language, in general, among the brands considered and the three categories analysed (i.e., clothing, cosmetics and jewellery), the ads of international brands that appear in the Chinese editions of *Vogue* in the clothing and jewellery categories are never translated into the local language and no textual information is used, therefore demonstrating greater standardisation.

By contrast, cosmetics made good use of textual communication and translation. Unlike the intrinsic features of clothing and jewellery, which tend to sell themselves without verbal or textual expression, cosmetics clearly need textual expression to inform the prospective purchaser. We found a huge difference in product typology advertised across the two countries in the cosmetic sector. While *Vogue Italia* focusses more on foundation products, *Vogue China* clearly focusses more on product typology: whitening products and anti-ageing products. Moreover, whereas in Italy cosmetics brands generally advertise a single product, in China a range of different products within the same brand are advertised together. Nevertheless, both countries' editions pay equal attention to explanation of product benefits and characteristics, even though the overall product range differs appreciably.

Conclusion and managerial implications

Although our findings cannot be generalized for all magazine ads, they do provide critical insights into luxury practitioners who pursue market penetration in both countries and reciprocity: Italian market penetration for Chinese brands and Chinese market penetration for Italian brands. The purpose of this study is to contribute to the debate on standardised versus specialised approaches to international advertising by means of cross-cultural content analysis that compares print advertising.

Firms that are used to advertising locally and would like to diversify and invest in China should first understand the sector they are entering and the embedded cultural values of the Chinese people. For example, a lot of Chinese cosmetics ads relate to products that are not typical in the West such as whitening creams. Sales of such products are highly dependent on cultures that deem a white and pure skin a symbol of beauty. The implications are many for firms wishing to promote such products. It would mean creating *ad hoc* ads, selecting credible and attractive celebrities to promote them, and highlighting values and benefits that would not be politically correct in the West (i.e., white skin).

While information about points of sale is given in Chinese ads, in Italy it is missing. This highlights the importance of having a physical presence, which is evidence of the authenticity and strength of the brand. This is important in emerging countries where people are not used to comparing brands.

Our research shows there is no need to change the body copy for apparel, just adapt some elements. Indeed, languages can be mixed to adapt the ad and the original language can be used for headlines or claims if the country of origin is paramount. Our analysis leads us to suggest using both languages (Chinese and the brand's mother language) in the body copy.

When reading our results, it is important to remember the target audience of *Vogue*. In China it targets open-minded city-dwelling young people with disposable income and a desire to live a fashionable life. In Italy the target audience comprises mostly women who enjoy reading the ads, keep up to date with fashion and aspire to a high social status.

We hope our study opens up new possibilities for future studies to include local brands, both Italian and Chinese, and not only international ones. This is especially true of the jewellery sector, which highlighted the considerable presence of local brands in the Chinese edition of *Vogue*. Moreover, further investigations about the most effective way to use local language in the marketing strategy of these brands would be of great help for marketeers who want to approach the unique Chinese market in the near future. Our study confirms that strategy changes according to the country of origin of the brand analyzed, as already shown in the literature (Graham et al., 1993).

Notes

1. See National Bureau of Statistics (2008) (*http://www.stats.gov.cn/english/*) [accessed on 31 May 2012].
2. This is a weighted forecast of main media adspend covering many markets: Australia, Brazil, Canada, China, France, Germany, India, Italy, Japan, Russia, Spain, the US and the UK.
3. Nielsen Professional Services records retail transactions at stores, monitors households, scans products, tracks TV programs, follows web-surfing habits, analyses over 85 per cent of world advertising, measures brand 'buzz' and monitors the habits of cellphone users.
4. See Nielsen Media Research (2013), *il mercato pubblicitario italiano nell'anno 2012* (the Italian advertising market from January to December 2012) [in Italian].
5. The beauty ideal is a social construct that physical attractiveness is among a woman's most important assets and something to which women should aspire.
6. Body copy is the written text of an ad.

7. For Italy the data are provided by Audipress (*http://www.audipress.it/*).
8. Visit *http://www.internetworldstats.com*

References

Abernethy, A.M. and Franke, G.R. (1996) The information content of advertising: a meta-analysis. *Journal of Advertising*, **25**(2), 1–17.

Albers-Miller, N.D. (1996) Designing cross-cultural advertising research: a closer look at paired comparisons. *International Marketing Review*, **13**(5), 59–75.

Arrighi, G. (2008) *Adam Smith in Beijing: Lineages of the 21st Century*. Verso, London.

Belk, R.W. and Pollay, R.W. (1995) Materialism and status appeals in Japanese and US print advertising. *International Marketing Review*, **2**(4), 38–47.

Berger, J. (1972) *Ways of Seeing*. Penguin Books, London.

Biswas, A., Olsen, J. and Carlet, V. (1992) A comparison of print advertisements from the United States and France. *Journal of Advertising*, **21**(4), 73–81.

Cheng, H. and Frith, K.T. (2006) Going global: an analysis of global women's magazine ads in China. *Media International Australia Incorporating Culture & Policy*, **119**, 138–51.

Cheung, A. (2005) Visions of China. *Vogue UK*, **171**(2488): 113–18.

Colapinto, C. (2010) Moving to a multichannel and multiplatform company in the emerging and digital media eco-system: the case of Mediaset Group. *International Journal on Media Management*, **12**(2), 59–75.

CTR (2013) China's traditional media advertising market growth dropped below '5' in 2012. Available from: *http://www.ctrchina.cn* [accessed 24 June 2013].

Cutler, B.D., Javalgi, R.G. and Erramilli, M.K. (1992) The visual components of print advertising: a five-country cross-cultural analysis. *European Journal of Marketing*, **26**(4), 7–20.

Deans, P.C. and Miles, J.B. (2011) A framework to understanding social media trends in China. Paper presented at *11th International DSI and APDSI Joint Meeting, Taipei, Taiwan, 12–16 July*.

Dong, L.C. and Helms, M.M. (2001) Brand name translation model: a case analysis of US brands in China. *Journal of Brand Management*, **9**(2), 99–115.

Efendioglu, A.M. and Yip, V.F. (2004) Chinese and e-commerce: an exploratory study. *Journal of Business and Management*, **16**(1), 45–62.

EI (2010) *Consumer Lifestyles: China*. Euromonitor International, London.

Fam, K.S. and Grohs, R. (2007) Cultural values and effective executional techniques in advertising: a cross-country and product category study of urban young adults in Asia. *International Marketing Review*, **2**(5), 519–38.

Fan, R. (2010) Restoring the Confucian personality and filling the moral vacuum in contemporary China. *Reconstructionist Confucianism* (Philosophical Studies in Contemporary Culture No. 17). Springer-Verlag, New York, pp. 231–49

Forsythe, S., Kim, J.O. and Petee, T. (1999) Product cue usage in two Asian markets: a cross-cultural comparison. *Asia Pacific Journal of Management*, **16**(2): 275–91.

Frith, K.T. and Sengupta, S. (1991) Individualism and advertising: a cross-cultural comparison. *Media Asia*, **18**, 191–7.

Frith, K.T., Cheng, H. and Shaw, P. (2004) Race and beauty comparison of Asian and Western models in women magazine advertisements. *Sex Roles*, **50**(1/2), 53–61.

Frith, K., Cheng, H. and Shaw, P. (2005) The construction of beauty: a cross-cultural analysis of women's magazine advertising. *Journal of Communication*, 55(1): 56–70.

Graham, J.L., Kamins, M.A. and Oetomo, D.S. (1993) Content analysis of German and Japanese advertising in print media. *Journal of Advertising*, **22**(2), 5–15.

Greer, G. (1999) *The Whole Woman*. Doubleday, London.

Guo, S., Wang, M. and Leskovec, J. (2011) The role of social networks in online shopping: information passing, price of trust, and consumer choice. Paper presented at *12th ACM Conference on Electronic Commerce*. ACM, New York, pp. 157–66.

Hartley, J. and Montgomery, L. (2009) Fashion as consumer entrepreneurship: emerging risk culture, social network markets, and the launch of *Vogue* in China. *Chinese Journal of Communication*, **2**(1), 61–76.

Hite, R.E. and Fraser, C. (1988) International advertising strategies for multinational corporations. *Journal of Advertising*, **28**(4), 9–17.

Hofstede, G. (1997) *Cultures and Organizations: Software of the Mind*. McGraw-Hill, New York.

Javalgi, R.G., Cutler, B.D. and Malhotra, N.K. (1995) Print advertising at the component level: a cross-cultural comparison of the United States and Japan. *Journal of Business Research*, **34**(2), 117–24.

Ji, M.F. and McNeal, J.U. (2001) How Chinese children's commercials differ from those of the United States: a content analysis. *Journal of Advertising*, **30**(3), 79–92.

Kolbe, R.H. and Burnett, M.S. (1991) Content-analysis research: an examination of applications with directives for improving research reliability and objectivity. *Journal of Consumer Research*, **18**(3), 40–8.

Leung, Y.M. (2003) Celebrities and commercials. *Media Digest – RTHK*. Available from: *http://www.rthk.org.hk/mediadigest* [accessed 4 September 2012] [Radio Television Hong Kong].

Maynard, M.L. and Taylor, C.R. (1999) Girlish images across cultures: analyzing Japanese versus U.S. seventeen magazine ads. *Journal of Advertising*, **28**(1), 39–48.

Miciak, A.R. and Shanklin, W.L. (1994) Choosing celebrity endorsers. *Marketing Management*, **3**(3), 50–9.

Moore, C.M. et al. (2010) Flagship stores as a market entry method: the perspective of luxury fashion retailing. *European Journal of Marketing*, **44**(1/2), 139–61. Available from: *http://dx.doi.org/10.1108/03090561011008646*

Mueller, B. (2004) *Dynamics of International Advertising: Theoretical and Practical Perspectives*. Peter Lang Publishing, New York.

Nelson, M.R. and Paek, H.J. (2007) A content analysis of advertising in a global magazine across seven countries: implications for global advertising strategies. *International Marketing Review*, **4**(1): 64–86.

Okazi, S. and Rivas, J.A. (2002) A content analysis of multinationals' web communication strategies: cross-cultural research framework and pre-testing. *Internet Research*, **12**(5), 380–90.

Rochet, J.C. and Tirole, J. (2002) Platform competition in two-sided markets. *RAND Journal of Economics*, **23**(3), 334–49.

Terpstra, V. and Sarathy, R. (1997) *International Marketing*. Dryden Press/ Harcourt Brace College Publishers, Orlando, FL.

Wang, C.L. and Chan, A.K.K. (2001) A content analysis of connectedness vs. separateness themes used in US and PRC print advertisements. *International Marketing Review*, **18**(2), 145–60.

Wang, C.L. and Lin, X. (2009) Migration of Chinese consumption values: traditions, modernization, and cultural resistance. *Journal of Business Ethics*, **88**(3), 399–409.

Warc (2013) Consensus ad forecast. Available from: *http://www.warc.com/* [accessed 4 June 2013].

Yifan, W. (2007) *Brand in China*. China International Press, Beijing.

Yin, J. (1999) International advertising strategies in China: a worldwide survey of foreign advertisers. *Journal of Advertising Research*, **39**(6), 25–35.

Zhang, J. and Shavitt, S. (2003) Cultural values in advertisements to the Chinese X-generation: promoting modernity and individualism. *Journal of Advertising*, **32**(1), 21–31.

Zhao, Y. (2008) *Communication in China: Political Economy, Power, and Conflict*. Rowman & Littlefield, London.

13

Asian growing markets and competition: evidence in the Chinese wine market

Roberta Capitello, Lara Agnoli and Diego Begalli

Abstract: Chinese society is becoming a consumer society thanks to economic development, which has brought about a revolution in values. The demand for luxury and branded products cannot be fully satisfied by domestic production. Chinese consumers are facing progressive westernisation such as the demand for imported wine, which is perceived as a luxury product. This study highlights the factors determining the growth in demand for imported wine, the impact these factors have on competitive relations among exporting countries and wine regions, and the opportunities and constraints facing the business development of the main competitors. Group influence on choices, the new 'cultural revolution' and the desire for achievement and modernity have emerged as drivers of the demand for imported wine, the pursuit of luxury, the wish for westernisation and the perception of a foreign product's country of origin (COO). France has emerged as the foreign supplier who benefits most from a strong and undisputed reputation, especially in bottled and sparkling wines. However, Chinese consumers are moving towards new suppliers and product differentiation, opening up new business opportunities.

Key words: China, Chinese consumers, wine, luxury, westernisation, country of origin (COO), wine import.

Wine in Asian markets

The world wine industry is rapidly changing. According to Banks and Overton (2010), the geographies of wine consumption and production are widening and transforming. The former Old World–New World distinction is no longer well grounded, and the emerging 'Third World of wine' is so heterogeneous that it cannot be considered a new category (Banks and Overton, 2010). The complexity and dynamism of the wine industry has generated 'multiple worlds of wine', characterised by the fast development of new wine-producing areas, expanding markets, consumer preference transformations, exchanges of ideas, know-how and resources, search for differentiation and new quality cues.

The three most important wine-producing countries (France, Italy and Spain), which dominated the world wine industry in the past, covered about 44 per cent (54 per cent in 2000) of total production in 2012, which was 252 million hectolitres in 2012 (OIV, 2013). They have to compete intensively with the so-called 'New World' in the international market (the United States, Australia, Chile, Argentina, South Africa and New Zealand). The latter countries accounted for about 30 per cent (20 per cent in 2000) of world wine production in 2012 (OIV, 2013). Different elements characterised their development paths: use of local varieties versus international varieties; shift from bulk wines to bottled wines; differentiation through the origin; investment in vineyard improvement and winemaking technology; know-how exchanges with winemakers from the 'Old World'; private–public synergies; innovation in marketing and promotion.

In recent years, viticulture and winemaking have also consistently spread across some Third World countries, mainly China and India (Banks and Overton, 2010). Even though still in its initial stages, viticulture is also developing in other Asian countries, such as Thailand and Vietnam. It is being pushed by economic development, higher per-capita income and the perception of wine as a status symbol. This last factor seems to be the main lever attracting new investment in the wine industry.

China will emerge further and faster to become the third largest competitive 'pole' in the world for wine. Since 2012 China has become the fifth wine producer in the world (14.9 million hectolitres), with an increase of 42% in the period 2000–12 (OIV, 2013).

The geography of wine consumption has changed markedly. Today, the main markets include the United States, Germany, China and the United Kingdom, in addition to France and Italy. World wine consumption (243 million hectolitres in 2012) increased 8 per cent in the period 2000 to 2012 (OIV, 2013), encouraged by new consumer countries. While the traditional producing and consuming countries witnessed a drop in wine consumption in their own countries, consumers in developing economies seek variety, preferring wine to other beverages.

Marketline (2012) identifies the Asia-Pacific region as one of the most attractive wine markets. Compared with 2011, the wine market is expected to increase in value by 64.5 per cent, reaching US $60.7 billion in retail sales by 2016. In the same period, market volume is expected to increase to 3.6 billion litres, a growth of 49.5 per cent. These forecasts confirm the growing trend already highlighted by this market area between 2007 and 2011 (+46.8 per cent in value and +53.2 per cent in volume), at the end of which China had a market share of 50 per cent of the value of the Asia-Pacific wine market, followed by Japan (15.2 per cent), South Korea (1.7 per cent) and India (0.9 per cent) (Marketline, 2012).

The above changes in wine production and consumption have led to a sharp increase in international trade (+52.8 per cent in value and +45.0 per cent in volume during the period 2003–11). A breakdown by continent shows the dynamics of the new worlds of wine (Table 13.1). Europe is still an important macro-area capable of triggering significant trade flows, due to increased consumption in northern and Eastern European countries. However, the recent economic and financial crisis has led to consumers paying more attention to price, resulting in a reduction of the market share in value. In the Americas, the global financial crisis has been the main driver of declining imports, which were offset by growing consumer appreciation of product quality and greater willingness to pay. Asia represents a significant opportunity for foreign products and China will become a fast-growing market for the wine sector (OIV, 2013).

Table 13.1 shows that Asian markets are very attractive destinations for New and Old World producers, which have high expectations for these new opportunities, given the growth rate of Asian economies and their interest in wine. The main Asian importing countries are China, Japan, Hong Kong, Singapore and the Republic of Korea (South Korea), which represented 93.8 per cent of the value of Asian wine imports and 14.4 per cent of global wine imports in 2011. In the decade 2002–11, these countries increased their imports in both quantity and value (Figure 13.1). In 2011, China accounted for 29.0 per cent of the value and 48.4 per cent of the quantity. In all major Asian markets, there has been a significant increase in import prices (Table 13.2). China remains one of the most desirable destinations, given the breadth and potential of its market.

The aim of this chapter is to focus on the Chinese wine market as a significant case study in the Asia-Pacific region, to understand: (i) the factors driving the growth in demand for imported wine; (ii) how these factors affect competitive relations among exporting countries and wine regions; and (iii) the emergent opportunities and constraints facing

Table 13.1 Wine imports in the five continents

	Value ($m)			Volume (000 hl)		
	2002	2011	Δ% 2002–11	2002	2011	Δ% 2002–11
Europe	9,445	18,570	96.6	49,696	70,456	41.8
America	3,586	7,755	116.3	30,168	16,173	–46.4
Asia	1,089	4,945	354.2	2,573	7,558	193.7
Africa	32	244	666.8	563	1,585	181.3
Oceania	152	699	361.0	714	1,206	68.8

Source: an elaboration of UN Comtrade data (2013).[1]

business development by the main competitors, in the light of the quantitative and qualitative development of the Chinese wine market.

This chapter is organised as follows: the next section 'Chinese consumers' will look at the evolution of Chinese consumer behaviour, and the increasing focus on product quality, Western luxury and origins; the following section 'Chinese wine consumers' will deal with the relationship between the Chinese consumer and wine; there then follows a section 'Demand for imported wine in China' that focusses on the Chinese import market. The characteristics of this market and the competitive relationships among products, countries and wine regions will be highlighted through the results of empirical analyses. Finally, the section 'Conclusions' points out likely competitive scenarios and outlines managerial implications for wine businesses and institutions.

Chinese consumers

China's strong social hierarchy, subject as it is to class divisions, and the influence of a reference social group on choices are important factors to consider when studying Chinese consumers. Their awareness of belonging to a group is deep rooted; group members have the same tastes, habits, ways of spending free time and income. As He et al. (2010) state, consumption utility does not come purely from product attributes, but from the will of the individual to achieve and maintain a certain social

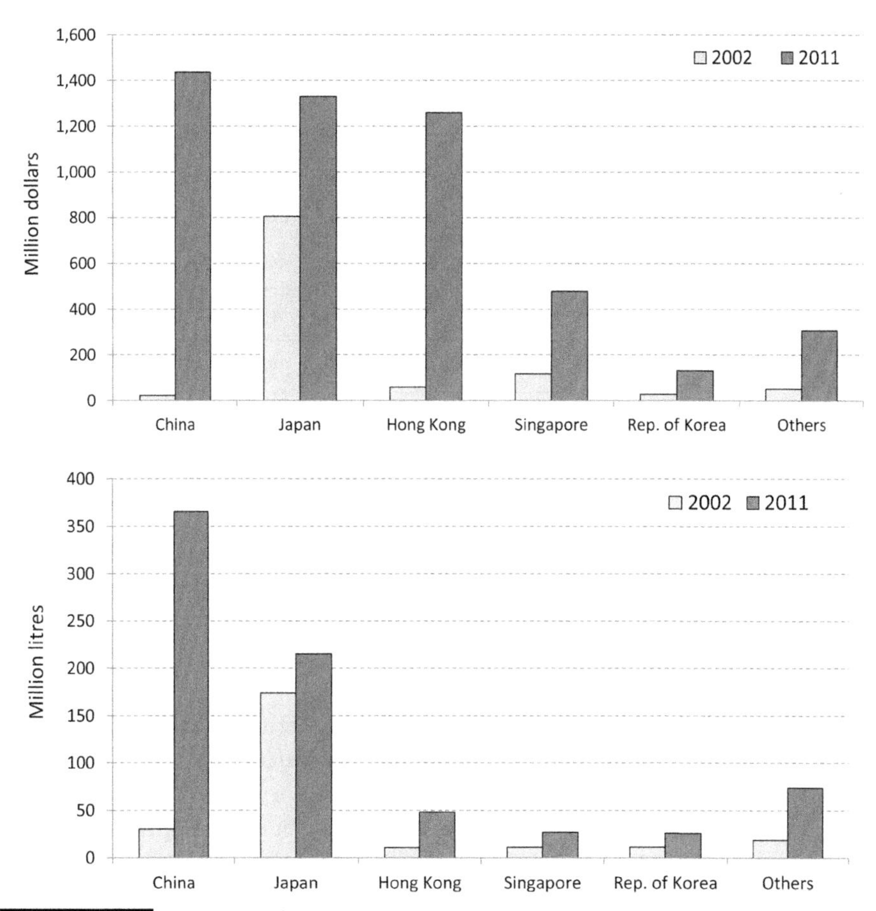

Figure 13.1 **Top 5 importer Asian countries ($m and million litres)**

Source: an elaboration of UN Comtrade data (2013).

identity. In this respect, brand is an important cue, communicating a specific identity and interaction with the group. Therefore, a materialistic culture exerts a strong influence, despite apparently contrasting with traditional Confucian values (Wang et al., 2013).

Thanks to these values, the Chinese consumer is brand loyal, slowly adopts the products of new markets, has a high propensity to save and a low propensity to complain when dissatisfied with a purchase (Lin and Wang, 2010). However, economic development has driven the country towards a new 'cultural revolution', and has transformed Chinese society into a consumer society, resulting in a revolution of values. According to Wang et al. (2013), the growth of hedonistic values linked to consumption is a main indicator of the emerging materialistic culture in

Table 13.2 Average price of wine in the Top 5 importer Asian countries ($/l)

	2002	2011
China	0.76	3.93
Japan	4.63	6.18
Hong Kong	5.49	26.13
Singapore	10.42	17.86
Republic of Korea (South Korea)	2.55	5.08
Others	2.74	4.16

Source: an elaboration of UN Comtrade data (2013).

China. These values are based on fun, gratification and pleasure, at the expense of utilitarian values dictated by tradition that aim to satisfy basic needs. The values of modern China lead the consumer to novelty seeking, responsiveness to promotion stimuli, brand consciousness and preference for foreign brands (Wang et al., 2013).

The conflicts between traditional and modern values are highlighted by Lin and Wang (2010). These contrasts affect consumption, which is characterised by the coexistence of a preference for self-constraint and thriftiness, for self-expression and extravagance, in the upper and middle classes. According to Podoshen et al. (2011), three main values coexist in the Chinese contemporary consumer and in young consumers: communistic values, which emphasise personal sacrifice and contribution to the state; the Confucian values of thrift and saving to meet long-term needs; and materialistic values, which encourage spending money to meet personal needs.

More visceral peculiarities than cultural values distinguish the Chinese from the Western consumer. According to scholars (Jacobs et al., 1993; Morgan and Reichert, 1999), Asian languages and writing techniques have different effects on brain use and, consequently, the perception of advertising stimuli. While Western populations would mainly use the left-brain hemisphere, which controls word functions and involves syntax, phonology and analytical functions, Asian populations would be more likely to use the brain's right side, which involves semantic determinations, non-verbal communication and musical and spatial–visual perceptions. According to Cui et al. (2013), this would lead the Chinese consumer to prefer transformational and integrated advertising than informational advertising, and to be more involved in affective processing than in cognitive thoughts.

Another difference between the Chinese and Western consumer is the vision of 'self'. According to Western views of the self, consumption behaviour is driven by taste, values, skills and preferences. Chinese culture considers the 'self' as the centre of relationships, and the identity of an individual comes from one's family, profession, social relations and culture, with a strong effect on consumption (Podoshen et al., 2011).

A mistake to avoid when studying Chinese consumers is to include them in a single unique profile. Huge differences exist between individuals living in urban areas and in rural areas. While in urban areas a consumer culture is emerging, rural areas are still characterised by traditional consumption patterns (Lin and Wang, 2010). Many Western companies are being established in urban and coastal development areas. Consumers from these areas are oriented towards achievement and modernity, which inexorably leads to the consumption of foreign products (Lin and Wang, 2010).

Together with coastal and urban consumers, there are millions of peasant consumers, who Baoku et al. (2010) divide into three groups, according to their consumption awareness: the 'confused by over-choice' have low incomes and do not distinguish between different shops and brands; the 'fashion and impulsive' have fun, are excited to try new products and are attentive to fashion and new trends; the 'perfect' consumers are rational, have high standards and expectations, look for quality and good value for money in a product.

Foreign companies wishing to enter China must consider three key factors that attract Chinese consumers to imported products: the pursuit of luxury, the wish for westernisation and the perception of foreign products and country of origin (COO).

The pursuit of luxury

Today, China is one of the Top 3 markets for luxury products, together with the United States and Japan. In the 1990s, as a result of the 'open-door policy', China opened up to foreign markets and the supply of luxury goods increased.

Today, the market for luxury goods is experiencing growth in China, fuelled by increasing incomes of the middle class, which consists mainly of young consumers.

Despite the economic crisis that has affected many Western countries, China is becoming a huge market outlet for high-fashion brands and other luxury products. According to Lin and Wang (2010), 60 per cent of China's population is under 35 years old. The one-child policy has created a young generation often spoiled by their parents – who grew up during the Cultural Revolution and focussed their broken aspirations on their children. Parents spend most of the family income to meet the needs of only sons or only daughters, and give them a high level of education. So, China's growing middle class is from 25 to 44 years old, has a good education and high income, which is largely spent on luxury goods. This new Chinese generation, the one-child generation, is less inclined to save and more prone to break with communist values than previous generations (Lin and Wang, 2010). They are more likely to impulse-purchase and desire power and prestige to impress their reference social group (Li et al., 2009; Zhao and Belk, 2007).

According to Lu (2008), a brand's social recognition is the basis of luxury good consumption for Chinese consumers; luxury reveals their success and elevates their social status.

Zahn and He's study (2012) surveyed the consumption of luxury goods by the Chinese middle class, testing the relationship between psychological traits and attitudes towards well-known luxury brands. They identified value consciousness, susceptibility to normative influences and the need for uniqueness as key influencing characteristics.

Despite the growing pursuit of luxury, a KPMG (2007) study demonstrated a lack of knowledge about this market by the Chinese consumer, who can nominate only one, or at most two, luxury brands for each product category.

He et al. (2010) analysed affluent Chinese consumers and broke them down into three segments: consumers with a salient 'need for uniqueness', who consume goods to stand apart from others; price-conscious consumers, who are overconfident in their purchase decisions, and are often impulse purchasers; and consumers oriented towards public interest.

The demand for luxury and branded products cannot be fully satisfied by domestic production. This represents a great opportunity for foreign businesses, but they face a politically motivated rejection of foreign products and growing nationalistic sentiments (Bi et al., 2012).

The wish for westernisation

Although the Chinese consumer is historically ethnocentric and dislikes Western commodities, recent economic changes and the symbolic meaning of Western brands have led the Chinese upper and middle class to adopt Western lifestyles and consumption patterns to show social status (Lin and Wang, 2010). In addition to an increase in the consumption of luxury goods, the new wealth has led consumer demand for products representing icons of Western consumerism (Banks and Overton, 2010).

Chinese consumers have long been restricted in their consumption choices, and are now looking to the West to break with the uniformity and monotony of Chinese society (Croll, 2006). Open criticism of China's revolutionary past by the majority of the population attained prominence with the *Heshang Phenomenon* (*River Elegy* in English), a six-part documentary broadcast by China Central Television in 1988. This documentary depicted the decline of traditional Chinese culture and criticised the political system (Chen, 1992). The increasing use of Western-style accessories and cosmetics changed Chinese concepts of beauty; influenced by Western movies, advertising and television shows, Western products represented a new-found freedom (Podoshen et al., 2011). To be one of the first to own a Western luxury good demonstrated individualism and was envied by others (Croll, 2006). Western-style consumption especially affects the younger generation, who have mainly been influenced by Western advertising (Croll, 2006).

The Westernisation of Chinese consumers also involves dietary changes. Rapid economic and income growth, urbanisation and globalisation are causing a dramatic change in diet towards Western patterns, characterised by greater consumption of wheat, temperate fruit and vegetables, high protein and energy-dense foods (Curtis et al., 2003; Pingali, 2006). This process is accelerated by the rapid spread of global supermarket chains (Pingali, 2006).

Perception of foreign products and country of origin

As stated by Li et al. (2012), a country's image influences the attractiveness of that country's entire production, its competitiveness at the global level and consumer perceptions. Several studies about COO effects conducted in developed countries reveal that consumers prefer domestic over foreign products, especially when they lack information about the product (Elliott and Camoron, 1994). Conversely, in developing countries such as China, consumers generally perceive foreign products – especially those produced in developed countries – to be of higher quality than domestic products (Li et al., 1997; Sharma, 2011).

As stated by Zhou and Hui (2003), thanks to the open-door policy adopted by China since the 1990s, many Chinese people associate foreign products with sophistication, modernity, novelty and faddishness, and – as stated by Gong (2003) – they consider imported products more prestigious than domestic products.

Since foreign brands entered the Chinese market in the early 1980s, they have earned a reputation for quality and are considered status symbols (He et al., 2010; Heslop and Papadopoulos, 1993). This aspect is particularly important for the Chinese consumer, who is very attentive to image as perceived by others as well as the status and prestige gained in society stemming from the symbolic values embedded in foreign products (Knight et al., 2008; Zhou and Hui, 2003). According to Knight et al. (2008), the higher quality attributed to foreign products by Chinese consumers derives from the awareness that they have passed stringent quarantine inspections at customs and enjoy more sophisticated traceability systems.

He et al. (2010) highlight the link between the values and attitudes of Chinese consumers preferring foreign brands, and point out that a strong need for achievement leads them towards imported products. Li et al. (2012) show the effects of consumer ethnocentrism – namely, beliefs about the appropriateness and morality of purchasing foreign products – on the propensity to purchase foreign and domestic products. Qing et al. (2012) studied the purchase intention of imported fresh fruit and considered ethnocentrism as an important factor in driving Chinese consumers towards domestic products. Conversely, according to the study of Bi et al. (2012), Chinese consumers would not be much affected by this adverse feeling in consumption choices, and foreign production can benefit from this. A study by Ren et al. (2011) about imported soy-based dietary supplements highlights that attitude, perceived behavioural control and dine-out sociability positively influence the consumption intentions of Chinese consumers. Wang et al. (2013) showed that the effect of consumer animosity or antipathy towards a country, related to previous or ongoing military, political or economic events, was tempered both by a consumer's personal values (materialism) and social influences (susceptibility to moral influence).

Chinese wine consumers

Historical records show that the consumption of alcoholic beverages has been part of Chinese culture going back thousands of years, and is now a part of everyday life (Tang et al., 2013). In particular, vine cultivation and winemaking have been practised from the first century BC (Kjellgren,

2004); in modern times wine styles and production techniques are evolving. The old styles and brands are expanding and are trying to learn from European styles and to imitate their production models (Banks and Overton, 2010).

Wine from a foreign country is perceived as a luxury product by Chinese consumers, a symbol of Western lifestyles, a means of showing off during important occasions and a product of higher quality than domestic wine. Chinese consumers are willing to pay for imported quality products and are attracted to a modern lifestyle (Li et al., 2011). According to Knight et al. (2008), the Chinese consumer chooses imported wine, although it is more expensive, for reasons related to social standing and to the perception of it being higher quality than domestic wine.

Wine, especially when imported, has been adopted as a marker of wealth and sophistication and its consumption is a sign of wealth, elegance, worldliness and social status (Banks and Overton, 2010; Hu et al., 2008; Li et al., 2011). Wine consumption has symbolic value: imported quality wines with a brand reputation are preferred, used to impress guests and satisfy an individual's social standing. Wine promotes good *mianzi*, or 'saving face' (i.e., keeping up appearances) in front of others (Liu and Murphy, 2007).

According to Knight et al. (2008), Chinese consumers typically buy imported wine as a gift. Young people often purchase imported products as gifts for parents or older relatives to demonstrate filial piety, an important Confucian value. The purchase of imported products reduces the complexity of assessing a gift for those who receive it and decreases the social risk for those who make the gift.

According to Yu et al. (2009), wine consumption, particularly red wine, is on the increase. The reasons for this are many: social, the effects of self-esteem, the trend toward westernisation and health benefits. Other studies also highlight health benefits as promoting wine consumption for Chinese consumers (Balestrini and Gamble, 2006; Li et al., 2011; Somogyi et al., 2011). Links between the medical and nutritional benefits of food are considered very important. The healthy dimension of wine is often attributed to the concept of *ch'i*, 'strength' or 'energy'. *Ch'i* pervades a person's body and ensures health. People drink wine because it provides the body with *ch'i*, allowing the body to be in harmony with one's self and the universe (Ngai and Cho, 2012).

Balestrini and Gamble (2006) make the point that Chinese consumers mainly purchase wine for sensory reasons. They do not consider it as a means of quenching their thirst, as do consumers in some European countries. Rather they consider it as suitable for social occasions.

From the sensory perspective, according to Knight et al. (2008), Chinese consumers have a more developed sense of smell than taste, as a result of drinking tea and the widespread practice of *gan bei-ing*.[2] Yu et al. (2009) place this sensory factor among the Top 3 elements driving Chinese consumers to purchase wine, together with brand name and origin.

Despite increased interest in the product, several studies highlight the lack of knowledge that Chinese consumers have about wine, as exemplified by some Chinese consumers only knowing of red wine (Knight et al., 2008; Li et al., 2011; Liu and Murphy, 2007). It is also not uncommon for wine to be drunk with ice or mixed with fruit juice or soft drinks (Knight et al., 2008). When product knowledge is low, the price or COO become quality cues to avoid social risk. The COO is critical for Chinese consumers to determine a wine's quality, as much as the price, according to Hu et al. (2008). It is much more important according to Balestrini and Gamble (2006). According to Knight et al. (2008), the COO of a wine is highly integrated with product perception, and takes pride of place in the mind. According to Balestrini and Gamble (2006), Chinese consumers give much more importance to the COO when the wine is purchased for special occasions than for private consumption. However, when they purchase wine for social occasions, they base their choices on quality, taste and image. Consumers are willing to pay a lot on such occasions, hence their focus on expensive imported wines.

France enjoys the reputation of being the best producer of wines by the Chinese (Balestrini and Gamble, 2006; Hu et al., 2008; Knight et al., 2008; Mitry et al., 2009). Consumers consider French wines the best and perceive them as 'safe'. They are able to avoid the risk of losing face by buying a product that others might consider low class (Knight et al. 2008). Australia, Italy, Spain and the United States take a back seat; however, they all enjoy a better reputation than local Chinese wines (Balestrini and Gamble, 2006).

The upper middle class, who live in the largest cities, and young professionals in particular, are the target of wine-marketing campaigns in China (Jenster and Cheng, 2008; Liu and Murphy, 2007). Rabobank (2010) identifies 11 cities, divided into two tiers,[3] which are estimated to account for 76 per cent of imported wine sales by volume.

The importance and power of a reference social group in all aspects of Chinese life are very significant; the study of Balestrini and Gamble (2006) highlights the most important information cue for a Chinese consumer to assess a wine's quality is peer advice. Further, the type of event is a very important factor in the purchasing of wine and in deciding the price, vintage and origin (Li et al., 2011; Liu and Murphy, 2007).

Demand for imported wine in China

The dynamics of Chinese consumer behaviour have led to a growing dependence on the international market. This is a very recent phenomenon and mainly involves bottled wines. Since 2006, imports of bottled wine have exponentially increased, more than 10 times in volume and more than 16 times in value in the period 2007–11. This wine category is responsible for the increase in value of wine imports to China, since the difference (mainly represented by bulk wine) between total imports and imports of bottled wine remained constant during this growing phase (Figure 13.2). However, the price plays an important role in this trend, since there is a minor flattening of the difference between total imports of wine and bottled wine when analysing them by quantity.

The year zero for wine in China seems to be 2006, when there was a radical large-scale change towards wine by Chinese consumers. Attention definitely turned towards imported wines, although bulk imported wines were often used to produce domestic wine. The extent of this can be shown by the fact that bottled wine represented 13 per cent of total wine imports by quantity in 2002 and as much as 66 per cent in 2011; in the same period its value grew from 40 to 88 per cent. Business expectations towards this new market outlet can be understood by considering that almost all of this growth took place in the period 2006–11. This had a major impact on the competitiveness relationship among the world's leading wine producers – and their export development perspectives – who had to take into consideration the likelihood of there being approximately 200 million potential wine consumers in 2010, with an annual per-capita consumption of 5.5 litres (Sumegi, 2011).

The size of the Chinese market coupled with deep changes in consumer preferences and habits highlight the importance of analysing the competitiveness relationship among the main world players so that we can ascertain whether the opening of new markets in China will lead to significant changes in the market shares of origin sources (countries and/or wine regions) and in the leadership for different product categories.

Analysis of the market shares of the Top 5 wine exporters in the decade 2002–11 highlights the following trends (Table 13.3): (i) the market concentration of each wine category; (ii) the strengthening of French leadership against the main competitors in both bottled and sparkling wine; (iii) the new role of Chile as a supplier of bottled wine (replacing the US) and the new role of Spain as a supplier of bulk wine (again replacing the US); (iv) increased Australian competitiveness in bulk wine; and (v) the

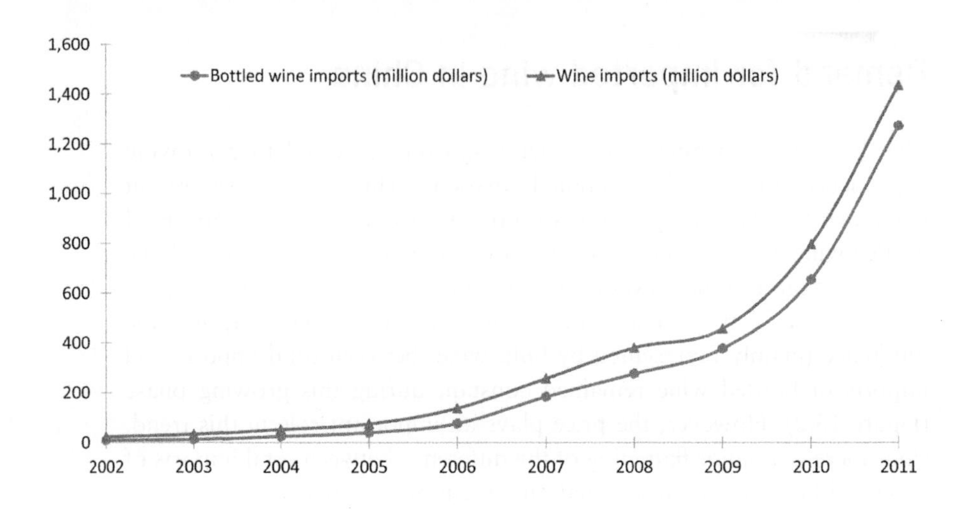

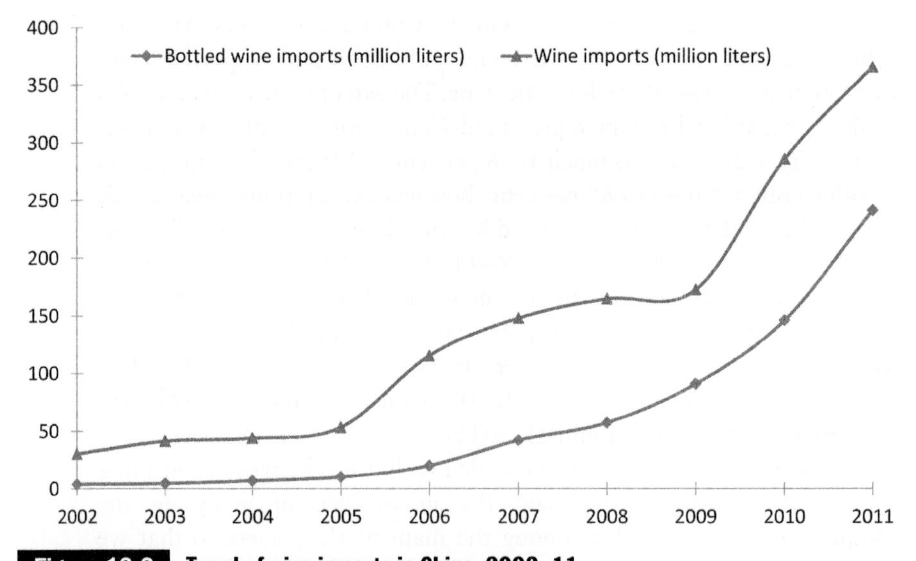

Figure 13.2 **Trend of wine imports in China, 2002–11**

Source: an elaboration of UN Comtrade data (2013).[5,6]

low-price strategy adopted by Spain for exports of bulk wine and the high-price strategy adopted by Australia.

We can analyse the competitiveness relationships between goods (wine categories), sources (countries) and products (wine category per country) by estimating their price, expenditure and cross-price elasticity. This allows us to identify dynamic elements in the Chinese market.

Table 13.3 Market share by product and source

Value 2002	Quantity 2002	Value 2011	Quantity 2011
	Still bottled wine		
C5 = 83.9%	C5 = 81.9%	C5 = 87.0%	C5 = 85.2%
France (42.4%)	France (40.1%)	France (55.4%)	France (48.8%)
Australia (16.5%)	Australia (16.2%)	Australia (15.2%)	Australia (13.5%)
USA (12.4%)	USA (11.4%)	Italy (6.1%)	Spain (7.9%)
Italy (7.8%)	Italy (7.8%)	Chile (5.4%)	Italy (7.8%)
Spain (4.8%)	Spain (6.4%)	Spain (4.9%)	Chile (7.2%)
	Bulk wine		
C5 = 92.4%	C5 = 85.9%	C5 = 92.0%	C5 = 93.1%
Chile (68.2%)	Chile (67.8%)	Spain (29.4%)	Spain (45.4%)
Spain (7.2%)	Spain (8.2%)	Chile (28.0%)	Chile (21.6%)
Italy (6.0%)	Italy (4.8%)	Australia (16.8%)	Australia (9.8%)
France (5.0%)	France (3.9%)	France (9.0%)	Italy (9.2%)
USA (1.5%)	USA (1.2%)	Italy (8.8%)	France (7.1%)
	Sparkling wine		
C5 = 91.0%	C5 = 69.2%	C5 = 96.8%	C5 = 91.8%
France (66.1%)	France (38.6%)	France (73.0%)	France (36.4%)
USA (8.6%)	USA (12.3%)	Italy (13.0%)	Italy (32.2%)
Germany (6.9%)	Italy (8.2%)	Australia (4.0%)	Spain (7.8%)
Italy (5.8%)	Germany (5.7%)	Spain (3.8%)	Australia (8.1%)
Australia (3.7%)	Australia (4.4%)	Germany (2.9%)	Germany (7.3%)

Table 13.4 shows the own-price elasticity of demand for the main products and sources estimated by the Restricted Source Differentiated Almost Ideal Demand System model (RSDAIDS) (Yang and Koo, 1994), which measures the responsiveness of demand to price.

Table 13.4 Marshallian own-price elasticity of demand for imported wines in China (January 2005–July 2012)

Product	Own-price elasticity
French still bottled wines	−0.562
Australian still bottled wines	−0.933
Italian still bottled wines	−1.309
Chilean bulk wines	−1.307
Australian bulk wines	−1.449
Italian bulk wines	−1.367
French sparkling wines	−0.488
Italian sparkling wines	−0.683

Source: an elaboration of UN Comtrade data (2013).

The three product categories analysed (still bottled, bulk and sparkling wine) have different price sensitivities: inelasticity for sparkling wines, elasticity for bulk wines, different responsiveness for still bottled wines. These indices confirm that Chinese consumers favour French wines. Australian still bottled wines are sensitive to price strategies. Italian wines suffer from competition by other suppliers and demand for them is sensitive to price policies. Bulk wine imports are price elastic because of market characteristics: fragmentation of market shares, homogeneous and unbranded products, and the volatility of commercial strategies. Rigidity in the price of sparkling wines, symbolic of luxury, confirms the leadership of France and Italy in satisfying demand, which is exigent in terms of product, brand and origin reputation, but not price sensitive.

Marshallian cross-price elasticity (Table 13.5) emphasises the market competition among the main followers (competitors) of France (the market leader) and the role of Australia, in particular. There are opportunities for growth for all suppliers in a developing market like China. The complementary role Australian wines play to French, Chilean and Italian wines is obvious. Expenditure on Australian wine is more sensitive to the product competition and pricing policies of other suppliers. These relations are asymmetric; in the provision of bulk wines Australia is affected by the replacement capacity of Italy (the follower), and

Table 13.5 Marshallian and Hicksian cross-price elasticity of the demand for imported wines in China (January 2005–July 2012)

Product	In response to a change in price of	Marshallian cross-price elasticity	Hicksian cross-price elasticity
Australian still bottled wines	French still bottled wines	−0.592	—
Australian still bottled wines	Italian still bottled wines	−0.226	+0.512
Australian bulk wines	Chilean bulk wines	−0.577	—
Chilean bulk wines	Australian bulk wines	+0.544	+0.565
Italian bulk wines	Australian bulk wines	+0.994	+1.381
Italian bulk wines	Chilean bulk wines	−0.411	—
French still bottled wines	Australian still bottled wines	—	+0.583
French still bottled wines	Italian still bottled wines	—	+0.591
Italian still bottled wines	French still bottled wines	—	+0.965
Italian still bottled wines	Australian still bottled wines	—	+0.607
Chilean bulk wines	Italian bulk wines	—	+0.167

Source: an elaboration of UN Comtrade data (2013).

Chile (the market leader). These market positions are confirmed by Italian bulk wines being complementary to Chilean ones.

Hicksian cross-price elasticity highlights mutual power relationships between France, Australia and Italy. Italian wines are sensitive to price changes by competitors and are substitutes for French and Australian wines. In contrast, French and Australian wines are less affected by Italian pricing strategies. Australian wines are not influenced by France's dominance.

Table 13.6 shows cross-price elasticity between products (wine category per source) and goods (wine category). Still bottled wines (in this case imported from France, Australia and Italy) are substitutes for bulk wine. Hicksian cross-price elasticity strengthens this relation. As these products meet the needs of different supply chains, their market relation derives from the growth of imports in China positively affecting both categories, although bottled wines derive the highest benefits. French wines enjoy a complementary effect to still bottled wine and sparkling wine, for which France is the market leader. This is due to the fact that both wines satisfy demand in the high-end segment. In this case the increase in demand also benefits both wine categories (French, in particular). Chinese expenditure on Italian sparkling wine tends to be substituted by still bottled wine. Bulk and still bottled wines are characterised by a complementarity relation, because in this case a growing market benefits bottled wine more than bulk wine.

Table 13.7 shows the elasticity of import demand to changes in expenditure. The competitive scenario that results is characterised by Chinese consumers moving towards new suppliers and product differentiation. The main imported wines are characterised by positive expenditure elasticity. The index of still bottled wines is below one, but reaches unity with Australian bulk wine. This shows that demand for these wines grows with increased expenditure, but at a lower rate. It confirms that increased expenditure on imported wine is the consequence of widening the product portfolio, which benefits both leading and following countries. The positive significant index of Italian bulk wine confirms the trend for import demand to diversify purchase from new supplier countries.

The demand for sparkling wine does not grow in proportion to expenditure – it exceeds it. This highlights the Chinese consumer's interest in different wine categories that were little appreciated in the past (white wines, sparkling wine), but which today reflect new consumer trends, meeting new highly sophisticated consumer needs. These consumers search for differentiation, brand and origin

Table 13.6 Marshallian and Hicksian cross-price elasticity between products and goods (January 2005-July 2012)

Product	In response to a change in price of	Marshallian cross-price elasticity	Hicksian cross-price elasticity
French still bottled wines	Bulk wines	+0.415	+0.608
Australian still bottled wines	Bulk wines	+0.678	+0.902
Italian still bottled wines	Bulk wines	+0.896	+1.090
French still bottled wines	Sparkling wines	−0.595	−0.560
Chilean bulk wines	Still bottled wines	−2.631	−2.561
Australian bulk wines	Still bottled wines	−1.125	—
French sparkling wines	Still bottled wines	−0.468	—
Italian sparkling wines	Still bottled wines	—	+1.349

Source: an elaboration of UN Comtrade data (2013).

Table 13.7 Expenditure elasticity of the demand for imported wines in China (January 2005–July 2012)

Product	Expenditure elasticity
French still bottled wines	+0.867
Australian still bottled wines	+1.009
Italian still bottled wines	+0.870
Australian bulk wines	+0.988
Italian bulk wines	+1.741
French sparkling wines	+1.240
Italian sparkling wines	+1.220

Source: an elaboration of UN Comtrade data (2013).

reputation, luxury goods, status symbols and engage in conspicuous consumption.

When we divide wine imports into COO and qualitative typology of wine (PDO, PGI, non-PDO and non-PGI),[4] not only can we gain further confirmation of the above analysis, but the perspectives and dynamics of the Chinese market can also be seen in detail, including the export strategies adopted by the main global players (Table 13.8).

Strong growth in the Chinese market and in consumer orientation towards Western products, symbols of status and luxury, is confirmed by the fact that PDO wines of the main European producing countries have increased out of proportion with those of the total market. The increase has very significantly affected red wines; however, between 2005 and 2011 white wines, which remained practically unknown until a few years ago, have significantly increased their penetration in Chinese markets. France is the undisputed leader in the PDO wine segment, with an export value more than 20 times higher than that of its main European competitor (Italy) as of 2011. In terms of value and of quantity, in particular, the aggregate New World is the main rival to France, with increases of about 20 times in volume and 30 times in value in the period 2005–11.

By analysing the average prices of exports we are able to consider Chinese market trends and the relationships between competitors in much greater depth. When it comes to PDO wines, Italy is most significantly oriented towards premium segments, despite its differential

Table 13.8 Chinese wine imports by COO and typology

	Value (€)		**Volume** (000 kg)		**Average price** (€/kg)	
	2005	**2011**	**2005**	**2011**	**2005**	**2011**
French PDO wines	9,862,221	387,269,883	1,440	56,412	6.85	6.86
White	682,657	14,260,830	122	2,358	5.59	6.05
Red	9,179,564	373,009,053	1,317	54,055	6.97	6.90
Italian PDO wines	773,834	18,994,249	196	4,476	3.96	4.24
White	82,189	5,743,652	38	1,385	2.16	4.15
Red	691,645	13,250,597	157	3,092	4.39	4.29
Spanish PDO wines	353,794	11,687,423	89	3,161	3.99	3.70
White	32,827	736,172	10	341	3.28	2.16
Red	320,967	10,951,251	79	2,820	4.08	3.88
German PDO white wines	909,740	5,935,058	200	1,535	4.56	3.87
European PGI wines	4,342,939	100,089,112	2,399	47,899	1.81	2.09
Other European PDO or PGI wines	2,613,763	50,380,542	977	18,463	2.68	2.73
European non-PDO and non-PGI wines	1,855,220	54,598,547	411	29,848	4.51	1.83
New World wines	12,767,672	332,783,909	4,629	86,311	2.76	3.86

Source: an elaboration of UN Comtrade data (2013) and Eurostat data (2013).[6]

with France remaining high. This improvement is driven by white wines, whose price doubled in the period. Conversely, Spain and Germany were more oriented towards significant price reduction, with a clear strategy to attack basic and popular segments; this was especially true of Spain. Finally, the comparison between non-PDO and non-PGI wines from Europe and the New World is interesting. The price of European wines has dropped considerably while the price of New World wines increased, highlighting the intention to directly compete with traditional European producers in the premium segment of PDO wines. In this segment, only France maintained a significantly higher premium price than that of its new competitors.

Conclusions

Economic development is transforming Chinese society into a consumer society that has brought about a revolution of values. Demand for luxury and branded products cannot be fully satisfied by domestic production; this has pushed Chinese consumers (especially the younger generation) towards progressive westernisation. It has also affected the demand for imported wine, which is perceived as a luxury product.

This study has highlighted the factors determining the growth in demand for imported wine, the impact they have had on competitive relations among exporting countries and wine regions, and the opportunities and constraints facing business development for the main competitors.

Since 2006 the Chinese wine market has undergone major development, resulting in China becoming one of the top producers, consumers and importers at the global level. Wineries from the New and Old World look to China as a great opportunity but also recognise its fast-growing competitive ability.

This study has given new insights into the cultural and socioeconomic factors that are driving the growth in demand for imported wine. It has identified some important trends that underpin the growing interest of the Chinese population in wine:

- a strong social hierarchy in which class differentiation and the influence of social reference groups affect choices;
- a new cultural revolution generated by economic development that pushes consumers to brand consciousness, responsiveness to promotion stimuli, novelty seeking and a preference for foreign brands;
- a consumer orientation towards achievement and modernity.

Three key factors – the pursuit of luxury, the wish for westernisation and the perception of a foreign product's COO – characterise the consumption choices of the new generation, as much with food as with wine. Wine fully fulfils this new cultural and consumption model, which has become a symbol of wealth, sophistication, comfort, elegance, worldliness and social status. In this context, the COO of a wine is an important quality cue. This is the reason France is the foreign supplier that benefits the most as a result of its undisputed reputation.

The size of the Chinese market as well as rapidly changing consumer preferences and habits are the reasons we chose to analyse competitiveness relationships among the world's main players and, by doing so, ascertain whether the opening of new markets in China will lead to significant changes in the market shares of origin sources and in the leadership for different product categories. In the future bottled wine will likely take centre stage as a result of its high market concentration, the undisputed leadership of France and rapid advance of Chile among the other followers.

By analysing own-price elasticity, cross-price elasticity and expenditure elasticity of demand we were able to elaborate the main opportunities and constraints facing global players in the Chinese market.

Own-price elasticity for bottled wine confirms Chinese consumers' love of French wines. Bulk wine imports are price elastic because of the fragmentation of market shares, the presence of homogeneous and unbranded products and the volatility of commercial strategies, making this segment more sensitive to competitive strategies based on prices, and therefore to changes in market shares. Rigidity in the price of sparkling wine confirms the leadership of France and Italy in satisfying Chinese demand.

Cross-price elasticity emphasises market competition among the main followers (competitors) of France (the market leader), despite there being opportunities for growth for all suppliers in a developing market like China. The new competitive scenario is characterised by a discerning Chinese consumer who is moving towards new suppliers and product differentiation; it opens up new business opportunities, especially for wines that demonstrate positive expenditure elasticity.

Finally, our brief focus on wine imports divided by COO and qualitative typology (PDO and PGI wines) highlights the need for further research into territorial sources, to gain a better understanding of the perspectives and dynamics of the Chinese market as well as the export strategies implemented by the main global players.

Notes

1. UN Comtrade data are available at *http://unstats.un.org/unsd/default.htm* [accessed 25 August 2013].
2. *Gan bei-ing* means drinking the contents of the glass in one shot, without relishing the drink. A toast on social occasions is often coupled with the word *gan bei*, which roughly translates as 'cheers' but more literally as 'dry the cup', under penalty of a forfeit of some kind.
3. Tier 1 includes Beijing, Guangzhou, Shanghai and Shenzhen, while Tier 2 embodies Chengdu, Hangzhou, Harbin, Nanjing, Qingdao, Tianjin and Wuhan.
4. PDO stands for Protected Designation of Origin and PGI for Protected Geographical Indication. These EU schemes are used to protect and promote the geographical names of wine, agricultural products and foodstuffs.
5. See Eurostat (2013). Available from: *http://epp.eurostat.ec.europa.eu/newxtweb/setupdimselection.do* [accessed 26 August 2013].
6. According to the coding of the Harmonized Commodity Description and Coding System (HS), bottled wine is classified as wine held in containers of up to two litres. Therefore, this chapter considers bulk wine as wine in containers that hold more than two litres.

References

Balestrini, P. and Gamble, P. (2006) Country-of-origin effects on Chinese wine consumers. *British Food Journal*, **108**(5), 396–412.

Banks, G. and Overton, J. (2010) Old World, New World, Third World? Reconceptualising the worlds of wine. *Journal of Wine Research*, **21**(1), 57–75.

Baoku, L., Cuixia, Z. and Weimin, B. (2010) An empirical study on the decision-making styles of the Chinese peasant consumers. *Journal of Consumer Marketing*, **27**(7), 629–37.

Bi, X., Gunessee, S., Hoffmann, R., Hui, W., Larner, J. et al. (2012) Chinese consumer ethnocentrism: a field experiment. *Journal of Consumer Behaviour*, **11**, 252–63.

Chen, X. (1992) Occidentalism as counterdiscourse: heshang in post-Mao China. *Critical Enquiry*, **18**, 686–712.

Croll, E. (2006) *China's New Consumers*. Routledge, New York.

Cui, G., Liu, H., Yang, X. and Wang, H. (2013) Culture, cognitive style and consumer response to informational vs. transformational advertising among East Asians: evidence from the PRC. *Asia Pacific Business Review*, **19**(1), 16–31.

Curtis, K.R., McCluskey, J.J. and Wahl, T.I. (2003) Westernization in China: a case study in processed potatoes. Paper presented at *American Agricultural Economics Association Annual Meeting, 27–30 July, Montreal, Canada.*

Elliott, G.R. and Camoron, R.C. (1994) Consumer perception of product quality and the country-of-origin effect. *Journal of International Marketing*, **2**(2), 49–62.

Gong, W. (2003) Chinese consumer behavior: a cultural framework and implications. *Journal of American Academy of Business*, **3**(1/2), 373–80.

He, Y., Zou, D. and Jin, L. (2010) Exploiting the goldmine: a lifestyle analysis of affluent Chinese consumers. *Journal of Consumer Marketing*, **27**(7), 615–28.

Heslop, L. and Papadopoulos, N. (1993) But who knows where or when: reflections on the images of countries and their products. In: N. Papadopoulos and L. Heslop (Eds), *Product-country Images: Impact and Role in International Marketing.* International Business Press, New York, pp. 39–75.

Hu, X., Li, L., Xie, C. and Zhou, J. (2008) The effects of country-of-origin on Chinese consumers' wine purchasing behavior. *Journal of Technology Management in China*, **3**, 292–306.

Jacobs, L., Keown, C. and Worthley, R. (1993) Right/left hemispheric orientation in Japan, China, and the United States: beware the difference! *Journal of International Consumer Marketing*, **5**(4), 93–106.

Jenster, P. and Cheng, Y. (2008) Dragon wine: developments in the Chinese wine industry. *International Journal of Wine Business Research*, **2**, 244–59.

Kjellgren, B. (2004) Drunken modernity: wine in China. *Anthropology of Food*, 3 December 2004. See also *Wine and Globalization/Vin et mondialisation.* Available from: *http://aof.revues.org/249* [accessed 24 August 2013].

Knight, J., Gao, H., Garrett, T. and Deans, K. (2008) Quest for social safety in imported foods in China: gatekeeper perceptions. *Appetite*, **50**, 146–57.

KPMG (2007) Luxury brands in China. Available from: *http://www.kpmg.com.cn/en/virtual_library/Consumer_markets/CM_Luxury_brand.pdf* [accessed 1 August 2013].

Li, D., Jiang, Y., An, S., Shen, Z. and Jin W. (2009) The influence of money attitudes on young consumers' compulsive buying. *Young Consumers*, **10**(2), 98–109.

Li, J-G., Jia, J-R., Taylor, D., Bruwer, J. and Li, E. (2011) The wine drinking behaviour of young adults: an exploratory study in China. *British Food Journal*, **113**, 1305–17.

Li, X., Yang, J., Wang, X. and Lei, D. (2012) The impact of country-of-origin image, consumer ethnocentrism and animosity on purchase intention. *Journal of Software*, **7**(10), 2263–8.

Li, Z., Fu, S. and Murray, L.W. (1997) Country and product images: the perceptions of consumers in the People's Republic of China. *Journal of International Consumer Marketing*, **10**(2), 115–39.

Lin, X. and Wang, C.L. (2010) The heterogeneity of Chinese consumer values: a dual structure explanation. *Cross Cultural Management: An International Journal*, **17**(3), 244–56.

Liu, F. and Murphy, J. (2007) A qualitative study of Chinese wine consumption and purchasing: implications for Australian wines. *International Journal of Wine Business Research*, **19**, 98–113.

Lu, X. (2008) *Elite China: Luxury Consumer Behavior in China.* John Wiley & Sons, Singapore.

Marketline (2012) Wine in China. Available from: *http://web.ebscohost.com/ehost/pdfviewer/pdfviewer?vid=3&hid=15&sid=36e7b065-ed3b-4f25-91ff-8f465c4b0c1b%40sessionmgr11* [accessed 25 July 2013].

Mitry, D., Smith, D.E. and Jenster, P.V. (2009) China's role in global competition in the wine industry: a new contestant and future trends. *International Journal of Wine Research*, **1**, 19–25.

Morgan, S.E. and Reichert, T. (1999) The message is in the metaphor: assessing the comprehension of metaphors in advertisements. *Journal of Advertising*, **28**(4), 1–12.

Ngai, J. and Cho, E. (2012) The young luxury consumers in China. *Young Consumers*, **13**(3), 255–66.

OIV (2013) Statistical report on world viticulture, 2013. Available from: *http://www.oiv.int/oiv/info/itstatistiquessecteurvitivinicole#secteur* [accessed 20 August 2013] [International Organisation of Vine and Wine].

Pingali, P. (2006) Westernization of Asian diets and the transformation of food systems: implications for research and policy. *Food Policy*, **32**, 281–98.

Podoshen, J.S., Li, L. and Zhang, J. (2011) Materialism and conspicuous consumption in China: a cross-cultural examination. *International Journal of Consumer Studies*, **35**(1), 17–25.

Qing, P., Lobo, A. and Chongguang, L. (2012) The impact of lifestyle and ethnocentrism on consumers' purchase intentions of fresh fruit in China. *Journal of Consumer Marketing*, **29**(1), 43–51.

Rabobank (2010) Rabobank Project Tannin Final Report. Available from: *http://www.wineaustralia.com/en/Signup.aspx?ContinueOriginalPage=/en/Winefacts%20Landing/Overseas%20Market%20Intelligence/China%20and%20Hong%20Kong.aspx* [accessed 28 March 2013].

Ren, J., Chung, J-E., Stoel, L. and Xu, Y. (2011) Chinese dietary culture influences consumers' intention to use imported soy-based dietary supplements: an application of the theory of planned behaviour. *International Journal of Consumer Studies*, **35**, 661–9.

Sharma, P. (2011) Country of origin effects in developed and emerging markets: exploring the contrasting roles of materialism and value consciousness. *Journal of International Business Studies*, **42**(2), 285–306.

Somogyi, S., Li, E., Johnson, T., Bruwer, J. and Bastian, S. (2011) The underlying motivations of Chinese wine consumer behaviour. *Asia Pacific Journal of Marketing and Logistics*, **23**, 473–85.

Sumegi, Z. (2011) Wine market and wine industry of China in the 21th century. Ph.D. dissertation, School of Management and Business Administration, Gödöll, Hungary.

Tang, H., Cai, W., Wang, H., Zhang, Q., Qian, L. et al. (2013). The association between cultural orientation and drinking behaviors among university students in Wuhan, China. *PLoS ONE*, **8**(1).

Wang, W., He, H. and Li, Y. (2013) Animosity and willingness to buy foreign products: moderating factors in decision-making of Chinese consumers. *Asia Pacific Business Review*, **19**(1), 32–52.

Yang, S-R. and Koo, W.W. (1994) Japanese meat import demand estimation with the source differentiated AIDS model. *Journal of Agricultural and Resource Economics*, **19**(2), 396–408.

Yu, Y., Sun, H., Goodman, S., Chen, S. and Ma, H. (2009) Chinese choices: a survey of wine consumers in Beijing. *International Journal of Wine Business Research*, **21**, 155–68.

Zahn, L. and He, Y. (2012) Understanding luxury consumption in China: consumer perceptions of best-known brands. *Journal of Business Research*, **65**, 1452–60.

Zhao, X. and Belk, R.W. (2007) Live from shopping malls: blogs and Chinese consumer desire. *Advances in Consumer Research*, **34**, 131–7.

Zhou, L. and Hui, M. (2003) Symbolic value of foreign products in the People's Republic of China. *Journal of International Marketing*, **11**(2), 36–58.

Epilogue

Abstract: Since the beginning of the twenty-first century Chinese business has entered a new stage, that of overseas direct investment (ODI). Factors impelling Chinese companies to invest include domestic enforcement of environmental legislation, yuan appreciation, rising wage levels and the need to acquire technology, even though the quest for energy and minerals was the initial impetus. The state sector and increasingly private-owned enterprises (POEs) are active. The EU and the United States are loci where the search is for innovative capacity in both manufacturing and services. A further objective is market reconnaissance. To this end companies like Huawei have sought localisation, employing local managers. Given former colonial links, Europe may also prove a conduit to Africa, where the Chinese are active in infrastructural development. As in Europe, Chinese companies such as car manufacturers are engaged in technological cooperation in the United States, targetting markets in China and overseas.

Key words: innovation, localisation, overseas direct investment (ODI), private-owned enterprises (POEs), research and development (R&D), state-owned enterprises (SOEs).

The chapters in this book have focused on the evolution of Chinese management, whether in manufacturing or services, including the impact of foreign direct investment. Since the early years of the twenty-first century, however, the globalisation of Chinese business could be said to have entered a new stage, with the initiation of China's overseas direct investment (ODI) and in recent years this trend has accelerated.

There are commonalities in the motives for such investment among manufacturers and service providers. Some observers have suggested that the Chinese economy has surpassed the threshold of US $8000 per-capita income, the globally accepted level at which domestic consumers demand better products and services (Moody et al., 2013). In the 1980s and 1990s China became a global workshop for labour-intensive low–profit margin products targeted at foreign and increasingly domestic markets. But, as mentioned in the introduction to this book, there are increasing pressures in favour of producing high-quality value-added goods, especially consumer durables. Moreover, environmental legislation, where enforced, raised costs for labour-intensive industries that pollute. In addition, formerly a low-valued yuan lessened the incentive for innovation and brand building but the currency's appreciation will enhance the importance of high-level manufacturing for sales on both domestic and foreign markets. Assuming that the yuan will appreciate over time, a premium will be placed on R&D to target upmarket sectors in order to compete on global and, increasingly, Chinese markets. Consequently, there is growing impetus to invest overseas, with a tendency to locate offshore in Asian labour-intensive sectors which Chinese wage levels are making uncompetitive, with manufacturers at the same time seeking the advantage of acquiring technology from foreign partners in Europe and the United States (Zhao, 2013; Zhou, 2013).

The initial factor in ODI was China's need for energy and minerals to fuel its industries as domestic sources of supply proved inadequate. A research report by the international business adviser KPMG defined three major stages in overseas investment by state-owned enterprises (SOEs). The first in the 1970s and 1980s focused on the establishment of overseas branches, representative offices and foreign trade companies. The second between 1991 and 2003 involved setting up purchasing channels and sales networks. It has been at the third stage, since 2004, that overseas acquisitions have been secured (Moody and Chen, 2013).

The impetus for the merger and acquisition (M&A) strategy came from SOEs which enjoyed support and funding from government. That link, however, has often proved a disadvantage, given fears of Chinese control over strategic industries on the part of European and American authorities. Some African leaders see evidence of neo-colonialism in the extraction of natural resources by China, even though such fears must be balanced against Chinese participation in beneficial infrastructural projects on the continent. Any such suspicions can be heightened by the Chinese government role. The foreign enterprises targeted have been those with access to national resources or proprietary technology but such strategies have not always been successful. There is, however, potential for private firms (Rich and Recker, 2013; Wu, 2013). Nevertheless, most of the US $68 billion the Chinese invested overseas in 2010 came from SOEs (Ma, 2012).

In contrast, Chinese private-owned enterprises (POEs), in general, though contributing 60 per cent to China's domestic GDP, have been slower to engage in ODI. In fact, POEs have faced a number of challenges: they face difficulties in raising capital; they lack the abovementioned advantages of SOEs; they have less experience and fear that their brand lacks recognition overseas. They nevertheless recognise that, apart from the question of rising costs, they are forced to seek new markets and associated marketing networks, with the overall objective of global competitiveness. Another important issue is the acquisition of technology and branding to attain competitiveness in China's domestic market. A Chinese stake in a foreign company may also help both parties to adjust to and localise in an overseas environment (Moody and Chen, 2013). Participation in ODI is thus changing; in the first six months of 2013, for instance, four of the ten outward M&A deals were concluded with private companies. Three of China's major global investor players are private: the telecommunications company, Huawei, the computer company, Lenovo and the electrical goods producer, Haier. Such investment is discussed below (Moody and Chen, 2013).

These trends are necessarily reflected in recent increases in the volume, sectoral composition and geographical direction of China's ODI. According to the Dragon Index, published by A CAPITAL, China's global investment rose to US $77.2 billion in 2012, an increase of 14 per cent over the previous year's US $68 billion. While Asia remains a major destination for China's ODI, in part reflecting China's participation in ASEAN-led economic and free trade agreements, the focus in this epilogue is on the advanced industrial countries of the EU and the United States which are natural future locations, given their supremacy in R&D, even though there is evidence that innovation power is growing in China itself. According to the 2012 *Statistical Bulletin of China's Outward Foreign Direct Investment*, the cumulative or outstanding total of China's ODI stood at US $531.94 billion that year. The Dragon Index shows that resources such as minerals remain a major component of China's ODI, accounting for about US $243 billion or 58 per cent of the total in 2012 but the most rapid growth in that year was in services, the US $11 billion total representing an increase of 165 per cent over the US $4.8 billion in 2011. While much resource extraction by Chinese enterprises takes place in the developing countries of Asia and Africa, the service sector is an increasingly important element in China's ODI in advanced industrial countries (Li, 2013; Steinbock, 2013; Zhao, 2013).

Consequently, the EU and the US are proving magnets for Chinese ODI, given their continuing pre-eminence in R&D and their vast potential markets. Significantly, according to the Dragon Index, Europe was a preferred destination, with 33 per cent of all Chinese ODI being channelled towards the continent, a figure double that in the US in 2012.

In addition, 51 per cent of all service sector investment went to Europe, and China also accounted for 61 per cent of all non-resource acquisition deals there (Zhao, 2013).

The United Kingdom and Germany can be seen as the gateway to the rest of Europe for China's ODI. In spite of the need to regulate the British banking system in the wake of the post-2008 economic crisis, the United Kingdom is regarded as expert in financial business services which received about 17 per cent of all Chinese ODI in that country between 1997 and 2007, with a steadily rising share. In addition, rising Chinese investment in areas like information technology are likely to continue (Rossi and Burghart, 2009). Examples, however, may be cited in a range of sectors, both in services and manufacturing. China Investment Corporation recently bought an 8.68 per cent stake in the UK utility group, Thames Water, as well as 10 per cent of London's Heathrow Airport. In 2005 SAIC Motor Corporation acquired the car manufacturer, MG Rover, while Zhuzhou CSR Times Electric bought British semiconductor manufacturer Dynex in 2008 (Liu, 2013).

Thus, within the above perspectives, as indicated earlier, Britain may be seen as a gateway to Europe. The presence of China's companies on the continent is, however, motivated not only by the attempt to avoid potential tariff barriers and acquire manufacturing expertise and information technologies but simultaneously to create and maintain markets through reconnaissance of consumer preferences.

China's investment in Germany may serve as a case in point and show the extent to which its companies are adapting to the European market. Dusseldorf, Cologne and the North Rhine Westphalia area in general have been seen as ideal conduits to penetrate markets elsewhere in Europe because of excellent transportation infrastructure. Moreover, as more and more companies locate in the region, a social infrastructure develops, just as Japanese businessmen's clubs and schools began to develop in Asia and Europe during the 1980s and 1990s, even if such potential exclusiveness can be seen as a disadvantage in terms of adaptation to the local community. In industrial terms, of course, area concentration of supplier and customer firms is a distinct asset. This is a growing feature of the Chinese presence in Dusseldorf. In fact, developments in the city show how Chinese ODI is evolving. Most of the Chinese companies in the city are moving from manufacturing low-price goods to high-tech value-added products. A success story in the technological field is Huawei which began its European operations in 2002, and since 2011 the continent has been the largest market outside China, accounting for about 13 per cent of its global revenue in 2012.

Importantly, Huawei has entered the localisation stage, with 70 per cent of its 7000 employees in Europe locally sourced, and that policy will continue. This process of localisation (i.e., employing local management and workforce) is intended to facilitate understanding of local culture, build labour relations and liaise with local government, issues faced by foreign investors in China itself since the open-door policy initiated in the 1980s. Chinese companies, in their move to Europe, have sought to upgrade their technology to overcome a residual image of low-priced low-quality products. In the 1980s the editor of this volume, in undertaking research into Sino-German trade in the then Federal Republic of Germany, interviewed traders who suggested that Chinese manufacturers would not succeed in European markets until design, quality and branding were improved, given the context of China's move from a seller's to a buyer's market. The key to overcoming this negative image is branding which is just as important as quality and price (Tuo, 2013).

There is, however, undoubtedly another agenda in Chinese investment in Europe. Given former colonial links and experience of doing business there, European countries may serve as a conduit for Chinese business in Africa. There are also potential strategic links between Chinese and European companies in market targetting. Market opportunities for Chinese investors in Africa would appear to abound; consumer articles like household appliances are increasingly in demand as economies grow. Chinese expertise could benefit African agriculture through the utilisation of cheap labour, with resulting higher yields and financial returns, thus benefitting both sides. Increased access to African countries, however, will demand improved transport services. Chinese activity in this field is indicated by the acquisition by HNA Group, China's fourth largest airline conglomerate, in October 2012 of a 48 per cent stake in Aigle Azur, a French private airline, in order to facilitate the Chinese side's network expansion (Wu, 2013; Zhao, 2013).

In fact, Africa's poor infrastructure is an undoubted impediment to trade and investment, and Chinese investors may be advantaged for two reasons. The Chinese are not new to Africa's infrastructural development; in the 1960s Chinese engineers built the Tan Zam railway in East Africa, attempting to create a long-term climate of goodwill. Second, in recent years China's own physical infrastructure has expanded enormously, and both SOEs and private enterprises are well prepared for involvement in Africa. In turn, these developments could pave the way for China's companies to cooperate with African countries in such areas as tourism, itself dependent on logistics and telecommunications (Wu, 2013).

In summary, however, while Europe may serve as a conduit to African markets, the prime attraction for Chinese investors has been the perceived technological superiority of selected European industries. China's ODI in the United States is informed by similar motives. In this epilogue the specific focus is the car industry, mandated as a priority in the 12th Five Year Plan. In the early years of reform automobile manufacturing in China benefitted from FDI in joint ventures with makers like Volkswagen and Peugeot. Generally speaking, it is still the case that Chinese managers and directors in engineering at original equipment manufacturers have limited experience, most of which derives from reverse engineering (i.e., copying) and have not been involved in vehicle development *per se*. Consequently, Chinese car equipment makers have invested in Detroit to take advantage of abundant engineering skills to increase their knowledge of manufacturing. Such firms are gaining production experience by conducting R&D for parent companies in China as well as producing components for American manufacturers. While, in order to raise quality, American car parts are still imported by China, recent Chinese acquisitions of US component companies are designed to target technology and innovation which will improve operations in China itself, an example being the purchase by Beijing West Industries, a joint venture between two Chinese SOEs, of the suspension and brake units of Delphi Corporation for US $100 million in 2009. The immediate objective, of course, is to build vehicles in China to supply the growing middle class but ultimately the objective is to target global markets, following the precedent of Japanese and South Korean producers (Barris, 2013).

ODI represents the latest stage in the globalisation of Chinese business. This epilogue has highlighted the impetus, motives, phases and actors informing that process. It was shown that both state and private sectors have shared similar motives, with the latter playing a growing role in China's ODI. The quest for natural resources and state-of-the-art technology to upgrade Chinese industries has determined the geographical locus of investment. Given the ongoing maturation of the Chinese economy and the growth of a domestic market attendant upon middle-class income, China's industry and business must enhance competitiveness. In doing so they may become rivals for Western companies. Chinese competitiveness will also be crucial in targetting the global marketplace, as Western countries climb out of recession. To date, as demonstrated by the car industry, China is still heavily dependent on Western countries for technological upgrading but the key to domestic success in production development is innovation. Chinese domestic patents are growing in importance but such innovation must be maintained.

It has often been observed that democratic societies, because of freedom of expression, are likely to be more inventive and innovative. Certainly, the maintenance of a one-party state in China has not prevented a transition to a free market economy, although state enterprises still remain predominant in certain domestic economic sectors and play a major role in ODI.

While many of China's outward investors are still not truly multinational, they may yet become intense global competitors with Western companies. One of the keys to the success of Chinese invested ventures overseas is effective human resource management, as localisation increases. In this context, at central government level, Chinese leaders are becoming increasingly aware of 'soft power', as evidenced by the establishment of Confucius Institutes in Western countries; these are designed to promote understanding of China's language and culture and, by implication, gain support for the country's business presence. In the 1990s the managerial effectiveness of Japanese ventures, for example, in Britain, was considered by many as the model to be emulated by domestic enterprises. While it seems unlikely that Chinese outward invested enterprises will play such a role of mentor in the foreseeable future, it seems more likely that hybrid styles of management may emerge, just as they have in Sino-foreign ventures in China itself. This could reflect a later stage in the globalisation of Chinese business.

References

Barris, M. (2013) Detroit is magnet for China's auto industry. *China Daily European Weekly*, 9–15 August.

Li, J.B. (2013) China vaults to world's 3rd largest investor. *China Daily European Weekly*, 13–19 September.

Liu, C. (2013) Visible progress in 'invisible' sectors. *China Daily European Weekly*, 6–12 September.

Ma, J. (2012) State owned enterprises: partners and competitors. *China Business Review*, **39**(1), 36–40.

Moody, A. and Chen, Y.Q. (2013) Going overseas is key for development. *China Daily European Weekly*, 30 August–6 September.

Moody, A., Chen, Y.Q. and Song, W.W. (2013) Private push. *China Daily European Weekly*, 30 August–6 September.

Rich, T. and Recker, S. (2013) Understanding Sino-African relations: neo-colonialism or a new era? *Journal of International and Area Studies*, **20**(1) 61–76.

Rossi, V. and Burghart, N. (2009) Chinese investment in Europe: a shift to services. *China Business Review*, **36**(5), 26–7, 41.

Steinbock, D. (2013) New growth model, new investment. *China Daily European Weekly*, 24–30 May.

Tuo, Y.N. (2013) Gateway to Europe. *China Daily European Weekly*, 24–30 May.

Wu, J.G. (2013) Private firms can bloom globally. *China Daily European Weekly*, 30 August–5 September.

Zhao, Y.R. (2013) Outward investment continues. *China Daily European Weekly*, 24–30 May.

Zhou, F. (2013) Set no limit for rising yuan. *China Daily European Weekly*, 21–27 June.

Index

Printed and bound by CPI Group (UK) Ltd, Croydon, CR0 4YY
08/05/2025
01864974-0003